ETHICS IN REHABILITATION COUNSELING

A CASE STUDY APPROACH

EDITED BY

JOSEPH F. STANO, Ph.D., LRC

PUBLISHED BY

ASPEN PROFESSIONAL SERVICES
63 DUFFERS DRIVE
LINN CREEK, MO 65052

2022

Ethics in Rehabilitation: A Case Study Approach

[edited by] Joseph F. Stano

ISBN 978-1-07332488-4-6

Cover designed by M Jean Andrew, J.D.

To Secure Additional Copies • Contact:

Aspen Professional Services
63 Duffers Drive
Linn Creek, MO 65052
jandrew@socket.net
573.317.0907
Cell: 573.286.0418
FAX: 573.873.2116

Aspenprofessionalservices.com

TABLE OF CONTENTS

TABLE OF CONTENTS (Cont'd.)

THE EDITOR

Joseph F. Stano, Ph.D., LRC

My career spanned forty-five years as a counselor and as a full time faculty member. I started my career as a vocational rehabilitation counselor specializing in addictions. I then spent forty years of my career as a full time faculty member at Springfield College. I was initially hired in the Rehabilitation Counseling program to develop addictions courses and to teach in both the undergraduate and graduate programs. Eventually, I was asked to be the coordinator of the graduate programs. Due to my background in statistical analysis and evaluation I spent a majority of my time teaching in the mathematics program for several years. I was then asked to start an undergraduate program in Health Science. This was my primary focus over the last ten years of my teaching career. This program grew to 200 hundred students by the time of my retirement.

I now spend my time reading extensively. It is the first time since high school that I can read all that I want for pleasure. I humorously say that I would like to read all the nonfiction books ever written as well as many of the fiction ones. My wife and I tend one acre of flower gardens as well as a koi pond and three other water features. We enjoy traveling extensively. I love staying in contact with friends, colleagues, and former students literally all over the world.

THE AUTHORS

MICHAEL P. ACCORDINO, D.Ed., CRC., LMHC., is Professor of Counseling/Clinical Mental Health Counseling (CMHC) Coordinator in the Department of Counseling at Springfield College. He has worked in the field of psychiatric rehabilitation (community residential rehabilitation and partial hospitalization programs) for seven years and has been a rehabilitation educator for 23 years. Dr. Accordino has published articles pertaining to treatment outcomes of psychiatric rehabilitation facilities, vocational rehabilitation of people with psychiatric disabilities and has conducted communication skills training in community mental health and prison settings. He has also presented nationally and internationally on the same topics.

ALISON BARANAUSKAS, B.S., is a graduate student in the Rehabilitation Counseling Program at Springfield College. She is a graduate associate for the Counseling Department and an intern at the Massachusetts Rehabilitation Commission.

PAUL BOURGEOIS, PhD, CRC, NCC, is an Assistant Professor in the Department of Psychology and Coordinator of the Clinical Mental Health Counseling Program at the University of New Haven. Dr. Bourgeois holds a PhD in Rehabilitation Counselor Education from the University of Arizona. He has published and presented widely on issues related to professional ethical behavior and professional issues in counseling. Currently, his research is focused on ethical issues in counseling involving the use of technology and ethical workplace culture within counseling organizations. He is a Certified Rehabilitation Counselor and National Certified Counselor. Dr. Bourgeois is active in numerous professional organizations including the American Counseling Association, Association for Counselor Education and Supervision, and National Council on Rehabilitation Education.

DANIEL L. BOUTIN, Ph.D., CRC, NCC, is an associate professor in the School of Interdisciplinary Health Professions at Northern Illinois University. He received his Ph.D. in counselor education from The Pennsylvania State University and M.S. in rehabilitation counseling from Springfield College (MA). Dr. Boutin has published articles on the impact of vocational rehabilitation services for persons with disabilities. He is an ad hoc reviewer for several scholarly rehabilitation journals and a past board member for the National Rehabilitation Association.

(Author's Cont'd.)

Amanda Boyd has a master's degree in Rehabilitation and Mental Health Counseling from the Illinois Institute of Technology and is currently a doctoral candidate in the Rehabilitation Counseling Education program. She is a Licensed Clinical Professional Counselor (LCPC) and Certified Rehabilitation Counselor (CRC) that specializes in vocational and mental health counseling with transition-aged youth in the therapeutic day school setting. Her research interests involve the development/adaptation of interventions designed to increase post-secondary outcomes for individuals with ASD.

Emily A. Brinck, Ph.D., is a researcher in the Wisconsin Center for Educational Research (WCER) Center at the University of Wisconsin-Madison on the Vocational Rehabilitation Technical Assistance Center for Quality Employment (VRTAC-QE) grant. Prior to working for Wisconsin, she was previousy an Assistant Professor and Director of the Rehabilitation & Human Services program at the University of North Dakota and University of Maine at Farmington. She received her Ph.D. in Rehabilitation Counselor Education from the University of Wisconsin-Madison, her Master's in Management from Indiana University, Intervention Specialist, Miami University. Dr. Brinck has had the opportunity to work on the Wisconsin program, Promoting the Readiness of Minors in Supplemental Security Income (PROMISE), as well as the Rehabilitation Research and Training Center on Employer Practices grants. She has published numerous research articles. Her research interest includes interagency collaboration between schools, vocational Rehabilitation, and employers; transition services to post-secondary rehabilitation, and employers; transition services to post-secondary employment and education; and counselor supervision.

Nicholas Cioe, Ph.D., CRC, CBIST, has been the Director of Rehabilitation Counseling at Assumption University in Worcester, MA since 2016. In addition to counselor education, he specializes in post-acute brain injury rehabilitation, treatment of co-existing substance use disorders and disabilities with cognitive impairment and preparing students to work with veterans. He is also the Coordinator of the Special Ops: Service Members, Veterans, and their families (SMVF), graduate certificate program that is designed to up-skill individuals interested in addressing the needs of SMVF. He is a Certified Rehabilitation Counselor (CRC) and Certified Brain Injury Specialist Trainer (CBIST).

AUTHOR'S (CONT'D.)

BRIAN CLARKE is a practicing mental health counselor and graduated from Northern Arizona University with a master's in clinical Mental Health Counseling. His clinical experience is diverse, from private community practice and crisis counseling, to providing clinical supervision and training. Brian is a PhD candidate and Graduate Teaching Associate in Counselor Education at the University of Arizona. He has served on the Association for Counselor Education and Supervision (ACES) graduate student board and as a graduate student representative on the Western Association for Counselor Education and Supervision (WACES) board. His current research is focused primarily on the implications and practice of mindfulness in counselor training, and applied ethics in counseling practice and education.

ALLISON R. FLEMING, PhD, CRC, is an Associate Professor of Rehabilitation and Human Services and Counselor Education at Penn State University. Allison received her master's degree in rehabilitation counseling from Springfield College in 2004 and became a Certified Rehabilitation Counselor (CRC) that same year. She has worked in the rehabilitation field as a counselor, researcher, and educator for the last 16 years. Prior to pursuing an academic career, Allison worked as a vocational rehabilitation counselor for the Commonwealth of Massachusetts in Boston. Following that experience, she also worked for the Institute for Community Inclusion providing continuing education in best practices in employment services to rehabilitation counselors and community rehabilitation staff around New England. She received her PhD in Rehabilitation Counselor Education at Michigan State University in 2012 and has been on the faculty at the University of Kentucky and Penn State. She is currently serving as First VP of the National Council for Rehabilitation Education, and on the research advisory board of the Gregory S. Fehribach Center at Eskinaze Health.

LINDSEY FULLMER, Ph.D, CRC, NCC, is an Assistant Professor of Counseling in the Department of Counseling at Springfield College. Dr. Fullmer has worked in the field of psychiatric rehabilitation for 10 years and has also worked for three years as a supervisor at a training clinic for a counselor education program. She has published articles and presented nationally on topics pertaining to college student mental health and reentry readiness for individuals experiencing incarceration. Dr. Fullmer is a member of the Massachusetts Prison Education Consortium and is a mentor for women at a community reentry program.

AUTHOR'S (CONT'D.)

MICHAEL HARTLEY, M.S., Ph.D., is an associate professor in the Department of Disability and Psychoeducational Studies at The University of Arizona. He earned an M.S. degree in Rehabilitation Psychology from The University of Wisconsin-Madison and a Ph.D. degree in Rehabilitation Counselor Education from The University of Iowa. In the past, he has worked as a rehabilitation counselor to assist individuals who met a nursing home level of care to live and work independently in the community. He also has experience working as a college counselor and university disability counselor as well as the interim director of a Center of Independent Living (CIL). Dr. Hartley is engaged in professional and ethical issues, having served on an American Counseling Association (ACA) and a Commission of Rehabilitation Counselor Certification (CRCC) taskforce to revise codes of ethics regulating the practice of counseling. His research, teaching, and service all revolve around critically framing the application of ethical principles within a dominant cultural context that has historically devalued and restricted the lives of people with disabilities. Much of his work targets distributive justice issues and therefore his scholarship on ethics has expanded to include the importance of promoting resilience and of advocating against ableism.

HEAVEN HOLLENDER, PH.D, CRC, CBIS is a Clinical Assistant Professor at Indiana University Purdue University Indianapolis. Prior to this position she worked in healthcare for over 10 years for a post-acute rehabilitation program for brain injury, spinal cord, and neurological disorders and disabilities. During these positions she has served as a program director and administrator, supervised staff including nursing, case managers, rehabilitation counselors, speech, occupational and physical therapists, dietitians, conducted program evaluation, directed case management, and aligned the program to state and federal regulations. Furthermore, she is a Certified Rehabilitation Counselor (CRC) and Certified Brain Injury Specialist (CBIS).

BRANDON HUNT, PhD, LPC, NCC, is a professor of counselor education at Georgia Southern University and a practicing clinical supervisor. Her scholarship focuses on counselor training, as well as counselor knowledge and attitudes toward clients, and she teaches courses on clinical mental health counseling, sexuality and counseling, and clinical internship. She has served on the editorial board for a number of counseling journals including the "Journal of Counseling & Development" and served on the board of directors for CACREP and NBCC.

AUTHOR'S (CONT'D.)

CHERIE L. KING, M.S., PH.D, CRC, CDMS received her doctoral degree in Rehabilitation Counselor Education from Boston University. She also has a bachelor's and master's degree in Rehabilitation Counseling from Springfield College. Dr. King has been on CCSU's faculty since 2003. She is an Associate Professor and Chairperson of the Counselor Education and Family Therapy Department and Coordinator of the Advanced Official Certificate Program in Professional Counseling (OCP). She has over 30 years of experience in the counseling field as a practitioner in various capacities including mental health, rehabilitation, disability management, and as a forensic rehabilitation expert. She is a nationally Certified Rehabilitation Counselor (CRC) and Certified Disability Management specialist (CDMS).

ANDREA PERKINS NERLICH, Ph.D an associate professor and the graduate director of the Rehabilitation Counseling Programs at Hofstra University. She completed her doctorate in rehabilitation counselor education from Michigan State University and received a Bachelor and Master's degree in rehabilitation counseling from Springfield College (MA). She is nationally certified as a rehabilitation counselor (CRC) and vocational evaluation specialist (CVE). Her passions and research interests include transition services, vocational evaluation and career assessment, collaboration models, advocacy, disability justice and health equity, mentoring, and student and professional development and identity.

ROXANNA NASSERI PEBDANI, Ph.D, CRC, SFHEA, is Acting Head of the Discipline of Rehabilitation Counselling in the School of Health Sciences at the University of Sydney. She is a Certified Rehabilitation Counselor and a Fellow of the Higher Education Academy. She has authored or co-authored 30 journal articles and book chapters and has conducted over 30 presentations at local, national, and international conferences. Dr. Pebdani's research interests are in women's issues in disability, specifically pregnancy and fertility. Dr. Pebdani also conducts research on sexuality and disability. Her other streams of research include supervision and pedagogy in counselling as well as interdisciplinary research on the effect of exercise on the quality of life of individuals with disabilities. Dr. Pebdani is a mother of two and an avid cyclist.

Author's (Cont'd.)

Sang Qin is a certified rehabilitation counselor and a licensed professional counselor in Illinois. She has a master's degree in Rehabilitation and Mental Health Counseling and is pursuing her doctoral degree in Rehabilitation Counseling Education at the Illinois Institute of Technology. Sang is a clinical research associate at the Chicago Health Disparities Center (CHDC) and the National Consortium for Stigma and Empowerment (NCSE). Her research focuses on improving health equity and increasing the knowledge of psychiatric rehabilitation.

Linda R. Shaw, Ph.D., LPC, LMHC, CRC, is a Professor in the Counseling program at the University of Arizona, where she teaches classes in group counseling, ethics, and advocacy and leadership. She previously served as the Director of the University of Arizona Doctoral program and Department Head of Disability and Psychoeducational Studies, as well as Department Head of the Rehabilitation Counseling Department at the University of Florida. She served as a member of the Association for Specialists in Group Work's (ASGW) Guidelines Task Force, the American Counseling Association (ACA) Ethics Revision Task Force for the 2014 ACA Code of Ethics revision, and as the Chair of the Commission on Rehabilitation Counseling's (CRCC) Code of Ethics Revision Task Force for the 2017 revision. Dr. Shaw is a past-president of both ARCA and CORE and was the ARCA Representative to the 20/20 workgroup. She served as Vice-Chair of the Commission on Rehabilitation Counselor Certification (CRCC) and as chair of the Ethics Committee for CRCC. Dr. Shaw's research focuses on ethics in counseling and healthcare, disability human rights, professional issues in rehabilitation counseling and group counseling.

James L. Soldner, Ph.D., CRC, is an Associate Professor and Graduate Program Director of the Rehabilitation Counseling Program at the University of Massachusetts Boston (UMB) in the School for Global Inclusion and Social Development (SGISD). He received his Ph.D. in Rehabilitation from Southern Illinois University Carbondale. Dr. Soldner conducts scholarly research, teaches graduate coursework, and is involved in various service activities within SGISD, UMB and the broader professional fields of rehabilitation and behavior analysis. His research focus includes the applications of behavior analysis to rehabilitation, clinical supervision, evidence-based practice in rehabilitation, rehabilitation administration and leadership, brain injury rehabilitation, and the scholarship of teaching and learning.

Dr. Soldner serves on the editorial review board for the Journal of Rehabilitation, Rehabilitation Counselors and Educators Journal, and is a guest editor for varied behavioral and rehabilitation-related scholarly journals on an ongoing basis. He has facilitated 80+ presentations at academic conferences and training seminars at the local, state, national, and international levels. He has an extensive clinical background providing services to individuals with disabilities in a wide variety of rehabilitation and educational settings.

MATTHEW E. SPRONG, PH.D., CRC, LCPC, CADC, CLCP, CVE

Dr. Sprong is the Supervisory Vocational Rehabilitation Counselor in the VHA Vocational Rehabilitation Program at VA Illiana Health Care System and Assistant Professor in the Clinical Mental Health Counseling program at Lock Haven University. He specializes in addictive behaviors including substance-related disorders with co-existing psychiatric and physical disabilities, video gaming behavioral functions, and rehabilitation counseling service delivery issues with Veterans who have addictions. He is a Licensed Clinical Professional Counselor (LCPC), Certified Alcohol & other Drug Counselor (CADC), Certified Life Care Planner (CLCP), and Certified Vocational Evaluator (CVE) Specialist.

ERICA L. WONDOLOWSKI, Ph.D., CRC, is the Program Director and

Associate Professor of Rehabilitation Science at Arkansas Tech University. Dr. Wondolowski holds a Ph.D. in Rehabilitation Counselor Education (Michigan State University) and previously worked for the Massachusetts Rehabilitation Commission. Her research interests include sexual health and expression of persons with disabilities, diversity, equity, and inclusion, in addition to social justice law and movements.

PRIYANKA YALAMANCHILI, PH.D., CRC, works as an Assistant

Professorand Rehabilitation Counseling Clinical Coordinator at California StateUniversity, San Bernardino. She earned her Ph.D. degree in Rehabilitation Counseling at Southern Illinois University Carbondale and is a Certified Rehabilitation Counselor. She teaches courses related to individual and group counseling skills, counseling theories, psychiatric rehabilitation, addictions and co-existing disabilities, case management, job placement, and medical and psychosocial aspects of disability. Dr. Yalamanchili's research includes understanding cultural competencies from the perspective of clients receiving services from community agencies, and teaching pedagogies used to enhance interdisciplinary collaboration. She serves

Author's (Cont'd.)

on the board for the National Council on Rehabilitation Education NCRE) and as a peer reviewer for the Journal of Applied Rehabilitation Counseling, Journal of applied Rehabilitation Counseling, Journal of Rehabilitation Administration, and the Rehabilitation Counseling Bulletin.

Cindy Zabinski, LMHC, CRC, ACS is the owner of a group counseling practice where she oversees and supervises a team providing individual, couples, family, and group counseling. Her clinical focus is in the areas of eating disorders, body image, addictions, trauma, and infertility. She is a certified EMDR therapist and a consultant-in-training. She is passionate about the training of new counselors and professional development of licensed counselors, offering clinical supervision and internships as part of her practice and providing service to the field through writing, presentations, teaching, and involvement in several professional organizations.

This page intentionally left blank.

CHAPTER 1

BASIC CONSTRUCTS OF ETHICS

ERICA L. WONDOLOWSKI

INTRODUCTION

Beginning at birth, every person begins to integrate the knowledge provided to them by trusted adults with their own experiences and interactions with the world. This process assists individuals in determining what qualifies an act, thought, and verbal exchange as good or bad. As a child, one is subject to the definitions and qualifications provided to them by the authority figure(s) in their life. As one matures, becomes a more independent thinker, and has more diversified experiences, their own definitions and qualifications will emerge. These constructs eventually translate into a personal code of ethics, or manner of governing how one chooses to interact with the world.

In the professional realm, the code of ethics which governs how we interact with the world as a rehabilitation counselor is informed by sociocultural, contextual, and historical factors. In maintaining a standard expectation of conduct, the Commission on Rehabilitation Counselor Certification (CRCC) serves as a gatekeeper, ensures quality care and service provision, while also staying apprised of relevant changes in those sociocultural, contextual, and historical factors which may impact the applicability of the current Code of Ethics[1] (Code).

While one's personal ethics may be impacted by those they uphold as a professional, those outlined by the CRCC as a governing body are considered non-negotiable for those who hold the Certified Rehabilitation Counselor (CRC) or Canadian Certified Rehabilitation Counselor (CCRC) credential. Furthermore, failure to maintain a working knowledge and understanding of the standards outlined in the Code only increases the likelihood that one will conduct themselves unethically. It is therefore crucial to fully explore the construct of ethics, beginning with the basic definition.

THE DEFINITION OF ETHIC(S)

The first definition of *ethic(s)*[2] is *the discipline dealing with what is good or bad and with moral duty and obligation.* There are two aspects of this definition which need to be addressed; the first is *...dealing with what is good or bad.* For this component of the definition to be made operational one, or a group, needs first to determine the criterion which must be met for behavior to qualify as either good or bad. This can be viewed across several distinct, yet often intersecting contexts; those of one's profession, sociocultural background, and past and present historical contexts. Realistically, the professional context for ethical principles is driven by both the sociocultural and historical contexts in which they are carried out. Professions are a product of their place in time and the culture in which they originated.

The second part of this first definition is *...with moral duty and obligation.* Every professional in a given field, is charged with a moral duty and obligation to protect those that they provide services to, as well as maintaining the reputation and credibility of the profession as a whole. Rehabilitation counselors are charged with protecting their clients as they engage in service-provision and the counseling relationship. Clients entrust the rehabilitation professional with their care, often sharing confidential and sensitive information. For some clients, working with a rehabilitation counselor may result in an increased feeling of vulnerability. It is the subsequent actions taken by the rehabilitation professional that may shape the client's willingness to trust, share, and take risks in the future. Rehabilitation professionals, as facilitators of change within their clients, are charged with the obligation and moral responsibility, or duty, for providing quality service provision, always.

The second definition of *ethic(s)*[2] is *a set of moral principles; a theory or system of moral values*. The specific moral, or ethical, principles will be explicated in a later chapter. It is important to note that these principles and values also should be viewed via the context of both culture and history. As an example, think of how much technology has both affected and changed the world. Less than 30 years ago, cell phones were considered a luxury that only the affluent could afford, as opposed to today's culture where cellphone ownership is, to a certain degree, expected. As the historical context changes, so does the sociocultural context. The first mass-produced black and white television sets first began integrating into everyday American life following the end of World War II, less than a century ago, yet since that time the evolution of the television and related broadcasting has been significant. As relevant news became more readily available, information exchange increased in speed and frequency, and the ability to view and interact with persons outside one's local area became available, the sociocultural context within each person lives is affected.

The third definition of *ethic(s)*[2,3] is *the principles of conduct governing an individual or group*. The *principles of conduct* are, in practice, the code of ethics for a given profession. Those within a profession are held to those principles outlined by a governing entity, or body, which oversee the creation, implementation, and adjudication of said principles. For CRC and CCRC designees, the CRCC is that governing body. For those counselors who are licensed in their respective state, the state licensure board is the governing body. In adhering and upholding those principles of conduct prescribed to them by the governing entity, the profession is better positioned to provide standardized care emphasizing the protection of the client and credibility of the profession. Today's practitioner has the responsibility to both maintain the ethical canons of their profession and to participate in opportunities whereby their Code is revised due to the evolution of sociocultural, historical, and contextual factors over time.

With a clearer understanding of the definition of ethic(s), one must now seek to understand the process by which ethical codes of conduct are developed.

GUIDING PRINCIPLES

Though many professions maintain and uphold their own code of ethics, those within the healthcare-related professions draw from several universal tenets or principles as a guide. The basic principles are beneficence (i.e., promote client wellbeing), nonmaleficence (i.e., do no harm), fidelity (i.e., to honor that which one is entrusted with), responsibility, integrity, justice (i.e., to be fair), veracity (i.e., to be honest), and respect for people's rights and dignity. While these principles will be further outlined in a later chapter, the terms are introduced here so that they are understood as the *guiding principles* of the rehabilitation counseling profession and of the individual rehabilitation counseling professional.

Throughout history, there have been many constructs and frameworks developed to guide behavior and how one interacts with society. Frameworks exist for government, specific professions, and those outlined in spiritual and faith-based texts. Though these constructs may be perceived as universal, they are also products of the historical, contextual, and sociocultural contexts in which they were developed. Becoming more specific now, one must seek to understand the process by which ethical standards are applied in practice.

APPLIED ETHICS

Applied ethics focuses on taking concepts from the conceptual, where ideas are formed and informed by existing research, and enacting them in practice to determine their level of effectiveness. While an idea may look as though it cannot fail on paper, the idea may very well not succeed for one reason or another, when carried out. Historically, philosophizing without a predetermined application in mind allowed those who so desired to spend a life in deep contemplation of the more abstract Meta issues such as, (a) What is the meaning of life?; (b) What is the meaning of good and evil?; (c) What is the meaning of pain and suffering?; (d) What is justice?; and (e) What is love? As the sociocultural, historical, and contextual constructs transform over time, many individuals designated less time for contemplative reflection in exchange for an increased focus on achieving goals, fulfilling daily obligations, managing a full schedule masterfully.

It can be argued that any profession's code of ethics is an example of applied ethics. Therefore, it follows that the CRCC's Code is an example of applied ethics for rehabilitation counseling professionals. Rehabilitation counseling practitioners must first thoroughly familiarize themselves with the Code and seek to have a functional understanding of how the Code applies to their profession. Claiming ignorance in light of an allegation of ethical misconduct is unacceptable. As such, the Code serves as an integral component upon which rehabilitation counselor education curricula is based. While the Code is and should be integrated in as many classes as is appropriate, it is within the experiential learning (e.g., practicum, fieldwork, internship) opportunities where the student is able to take what was taught on a conceptual level within the classroom, and see it being applied to situations they may be involved with.

4

Over the course of a rehabilitation counselor's career, several situations are likely to arise. First, they will have the opportunity to gain practical professional experience as they continue to interact with a diverse clientele. As a result of these interactions, the rehabilitation counseling professional may be exposed to a variety of ethical quandaries with which they need to understand and address. Second, due to these experiences, and continuing clinical supervision, the rehabilitation counseling professional develops a greater appreciation for the intricacies of the ethical standards as well as their application in clinical rehabilitation counseling environments. Third, the rehabilitation counseling professional becomes more aware of ethical concerns as they arise in these professional environments, at the time that they occur. This awareness allows the rehabilitation counseling profession to be increasingly effective when providing services to clients and allows the professional to anticipate *potential* situations where ethical misconduct could occur. Fourth, the client often is a secondary beneficiary of their rehabilitation counseling professional's heightened sense of awareness and sensitivity. As this awareness increases, client's may feel as though their quality of service, their rehabilitation counselor's level of professionalism, and the client's likelihood of achieving their goals has significantly increased. This synergistic process results in increased client satisfaction and betterment of the profession, overall.

Engaging in developmental processes such as that outlined above illustrates the importance of having a Code which utilized applied ethics, and that seeks to respond to the transformation of sociocultural, historical, and contextual factors over time. It remains a primary goal for rehabilitation counseling educators to ensure that the community of clients is provided with rehabilitation counseling professionals who exemplify the highest standards of competence and ethical behavior, while also holding one another accountable of the same expectation.

The rehabilitation counseling professional frequently operates within a complex environment, which is subject to evolution and change. Furthermore, due to diverse medical histories of the clients served by rehabilitation counseling professionals, one must also operate at the nexus of Bioethics and Healthcare Ethics. Rehabilitation counseling professionals must be well versed in the across and within each of these fields. For example, a bioethical dilemma which a rehabilitation counseling professional may find themselves presented is the utilization of cochlear implants by persons who have significant hearing loss. This is a controversial intervention in the Deaf community, with cochlear implants being often viewed as an absolute and outright rejection of the Deaf culture. There are no straightforward and clear resolutions to this dilemma. Similarly, the Rehabilitation Counseling professional must address, with their client, concerns surrounding engaging in experimental medical procedures in addition to whether a procedure is necessary from a cost-benefit and quality of life perspective, respectively.

The rehabilitation counseling professional is akin to that of a circus ringmaster; as the ringmaster stands in the center of the arena, they are simultaneously directing the acrobats above them, the lion tamer next to them, and the elephant displaying his repertoire of tricks for all to see. Failure to successfully divide one's attention as needed, or to neglect to direct one particular act, and the whole show may very well fall apart. Similarly, the rehabilitation counseling professional often manages several ongoing services for any one client. As such, the professional must coordinate and monitor said services, provide upkeep of the case management areas just as documenting case notes, attend care team meetings when applicable, in addition to supporting the client with consistent guidance and insight. All of which require contextual, sociocultural, and historical awareness and sensitivity. One would be correct to ascertain that to successfully accomplish these tasks is no easy feat. Consider the ramifications if a gross misstep were to occur; the rehabilitation counseling professional may become overwhelmed, may feel as though they cannot recover from said misstep, or may begin to take their frustrations out on their clients or colleagues. Furthermore, if the professional is feeling overwhelmed, they may begin to cut corners to expedite a given process or procedure and subsequently begin committing ethical violations as a result. While the provision of services can, at times, feel overwhelming it is through the integration of self-care practices that one staves off burnout and prevents making ethical missteps as a result.

Rehabilitation counseling professionals accept all the obligations and responsibilities outlined within the Code when they earn the CRC or CCRC credential. Clients seek out rehabilitation counseling professionals, often, in times of great vulnerability and proceed to entrust these professionals with highly sensitive and confidential details of their lives. It is crucial that the rehabilitation counseling professional appreciate the risk that the client is taking to better themselves, and how the quality of services provided directly correlates to the quality of life that the client has, currently and in the future. As rehabilitation counseling professionals engage in their daily activities, the ethical standards of conduct as prescribed in the Code should be kept at the forefront of the mind, guiding not only the acts, thoughts, and words they exchange in a professional setting but also in those environments when they are no longer considered at work, believe they are alone, or that no one is looking. Consider how a client may perceive their rehabilitation counselor should they find them highly intoxicated and having difficulty walking at the local grocery store. While the professional is not at work and is not responsible for seeing clients at that time, their behavior still reflects poorly on them and the entire profession. As CRC or CCRC designees, one is not only a gatekeeper for the profession ensuring that those who are accepted into this select group meet the necessary requirements but also, a guardian. As a guardian, every CRC and CCRC holder has a duty in making sure that those who have been accepted into the profession continue to provide quality services to their clients, upholding the ethical principles as outlined in the Code, and to raise up the rehabilitation counseling profession in *all* that they do.

DISCUSSION QUESTIONS

1. Reflect on the last 24 hours. Chances are, you made an ethical decision at some point.

   a. What was the situation and your possible choices of action?

   b. Which decision did you make, and why?

   c. To whom or what, do you attribute with determining whether your decision was good or bad (e.g., yourself, your upbringing, trusted adult, experience, spirituality/faith/religion)

2. Reflect on the time you spend watching television and/or engaging with a cellphone. If neither television nor cellphone use applies to you, choose a different modern technology to reflect on.

   a. How has your time spent with the technology enhanced your life, if at all?

   b. How has your time spent with the technology proven to detract from your life, if at all?

   c. How, if at all, has the presence of this technology influenced the way you live (e.g., how you dress, speak, habits)?

   d. What might your life look like if the technology had never been introduced to you?

3. Sit in a quiet room, with no distractions. Ensure you will not be disturbed for 20 minutes. When you are ready, find a comfortable place to sit or lie down and reflect on one of the following meta issues for 10 minutes. You may wish to set a timer/alarm, so you do not feel the need to check the clock. If at any time you find your mind drifting from the issue, gently redirect it back as many times as you need to.

   a. What is the meaning of life and who/what determines that meaning?

   b. Is there such a thing as good and evil, and is it a spectrum one falls within or are you simply one or the other?

   c. What is the meaning of pain and suffering?

   d. What is justice?

   e. What does it mean to love and to be loved?

REFERENCES

[1]Commission on Rehabilitation Counselor Certification. (2017). *Code of professional ethics for rehabilitation counselors.* https://crccertification.com/wpContent/uploads/2021/03/CRC_CodeEthics_Eff2017-FinaLnewdiesign.pdf

[2]Merriam-Webster. (n.d.). Ethic. In *Merriam-Webster.com dictionary*. Retrieved March 3, 2021, from https://www.merriam-webster.com/dictionary/ethic

[3]Merriam-Webster. (n.d.). Ethics. In *Merriam-Webster.com medical dictionary*. Retrieved March 16, 2021, from https://www.merriam-webster.com/medical/ethics

CHAPTER 2

THE COMMON MORAL SYSTEM

ERICA L. WONDOLOWSKI

THE COMMON MORAL SYSTEM

As discussed in Chapter 1, all professional codes of ethical conduct are shaped by the existing contextual, sociocultural, and historical factors during which they are developed or revised. The concept of a *Common Moral System* refers to an intuitive standard of behavior, frequently assumed to be consistent in nature, but equally influenced by contextual, sociocultural, and historical factors of the time at which it is executed. One must first analyze the means for the terms *common, moral,* and *system* before moving toward a greater understanding of the overall concept.

According to the Merriam-Webster Dictionary,[3,4,5]

Common is defined as:
➤ of or relating to a community at large; and

➤ of the best known or most frequently seen kind.

Moral is defined as:
➤ of or relating to principles of right and wrong in behavior;

➤ expressing or teaching a conception of right behavior;

➤ sanctioned by or operative on one's conscience or ethical judgment; and

➤ capable of right and wrong action.

System is defined as:
➤ a regularly interacting or interdependent group of items forming a unified whole;

➤ a group of interacting bodies under the influence of related forces;

➤ a group of devices or artificial objects or an organization forming a network especially for distributing something or serving a common purpose; and

➤ an organized set of doctrines, ideas, or principles usually intended to explain the arrangement or working of a systematic whole.

EXPLICATION OF *COMMON*

The first component of the definition of *common* refers to ...*relating to a community at large*. From a *macro-perspective*, the term of community can be viewed as a synonym for society. While something can be common for one person, this personal perspective is both myopic and non-comprehensive. If society were comprised of individuals who only pursued their own interests, the result would be chaotic, rather than democratic. Instead, each person must balance their own personal wish for fulfillment with the interests of the greater society. Alternatively, the *micro-perspective* refers to that of a group of like-minded individuals who decide the parameters of their concern and responsibility. The profession of rehabilitation counseling is one such group, bounded by the established role, function, and Code which inform the services one provides.

The second component of the definition of *common* refers to–*the best-known kind.* While there may be multiple options available, the best-known refers specifically to an option that is not only used frequently but has a high rate of success when executed. As both gatekeepers and guardians, rehabilitation counseling professionals are charged with safeguarding the interests of their clients and that of the profession. To do so, one must acknowledge and embrace that it is not enough to act ethically when working in the capacity of a rehabilitation professional, but in all that they do. Imagine a small, round, glass fishbowl filled with water, some decorative stones, perhaps a sprig of fake flora, and a pet goldfish, Gil, who is perfectly content swimming around his habitat. Gil is always subject to observation in his glass home because there is nothing within the fishbowl where he could hide, try as he may. For leaders and professionals in any field, this is also the case. Whether at the office or grocery shopping, out for a social gathering with friends or meeting with the rest of a care team, one can and should anticipate that there will be another who will bear witness to their actions and words. An analogy heavily referred to in leadership literature, the fishbowl "means you have to behave with integrity all the time and do the right thing, even when you don't feel like it"[6,p.152] because "in this fishbowl world, it is extremely easy for reputations to be quickly and completely shredded."[6,p.135]

EXPLICATION OF *MORAL*

Everyone seemingly has a personal definition of *moral.* The wellspring of this definition is rooted in the *personal* experiences of that individual, reinforced by the formal and informal information they collect over time from trusted and respected individuals and guiding principles of their faith/spirituality. While a personal definition is important as a component of development and in directing behavior, it is a micro-perspective, and therefore not sufficient for guiding the actions of multiple individuals within a profession. As a healthcare provider, the rehabilitation counseling professional must be aware and keyed in to the macro-needs of the field.

The first component of the definition of *moral* refers to–*of or relating to principles of right or wrong behavior.* When determining *right* and *wrong behavior,* one must take into consideration the sociocultural, historical, and contextual factors in which they are examined. In 1919 the 18th Amendment was ratified, establishing prohibition, and making alcohol illegal in the U.S. regardless of age. Ratified 12 years later, the 21st Amendment repealed the 18th Amendment, thus ending prohibition. Depending on whether you were seen drinking alcoholic beverages in 1921 or in 1934, you may or may not have been arrested.

While the legal system of a country is shaped within the historical context in which legislation is passed, one must be remembered that the needs of a society change over time. For example, the CRCC Code was first approved and adopted by the Board of Directors in 1987.[2] Eight years later, shortly following the advent of the World Wide Web and commercial release of internet access, the Pew Research Center[7] reported that nearly half (42%) of all adults in the U.S. had never heard of the internet, and an additional 21% knew only of a vague association with computer use. The CRCC had no reason to include what is currently Section J, *Technology, Social Media, and Distance Counseling*, in the initial release of the Code because the historical and sociocultural factors did not dictate a need at that time. It was not until 2002, when the Code was first revised,[3] that the CRCC began to address the use of computer technology in practice, with specific substandards written related to confidentiality, informed consent, and professional responsibility. As the technologies advanced and became more readily accessible by the public so, too, did the Code. Many are thankful for the ongoing evolution of the Code, particularly around technology and distance counseling, given the onset of the COVID-19 Pandemic in 2020 during which Pierce, et. al.[8] report over a 26-fold increase in outpatient telehealth mental health counseling provision.

The second component of the definition of *moral* refers to–*expressing or teaching a conception of right behavior*. This definition can be interpreted in a variety of ways, however here the term *expressing* implies that right behavior must be carried out in a manner that is visible to others, aligned with current, relevant legislation at the state and nation level, such that the Code is memorialized in a formal document and available to those who wish to view it. Rehabilitation counselor educators, all of whom are invited to participate in the process of ethical code revisions alongside rehabilitation counseling professionals, underscore the importance of *teaching* in this definition as the required curriculum for rehabilitation counseling students includes considerable classroom instruction in the ethics, in addition to supervised application in the field during their practicum, fieldwork, and internships.

The third component of the definition of *moral* refers to–*sanctioned by or operative on one's conscience or ethical judgment*. The purpose of a formal educational curriculum is not only to expose the students to the knowledge base which comprises a professional field of endeavor, but also to nurture the development of a professional identity. The rehabilitation counseling student not only learns the ethical dilemmas which a professional commonly encounters at a conceptual level, but through the process of clinical supervision, the student also is exposed to the process of ethical decision-making in a clinical setting. The development of *ethical judgment* matures over the course of one's career. One never achieves absolute competency in the area of clinical judgment due to the fact that each client and the concerns they bring into the counseling relationship, are unique.

The fourth component of the definition of *moral* refers to–*capable of right and wrong action*. That is not to say that one will always *choose* to take the right action, but that an individual is aware of the difference between right and wrong.

Even if a given professional were to be held to the most detailed and thorough code of ethics, it can be anticipated that the complexity of human behavior and constantly evolving contextual and sociocultural considerations will result in situations that are convoluted in nature, and subsequently not directly addressed in the code of ethics that a professional is responsible to uphold. There are often not any clear-cut decisions concerning a behavioral course of action. If human behavior was simplistic and straightforward, ethical conduct could be taught like the principles of simple arithmetic, where there exist four fundamental arithmetic operations with uniform functions. Unfortunately, the complexity of human behavior must be approached differently, and requires fewer clear delimiters.

EXPLICATION OF *SYSTEM*

Just as each person seemingly has their personal definition of *moral* it can also be assumed that they have a conceptualization of *system*. The use of the term *system* must have a specific context. For example, each person is simultaneously operating in multiple systems, where each system has a task or set of tasks associated with it, often proving to efficiently maximize achievement of said task(s). Here the focus is upon definitions of *system* as they apply to the understanding and resolution of ethical quandaries.

The first component of the word *system* refers to–*a regularly interacting or interdependent group of items forming a unified whole*. Consider for a moment what constitutes a code of ethics. It is not simply a categorical listing of actions a professional does or does not take; that is a list—it is not a code. The implication of the term *code*, as it is with this first definition, is that the components of said code are interdependent and intersectional, and whether one component is implemented or not directly influences whether a different component can be effectively implemented.

The second component of the word *system* refers to– *a group of interacting bodies under the influence of related forces.* Consistent with the theme above, the standards of conduct addressed in a system have, as a prerequisite, an inherent interdependence. The ethical concerns and situations which commonly arise in working with persons with disabilities have common thematic elements. The first thematic element specific to the rehabilitation counseling professional is that of a disability. It is true that each individual experiences their specific disabling condition in a unique way. That is, dependent upon the course, prognosis, nature of onset, duration, and frequency, among others, and how those factors interact within each client. There may be, however, common elements of an experience which provides the opportunity for subsets of individuals with a shared diagnosis to exchange. This is often the basis for patient education and support groups. A *system* of rehabilitation counseling ethics must include reference to both the commonalities of human existence and the unique facets of the individual experience. These *related forces* constitute the basis and need for the Code.

The third component of the word *system* refers to–*a group of devices or artificial objects or an organization forming a network especially for distributing something or serving a common purpose*. The focus here is upon *an organization forming a network for...serving a common purpose.* Professionals form organizations. The primary purpose of a professional organization is to serve as guardian and gatekeeper of the interests of that profession. The CRCC, as a professional governing body, serves the interest of two equally important constituencies: those members who have been designated with the CRC and CCRC designation, and the clients who are provided services via those designees. The Code is reflective of means by which the designees are to protect themselves, while also providing quality care and avoiding situations where harm may come to a client. Furthermore, the Code applies to students within a rehabilitation counseling program, providing protections similar to those provided to a client, and providing guidelines which help to protect faculty, similar to the counselor.

The fourth component of the word *system* refers to–*an organized set of doctrines, ideas, or principles usually intended to explain the arrangement or working of a systematic whole*. Here, let the focus be upon *an organized set of...principles usually intended to explain the arrangement or working of a systematic whole*. This is, simplistically put, the purpose and definition of a set of ethical canons. The Code serves as the immutable template for guiding the professional behavior of rehabilitation counseling professionals. Though the professional may not find the exact solution to each ethical dilemma they find themselves confronting in the Code, by referring to this document, and seeking appropriate consultation, the rehabilitation counseling professional is provided the information needed to construct a response that will place the wellbeing of the client, first. The response is thus a triple systematic. The code of ethics is, in and of itself, a systematic codification of operating principles, which is a systematic resolution of both the professional's and the client's dilemma. Last, these processes are conducted within the larger context of the systematically operating culture.

EXPLICATION OF THE NEXUS OF *COMMON*, *MORAL*, AND *SYSTEM*

Historically, mankind was primarily concerned with day-to-day survival, often migrating with their family groups, as the seasons changed. It can be hypothesized that even then, a basic understanding of what constituted good and bad, or right and wrong, existed. For mankind to survive to present day, a recognition of the critical need for interdependence and trust, to some degree, was necessary for survival. From interdependence and trust to a concept of shared experience, or commonality, then easily evolves into a framework of ethics and morality. Humanity would have failed to thrive for as long as it has, if there was no such framework preventing individuals from anarchy.

As groups of individuals began to settle in one geographic place and reside there year-round, they acquired more possessions than they had before, and options in terms of livelihood became more diverse. It is known that in several cultures and nations, including that of the U.S., some had accumulated so much in terms of assets, that they were able to purchase and enslave others. There were, unfortunately, innumerable abuses of others within these societies. To transcend these systems, even to a small degree, a sense of commonality needed to be established. One needed to recognize that no one person was above or below another, and that they are multiple shared experiences regardless of socioeconomic status, race, ethnicity, religion, and so on. As transportation and correspondence advances were made, cultures and societies were able to share, borrow, and learn from one another, resulting in the development of multiple systems over time.

Social and technological advances have only increased the complexity of human existence, and subsequently, the complexity of their interactions with one another. The nature by which humanity interacts with one another is also continuously evolving. While the formal profession of counseling came into existence only in recent history, there have been individuals throughout history who have performed many of the same functions. Often, and depending on the culture, these were individuals affiliated with a spiritual or religious group. Indeed, spiritual guides still function today in all cultures.

While the profession of rehabilitation counseling was established in the early 1900s, it became formalized with the passage of the Rehabilitation Act of 1954. The federal government began awarding grants to colleges and universities to train individuals to provide services to individuals with disabilities. Increased professionalism has continued at a frenetic pace since then, including the development of the CRCC Code for rehabilitation counseling professionals. Concurrently, members of the profession kept focus on those binding themes, the common moral system, used to guide the development of that Code over time.

DISCUSSION QUESTIONS

1. Think about a group you belong to (i.e., sorority/fraternity, faith/spirituality-based).

   a. Who decide(s/d) what the parameters of the group were? What process did they take to reach that conclusion?

   b. Is there an exemplar for your group of what it means to be "the best"? Who or what decided what qualified that exemplar?

2. Recall when you were 10-12 years old, and your behavior at that time.

    a. For much of the time, at that age, would your behavior be considered right or wrong?

      - Who determined what constituted right and wrong at that time?
      - Would that same behavior still qualify as right or wrong today, at your current age? Why or why not?

    b. Can you recall…
      - a behavior which was considered right or correct at 10-12 years of age, but is not now?

      What changed from 10-12 years of age until today, to reverse what that behavior qualified as?

      - a behavior which was considered wrong or bad at 10-12 years of age, but is not now?

      What changed from 10-12 years of age until today, to reverse what that behavior qualified as?

3. If you are in a room with other people in it, *observe* the person nearest you. If you are alone, recall the last person you *saw*.

    a. What do you believe you have in common with them?
      - From a micro-perspective?
      - From a macro-perspective?

    b. What do you believe differentiates you from them?
      - From a micro-perspective?
      - From a macro-perspective?

    c. How may these commonalities and differences dictate how you interact with this person if you were to try to hold a conversation?
      - Why?

REFERENCES

[1]Commission on Rehabilitation Counselor Certification. (2002). Code of professional ethics for rehabilitation counselors. https://doi.org/10.1037/amp0000722

[2]Commission on Rehabilitation Counselor Certification. (2021). *About us.* https://crccertification.com/about-crcc/

[3]Merriam-Webster. (n.d.). Common. In *Merriam-Webster.com dictionary*. Retrieved April 14, 2021, from https://www.merriam-webster.com/dictionary/common

[4]Merriam-Webster. (n.d.). Moral. In *Merriam-Webster.com dictionary*. Retrieved April 14, 2021, from https://www.merriam-webster.com/dictionary/moral

[5]Merriam-Webster. (n.d.). System. In *Merriam-Webster.com dictionary*. Retrieved April 16, 2021, from https://www.merriam-webster.com/dictionary/system

[6]Murray, K. (2011). *The language of leaders: How top CEOs communicate to inspire, influence and achieve results.* Kogan Page.

[7]Pew Research Center. (1995, October 16). *Americans going online...Explosive growth, uncertain destinations.* https://www.pewresearch.org/politics/1995/10/16/americans-going-online-explosive-growth-uncertain-destinations/

[8]Pierce, B.S., Perrin, P.B., Tyler, C.M., McKee, G.B., & Watson, J.D. (2021). The COVID-19 telepsychology revolution: A national study of pandemic-based changes in U.S. mental health care delivery. *American Psychologist, 76*(1), 14-25. https://doi.org/10.1037/amp0000722

CHAPTER 3

PRINCIPLES OF ETHICS

NICHOLAS CIOE

PRIYANKA YALAMANCHILI

MATTHEW E. SPRONG

The rehabilitation counseling discipline incorporates a "holistic" approach to counseling. It is "a profession that assists persons with disabilities in adapting to the environment, assists in accommodating the needs of the individual, and works toward full participation of persons with disabilities in all aspects of society, especially work,"[36,p.83] The goal of rehabilitation counseling is to help persons with disabilities live useful and satisfied lives.[38] With a primary focus on purpose and meaning, the rehabilitation model emphasizes identification of barriers or challenges (e.g., vocational, medical, psychological, social/environmental, spiritual or religious, cultural) faced by persons with disabilities and reduction or elimination of such barriers. By reducing or eliminating multiple barriers, the individual's perceived quality of life will improve.[27] This differs from other approaches that may focus on one specific obstacle (e.g., mental health). Despite its "holistic" approach to counseling, the discipline of rehabilitation counseling is newer and less established than other professions (e.g., Social Work, Psychology) and threatened by dominating counseling models (e.g., Mental Health Counseling). Although the profession is 100 years old (formally established by the Smith Fess-Act in 1920), it continues to struggle with recognition and establishing a shared understanding about how it benefits society.

The Rehabilitation Counseling profession is traditionally understood to function within the vocational rehabilitation (VR) arena with focus on helping persons with disabilities obtain and maintain employment and provide advocacy related to the Rehabilitation Act of 1973 and the Americans with Disabilities Act, among others services.[30] However, the disciplines' philosophical underpinnings (focus on ability versus deficit) and counselor education programs (broadened content and experiential opportunities) have helped rehabilitation counseling professionals find success outside of state/federal VR systems, especially related to substance use disorders and addiction, community rehabilitation, disability insurance, disability specific (congenital and acquired) and culture specific (e.g., military) rehabilitation, clinical rehabilitation, and mental health counseling. Success and diversification of role have further blurred the profession's "boundaries" and this continued struggle will present obstacles when competing against other counseling and helping professions. Other unique obstacles include continued:

1. improvement in defining rehabilitation counseling,

2. utilization of research-based/empirically supported best practices, and

3. updating the professional codes of ethics.

The primary emphasis of this chapter will be on the principles of ethics and how ethics guide our profession.

COMMISSION ON REHABILITATION COUNSELOR CERTIFICATION (CRCC)

The CRCC is one of the most established credentialing mechanisms in the counseling and rehabilitation profession and was developed in 1974 to provide credentialing to rehabilitation counselors' nationwide.[21] Rehabilitation counselors, and those graduating from closely related fields, are able to obtain certification through the CRCC, which demonstrates that the professional has the knowledge, skills, attitudes, and competencies needed to assist persons with disabilities. The purpose of becoming a certified rehabilitation counselor (CRC) is to provide assurance to people with disabilities that the counselors providing them with the rehabilitation services are of good moral character and meet the standards formed by the credentialing body and the standards of the field in general.[36] Tarvydas and Leahy,[36] suggested that in addition to the CRC credential, rehabilitation counselors could also get different credentials such as Certified Case Manager (CCM) or Certified Disability Management Specialist (CDMS). However, the rehabilitation counseling discipline has evolved from a traditional VR employment context to one that is multi-dimensional (e.g., rehabilitation counselors are working in clinical mental health settings).

Even though the CRC credential has served rehabilitation counselors well for a number of years, rehabilitation counselors should also be aware of the requirements in their state regarding licensure.[22] The most common licensure obtained by rehabilitation counselors is that of the Licensed Professional Counselor (LPC). Some other licenses obtained by rehabilitation counselors are Licensed Mental Health Counselor (LMHC) and Licensed Clinical Professional Counselor (LCPC).[22] The move toward individual state licensure in place of national certification is tied to federal/state funding agreements for Medicaid and Medicare services. States receive matching federal funds for health care related services and federal dispersal is predicated on licensure within the state where the services were provided. While some states have reciprocity between the CRC certification exam and state licensure, many states do not and require courses in addition to 48-credit hour rehabilitation counselor training program as prerequisites for licensure exams.

The change in professional roles has begun to shift from an accreditation standpoint as well. For instance, a more formal protocol is being developed that helps rehabilitation counselors enter clinical mental health counseling without the burden of proving that we have the same competencies as students graduating from mental health counselor training programs. This is primarily due to the merging of the Council of Rehabilitation Educators (CORE)—the long standing accrediting body for rehabilitation counselor education programs and the Council for Accreditation of Counseling and Related Educational Programs (CACREP) and their prior collaboration in developing mutually supported accreditation standards (i.e., clinical rehabilitation counseling standards [CLRC]).

ETHICS IN REHABILITATION COUNSELING

As evident by the new professional code of ethics (2017), the Commission on Rehabilitation Counselor's Certification (CRCC) needs to regularly update the code of professional ethics. To guide these standards the CRCC formulated a Code of Ethics for rehabilitation counselors that define the rehabilitation counseling field as client centered, sensitive to an array of disabilities, vocationally inclusive, and open to collaboration with other disciplines in and outside the counseling field.[36] The CRCC has also recognized a potential shift in employment given the two CACREP specialty areas (General Rehabilitation Counseling and Clinical Rehabilitation Counseling) and aligned the latest CRCC code of ethics with the revised American Counseling Association's (ACA) code of ethics. The reason for aligning with the ACA code of ethics is because rehabilitation counselors' work in various employment settings and oftentimes obtain state licensure. If rehabilitation counselors have both certification from the CRCC and state licensure, they need to abide by both the CRCC and ACA's code of professional ethics. Therefore, consistency between the two codes avoids potential conflicts.

To best meet the needs of individuals from different cultural backgrounds, Middleton, et al.,[23] suggested that researchers should continue to examine and implement different teaching strategies to better train rehabilitation counselors to be culturally competent with skills to address the needs of minority clients with disabilities. Parallel to the increase in individuals from different cultural backgrounds, there is an increase in the number of consumers with coexisting disabilities or dual diagnoses.[1] Benshoff, et al.,[1] suggested the intricacies involved in dealing with clients with dual diagnoses or coexisting disabilities are overly complex, making it necessary to increase the counseling skills of rehabilitation counselors to meet these needs. Thus, in order to keep up with the changing needs of individuals with severe disabilities, veterans, a shifting economy, and the diversification of the workforce it is important that CACREP keep working toward refining its educational standards to help train highly skilled rehabilitation counselors. Furthermore, the CRCC must continue to update and modify the code of professional ethics to reflect the diversification of employment for rehabilitation counselors.

The importance of ethics in rehabilitation counseling is not only related to being recognized as a legitimate profession, but also vital in providing effective service delivery. As will be demonstrated throughout this chapter, ethics are essential in helping rehabilitation counselors provide services that have been widely accepted by other professionals. Likewise, the code of professional ethics not only helps rehabilitation counselors, but also guides ethical behavior among students in rehabilitation counselor training programs. Oftentimes, rehabilitation counselors have a personal value system that may influence both service delivery and how they view the rehabilitation counseling relationship. Therefore, a professional code of ethics is used to display what is considered appropriate and inappropriate behavior according to a panel of established rehabilitation professionals, rather than one individual.

The code of professional ethics for rehabilitation counselors was established to enforce competencies in service delivery to persons with disabilities. Obtaining certification demonstrates mastery of specific skills to provide effective service delivery, but also to enforce that rehabilitation counselors will abide by the CRCC code of ethics. The code of ethics and effective service delivery go hand in hand in that the code expects that rehabilitation counselors must "demonstrate beliefs, attitudes, knowledge, and skills, to provide competent counseling services and to work collaboratively with diverse groups of individuals."[8, p.1] The preamble of the code of professional ethics states that our primary obligation is to serve and have the best interest of the client. If rehabilitation counselors do not possess the competencies needed in certain areas (e.g., forensic rehabilitation), they must recuse themselves from serving in this capacity until the competencies are acquired (e.g., further training, locating a mentor). As stated in the preamble, the primary values that rehabilitation counselors must abide by include:

> respecting human rights and dignity,

> ensuring the integrity of all professional relationships,

> acting to alleviate personal distress and suffering,

> enhancing the quality of professional knowledge and its application to increase professional and personal effectiveness,

> appreciating the diversity of human experience and culture, and

> advocating for the fair and adequate provision of services.[p.1]

These values were considered when developing the ethical standards and standards found within the professional code of ethics.

Ethical duties. In addition to using the aforementioned values in developing the ethical standards for rehabilitation counselors, there also exists an apparent need to consider to whom or what our ethical duties apply. We assert that we have five primary duties, including a duty to society, duty to persons with disabilities, duty to the rehabilitation counseling profession, a duty to our colleagues, and duty to our students (if we serve as counselor educators or supervisors during clinical training).

Duty to society. With respect to society, many tax dollars are allocated to human service professions. Specifically, within rehabilitation counseling, we are expected to make the best use of the dollars by providing effective and efficient services. The professional code of ethics can be used as a tool to help guide the meeting of societal expectations. For instance, it is an ethical imperative to be competent in the services provided and have knowledge and training in best practices.

Duty to persons with disabilities. People with congenital or acquired disabilities must manage many personal and societal attitudes that influence the perceived quality of life of individuals with disabilities.[33] (See Smart, *Disability, Society, and the Individual* for information related to disability attitudes). Our job is to help persons with disabilities respond to their disability by facilitating independence and supporting efforts to maximize potential and achieve rehabilitation goals. The ethical guide requires the provision of best practices in the most effective and efficient method available. Persons with disabilities rely on our knowledge, skills, and abilities to help them achieve their rehabilitation goals. Failing to practice appropriate ethical behavior (adherence to ethical principles) may result in clients not receiving effective service delivery. Perhaps the most likely unknowing violation of ethical practice is regarding cultural norms. There can be challenges in acquiring meaningful education directly from differing cultures because of a natural resistance to outsiders. Obtaining education about the culture and approaching individuals in a respectful manner is in line with ethical practice. Despite sometimes being uncomfortable, avoidance of these opportunities is inconsistent with ethical practice and extremely valuable career development opportunities.

Duty to the profession. Rehabilitation counselors have the duty to uphold the profession. For a profession to be viewed as a profession, it must be differentiated from other professions.[13,18] Confusion in defining rehabilitation counseling [e.g., vocational vs. mental health][26] presents a challenge. "Professions" have a code of professional ethics. Despite meeting some pre-established criteria of what defines a profession, if the professionals working within the field are incompetent and viewed as unethical, credibility associated with the profession will diminish. The CRCC code of professional ethics clearly suggests that rehabilitation counselors must provide competent services and have the interest and welfare of the client in mind when providing service delivery. Therefore, it is essential for rehabilitation counselors to continue to evaluate the CRCC code of professional ethics and to hold colleagues and oneself accountable when ethical violations occur.

Duty to colleagues. The commitment to counsel effectively requires immersion in other's experience of adjustment, which can be draining. Support, among other professional courtesies (e.g., respect, collaboration) is essential to ethical practice. The frequency of interaction with other CRCs is a marker of fulfillment of this expectation. Conferences, speaking presentations, educational engagement, providing supervision, and mentoring provide ongoing opportunities to fulfill this duty. There will understandably be differences of opinion, competition, and professional tension. An ethical approach to these situations is not necessarily established by the initial response but certainly by the ongoing interaction and effort to act professionally. The CRCC Code of Ethics[8] clearly states that Rehabilitation counselors have an ethical obligation to challenge colleagues when they are providing incompetent services. However, efforts should always be made to communicate politely with colleagues whenever behavior seems to fall outside of professional and certain ethical boundaries.

Duty to students. There is a duty to students if employed in an educational setting or serve as a supervisor in clinical training. It is the responsibility of educators to help students obtain the necessary competencies to provide effective service delivery and to continue to honor the profession by engaging in appropriate ethical behavior. Van Hoose and Kottler,[37] adapted Kohlberg's system of moral development stages and described a number of assumptions of ethical behavior.[12] One assumption, among others, is that "the counselor's functioning is not solely at one stage-this functioning may be affected by situational, educational, and other variables."[p.79] Although educational settings may not be the only mechanism in helping students engage in appropriate ethical behavior, educators can serve as a medium to helping students understand the profession's standpoint on appropriate ethical behavior and allow students to learn and apply the ethical code in specific contexts.

COMPONENTS OF THE CRCC PROFESSIONAL CODE OF ETHICS

The CRCC officially developed its first code of professional ethics in 1987, with major revisions occurring in 2002, 2010 and 2017. The professional code of ethics allows rehabilitation counselors to maintain their duties to these specific areas by providing guidelines of appropriate ethical behaviors. Herlihy and Corey,[16] suggested that professional codes of ethics serve three primary objectives[11] including:

1. educate professionals about sound ethical conduct,

2. hold rehabilitation counselors accountable, and

3. serve as catalysts for improving practice.

Therefore, the CRCC identified 12 key components included in the professional code of ethics, which are fundamental to providing effective service delivery. Each area contains numerous sub-standards that address the potential issues that could arise and help rehabilitation counselors prevent ethical violations. These key components will be discussed in later chapters within this book, but include areas such as:

1. the counseling relationship,

2. confidentiality, privileged communication, and privacy,

3. advocacy and accessibility,

4. professional responsibility,

24

5. relationships with other professionals and employers,

6. forensic services,

7. assessment and evaluation,

8. supervision, training, and teaching,

9. research and publication,

10. technology, social media, and distance counseling,

11. business practices, and

12. resolving ethical issues.

The components of the CRCC code of ethics are quite comprehensive, but the CRCC board recognizes that ethics must continue to evolve to accommodate changes in service delivery. For example, the technology concerns of today (e.g., distance counseling) were not necessarily of concern in the 1980s, due to the limited access to technology for consumers, or slow-internet connections.[24]

MOST FREQUENT REPORTED ETHICAL PROBLEMS

The CRCC ethics committee reviews complaints filed against certified rehabilitation counselors and assists in evaluating the code of professional ethics to determine if updates or modifications are needed to guide rehabilitation counselors and to reduce future complaints. For example, prior to the 2010 CRCC professional code of ethics, there was limited support to those working within Forensic Rehabilitation, and the current code of ethics demonstrates conflict with regard to who is the client in the forensic relationship. Since data collection began in 1993-1994 related to ethical violation complaints towards certified rehabilitation counselors, there have been 169 cases adjudicated, 51 cease and desist orders issued, and 143 advisory opinions issued.[19] Furthermore, the CRCC reports that the quantity of actions taken include 15 letters of instruction (note: used for minor violation), 10 reprimands, 6 CRCs were placed on probation, 7 CRCs had their certification suspended, and 22 CRCs had their certification revoked. The most common reported ethical violations included competence and conduct with clients, business practices, and professional practice.

VIRTUE ETHICS VS PRINCIPLE ETHICS

Counseling professional ethicists have analyzed the relationship between Virtue Ethics–emphasis on the moral character, and Principle Ethics–approach focused on the importance of general principles (e.g., autonomy, beneficence, nonmaleficence, fidelity, justice, veracity). Principle ethics are more suited for acting and deciding, increasing the possibility for idiosyncratic decision making. Bersoff[2] argued against adopting virtue ethics as a guiding concept in the development of counseling guidelines.

Virtue ethics focuses on the character traits of the counselor and nonobligatory ideals to which professionals aspire rather than on solving specific ethical dilemmas. In the absence of an ethical dilemma, virtue ethics compels the professional to be conscious of ethical behavior.[11] The difference between virtue and principle ethics is whether or not the focus of the question is on the situation (principle) or the person (virtue). In most applicable non-philosophical uses of the term ethics, people are conceptualizing principle ethics–a set of obligations and a method that focuses on moral issues with the goals of:

1. solving a particular dilemma or set of dilemmas, and

2. establishing a framework to guide future ethical thinking and behavior.[11]

The CRCC Code of Ethics uses six Principle Ethics (autonomy, beneficence, non-maleficence, fidelity, justice, veracity) as the basis of their code for professional ethical behavior.

AUTONOMY refers to an individual's freedom to choose a course of action. Within this ethical principle, rehabilitation counselors respect the individual's ability to make decisions free from the constraint of others.[11] It should be noted that for a client to make decisions, they need to have all of the information available. The rehabilitation counselor must make every effort to help clients understand the factors associated with and consequences for their decisions (e.g., employment, quality of life, change in benefits). The counselor should also prepare to support clients if their choices do not lead to desired outcomes so that the right to make decisions contributes to personal growth instead of failure. Autonomy is vital to the rehabilitation counseling relationship, as client autonomy predicts treatment engagement and success.[12]

BENEFICENCE refers to the notion of "doing good" to the client and taking action to improve the situation of others.[20] The principle of beneficence refers to promoting the client's well-being, and rehabilitation counselors engage in professional activities to foster skill development that benefits the client. Regular engagement in professional development, conducting systematic monitoring of practice and outcomes, and practicing continuous self-assessment to determine if personal values are negatively influencing service delivery are examples of ways that rehabilitation counselors align with this prinicple.[12]

NON-MALEFICENCE refers to the commitment of a rehabilitation counselor to avoid harm to the client. This may include sexual, financial, emotional, exploitation, and lack of competency in service delivery. Rehabilitation counselors also have an ethical obligation to challenge colleagues when they are providing incompetent services,[8] (e.g., allowing incompetent rehabilitation counselors to continue providing ineffective and incompetent service delivery jeopardizes the profession's credibility).

FIDELITY refers to the rehabilitation counselor establishing a therapeutic relationship with the client based on trust and non-judgment.[4] This includes staying current on evidence-based practices and incorporating these into service delivery. This ethical principle involves being faithful, loyal, truthful, and respectful to the client, while agreeing to keep promises made to the client (e.g., if the rehabilitation counselor agrees to investigate whether the client will be approved for post-secondary educational expenses by a specific date, the rehabilitation counselor should make all attempts to complete the task by this date).[12]

JUSTICE refers to the notion that we are fair to our clients. Bosede[7] suggested that this ethical principle is based on three assumptions: impartiality, equality, and reciprocity (treat people as you wish to be treated). A violation of this ethical principle may be demonstrated by a rehabilitation counselor providing more post-secondary educational services to clients of the same race compared to another race (with all other factors being equal). When providing services, rehabilitation counselors offer everyone equal opportunities. Understandably, in a resource limited environment, rehabilitation counselors must consider many factors and be able to support their allocation of resource decisions.

VERACITY is the principle of truth telling, which is essential to honor the person's autonomy.[38] Welfel[38] suggested that truth telling is violated by the act of lying, providing erroneous information to the client, or omitting all or some portions of the truth. Therefore, violating this ethical principle can eliminate or reduce a client's right to make decisions related to the rehabilitation plan by withholding or providing false information to the client.

ETHICAL CONFLICT. Rehabilitation counseling service delivery guided by the ethical principles will still result in conflicts. There are often times when conflict resolution and negotiation strategies are needed when developing rehabilitation goals (e.g., the expectations and perceptions of the counselor and client are different). The counselor needs to honor the individual's ability to make choices related to the rehabilitation plan (autonomy) but also be beneficent and non-maleficent. What happens if the rehabilitation plan is not in the client's best interest or welfare? This type of situation can be referred to as an ethical conflict.[19] It is necessary, in this situation, to provide a detailed conflict resolution model to help reduce the tension within the working therapeutic relationship (see Koch, et al.,[19] to access the conflict resolution model).

RESOLVING ETHICAL ISSUES

All resolutions of ethical issues should occur using an ethical decision-making model (*see* Corey, et al.;[11] Tarvydas;[36] Steinman, et al,;[34] Weifel;[38]

Rubin, et al.[31]). There is significant similarity among established decision-making models for rehabilitation counselors, but almost all presuppose the decision maker has already examined any conflict between personal and professional values. The examination of this conflict is an essential prerequisite to any attempt to solve an ethical issue as the argument for one or another course of action is necessarily tied to the decision maker's assessment of value to one or another principle. Importantly, the examination of a conflict does not imply a violation of the code but rather a natural tendency to hold in higher regard one principle over another. Additionally, a tendency to favor the importance of one principle (e.g., autonomy) over another (e.g., justice) will likely change given alternative circumstances and influencing factors. Knowledge of tendencies based on personal values is the first step toward effective ethical decision-making.

Counselors must refrain from having their personal values interfere with the profession's values.[12] Yet, some experts have suggested that "separating moral outlook and choices from professional skills and practices is both deceptive and deleterious to one of psychotherapy's major sources of legitimacy, direction and power."[12, p.69] Furthermore, the challenge of attempting to separate one's personal values from professional service delivery is quite difficult, as often times counseling involves values.

Personal values can be described as a person's implicit or explicit standards of choice, principles, or standards of behavior, and the judgment of what is important.[37] Since personal values can often interfere with our interpretation of "Best Practices," using a group of professionals from the discipline will help settle what constitutes "best ethical practices." The profession's values (outlined in the preamble of the CRCC code of ethics) are established by a group of scholars within the profession (e.g., rehabilitation counselor educators and researchers, professionals working within the rehabilitation counseling field). Professional identity involves the counselor self-reflecting so that a level of understanding can be obtained in relation to how their own self-concept and values enable them to articulate their role, philosophy, and approach to others within their chosen field.[15,5,32] Corey, et al.,[11] suggested that counselors should practice self-assessment and self-reflection of their personal values and consider how these personal values may influence the service delivery that they provide. Self-Assessment/Reflection is vital as continuous self-reflection may lead to self-discovery of potential conflict between the two values (i.e., personal vs. professional).

SELF-ASSESSMENT OF PRACTICE

There is a certain degree of independence experienced by CRCs. The rehabilitation counseling certification carries with it an expression of specialized skills that those not similarly trained or without commensurate experience are unable, or at least unlikely, to challenge. While the profession uses these advantages to distinguish its value, there is an inherent responsibility for ongoing self-assessment of practice to assure adherence to the profession's guiding code of ethics. As such, self-assessment is a necessary exercise that all CRC professionals should initiate at least annually.

The CRCC has established requirements for a minimum of 10-hours of continued education related to ethics prior to having the CRC renewed [note: renewal is every 5 years and requires 100 CEUs[8]] (see www.crccertification.com). Theoretically, fulfillment of these required ethical CEUs would suffice for self-assessment, but practically, acquisition of CEUs does not translate into meaningful self-assessment. A meaningful self-assessment should include at the very least, re-reading the entire code of ethics and, in doing so, assessing how one's professional performance aligns with the code. Identifying an area where performance and code seem inconsistent does not necessarily mean there has been an ethical violation. Rather, the act of engaging in self-assessment is, in and of itself, an act consistent with the expectations of the code and provides an opportunity for identification of potential inconsistency to allow for improvement rather than punishment.

Self-Assessment is also vital to reduce the likelihood of transference or countertransference within the counseling relationship. *Transference* can be described as feelings and barriers that the client presents in the counseling session and transfers these feelings or barriers onto the counselor.[10] For example, a client who was diagnosed with a substance related disorder (DSM 5) may have hostility toward family members because they are always "annoying" the client about his or her drug use. If the counselor confronts the client in a similar manner during the counseling relationship, this could create anxiety and hostility and diminish the therapeutic relationship (for alternative approaches please see materials related to motivational interviewing and the therapeutic technique of evoking "change talk" when working with clients who present substance related barriers).

Countertransference can be described as the reactions and responses directed from the counselor to the client.[10] This often occurs when the counselor has boundary-related issues or other unresolved issues. For example, a counselor may have had a past abusive relationship and the counselor may have failed to seek help in resolving or working on the feelings related to this past event. If the counselor has not worked on the challenges related to the past abusive relationship, the counselor may have difficulty remaining objective if a client is disclosing information that occurred in a similar context. Additionally, the counselor may unconsciously impose their values onto their client.

USING SUPERVISORS AND PEERS

The use of supervisors and peers is a key component to ethical practice. While engaging in self-assessment is important because of the professional freedom experienced by a CRC, even the biggest self-critic will struggle to break from his or her personal value hierarchy. The use of peers and supervisors facilitates the challenging of one's personal value hierarchy based on the likelihood that the other's value hierarchy is different. In this sense, a person is most likely to grow if they engage others in a manner that challenges their established position. This is especially important when participating in the ethical decision-making process.

Rehabilitation counselor supervisors execute a variety of roles, duties, and responsibilities that typically place them in an emissary position between the employing agency or organization and the rehabilitation practitioner. Although supervisors have responsibilities for the interests of the employer and the professional growth of the supervisee, the client's welfare must still be primary.[28] Section G.1.d of the Code of Ethics requires the supervisor to provide direct supervision that is adequate to ensure that the rehabilitation counseling services provided by others are sufficient and do not cause harm to the client.[8] Ultimately, the supervisor is accountable, both ethically and legally, for the services and actions of the rehabilitation trainees or practitioners under her or his supervision.

In view of the fact that rehabilitation counselor supervision is a complex and significant professional activity, it requires a high level of demonstrated competence. The Code obligates supervisors to "supervise only within the boundaries of their competence, based on their education, training, supervised experience, state and national professional credentials, and appropriate professional experience" (Section G.1.c). Supervisors must also keep current in their own specialties and be aware of advances that are being made in the general area of clinical supervision.[29] As with rehabilitation counselors, supervisors are obligated to renew and update their skills to maintain an acceptable level of professional competence.

Rehabilitation supervisors need to assess continually the usefulness of the services a client receives as well as the professional development of the rehabilitation trainees or practitioners whom they supervise. They are responsible for providing a fair and considerate appraisal of the individual's strengths, weaknesses, and their advancement as a professional. Further, rehabilitation supervisors need to communicate this information back to the supervisee in a clear, unequivocal, and timely manner.[3] Failure to provide evaluative feedback raises a serious ethical concern because the supervisor fails to provide one of the most essential tasks of supervision,[25] and this can compromise both the supervisee's growth as a counselor and the client's progress in counseling.

Personal issues should be addressed in supervision only in terms of the impact these issues have on clients and on professional functioning. Rehabilitation counselor supervisors are ethically responsible for ensuring that the supervisory relationship provides a safe and supportive opportunity for learning and their role and objectivity are not blurred by dual relationships (such as sexual intimacies). In the case of a dual relationship arising in supervision, the supervisee should seek personal counseling and determine ways to maintain the integrity of the supervisory professional relationship with his or her supervisor.[25] Supervisors have an ethical responsibility for the welfare of the clients who meet with their supervisees.[6] This requires that both the client and the supervisee clearly understand what will be kept confidential in relation to the process of supervision. In addition, the supervisor and supervisee are obligated to ensure that clients are accurately informed and clearly understand the supervisee's qualifications and credentials so that they can make informed choices.[8,28]

The principle of informed consent also extends to the supervisor and supervisee relationship. Just as the supervisee is responsible for securing the client's informed consent, the supervisor is responsible for ensuring that the supervisee understands and consents to the conditions of the supervisory relationship.[29] Use of a written agreement of supervision can further formalize and clarify the supervisor–supervisee relationship. This agreement can also serve to negate conflicts or misunderstandings that may arise in the supervisory relationship, provide a basis for resolution of conflicts, and increase accountability.

Standard H.2.b. of the Code requires rehabilitation counselor supervisors to be "aware of and address the role of cultural diversity in the supervisory relationship." Addressing cultural issues and issues of power within the supervisory relationship is a critical step in helping supervisees recognize and address similar issues with their clients. Given the diversity of clients served by rehabilitation counselors and the societal inequities often faced by those clients, it is imperative that supervisors work with supervisees to recognize the impact of cultural factors on assessment, counseling, and supervisory processes.[14]

To provide competent supervision, supervisors need to recognize the strengths, as well as the limitations, of their training, education, and experience and to supervise only within the boundaries of their competence. Evaluation and due process compel supervisors to provide supervisees with honest, consistent feedback and a means for addressing concerns appropriate for development of an acceptable level of professional competence. In addition, supervisors have special ethical obligations in the context of the supervisor–supervisee relationship. Supervisors need to ensure that this relationship provides for a safe and supportive opportunity to learn and does not abuse, exploit, or harm the supervisee in any way. Supervisors must also be clear about the nature and expectations of the supervisory relationship and ensure that the supervisee understands and agrees to the conditions of supervision.

By providing competent supervision and a safe and supportive opportunity to learn, assuring high standards and quality of service delivery, and demonstrating an ethical and respectful treatment of clients and supervisees, supervisors are demonstrating their commitment to the profession and the ethical standards related to the supervisory process. This, in turn, will shape how the supervisees will ultimately treat their clients as well as their own trainees in the future.[3]

USING AN ETHICAL DECISION-MAKING MODEL

Resolution of ethical issues is the most widely conceptualized purpose of a profession's code of ethics. Despite this conception, most codes, and certainly the CRCC Code, do not provide prescriptive answers to most ethical issues. For this reason, the word dilemma–a situation in which you must make a difficult choice,[12] is most often used when discussing ethical decision making. One such model[17] provides a framework for rehabilitation counselors to internalize potential conflict and practice a conflict resolution between the personal and profession's value difference. Kinnier[17] suggested using rational strategies, including:

1. defining the conflict clearly,

2. gathering information systematically,

3. comparing alternatives and considering consequences logically, and

4. eliminating alternatives systematically.

Kinnier[17] also suggested incorporating intuition-enhancing strategies, such as emotional focusing and incubation (e.g., vision question, meditation), among others.[p.24] Other models to help rehabilitation counselors consider the best option for service delivery when multiple ethical standards conflict with one another are the ethical decision-making models, which allow for more in-depth analysis of the ethical dilemma.

There are several ethical decision-making models that a rehabilitation counselor can use to assess the best approach to providing service delivery when two ethical standards conflict with each other,[12, pp.90-91] such as:

- Corey, Corey, & Callanan,[11]

- Forester-Miller & Davis (1996),

- Hill, Glaser, & Harden (1995),

- Keith-Spiegel & Koocher (1985),

- Welfel (2002),

- Steinman, Richardson, & McEnroe (1998),

- Stadler (1986),

- Corey, et al., (1998),

- Tarvydas, (1998),

- Weifel, (1998), and

- Rubin[31]

Although there are some similarities between the different ethical decision-making models listed above, rehabilitation counselors should evaluate each model and identify the strengths and limitations of choosing one model over the others. Despite the notion that some scholars may argue one model is more useful than another, we will demonstrate application of a generalized 7-step model for ethical decision making.

1. identification of the problem,

2. identification of the potential solutions,

3. review of the ethical code for guidance,

4. project and assess the potential consequences for each solution,

5. solicit feedback from others,

6. select and implement a course of action,

7. reflect on the decision and consequences.

CASE STUDY

FAILURE TO PROPERLY DOCUMENT, AND FALSIFYING RECORDS

You are currently employed as a rehabilitation counselor at a community-rehabilitation facility that provides job placement/development, vocational evaluations, independent living, behavior analysis, GED prep-work, and counseling services. The agency is preparing for an upcoming accreditation (i.e., Commission on Accreditation of Rehabilitation Facilities [CARF]) and you have been tasked with preparing the case notes/treatment plans for review by the CARF review team. Upon your review of case notes, you recognize that the agency did not keep any documentation/treatment plans for clients receiving counseling services, or case documentation for independent living skills being taught/learned. You meet with the program director and are informed that you will need to start having rehabilitation counselors develop case notes based on their recollection of meeting with clients and will have to date the notes based on when the meeting occurred, not when the note was written. The program director was nervous that CARF would make a recommendation, so it was important to modify the date. You asked about clients served from rehabilitation counselors that have since retired, and he informed you that you should contact them and see if they can write some case notes or provide you information so you could write them.

STEP 1. IDENTIFY THE PROBLEM

One of the primary issues is that appropriate case documentation had not occurred, and you are being directed to falsify documents for preparation for CARF accreditation review. Other issues may include inappropriately discussing client information with members that were not a part of the treatment team and writing incorrect information that could potentially be used if records were subpoenaed or requested by other medical/mental health professionals.

STEP 2. IDENTIFY POTENTIAL SOLUTIONS:

As the rehabilitation counselor, you could:

1. meet with the former clients to discuss prior counseling sessions,

2. contact rehabilitation counselors (current and retired) to ask for assistance in creating case notes/Tx plan based on prior sessions and date them when the session occurred,

3. create treatment/case notes and based on prior sessions but mark the date created as the current date, or

4. implement a strategy to complete case documentation (including treatment planning) moving forward with clients that are referred.

STEP 3. REVIEW THE ETHICAL CODE FOR GUIDANCE AND/OR STATE LEGISLATION (note: each state has different rules/regulations)

SECTION B: CONFIDENTIALITY, PRIVILEGED COMMUNICATION, AND PRIVACY

B.6. RECORDS AND DOCUMENTATION

B.6.A. REQUIREMENT OF RECORDS AND DOCUMENTATION

Rehabilitation counselors include sufficient and timely documentation in the records of their clients to facilitate the delivery and continuity of needed services. Rehabilitation counselors make reasonable efforts to ensure that documentation in records accurately reflects progress and services provided to clients. If errors are made in records, rehabilitation counselors take steps to properly note the correction of such errors according to organizational policies.

SECTION D: PROFESSIONAL COMPETENCE

D.4. Professional Credentials

D.4.G. Veracity
Rehabilitation counselors do not engage in any act or omission of a dishonest, deceitful, or fraudulent nature in the conduct of their professional activities.

SECTION E: RELATIONSHIPS WITH OTHER PROFESSIONALS AND EMPLOYERS

E.1. Relationships with Colleagues, Employers, and Employees

E.1.B. Negative Employment Conditions
The acceptance of employment in an organization implies that rehabilitation counselors are in agreement with its general policies and principles. Rehabilitation counselors alert their employers of unethical policies and practices. They attempt to effect changes in such policies or procedures through constructive action within the organization. When such policies are inconsistent with the Code, potentially disruptive or damaging to clients, and/or limit the effectiveness of services provided, rehabilitation counselors take necessary action if change cannot be affected. Such action may include referral to appropriate certification, accreditation, or licensure organizations. Ultimately, voluntary termination of employment may be the necessary action.

SECTION K: BUSINESS PRACTICES

K.2. CLIENT RECORDS

K.2.A. RECORDS AND DOCUMENTATION

Regardless of format, rehabilitation counselors create, protect, and maintain documentation necessary for rendering professional services. Rehabilitation counselors include sufficient and timely documentation to facilitate the delivery and continuity of services. Rehabilitation counselors make reasonable efforts to ensure that documentation accurately reflects client progress and the services provided, including who provided the services. If records or documentation need to be altered, it is done so according to organizational policy and in a manner that preserves the original information. Alterations are accompanied by the date of change, the identity of who made the change, and the rationale for the change.

STEP 4. PROJECT AND ASSESS THE POTENTIAL CONSEQUENCES FOR EACH SOLUTION

TABLE 1

Potential Action	Positive Outcome	Negative Outcome
Meet with the former clients to discuss prior counseling sessions	Client may provide information to properly document prior sessions/meetings	Client provides inaccurate information, Client refuses, bad CARF review
Contact rehabilitation counselors (current and retired) to ask for assistance in creating case notes/Tx plan based on prior sessions and date them when the session occurred,	Rehabilitation counselors provide old documentation or are able to provide information to help agency document prior occurrences, CARF accreditation is positive experience	Rehabilitation counselors provide inaccurate information, notes are created and are used in other settings (e.g., social security hearings, litigation, future mental health treatment)
Create treatment/case notes and based on prior sessions but mark	Case note/Tx plan creation are being appropriately documented by the date they were created	CARF accreditation review may result in inadequate findings, information provided might be inaccurate

the date created as the current date, or		
Implement a strategy to complete case documentation (including treatment planning) moving forward with clients that are referred.	Appropriate case documentation/Tx plan creation protocols will be used moving forward and the issues should be alleviated.	Does not resolve current issue, CARF reaccreditation review is impacted.

STEP 5. SOLICIT FEEDBACK FROM OTHERS
Review your process with a supervisor, peer, and legal counsel. Ask for input. Note: It may be inappropriate to only rely on the program director, given his directives regarding the issues.

STEP 6. SELECT AND IMPLEMENT A COURSE OF ACTION
Meet with the program director, provide a written justification regarding the course of action you intend to take. Additionally, other suggestions to resolve the case documentation issue could be discussed other than the directive given.

STEP 7. REFLECT ON THE DECISION AND ITS CONSEQUENCES
Reviewed and discussed at monthly meeting

ETHICAL CONSIDERATIONS FOR REHABILITATION COUNSELORS

HOW TO REPORT ETHICAL ISSUES
The CRCC[9] has established a grievance process to allow individuals to file a grievance or complaint against an individual who has violated the code of professional ethics.[9] The grievance and complaint form provides information related to the grievance/complaint process (e.g., conduct of hearing and presentation of evidence). Those filing the complaint are requested to complete five sections, including:

1. contact information (e.g., complainant's name, address, phone number),

2. name of CRC who has allegedly violated the ethical code,

3. information pertaining to the client (following the grievance process with the agency first), information pertaining to the professional colleague (discuss the situation with the CRC first), and are the ethical violation complaints being examined from other licensing or certifying organizations and/or civil lawsuits (e.g., state licensing board, civil lawsuit),

4. request for the complainant to cite specific ethical standard(s) that have been violated from the CRCC code of professional ethics, and

5. request for the complainant to cite the nature of the complaint and specific dates of when these events occurred.

The complainant is then requested to sign and date the complaint form and submit it for review. As aforementioned, it is essential to discuss the ethical violations with the colleague prior to filing a formal complaint. In many instances, this may reduce the continuation of unethical behavior and no formal complaint need be filed. However, if the unethical behavior continues, then a formal complaint may be needed.

USING DECLARATION OF PROFESSIONAL SERVICE

A declaration of professional service is beneficial because it provides clients with information pertaining to the areas of expertise, professional relationships and boundaries, and other pertinent information related to service delivery. Clients who clearly understand the purpose, nature, and structure of rehabilitation services as communicated in an intake interview report higher confidence in their rehabilitation counselors.[2] The rehabilitation counselor must make a sincere effort to provide the information in a way that makes it personally relevant to each client. An intake interview in which the rehabilitation counselor reads jargon-filled statements and generic policy information to a client reduces the chances that the client will consider the content of the session personally meaningful and may actually reduce the likelihood of the information being encoded into long-term memory.[35] While all the important "bases" need to be covered, the rehabilitation counselor can adapt the way the information is provided based on the client's experience with rehabilitation or other health care services, the client's particular needs and/or goals, and the client's expectations of the rehabilitation counselor or agency.[5]

The CRCC provides examples of professional disclosure forms (see CRCC,[7] disclosure & release forms) for different work contexts (i.e., private sector-forensic; private sector-worker's comp/LTD; public sector; technology and distance counseling; release of information). The example worksheet (Public Sector) describes the purpose of public VR and the desired outcome (i.e., employment), who the client will be working with (e.g., rehabilitation counselor), eligibility requirements for services, and specific terms that will be explained by the rehabilitation counselor (e.g., evaluation for vocational needs;

counseling and guidance; educational training). The professional disclosure form also indicates the roles and responsibilities of the rehabilitation counselor and client, confidentiality and limitations regarding confidentiality, and risks and benefits associated with services, among others. However, it will be beneficial to incorporate a boundary-related interaction (e.g., non-personal interactions) policy and code of conduct, and a potential social media policy (if this type of service delivery is used by the rehabilitation counselor or if the client attempts to contact the rehabilitation counselor in a non-professional interaction) so that the client is well aware that the relationship will be professional in nature.

CONCLUSION

Throughout history, tremendous effort has been made to establish the rehabilitation profession. A code of professional ethics establishes credibility for the profession by providing guidance and expectations to rehabilitation counselors in relation to service delivery. The CRCC must continue to update the code of professional ethics to provide guidance to rehabilitation counselors who branch out from traditional VR employment (e.g., mental health counseling).

In 2014, the ACA code of professional ethics was revised with an attempt to replace value-based standards with competency-based standards. Since the CRCC ethical task force utilizes the ACA's code of professional ethics, one can expect consideration of the revised ACA code of ethics to be part of the CRCC code of ethics review and revision process. This is especially relevant regarding competency-based standards in relation to culturally appropriate service delivery. Demonstrating respect for cultural backgrounds does not simply include asking the client about his or her culture; respect for cultural backgrounds requires infusion of culture into each component of the rehabilitation process, including intake interviewing, functional assessments, rehabilitation plans, and outcome measurement.

Ethical practice is an expectation and very few individuals involved in the provision of rehabilitation services set out with the intention of violating ethical guidelines. However, many external and internal factors influence the choices made by professionals. The code of ethics provides scaffolding to guide and encourage optimum service delivery, to best serve their profession, and to uphold the mission of rehabilitation counseling. Rehabilitation counselors must practice the strategies to increase compliance with professional ethical behavior, including:

> ➢ self-reflection techniques to determine if personal values are influencing service delivery,

➢ utilization of the ethical decision-making model to determine the best course of action when ethical violations occur, and

➢ continuing to review the CRCC code of professional ethics.

REFERENCES

[1]Benshoff, J., Robertson, S. J., Davis, S. J., & Koch, D. S. (2008). Professional identity and the CORE Standards. *Rehabilitation Education, 22*(4), 227-27.

[2]Bersoff, D. N. (Ed.). (1999). *Ethical conflicts in psychology.* Washington, DC: American Psychological Association.

[3]Blackwell, T. L., Strohmer, D. C., Belcas, E. M., & Burton, K. A. (2002). Ethics in rehabilitation counselor supervision. *Rehabilitation Counseling Bulletin, 45,* 240-247.

[4]Bosede, A. F. (2010). Ethical principles of guidance and counselling. *International Journal of Tropical Medicine, 5*(2), 50-5. doi: 10.92/ijtmed.2010.50.5

[5]Brott, P. E., & Myers, J. E. (1999). Development of professional school counselor identity: A grounded theory. *Professional School Counseling, 2*(5), 9.

[6]Cobia, D. C., & Boes, S. R. (2000). Professional disclosure statements and formal plans for supervision: Two strategies for minimizing the risk of ethical conflicts in post-master's supervision. *Journal of Counseling and Development, 78,* 29-296.

[7]Commission on Rehabilitation Counselor Certification. (2009). Disclosure and release forms. Retrieved from http://www.crccertification.com/pages/disclosure_and_release_forms/42.php

[8]Commission on Rehabilitation Counselor Certification. (2017). *Code of professional ethics for rehabilitation counselors.* Schaumburg, IL: Author.

[9]Commission on Rehabilitation Counselor Certification. (2012). CRCC guidelines and procedures for processing complaints. Retrieved from, http://www.crccertification.com/filebin/pdf/CRCC_GuidelinesForComplaints.pdf.

[10]Corey, G. (2020). *Theory and practice of counseling and psychotherapy* (10th ed.). Independence, KY: Cengage Learning.

[11]Corey, G., Corey, M. S., & Callanan, P. (2011). *Issues and ethics in the helping profession* (8th ed.). Pacific Grove, CA: Brooks/Cole.

[12]Cottone, R. R., & Tarvydas, V. M. (2007). *Counseling ethics and decision making* (rd ed.). Upper Saddle River, NJ: Pearson Education Inc.

[13]Friedson, E. (1994). *Professionalization reborn: Theory, prophecy, and policy.* Chicago: The University of Chicago Press.

[14]Glosoff, H., & Matrone, K. F. (2010). Ethical issues in rehabilitation counselor supervision and the new 2010 code of ethics. *Journal of Applied Rehabilitation Counseling, 41*(2), 54-59.

[15]Healey, A., & Hays, D. G. (2011, Spring). Defining counseling professional identity from a gendered perspective: Role conflict and development. Professional Issues in Counseling Journal. Retrieved from http://www.shsu.edu/--'piic/DefiningCounselingPro fessionalIdentityfromaGenderedPerspective.htm

[16]Herlihy, B., & Corey, G. (1996). *ACA ethical standards casebook* (5th ed.). Alexandria, VA: American Counseling Association.

[17]Kinnier, R. T. (1995). A reconceptualization of values clarification: Values conflict resolution. *Journal of Counseling & Development, 74*(1),18-24.

[18]Klegon, D. A. (1978). The Sociology of Professions: An Emerging Perspective. *Sociology of Work and Occupations 50*, 259–28.

[19]Koch, L. C., McReynolds, C., & Rumrill, P. D. (2004). Basic counseling skills for rehabilitation professionals. In F. Chan & K. Thomas (Eds.), Counseling theories and techniques for rehabilitation health professionals (pp. 227-24). New York, NY: Springer.

[20]LaFollette, H., & Persson, I. (201). *The Blackwell guide to ethical theory* (2nd ed.). Hobokeyn, NJ: John Wiley & Sons.

[21]Leahy, M. J., Chan, F., Saunders, J. L. (2003). Job functions and knowledge requirements of certified rehabilitation counselors in the 21st century. *Rehabilitation Counseling Bulletin, 46*, 66–81. doi: 10.1177/004552082646

[22]Leahy, M. J., & Holt, E. (199). Certification in rehabilitation counseling: History and process. *Rehabilitation Counseling Bulletin, 7*(2), 71-80. *Rehabilitation Counseling Bulletin, 52*, 95–106.

[23]Middleton, R. A., Rollings, C. W., Sanderson, P. L., Leung, P., Harley, D. A., Ebener, D., et al. (2000). Endorsement of professional multicultural rehabilitation competencies and standards: A call to action. *Rehabilitation Counseling Bulletin,4*, 219-240.

[24]Mui, N., Sprong, M. E., Chowdhury, D., Lee, S., & Flowers, C. (201). An ethical guide for rehabilitation administrators: Revising the NARL Code of Ethics. *Journal of Rehabilitation Administration, 7*(1), 19-24.

[25]Neufedlt, S. A. (1999). *Supervision strategies for first practicum* (rd ed.). Alexandria, VA: American Counseling Association. Professional practice: Supervisor qualifications and support.

[26]O'Brien, M., & Graham, M. (2009). Rehabilitation counseling in the state or federal program: Is there a future? *Rehabilitation Counseling Bulletin, 52*(2), 124-128.

[27]Parker, R. M., & Patterson, J. B. (2012). Rehabilitation Counseling: Basics and Beyond, (5th ed.). Austin, TX: PRO-ED.

[28]Pope, K. S., & Vasquez, M. J. T. (2011). *Ethics in psychotherapy and counseling: A practical guide (4th ed.).* Hoboken, NJ: John Wiley & Sons.

[29]Remley, T. P., Jr., & Herlihy, B. (2001). *Ethical, legal, and professional issues in counseling.* Upper Saddle River, NJ: Prentice Hall.

[30]Roessler, R. & Rubin, S. (2006). *Case management and rehabilitation counseling.* Austin, TX: PRO-ED.

[31]Rubin, S. E., & Roessler, R. T. (2008). Foundations of the vocational rehabilitation process (6th ed.). Austin, TX: Pro-ed.

[32]Shaw, L. R. & Kuehn, M. (2009) Rehabilitation counselor education accreditation: History, structure, and evolution. Special Joint Issue of the *Journal of Applied Rehabilitation Counseling and the Rehabilitation Counseling Bulletin, 52,* 69-76.

[33]Smart, J. F. (2008). Disability, society, and the individual. (2nd ed.). Austin, TX: Pro Ed.

[34]Steinman, S. O., Richardson, N. F., & McEnroe, T. (1998). *The ethical-decision making manual for helping professionals.* Brooks/Cole.

[35]Stewart, C. J., & Cash, W. B. Jr. (2011). *Interviewing: Principles and practice* (11th ed.). Boston, MA: McGraw-Hill.

[36]Tarvydas, V. M., & Leahy, M. J. (199). Licensure in rehabilitation counseling: A critical incident in professionalization. *Rehabilitation Counseling Bulletin, 7*(2), 92-108.

[37]Van Hoose, W. H., & Kottler, J. A. (1985). *Ethical and legal issues in counseling and psychotherapy* (2nd ed.). San Francisco, CA: Jossey Bass.

[38]Welfel, E. R. (2012). *Ethics in counseling & psychotherapy: Standards, research, and emerging issues.* Belmont, CA: Brooks/Cole.

[39]Wright, G. (1980). *Total Rehabilitation.* Little Brown & Co.

CHAPTER 4

THE COUNSELING RELATIONSHIP

HEAVEN HOLLENDER

EMILY A. BRINCK

MATTHEW E. SPRONG

SECTION A. THE COUNSELING RELATIONSHIP

The counseling relationship is perhaps the most important component of the work that rehabilitation counselors do; in fact, the creation and maintenance of a positive treatment alliance between the service provider and the client repeatedly emerges as one of the strongest predictors of treatment success in the helping professions.[24] The Commission on Rehabilitation Counselor Certification (CRCC) Ethics Task Force has established a set of ethical standards to help rehabilitation counselors effectively use best practices to guide the formation of this critical relationship. The purpose of this chapter is to explore *Section A* of the CRCC Code of Ethics covering "The Counseling Relationship."[10] The following excerpt was included in the CRCC Code of Professional Ethics, Section A Counseling Relationship.[10,p.6]

> *Rehabilitation counselors work in cooperation with their clients to promote client welfare and support them in developing and progressing toward their goals. Rehabilitation counselors understand that trust is the cornerstone of the counseling relationship, and they have the responsibility to respect and safeguard the client's right to privacy and confidentiality. Rehabilitation counselors respect the rights of clients to make their own decisions about matters that affect their own lives. Rehabilitation counselors make reasonable efforts to ensure clients are able to make informed choices about every aspect of the rehabilitation counseling process. Rehabilitation counselors actively attempt to understand the diverse cultural backgrounds of the clients they serve and do not discriminate in their provision of rehabilitation counseling services. Rehabilitation counselors also explore their own cultural identities and how these affect their values and beliefs.*

Each section of this chapter will start with the presentation and explanation of a *Section A* ethical sub-standard, which will then be followed by a brief case scenario where the ethical principles in question are tested. The *Section A* sub-standards include: (A.1.) Welfare of Those Served, (A.2.) Respecting Diversity, (A.3.) Client Rights, (A.4.) Avoiding Value Imposition, (A.5.) Roles and Relationships with Clients, (A.6.) Multiple Clients, (A.7.) Group Work, (A.8.) Termination and Referral, and (A.9.) End-of-Life Care for Terminally Ill Clients.[10] The Ethics Task Force determined that these nine principles are essential to establishing and maintaining a healthy and collaborative rehabilitation counseling relationship.

A.1 WELFARE OF THOSE SERVED BY REHABILITATION COUNSELORS

In any professional relationship, but especially within a rehabilitation counseling context, the welfare of the client deserves careful consideration and attention. Standard A.1 of the CRCC Code of Ethics[10] provides information related to:

> ➢ The primary responsibility of the rehabilitation counselor when providing service delivery to clients,

> ➢ The relationship when developing rehabilitation and/or counseling plans,

> ➢ The role in helping clients obtain and maintain employment, and

> ➢ Respecting the autonomy of the client.

A.1.a. PRIMARY RESPONSIBILITY
The primary responsibility of rehabilitation counselors is to respect the dignity and to promote the welfare of clients. Clients are defined as individuals with, or directly affected by a disability, functional limitation(s), or medical condition and who receive services from rehabilitation counselors. At times, rehabilitation counseling services may be provided to individuals other than those with a disability. When employed to render an opinion for a forensic purpose, rehabilitation counselors do not have clients. In a forensic setting, the evaluee is the person who is being evaluated (See Section F.).[10, p.6]

The "Primary Responsibility" sub-standard advises rehabilitation counselors to consider the welfare of their clients as the ultimate goal in professional interaction or provision of services. Rehabilitation counselors promote wellness throughout the duration of the counseling relationship, even if the client does not have a physical or psychiatric disability. This ethical standard is closely tied to the fundamental principle of *beneficence,* which underlies the core purpose of the CRCC Code of Ethics.[10] *Beneficence* is "to do good to others; to promote the well-being of clients."[10,p.5] This particular standard instructs rehabilitation counselors to consider carefully whether the benefits of a potential rehabilitation plan or provision of services outweighs any direct or indirect risks to the client's well-being.

The rehabilitation counselor should honor each client's decision-making ability, and refrain from interjecting personal opinions or advice during the decision-making process. Guidance offered to clients should be based on empirically-based interventions and client-centered goal-setting, considering the unique cultural experience of each client and their individual constellation of strengths and limitations.[12] Although it may be impossible to be completely conscious of the influence of personal values, attitudes, and beliefs when developing rehabilitation plans or providing services,[41] rehabilitation counselors must continuously utilize personal and professional self-reflection to minimize the impact of counselor values on service delivery.

A.1.b. REHABILITATION COUNSELING PLANS

Rehabilitation counselors and clients work together to develop integrated, individual, and mutually agreed-upon, written rehabilitation counseling plans that offer a reasonable promise of success and are consistent with the abilities and circumstances of clients. Rehabilitation counselors and clients regularly review rehabilitation and counseling plans to assess their continued viability and effectiveness and to revise them as needed.[10, p. 6]

In order to promote the welfare of clients, rehabilitation counselors must collaborate with said clients when developing rehabilitation goals and counseling plans. The rehabilitation plan should include detailed goals that are:

1. Mutually agreed upon between the rehabilitation counselor and client,

2. Measured in a specific manner to determine whether the goal was achieved or if progress toward the goal is being made,

3. Attainable by the client without setting unrealistically high or low expectations,

4. Results-oriented and meaningful to the client, and

5. Meant to be accomplished within an established time frame.[10]

Appropriate time frames for completion should be set for each goal, and if the client is unable to make substantive progress in the specified time, the rehabilitation counselor should identify the barriers that are preventing the client from achieving the goal. Collaboratively brainstorming about how to remove or overcome these barriers will reinforce the teamwork nature of the relationship. When rehabilitation counselors engage in collaborative goal-setting processes, the client is more likely to take ownership in the rehabilitation plan.[35]

Collaboration on treatment goals improves client motivation and also strengthens the working alliance.[36] Rehabilitation counselors should place the most emphasis on goals that reflect changes valued by the client, rather than prioritizing changes that the rehabilitation counselor feels are most important.[19] Clients whose worldviews, values, and belief systems have been carefully incorporated into their rehabilitation and counseling plans feel more invested in achieving the goals set forth in these plans.[35]

A.1.c. EMPLOYMENT NEEDS

Rehabilitation counselors work with clients to consider employment consistent with the overall abilities, functional capabilities and limitations, general temperament, interest and aptitude patterns, social skills, education, general qualifications, transferable skills, geographic locations, and other relevant characteristics and needs of clients. Rehabilitation counselors facilitate the placement of clients in positions consistent with their interest, culture, and their welfare. Rehabilitation counselors assist clients in understanding potential constraints on employment and placement choices (e.g., organizational policies, policies of external funding sources, legal requirements).[10,p.6]

Finding employment options that meet the needs of the both the client and the employer is essential when providing vocational rehabilitation services. Rehabilitation counselors must develop rehabilitation plans that allow clients to maximize their work potential while making sure the job position obtained fits the clients' interests and provides a good match for the clients' abilities, education, limitations, and personality style. Focusing on employment fit for only one of the characteristics listed in Standard A.1.c. will lower the chances of placement success. If an occupation is a good match for a client's functional capabilities and limitations but does not provide for optimal expression of the client's personality or social skills, the probability of the client succeeding in the position is decreased. The rehabilitation counselor cannot focus solely on the technical aspects of aptitudes, transferable skills, or functional limitations, because unless clients perceive the employment to be meaningful, they will likely not invest the needed effort to succeed in the position. Clients who find meaningful employment report higher subjective well-being and higher perceived quality of life.[16] Again, this standard does not only focus on client interests; rehabilitation counselors consider the welfare and needs of the employers they work with in order to maximize the benefits on each side of the economic equation.

A.1.d. AVOCATIONAL AND INDEPENDENT LIVING GOALS

Rehabilitation counselors work with clients to develop avocational and independent living goals consistent with their abilities, interests, culture, needs, and welfare.[10,p.6]

Independent living rehabilitation plans require several developmental activities so that individuals with disabilities can live as independent as possible. For example, an independent living assessment can be utilized to determine the barriers that an individual may have with different aspects of life.

For example, the World Health Organization's Disability Assessment Scale[55] identifies six domains of independent functioning, including cognition (understanding & communication), mobility (moving & getting around), self-care (hygiene, dressing, eating & staying alone), getting along (interacting with other people), life activities (domestic responsibilities, leisure, work & school), and participation (joining in community activities). As with any testing, a rehabilitation counselor should be aware that there are several domains of assessmnt.[38] Therefore, a rehabilitation counselor should use assessments, clinical interviews, peer-reviewed research articles, and work collaboratively with the client to develop avocational and independent living goals. Violation of this ethical principal would involve the rehabilitation counselor not taking into consideration the client's opinion and interests, as evidenced in a study where over half (55.4%) did not perceive that they had a choice in making their own choices when it came to choosing living arrangements.[40]

Rehabilitation Counselors should also take into consideration the clients abilities, interest, culture, needs, and welfare.[10,p.6] Each client is going to bring their own unique backgrounds, vocational experiences, and independent living experiences. Rehabilitation counselors can refer to the code of ethics A.2 Respecting diversity that address aspects on respecting culture and nondiscrimination towards clients.[10,p.7] Additional information and reference about A.2 can be found later in this chapter. It is important as rehabilitation counselors to recognize each client's abilities to help assist the client in developing their vocational and independent living goal.

A.1.e. AUTONOMY

Rehabilitation counselors respect the rights of clients to make decisions on their own behalf in accordance with their cultural identity and beliefs. Decision-making on behalf of clients that limits or diminish the autonomy of client is made only after careful deliberation. Rehabilitation counselors advocate for the resumption of responsibility by clients as quickly as possible.[10,p.7]

Rehabilitation counselors must always respect the autonomy of the client. This ethical principle establishes that clients have the ultimate decision in choosing their rehabilitation goals. Client autonomy predicts treatment engagement and success.[12] However, the rehabilitation counselor must also weigh the responsibility of helping the client to recognize and weigh how the potential choices will impact rehabilitation goals. If a client cannot realistically predict the consequences of an action on the outcome of a rehabilitation goal, allowing the client to proceed with that choice may diminish the client's autonomy in the long run. For example, if a client chooses to engage in behavior that puts him or her in a sensitive legal situation, the client's autonomy may be subsequently restricted by law enforcement, prohibiting attainment of meaningful employment or other goals. If a client's capacity to make reasonable and/or rational decisions has been compromised, or the client's disability has a strong likelihood of interfering with the evaluation of alternatives or the prediction of consequences, a decision may have to be made by the rehabilitation counselor on behalf of the client.

These situations should be evaluated carefully and in consultation with trusted colleagues and supervisors. The Code of Ethics[10] makes clear that any intervention on the part of the rehabilitation counselor in the decision-making process must be properly justified, clearly necessary, and as short-lived as possible. The resumption of responsibility on the part of the client should be the most immediate rehabilitation goal subsequent to loss of decision-making ability.

CASE STUDY

George is a vocational rehabilitation client who has been receiving services for six years. George has cerebral palsy and uses an automatic wheelchair for mobility. He has recently received his bachelor's degree in Rehabilitation Services. However, he has had great difficulty in finishing his degree, and graduated with a 2.5 GPA. George has received numerous accommodations from instructors to mitigate the effects of his attention deficit hyperactivity disorder (ADHD) and specific learning disability with impaired reading. George has a vocational rehabilitation goal of obtaining his doctoral degree in rehabilitation counseling. Achieving this goal would require admission into a doctoral program and a minimum of four years taking courses at the graduate level to obtain his master's and Doctorate degrees. George has taken the Graduate Record Examination (GRE) and has scored in the 2nd percentile in Quantitative, 1st percentile in Analytic Writing, and 4th percentile in Verbal Reasoning. Despite these low scores, he has been accepted into a master's level rehabilitation counseling program. His admission is provisional, which means he must maintain an acceptable GPA over the course of his first few semesters and has access to any needed support provided by the university. George's vocational rehabilitation counselor informed him that the likelihood of him being successful in a graduate program in general is low based on his difficulties in his undergraduate program, and that he believes George would be "wasting his time" pursuing advanced degrees. George believes he cannot find work that is meaningful to him with only a bachelor's degree. The vocational rehabilitation counselor suggests that George find another field of employment and tells George to "not to waste taxpayer money, the agency's time, or his own time" pursuing graduate study.

CASE STUDY DISCUSSION

The rehabilitation counselor has to weigh the five sub-standards of Standard A.1 against each other to determine the most appropriate rehabilitation plan for George. On one hand, the rehabilitation counselor must protect George's welfare (Standard A.1.a). George's GRE scores and difficulty completing his bachelor's degree may provide enough evidence to suggest that enrolling in graduate school could be setting him up for failure, overwhelm his capacity to cope with stress, or negatively influence his sense of self-efficacy. Graduate school may not be the best course of action to protect George's welfare, in other words. In addition, there appears to be evidence that George's abilities, functional capabilities and limitations, and aptitudes may be at odds with his interests and preferences. The vocational rehabilitation counselor must respect the collaborative nature of the rehabilitation plan (Standard A.1.b), which is not evident in the rehabilitation counselor's immediate dismissal of George's desire to pursue graduate study without investigating available support services that may assist George in accomplishing his goal. The poor choice of wording used by the rehabilitation counselor (e.g., "waste taxpayer money, the agency's time, or his own time") is a clear violation of the principle of *beneficence* underlying Standard A.1 and is likely to affect negatively the working alliance. The responsibility of the rehabilitation counselor to assist George in realistically predicting the consequences of his enrollment in graduate school must not involve automatic dismissal of client desires or shaming of the client. Proper assistance in generating a pro and con list for a rehabilitation goal involves asking pertinent questions and allowing clients to develop thoughtful answers.

If George insists that he knows the risks involved in enrolling in graduate school, the rehabilitation counselor may best honor his autonomy by letting George attempt the task and learn from the outcomes. Perhaps George will discover how challenging graduate school is and may alter his goal to obtain his master's degree, or he may consider not pursuing any advanced degree. Alternatively, given that the rehabilitation counselor is tasked with assisting George in accessing all available supportive services, George could utilize Academic Support Services, Disability Services, tutors, or other assistance to succeed in his original goal. Although the rehabilitation counselor initially views his goal of advanced education as unattainable, the counselor needs to respect the client's autonomy (Standard A.1.e). The most difficult ethical quandaries often arise when multiple ethical standards conflict and need prioritizing. Utilizing an ethical decision-making model,[37] consulting with colleagues or supervisors, or reviewing manuals on ethical conflicts in counseling[5] may assist rehabilitation counselors in reconciling these conflicting ethical standards.

A.2. Respecting Diversity

The racial composition of the United States population is changing at a rapid pace. Population models predict that two or more races are the fastest-growing racial group by 2060.[56] By the year 2060, one in three Americans will be a people of color other than White.[56] In addition to race, diverse self-identifications of sexual orientation, gender identity, marital status/partnership, religion, and socioeconomic status are being recognized as important components to consider when developing rehabilitation counseling treatment plans. This increased level of diversity requires that rehabilitation professionals be competent in meeting the needs of a multiethnic population. Rehabilitation counselors must acknowledge that theories of rehabilitation counseling reflect Western individualistic values and world views and must actively seek rehabilitation goals and services that fit with each client's unique culture, value, and belief system in order to maximize effectiveness.[50]

A.2.a Respecting Culture
Rehabilitation counselors demonstrate respect for the cultural identity of clients in developing and implementing rehabilitation and treatment plans, and providing and adapting interventions.[10,p.7]

There is no "one size fits all" rehabilitation counseling plan. While the rehabilitation counselor can and should integrate empirically-supported treatments into any client's treatment plan, the integration of culturally-appropriate interventions may be even more important to the overall success of the rehabilitation plan.[39] Having the knowledge and experience to adapt rehabilitation techniques, including the degree of directive or non-directive communication and amount of emphasis on the individual's cultural values and belief systems, is necessary for the modern rehabilitation counselor. Despite decades of research on the importance of incorporating culturally appropriate intervention strategies into psychotherapy, counseling, social work, and rehabilitation counseling, many agencies and individual practitioners continue to rely on Western European approaches that lead to less successful outcomes for clients.[33,56] Demonstrating respect for cultural backgrounds does not simply include asking the client about his or her culture; respect for cultural backgrounds requires infusion of culture into each component of the rehabilitation process, including intake interviewing, functional assessments, rehabilitation plans, and outcome measurement.

A.2.b. Nondiscrimination
Rehabilitation counselors do not condone or engage in prejudicial treatment of an individual or group based on their actual or perceived membership in a particular group, class, or category.[10,p.7]

This substandard closely resembles Title I of the Americans with Disabilities Act that prevents employment discrimination in federal agencies and private businesses who contract with the federal government. Some states have also adopted nondiscrimination policies when it comes to employment; however, many states do not expand these policies to protect individuals' sexual orientation, marital status/partnership, or gender identity. In fact, only 16 states provide protection against employment discrimination based on sexual orientation or gender identity.[2]

Rehabilitation counselors are held to a higher standard than employers, however, both because of the CRCC Code of Ethics[15] and legal precedents that indicate nondiscrimination is a core component to the field of counseling. A number of landmark legal cases have validated that neither legal nor ethical principles allow counselors, (mental health, rehabilitation, social work, or otherwise), to deny services to a client whose cultural, sexual, religious, gender, or racial identity is contrary to the value system of the counselor.[28]

One particular case, *Bruff v. North Mississippi Health Services, Inc.* examined a situation in which a counselor, based on her religious beliefs, wanted to refer a client who identified as homosexual to another counselor who did not share such religious objections. The counselor asserted that she was observing the American Counseling Association (ACA) Code of Ethics[1], Standard A.11.b. which states, "If counselors determine an inability to be of professional assistance to clients, they avoid entering or continuing counseling relationships."[10,p.7] *Bruff* reasoned that since she disagreed on moral grounds with the client's sexual orientation, another counselor would be more appropriate with and effective for that client. The United States Court of Appeals for the Fifth Circuit disagreed on a number of points and concluded that such a referral policy in mental health agencies would deter non-heterosexual clients from seeking treatment.

More recent legal cases have expanded on the precedent set in *Bruff v. North Mississippi Health Services, Inc.* When a student in the graduate counseling program at Eastern Michigan University was dismissed from the program after refusing to counsel clients "...on matters that conflicted with her religious beliefs,"[18,p.134] the student sued the university claiming that her religious freedom had been violated. Though the case was eventually settled out of court, the summary judgment issued by the initial court agreed with the ACA's position that "...referral is not to be based on the counselor's discomfort with the client's value system."[59,p.22] The court determined that "...the student was not required to change her views or religious beliefs; she was required to set them aside in the counselor–client relationship."[79, p.33]

Standard D.1.a of the CRCC Code of Ethics places the responsibility on the rehabilitation counselor to develop cultural competencies rather than refer clients who are different from them or who challenge their personal values or worldviews. The standard requires that, "counselors demonstrate beliefs, attitudes, knowledge, and skills pertinent to working with diverse client populations."[59,p.7] Students who feel they cannot place their own moral values behind the welfare of the client are justifiably kept from entering a profession that espouses social justice as an essential component to practice. Educators of rehabilitation counselors also have an ethical obligation to "...not endorse supervisees or trainees whom they believe to be impaired in any way that would interfere with the performance of the duties associated with the endorsement."[23,10, p.7] Standard A.2 Respecting Diversity and Standard A.4 Avoiding Harm and Avoiding Value Imposition have significant overlap in topic and content, so a comprehensive case study that incorporates both of these standards and their respective sub-standards will be discussed following the presentation of Standard A.4.

A.3. CLIENT RIGHTS

It is essential for the rehabilitation counselor to inform clients of their rights and any restrictions on these rights during initial contacts. Only when clients understand accurate information about the nature and potential limitations of the rehabilitation counseling relationship can clients evaluate whether they wish to engage in rehabilitation services. Educating clients about their rights will inform their decision-making processes and allow them to know what questions to ask to ensure their understanding of how services are delivered; this includes:

- ➤ Providing clients with a professional disclosure statement that discusses the qualifications and credentials of the rehabilitation counselor,

- ➤ Providing clients with the information relevant to make informed choices about rehabilitation goals,

- ➤ Communicating with clients in ways that are culturally sensitive,

- ➤ Explaining the procedures in place for service delivery if the client is unable to give consent, and

- ➤ Explaining the role of client support systems in the rehabilitation process.[10]

A.3.a. PROFESSIONAL DISCLOSURE STATEMENT
Rehabilitation counselors review with clients, both orally and in writing, the rights and responsibility of both the rehabilitation counseling and client. These are presented in a manner best suited to the needs of the client. Disclosure at the outset of the professional relationship minimally includes:

1. *The qualifications, credentials, and relevant experience of the rehabilitation counselor;*

2. *purposes, goals, techniques, limitations, and the nature of potential risks, and benefits of services;*

3. *frequency and length of services;*

4. *confidentiality and limitations regarding confidentiality (including how a supervisor and/or treatment team professional is involved);*

5. *contingencies for continuation of services upon the absence, incapacitation, or death of the rehabilitation counselor;*

6. *fees and/or payment arrangements;*

7. *record preservation and release policies;*

8. *risks associated with electronic communication; and,*

9. *legal issues affecting services.*

When necessary, rehabilitation counselors disclose other information consistent with organization and/or employer policies or legal requirements. Rehabilitation counselors recognize that disclosure of these issues may need to be reiterated or expanded upon throughout the professional relationship.[10,p.7]

Professional disclosure is essential to building a trusting relationship within the rehabilitation setting. In order to support a client's autonomy, (Standard A.1.d), the provision of accurate information about all aspects of the rehabilitation counseling relationship is necessary. Clients who clearly understand the purpose, nature, and structure of rehabilitation services as communicated in an intake interview report higher confidence in their rehabilitation counselors.[26] The rehabilitation counselor must make a sincere effort to provide the information in a way that makes it personally relevant to each client. An intake interview in which the rehabilitation counselor reads jargon-filled statements and generic policy information to a client reduces the chances that the client will consider the content of the session personally meaningful, and may actually reduce the likelihood of the information being encoded into long-term memory.[47] While all the important "bases" need to be covered, the rehabilitation counselor can adapt the way the information is provided based on the client's experience with rehabilitation or other health care services, the client's particular needs and/or goals, and the client's expectations of the rehabilitation counselor or agency.[43]

Particular attention must be paid to the limitations on confidentiality and the situations under which the rehabilitation counselor may be required to share the client's personal information with others. A client who does not understand that communications with the rehabilitation counselor are kept confidential (within legal and ethical limits) may choose not to share important personal information.[4] A client who does not understand the limits of confidentiality may feel betrayed when a situation arises that requires the rehabilitation counselor to break confidentiality, including an arrangement in which the rehabilitation counselor is being supervised for licensure or works with a treatment team. A clear understanding of the extent and limits of confidentiality builds client autonomy and also strengthens the therapeutic relationship between rehabilitation counselor and client.

A.3.b. INFORMED CONSENT

Rehabilitation counselors recognize that clients have the freedom to choose whether to enter or remain in a professional relationship. Rehabilitation counselors respect the rights of clients to participate in ongoing rehabilitation counseling planning and to make decisions to refuse any services or modality changes, while also ensuring that clients are advised of the consequences of such refusal. Rehabilitation counselors recognize that clients need information to make an informed decision regarding services and that professional disclosure must be an ongoing part of the rehabilitation counseling process so clients are able to provide informed consent. Rehabilitation counselors appropriately document discussions of disclosure and informed consent throughout the rehabilitation counseling relationship.[10,p.7]

Informed consent involves providing clients with all pertinent information regarding rehabilitation service delivery so that they can make appropriate decisions regarding rehabilitation plans and goals. In addition to understanding the services that are available, clients must be informed that they are able to discontinue any service they choose, although the specific consequences for such refusals must also be explicitly delineated. The rehabilitation counselor must keep accurate documentation of all discussions of informed consent and professional disclosures. Conversations about informed consent and disclosures should not end after the initial intake interview but should continue throughout the delivery of services. Periodically reminding clients of these issues serves two purposes:[42]

1. It reinforces the autonomy and agency of the client as an active participant in their rehabilitation plan.

2. It ensures multiple opportunities for the client to ask questions and solidify understanding of his or her rights in the rehabilitation counseling relationship. Rehabilitation counselors report all changes or modifications to the rehabilitation plan and the client's agreement or disagreement with the change(s).

A.3.c. INDIVIDUALIZED APPROACH TO COMMUNICATION
Rehabilitation counselors communicate information in ways that are both developmentally and culturally appropriate. Rehabilitation counselors arrange for qualified interpreter or translator when necessary to ensure comprehension by clients. Rehabilitation counselors consider cultural implications of informed consent procedures and, when possible, rehabilitation counselors adjust their practices accordingly.[10,p.7]

Rehabilitation counselors must be aware that all clients are unique individuals at different developmental stages and represent an ever-expanding array of cultures. The sheer quantity of information that must be communicated during a first session can be daunting for both the rehabilitation counselor and for the client. Done incorrectly, the client could leave feeling overwhelmed and confused, rather than properly informed. Communicating this vast amount of information in a developmentally or culturally inappropriate way will further complicate client understanding. A client may not be able to provide informed consent if language barriers make it difficult to communicate. Roessler and Rubin[43] recommend the following "rules" to avoid disruption in communication and subsequent inadequate informed consent:

Use language that corresponds with the client's background and level of comprehension. Avoid the use of confusing terminology and jargon. Guard against providing the client with too much information at "one shot" during the interview. Clients provided too much information at once can be overwhelmed.[43,p.54]

If a client is in need of a sign language interpreter or written materials in Braille format, the rehabilitation counselor should have access to and willingly provide these resources. If English is not the client's first language, a qualified interpreter may be needed to effectively communicate with the client. Rehabilitation counselors must use caution when selecting and utilizing an interpreter, however. Sue and Sue[50] provide a number of guidelines that will increase the effectiveness of using an interpreter with a client:

1. Communication will be more accurate if the interpreter shares the same dialect as the client and if there are minimal cultural differences between the interpreter and client.

2. Rehabilitation counselors should be familiar with the interpreters who are utilized, and the interpreter should have a basic understanding of the rehabilitation counselor's communication and counseling style.

3. The same interpreter should be used with the same client in order to ensure continuity and avoid disruption in the working alliance.

4. The counselor must realize that the use of an interpreter essentially creates a three-person relationship rather than a dyadic alliance. Since the client will most often be communicating directly with the interpreter, the client may initially feel closer to the interpreter rather than the rehabilitation counselor.

5. The interpreter must accurately understand the principle of confidentiality, and that he or she is held to the same ethical standards in this area as the rehabilitation counselor.

6. The rehabilitation counselor must be aware that the interpreter may feel affected emotionally by personal information shared by clients. The rehabilitation counselor must provide an appropriate space and amount of time for debriefing if the interpreter finds the information communicated during the session to be traumatic or disturbing.

7. The rehabilitation counselor must allow an adequate amount of time for sessions with clients who require interpreters.

Communication via interpreter proceeds at a slower pace, and often, information needs to be revisited a number of times for clarification and to ensure accurate understanding for all parties involved. For further information on interpreters in health care that specifically address issues of confidentiality and cultural competency, please see the national standards published by the National Council on Interpreting in Health Care.[35]

A.3.d. INABILITY TO GIVE CONSENT

When counseling minors or persons who lack the capacity to give voluntary informed consent, rehabilitation counselors seek the assent of clients and include clients in decision-making as appropriate. Rehabilitation counselors recognize the need to balance the:

1. *ethical rights of clients to make choices;*

2. *cognitive or legal capacity of clients to give consent or assent; and*

3. *legal rights and responsibilities of legal guardians, including parents who are legal guardians, or families (e.g., "next of kin" notification situations) to protect clients and make decisions on behalf of clients.*[10,p.7]

When a client is unable to give voluntary consent for services because of mental or legal incapacity, rehabilitation counselors must make every effort to obtain as much assent from the client as possible. Consent is a legal term that implies that the person giving consent is of sound mind, of a legal age, and is not under duress. Only adults (over 18 years of age) who do not have mental, intellectual, or other impairments can legally give consent for rehabilitation services. However, even if a client is legally unable to give consent, the rehabilitation counselor can seek the client's assent, which means giving his or her own, independent decision to seek and receive rehabilitation services.[3] In other words, even if a client is unable to give legal informed consent for services, the rehabilitation counselor can communicate the information detailed under Standard A.3.a (Professional Disclosure) in as much detail as the client's functional limitations and developmental level allow. The same principles that involve the ethical reasoning for providing clients with the ability to legally consent to services and providing as much information as possible about their rights and responsibilities underlie the principle of obtaining assent from clients who do not have such legal capacities. The more collaboration and agreement possible between counselor and client, the greater the chances of treatment success.[24] Difficulties may arise when there is a conflict between the wishes of those who are able to give legal consent for the client and the wishes of the client. In these cases, the rehabilitation counselor must respect the rights of the parent, guardian, or family agent who has legal authority to consent to treatment, while working to establish a working alliance with the client through relationship building, psychoeducation, and determination of the extent to which assent is possible.

A.3.e. SUPPORT NETWORK INVOLVEMENT

Rehabilitation counselors recognize that support by others may be important to clients. When appropriate and with consent from clients, rehabilitation counselors enlist the support and involvement of others (e.g., religious/spiritual/community leaders, family members, friends, and guardians).[10,p.8]

In some instances, the rehabilitation counselor may not work solely with an individual client, but also with the client's support system. The client may bring a partner or companion(s), family members or guardians, spiritual leaders, and others that the client wishes to be included in the rehabilitation process. Alternatively, clients may feel strongly about not including these individuals as part of the rehabilitation process. For example, families of clients whose cultures emphasize a collectivist perspective may expect to be included in all aspects of the rehabilitation counseling process. The rehabilitation counselor must also be aware that people who are considered to be "family" is extremely variable based on the client's cultural identity and affiliation. For example, it is not unusual for American Indian or African American clients to include extended family and close family friends in their conceptualization of "immediate family."[50] The rehabilitation counselor must take care not to impose his or her own definitions of "family" on clients being served. However, despite these wide variations in types of support systems, the rehabilitation counselor must first ask the client about the extent to which he or she wishes family or community leaders to be a part of the rehabilitation process. Exploration of the benefits and limitations of including the family and extended support system could be discussed with clients so that an informed decision can be made about the extent to which members of their support system are included in the rehabilitation process.

CASE STUDY

Janet is currently employed as a rehabilitation counselor supervisor at the local community rehabilitation program (CRP). She is primarily responsible for providing case management and counseling services to her clients. The agency currently serves 20 clients who receive independent living services (which include counseling/case management), and ten of these clients are on Janet's caseload. Janet's co-worker and supervisee, Bill, works with the other ten clients. Janet and Bill have formed a friendship throughout the past six years, as both were part of the same master's degree cohort. They graduated at the top of their class, studied for, and passed their Certified Rehabilitation Counselor (CRC) examinations, and both became employed at the same time at the local CRP.

On one social occasion, Janet, Bill, and a few other friends were out eating dinner. Janet and Bill were reminiscing about graduate school. During the conversation, Bill turned to Janet with a grin on his face and informed Janet that he lost his credential as a Licensed Clinical Professional Counselor (LCPC) because he failed to complete the continuing education (CEU) requirements. Janet presumed that Bill was joking around since he was always well organized and graduated at the top of their class. However, the following Monday evening, Janet was reviewing case documents and noticed that a few of Bill's younger clients were receiving applied behavior analysis (ABA) services from other employees in the CRP. Janet was unable to locate one informed consent that was supposed to be attached to a client file. Janet figured that Bill must have forgotten to attach these forms, although he rarely made these mistakes. After further investigation into

*the files, Janet remembered that Bill told her that he was not currently
an LCPC. She went to the state licensing website and verified that Bill
did not have his LCPC.*

*Janet held a meeting with Bill the following day to tell him that he
forgot to attach the informed consent form to a file and that she knew
he was no longer licensed. Bill told Janet that he did not have an
informed consent signed because the client's legal guardians refused
to consent to ABA services. Bill stated he believed they refused consent
because they did not understand what ABA services involved.
Furthermore, Bill stated that he did not spend much time discussing
what ABA services were because the parents were Hispanic, and he
figured that they would be confused since English was their second
language. Janet instructed Bill to hire a Spanish-speaking interpreter
because the parents indicated they wanted to be included in the
rehabilitation process. Janet addressed the LCPC issue and stated that
Bill's behavior was unethical because he was falsely providing
credentials on forms that are sent to the CRP funding source and
falsely providing credentials on the professional disclosure forms that
the clients sign prior to receiving services. Bill claimed that this lapse
in licensure was not a big deal because he was successfully closing
clients out for services and has recently received the Excellent
Counselor Award by the state funding source. Bill claimed that
because he has his CRC and the services he provides will remain
consistent throughout his career, he does not need to maintain his
LCPC. Janet informed Bill that the funding source required that
services be provided by rehabilitation counselors that have both their
CRC and LCPC, and that the agency's policy is to abide by the CRCC
Code of Ethics.*

CASE STUDY DISCUSSION

Informed consent is essential to the rehabilitation process because it
provides clients with information related to the services that they will receive
(Standard A.3.b.), and failure to disclose this information may result in the lack
of honoring the client's autonomy. If the client is unable to give consent (e.g.,
the client is a minor or unable to give voluntary consent) as indicated in the
above scenario (Standard A.3.d.), then a legal guardian needs to provide the
consent. It is evident that Bill failed to discuss properly the ABA services with
the parents of the client because of a language barrier even after they suggested
they did not want their child receiving those services. The rehabilitation
counselor did not communicate the information in a culturally appropriate
manner (Standard A.3.c.) by hiring a Spanish-speaking interpreter and failed to
involve the parents in specific decisions related to their child (Standard A.3.e.),
after the parents indicated they wanted to be involved in all phases of the
rehabilitation process. If Bill had hired a Spanish-speaking interpreter, he could

have explained clearly what ABA services were and how they would be helpful for their son.

Bill also falsely represented his credentials to all of the clients he had served during the previous year by providing a professional disclosure statement that had incorrect credentials (Standard A.3.a.) Bill falsely claims ownership of a license, which contradicts the CRCC Code of Ethics.[10] Janet's ethical obligation is to first confront Bill professionally as to the validity of this violation, and if Bill refuses to correct the ethical violation himself, she must report the violation to her supervisor(s), the state board governing Licensed Clinical Professional Counselors, and the board governing Certified Rehabilitation Counselors. In addition, she will need to disclose this information to the CRP funding source.

Bill's failure to represent accurately his qualifications and credentials could have impacts beyond the professional licensing and certification boards. For instance, because Bill was falsely signing his credentials on progress notes and treatment plans, insurance companies, and other funding sources may refuse reimbursement for services based on fraud.[12] Even though Bill believes that he is benefitting his clients, if the funding sources retract payment, the clients may be responsible for the costs of services. Although Bill feels he is competent in providing counseling services, certification and licensing examinations are useful in determining if a professional has specific competencies that are needed to be an effective counselor.[22] For instance, if Bill did not pass the section assessing proficiency in diagnosis, he may be unaware of how certain classes of drugs exhibit physiological and psychological effects during intoxication and withdrawal. This lack of knowledge could affect how the symptoms displayed by the client are diagnostically interpreted by Bill, potentially resulting in misdiagnosis. Misdiagnosis carries a number of important ramifications for clients, including improper treatment recommendations, permanent placement in a client's insurance file, and delayed implementation of proper interventions for the correct diagnosis.[7]

A.4. AVOIDING VALUE IMPOSITION

Rehabilitation counselors are aware of and avoid imposing their own values, attitudes, beliefs, and behavioral. Rehabilitation counselors respect the diversity of clients and seek training in areas in which they are at risk of imposing their values onto clients, especially when the rehabilitating counselor's values are inconsistent with the clients goals or are discriminatory in nature.[10,p.8]

The concept of avoiding harm in the counseling relationship can be tied to the ethical principle of non-malfeasance. *Non-malfeasance* refers to the commitment of a rehabilitation counselor to avoid harm to clients, trainees, supervisees, and research participants.[12,10, p.8] Harm may take many forms, but might include inappropriate sexual relationships, inappropriate financial relationships, emotional manipulation, client exploitation, and lack of competency in service delivery. Likewise, if a rehabilitation counselor does not maintain confidentiality (e.g., research, supervisor-supervisee relationship), then the client may experience negative repercussions. For example, if a rehabilitation counselor were working as a substance abuse counselor providing individual counseling services to an adolescent, and at the same time engaged in family counseling with the adolescent's immediate family, the issue of confidentiality could quickly become very complex. If the adolescent disclosed information during the individual counseling session and the rehabilitation counselor disclosed this information to the parents after agreeing not to disclose the information, the adolescent could lose trust in the counselor as well as face consequences from his parents.

Unavoidable or unanticipated harm may include counselors unconsciously imposing their values and beliefs onto clients or basing intervention selection and service delivery on the counselors' own worldviews. For example, if a rehabilitation counselor has the opinion (personal or professional) that a client would not be successful in attending post-secondary education; the counselor may withhold information about this option from the client. This example violates the principle of *Veracity*, which is purposely lying or withholding the truth.[10,p.17&59] Moreover, the rehabilitation counselor may unintentionally provide information related to services other than post-secondary education, or highlight the benefits associated with some options and minimize costs associated with other options. This type of behavior may lead to clients losing trust in the rehabilitation counselor, or not being able to choose fully their rehabilitation plans. This example violates the ethical principle of *Autonomy*, which is an individual's ability to choose the best course of action related to his or her rehabilitation plan.[10,p.5&11] Another example of unavoidable or unanticipated harm is in the case that the client commits suicide. Although this behavior may be unforeseeable, the rehabilitation counselor should always ask clients about suicidal ideation and develop safety plans with the clients who endorse suicidal ideation or intent, to help minimize risk.[50]

CASE STUDY

Julia, a 46-year-old Indigenous American woman, decided to seek rehabilitation counseling services after she experienced a disabling accident. When she arrived at the community rehabilitation program (CMP), she attempted to check-in at the front desk. However, the administrative assistant told her that she was 20 minutes late for her appointment and could not be seen that day. The administrative assistant gave her paperwork to fill out and bring back for another appointment scheduled the following week. Julia worried about her ability to return for the next appointment, because she lived nearly 30 miles out of town on her tribe's reservation and did not know if she would have money to pay for gas at that time. However, because she felt she needed the services provided at the CMP, she said nothing and agreed to return. Over the course of the week, Julia tried to save gas money to make the trip back to the CMP, but her sister needed money to buy food for her family and her family also celebrated her nephew's birthday with a large gathering. After these expenses, Julia had just enough money for gas to attend her appointment. Although Julia was ten minutes late to her appointment, the CMP agreed to allow her intake interview to take place, but she was warned that continued tardiness might impact her ability to receive services.

Mark, a 35-year-old Caucasian male, was assigned to be Julia's rehabilitation counselor. Mark noted in her chart that she had been late twice to appointments and that she had forgotten to bring the paperwork back to her second appointment. He began the interview by asking if Julia felt motivated to engage in rehabilitation counseling. Julia replied that she felt that the services would be beneficial. Mark nodded and said, "Sometimes clients who are hesitant about counseling are late to appointments and may not remember to do tasks like intake paperwork, so I just wanted to make sure you really wanted to be here."

Since Julia had been late, Mark felt pressed for time and launched immediately into the informed consent disclosure and standard intake interview questions. Mark noticed that Julia did not respond with much information to most of his questions and took quite a bit of time before she decided how to answer each of them. He also noticed that on some questions, she spent what he considered to be an excessive amount of time discussing irrelevant topics. Mark felt frustrated at the lack of cohesion in the interview and was worried about not being able to gather enough necessary information in the session. He told Julia, "I understand that you feel that this is important information, but there are certain details I need to get from you during this interview. I have to ask that we stay on topic for the remainder of the session. Is that ok?" Julia looked confused, but responded, "Sure."

After the intake interview concluded, Mark began writing his intake report. He still felt frustrated at the lack of information he was able to gather from Julia, and he was doubtful that she would be successful in rehabilitation counseling. When she disclosed that money and transportation to services would be potential issues, Mark responded that perhaps they could create a budget to ensure that she would have the necessary money for gas. He was surprised when Julia responded, "Budgets don't work in my house. If someone needs money, I give them money. It's how we are." At that point, Mark attempted to explain that Julia's recovery was a priority, and that she should feel

*that she is important enough to use her money for these services. Julia
did not respond. Mark felt that Julia was being resistant to his plan
and he felt that the exchange was another indication that Julia was not
invested in obtaining rehabilitation counseling services. He indicated
these observations in his intake report, and despite some indications
that Julia was eligible for multiple services provided by the CMP, he
recommended her for only one service to see if she was truly motivated
to obtain services. He reasoned that if she successfully completed this
one program then he would enroll her in more.*

CASE STUDY DISCUSSION

Differences in culture can lead to many inadvertent errors in
communication between rehabilitation counselors and clients. These differences
can also considerably increase barriers to treatment for clients who do not
identify with the future time-oriented, individualistic, and action-oriented
components of most rehabilitation counseling service programs.[29] The case
study above shows how differences in cultural values immediately put Julia's
success in rehabilitation counseling programs in jeopardy. Agencies run on
schedules and must pay attention to seeing the greatest number of clients and
deliver the best services possible despite often inadequate funding and/or
inadequate staffing numbers. Clients who do not show up for appointments or
who are often late are penalized by being removed from services or being put
back on a wait list, in order to maximize the agency's ability to provide services
for people who "really want" the services. In the United States, "time is viewed
as a commodity."[29,p.618] Rehabilitation counselors may assume that clients who
are late are not motivated for treatment or not engaged in services. However,
this assumption is often incorrect when applied to clients who come from
cultures who operate on a past or present time orientation rather than the future
time orientation that is valued in White culture.[50] The Code of Ethics Standards
A.2.a (Respecting Culture) and A.4. (Avoiding Value Imposition) are both
relevant to analyzing both the agency's and Mark's behaviors in this scenario.
By putting rigid restrictions on the amount of time Julia was allowed to be late
and still be seen, the agency unknowingly put a financial burden on her that
may have prevented her from even returning. Mark's well-intentioned
statement that Julia was "important enough" to use her money to obtain
rehabilitation counseling services neglects Julia's statement that her family
comes first when it comes to finances. Mark is exhibiting an individualistic
perspective by trying to encourage Julia to see herself as a priority, which
contradicts Julia's collectivistic perspective of valuing the family above self.
Although Mark believed he was motivating Julia, he most likely will fail to
form an effective therapeutic alliance with Julia if he continues to suggest
interventions that directly conflict with her expressed collectivistic value
system.

While it is inappropriate to generalize about any individual client's level of identification with his or her culture, it is also inappropriate to ignore how cultural differences may impact the client's perception of how rehabilitation counseling services are provided. Had Mark explored Julia's identification with her tribe and her specific cultural values, he may have understood that many American Indian tribes value nonverbal communication over verbal communication.[20] While Mark perceived Julia to be nonresponsive and perhaps resistant to his questions, it is likely her silence was a demonstration of respect, as *Indigenous American* may believe that learning occurs while listening.[50] In addition, many *Indigenous American* tribes value storytelling as a communication style. What Mark perceived to be Julia spending an inordinate amount of time on irrelevant topics may have been her way of trying to help Mark get to know her and her history. Recognizing and respecting these differences in communication styles will help Mark obtain necessary information while at the same time, building the therapeutic alliance.

The judgments that Mark made about Julia's communication and behavior subsequently influenced his decisions on what services to recommend. The Code of Ethics Standard A.4 is relevant to this particular situation, because even though Julia may be helped by being offered a number of different services for which she is eligible, Mark decided that her "motivation for treatment" was not sufficient. Denying or delaying services to clients based on cultural misunderstandings can most certainly do harm. Minorities tend to underutilize mental health services[51] and attend fewer sessions or drop out of therapy at higher rates than White clients.[17,54] These cultural misunderstandings may play a role in this underutilization of available services. Rehabilitation counselors must intimately understand their own cultural beliefs, attitudes, and values, and educate themselves as to how they may conflict with those of clients who are different from them.

A.5. ROLES AND RELATIONSHIPS WITH CLIENTS

The most effective role in building a therapeutic alliance is a counselor-client role. Engaging in relationships other than the counselor/client relationship may develop role confusion in which the client and counselor are confused. It can be difficult for not only the client but also the counselor to determine which role they serve in which context. Likewise, even if clear roles are established, it is difficult to stop the personal relationship from interfering with the professional relationship. Other unforeseen circumstances may include the loss of objectivity by the counselor, the development of an unsafe environment for the client (e.g., the personal relationship ends), transference and countertransference, and dependency and co-dependency related challenges of the counselor and the client.

An essential component of helping clients is to create a non-judgmental and safe environment for the client to interact and speak freely.[25] This process can be diminished if the counselor is unable to remain objective throughout the counseling process. Interacting with clients in non-professional relationships may lead to transference and countertransference when discussing the client's presenting barriers. Therefore, the CRCC code of ethics clearly states what is appropriate and inappropriate when considering nonprofessional relationships. Specifically, the CRCC code of ethics addresses the following areas:

1. sexual & romantic relationships with current, former, and certain former clients,

2. nonprofessional interactions or relationships other than sexual or romantic,

3. role changes in the professional relationship, and

4. receiving gifts.

All of these areas can diminish the counseling relationship and should be examined extensively prior to entering a counseling relationship, and when discussing roles and boundaries with clients. Below are a list of safeguards to avoid entering non-professional and potentially harmful relationship with the client.[60,p.258]

1. Have I adequately documented the decision-making process in the treatment records?

2. Did the practitioner obtain informed consent regarding the risks of engaging in the dual relationship?

3. Does the record show adequate evidence of professional consultation?

4. Does the record reflect a patient-oriented decision-making process?

5. Are the sources of consultation credible?

6. Do the diagnostic issues matter when considering a dual relationship?

7. Does knowledge of the patient support the establishment of a dual relationship?

8. Does one's therapist orientation matter when considering a dual relationship?

A.5.a. SEXUAL OR ROMANTIC RELATIONSHIPS ASSOCIATED WITH CURRENT CLIENTS

Rehabilitation counselors are prohibited from engaging in electronic and/or in-person sexual or romantic interactions or relationships with current clients, their romantic partners, or their immediate family members.[10,p.8]

Sexual or romantic relationships with the clients can be detrimental to the counseling relationship by diminishing the objectivity within the counseling relationship (Standard A.5.a.). For example, imagine a child made the accusation of sexual abuse against an aunt. This type of situation could divide the family (some believe the child; others believe the aunt). Imagine how difficult it would be for the counselor to remain objective if he or she was dating a family member of a client, with the family member believing the aunt, and the client believing the child. This type of situation can be difficult for a counselor to remain objective and non-judgmental due to the notion that the counselor has a personal connection to the situation. Another example could be if the client of a counselor were complaining about his or her family member, who is currently dating the counselor. This would be a conflict and could lead to a diminished therapeutic relationship.

Engaging in sexual or romantic relationships with current clients can also pose issues to the counseling relationship. The therapeutic relationship is built on trust,[25] and within the counseling relationship, clients will share stories and past events that bring out their thoughts, feelings, and behaviors related to such events or stories. In other words, clients become vulnerable in the counseling session and the counselor will be in a position where they can sexually exploit the client.[41] Moreover, common harmful client reactions of a sexual relationship between the counselor-client may include[41]

- ➢ ambivalence,

- ➢ cognitive dysfunction,

- ➢ emotional liability,

- ➢ emptiness and isolation,

- ➢ impaired ability to trust,

- ➢ guilt,

- ➢ increased suicidal risk,

- ➢ role reversal and boundary confusion,

- ➢ sexual confusion, and

- ➢ suppressed anger.

The authors noted that these reactions depend upon the client and their unique situation. For more information related to these potential harmful client reactions, read Pope's[41] chapter discussing "sex between therapist and clients."

A.5.b. SEXUAL OR ROMANTIC RELATIONSHIPS ASSOCIATED WITH FORMER CLIENTS

Rehabilitation counselors are prohibited from engaging in electronic and/or in-person sexual or romantic interactions or relationships with former clients, their romantic partners, or their immediate family members for a period of five years following the last professional contact. Even after five years, rehabilitation counselors give careful consideration to the potential for sexual or romantic relationships to cause harm to former clients. In cases of potential exploitation and/or harm, rehabilitation counselors avoid entering such interactions or relationships.[10,p.8]

A.5.c. SEXUAL OR ROMANTIC RELATIONSHIPS WITH VULNERABLE FORMER CLIENTS.

Rehabilitation counselors are prohibited from engaging in electronic and/or in-person sexual or romantic interactions or relationship with former clients, regardless of the length of time elapsed since termination of client relationships, if those clients: (1) have a history of physical, emotional, or sexual abuse; (2) have ever been diagnosed with any form of psychosis or personality disorder or marked cognitive impairment, or (3) are likely to remain in need of therapy due to the intensity or chronicity of a mental health condition.[10,p.8]

Engaging in sexual or romantic relationships with the client should be avoided (Standard A.5.b.). The CRCC clearly states that this must be avoided for at least five years after the last professional contact, but probably should be avoided in its entirety. One potential issue is that when there is a sexual or romantic relationship between the counselor and a former client, a professional relationship can never be established again. Furthermore, the client may have presented problems related to trauma from rape, domestic violence, etc., and the counselor may be able to exploit a sexual/romantic relationship by using information from prior counseling sessions. The client may have feelings of emptiness and isolation[53] and feel they were taken advantage of by their former counselor. Likewise, Pope[41] stated that a client involved in a sexual relationship with a counselor (e.g., past or current) may experience cognitive dysfunction (e.g., attention, memory, and concentration) because of the client's history of sexual trauma and may feel manipulated by the counselor due to a perceived power-differential and may result in unbidden thoughts, intrusive images, flashbacks, etc.

In an early study conducted by Pope and Vetter,[41] of the 958 clients who had been sexually involved with a therapist, "80% are harmed when the sexual involvement begins only after termination of therapy. About 11% required hospitalization; 14% attempted suicide; and 1% committed suicide. About 10% had experienced rape prior to sexual involvement with the therapist, and about a third had experienced incest or other child sex abuse. About 5% of these patients were minors at the time of the sexual involvement with the therapist. Of those harmed, only 17% recovered fully."[41,para.10] Likewise, clients may feel they do not have a voice to dismiss the potential relationship, because they may view the counselor as an authority figure, or the counselor's attraction is magnified by the inequality in power and control.[33]

A.5.d. SERVICE PROVISION SEXUAL OR ROMANTIC PARTNER

Rehabilitation counselors are prohibited from engaging in the provision of rehabilitation counseling services with persons with whom they have had a previous electronic and/or in-person sexual or romantic interaction or relationship.[10,p.8]

Rehabilitation counselors should never engage in counseling of former romantic or sexual partners. One potential issue that may result from engaging in such behavior is the inability to remain neutral and objective during the counseling process. Likewise, the rehabilitation counselor may be viewed as an equal, but also as subjective and judgmental. When the rehabilitation counselor challenges the client or attempts a therapeutic intervention, the client (former romantic partner) may view this as a personal attack rather than therapeutic. Additionally, the rehabilitation counselor and client may have difficulty transitioning into a different role (counselor-client), since they were previously romantically involved.

Imagine a client named Phoebe who was previously married to her counselor. Phoebe is discussing her inability to find companionship. Her ex-husband, Ross, starts reminding her of all the times she stayed out with friends and would often come home intoxicated. Ross reminds Phoebe of why their relationship ended. If Phoebe were seeing a counselor with no history of a relationship, perhaps this information would come out during a counseling session, and Phoebe might be able to make the connection between her behaviors and her inability to obtain companionship. Yet, if there is a past romantic relationship between the client/counselor, this could decrease the strength of the therapeutic relationship. Furthermore, Ross is unable to remain objective because he is inserting his personal experiences with Phoebe into the relationship. Phoebe could take this confrontation as a personal attack and an argument could arise. The rehabilitation counselor should conduct a risk-reward assessment of the possibility of counseling Phoebe and determine if a referral for counseling services from a separate counselor would be more beneficial to Phoebe.

A.5.e. SERVICE PROVISION WITH FRIENDS AND FAMILY MEMBERS
Rehabilitation counselors are prohibited from engaging in the provision of rehabilitation counseling services with friends or family members with whom they may have an inability to remain objective.[10, p.8]

Rehabilitation counselors should avoid engaging in a professional relationship with friends or family members where objectivity will be diminished. It would be inappropriate for a rehabilitation counselor to provide counseling to a friend or relative and might have difficulty with not viewing the client (relative/friend) in an appropriate manner. For example, suppose your cousin (Marine Veteran) is referred to your Compensated Work Therapy program within your Veteran Affairs (VA) Medical Center for assistance in securing employment in the federal government. Your family is happy that he is receiving help and hope he is able to find work as fast as possible. The program you are employed at, has a strict no drug policy, and he has tested positive for marijuana and cocaine. Given the dynamic of the relationship, you would be tasked with deciding whether to discharge him and upset your family or keep him in the program and possibly ruin your career. Non-professional relationships are sometimes referred to as *dual relationships*, where the counselor may be associated with the client in a professional counseling relationship but also in a non-professional relationship (e.g., client may also be a student, friend, family member, employee, or business associate of the therapist).[10]

A.5.f. PERSONAL VIRTUAL RELATIONSHIPS WITH CURRENT CLIENTS
Rehabilitation counselors are prohibited from engaging in personal virtual relationships with current clients (e.g., through social media). [10,p.8]

As society becomes more advanced in technology, there has been some focus on maintaining professional relationships with clients on social media platforms such as Facebook, Instagram, Snapchat, etc. If a professional has their personal page linked to a client, it may become known that they are receiving rehabilitation counseling services from you. For example, if you were to post a counseling-related memo on Facebook, the client might say, "I remember you telling me this during our session." This would eliminate the confidentiality component of the counseling relationship. Additionally, a social media relationship could tarnish the relationship if you were to post about a topic that conflicts with the client's values. For example, posting on topics such as vaccines, religion, and politics may trigger or elicit emotional responses that could tarnish the counseling relationship. One strategy that rehabilitation counselors can employ, is to create a comprehensive social media policy.[13] The policy should include statements such as, whether or not the rehabilitation counselor will accept friend requests, whether or not the messenger feature can be utilized on social media platforms (e.g., Facebook), and how HIPPA will be maintained in this capacity.[32] For example, if a rehabilitation counselor uses social media to consult with the client, how will the rehabilitation counselor ensure that the client is in fact the individual behind the account or messenger feature during the extent of the conversation. Although a social media policy is highly recommended, a rehabilitation counselor should avoid virtual relationships with current clients as directed by the ethical standard directly above. Sometimes, especially in small rural communities, this may occur frequently. For example, both the rehabilitation counselor and client may be invited to a wedding of a distant family member, or may, coincidentally, be seated close to each other at a local high school event. These are examples of non-professional interactions that were unintentional. Having a plan in place to discuss these potential conflicts during the intake (as aforementioned) will be helpful in resolving conflict such as this when it arises.

A.5.g. EXTENDING PROFESSIONAL BOUNDARIES

Rehabilitation counselors consider the risks and benefits of extending the boundaries of their professional relationships with current or former clients, their romantic partners, or their family members to include interactions not typical of professional rehabilitation counselor client relationships. In cases where rehabilitation counselors choose to extend these boundaries, they take appropriate professional precautions, such as seeking informed consent, consultation, and supervision to ensure that judgment is not impaired, and no harm occurs. With current clients, such interactions are initiated with appropriate consent from clients and are time-limited or context-specific. Examples include but are not limited to attending a formal ceremony (e.g., a wedding/commitment ceremony or graduation); purchasing a service or product provided by clients or former clients (excepting unrestricted bartering); hospital visits to ill family members; or mutual membership in professional associations, organizations, or communities.[10,p.8]

In some cases, rehabilitation counselors may face situations where they have the inability to avoid client interactions outside of the counseling relationship. For example, in small rural towns, a rehabilitation counselor may provide services to the family member of a dentist, medical doctor, or other community member where the client made it known that you are their counselor. Another example is when you go to a social event (e.g., town hall meeting or city council meeting) or engage in a fundraising activity where the client is also a member. Although the ethical issue is not necessarily being in the same place at the same time, an agency policy should be implemented that discusses what the process is if a situation arises where they are in the same location in a non-therapeutic environment. Such situations should be avoided unless it is a part of the treatment plan (e.g., client is receiving independent living skills training and you as their rehabilitation counselor take them shopping at a grocery store because their skill is to learn to budget for groceries) and therapeutic process. Prior to extending the professional boundaries with clients, it is important to consider the client's welfare and the long-term impact it might have on the client-counselor relationship.

A.5.h. DOCUMENTING BOUNDARY EXTENSIONS

If rehabilitation counselors expand boundaries as described in Standard A.5.g, they must officially document, prior to the interaction (when feasible), the rationale for such an interaction, the potential benefit, and anticipated consequences for the client or former client and other individuals significantly involved with the client or former client. When unintentional harm occurs to these individuals, rehabilitation counselors must show evidence of an attempt to remedy such harm.[10, p.9]

Another form of non-professional interaction that may occur is if the rehabilitation counselor and client were members of the same professional association, organizations, or communities, or community events. Regardless of where the non-professional interaction occurs, rehabilitation counselors need to document in a case note:

1. where the interaction occurred,

2. the extent of the interaction,

3. any confidentiality issues that might be in play,

4. were any ethical standards violated, and

5. how to resolve any conflict that developed as a result of the interaction.

Additionally, if the client inappropriately created the non-professional interaction, rehabilitation counselors need to review the policy on this type of interaction and possibly discuss the issues with the client (if it was inappropriate). For example, perhaps a client sees their rehabilitation counselor at a restaurant and starts telling people that this is their counselor, and then goes up to the counselor and attempts to have a conversation. These issues would need immediate discussion at the next appointment. All of this information should be documented as well.[43]

A.5.i. ROLE CHANGES IN THE PROFESSIONAL RELATIONSHIP

Rehabilitation counselors carefully evaluate and document the risks and benefits to clients before initiating role changes. If rehabilitation counselors change roles from the original or most recent contracted relationship, they discuss the implications of the role change with the client, including possible risks and benefits (e.g., financial, legal, personal, or therapeutic). They complete a new professional disclosure form with clients and explain the right to refuse services related to the change, as well as the availability of alternate service providers. Rehabilitation counselors refrain from frequent and/or indiscriminate role changes. If changing roles more than one time, rehabilitation counselors evaluate and document the risks and benefits of multiple changes. Examples of possible role changes include: (1) changing from individual to group, relationship, or family counseling, or vice versa; (2) changing from a rehabilitation counselor to a mediator role, or vice versa; (3) changing from a rehabilitation counselor to a researcher role (e.g., enlisting clients as research participants), or vice versa; and (4) changing from a non-forensic evaluative role or forensic role to a rehabilitation or therapeutic role, or vice versa.[10, p.9]

It is essential to discuss all benefits and limitations that may arise due to the role change so the client can make an informed decision. Role changes can be described as when the rehabilitation counselor shifts from one professional role to another professional role. For example, suppose a rehabilitation counselor is involved in providing individual counseling to a client but suddenly shifts to providing couples counseling to that client and his or her romantic partner. The client needs to be made aware of how the counseling relationship adjusts to accommodate this role change (e.g., who is the client and in whom does the counselor have the best interest?) A challenge in this type of role change for the counselor would be to avoid disclosing personal information from the individual sessions during the couples counseling (unless deemed appropriate and therapeutic by the client and counselor).

Role changes may occur during the VR process as well. For example, suppose a client named John is receiving VR services at the local State Rehabilitation Office. John informs his rehabilitation counselor that he would like to enroll in school to obtain his bachelor's degree in Rehabilitation Services. The rehabilitation counselor informs John that he also teaches a class in this program part-time, and that specific role changes must be discussed prior to him enrolling for classes. It is important to recognize that role changes do occur in rehabilitation counseling, and the strengths and limitations of these role changes must be discussed and dissected to avoid any harm to the therapeutic process.

A.5.j. ACCEPTING GIFTS

Rehabilitation counselors understand the challenges of accepting gifts from clients and recognize that in some cultures, small gifts are a token of respect and gratitude. When determining whether to accept gifts from clients, rehabilitation counselors take into account the cultural or community practice, therapeutic relationship, the monetary value of gifts, the client's motivation for giving gifts, and the motivation of the rehabilitation counselor for accepting or declining gifts. Rehabilitation counselors are aware of and comply with their employers' policies on accepting gifts.[10,pg.9]

The process of gift giving in counseling is not unusual; however, the ethical and therapeutic issues must be explored prior to a counselor accepting a gift. In some instances, the client may view the rehabilitation counselor as helpful in the rehabilitation process. The client may want to demonstrate appreciation of the services provided and want to give a gift to the rehabilitation counselor. Drew, et al.,[15] suggested that there are three general categories of giving gifts, including:

1. Gift giving is seen as a tip to the professional,

2. Gifts are given to address a perceived imbalance in the professional relationship, and

3. The gift may serve as a payment for sacrifice of the mental health professional.

Gerig[22] suggested that the professional must evaluate the level of therapeutic meaning and significance related to the gift, and consider the various questions[207-208] including but not limited to:

➤ What extent would acceptance of the gift be ethical?

➤ Will accepting this gift negatively affect the well-being of this client?

➤ Is there any potential for client exploitation due to the counselor-client role or power differential?

Prior to accepting or declining a gift, the rehabilitation counselor should also consider the cultural implications of engaging in such action. The rehabilitation counselor should document such instances of gift giving, whether accepted or declined, in the client's case file.

CASE STUDY

Lou is currently employed as a counselor at Two Rivers Counseling Support, a local agency in a small rural town. Lou recently ended a serious relationship with his romantic partner, Enrique. Lou has been pretty upset about how things ended after being a couple for the previous three years, but he wanted the experience of dating other people. Lou's best friend and private practice partner, Rosemary, suggested that Lou take some time off to work on his barriers related to the break up. Lou assured Rosemary that he will be fine, it will just take some time to get used to the new role.

Henry was referred to Lou approximately one month later, to receive counseling services after his cousin suggested that he see a counselor due to some potential anxiety-related issues. During the next few sessions, it appears that Henry is distraught because he has been unable to keep a relationship longer than a week. Henry identifies as a homosexual, which intrigues Lou because he has a tremendous amount of knowledge on the lesbian, gay, and bisexual community. Henry stated that there are not a lot of homosexuals within the small town in which they live and is afraid he will never settle down. Henry and Lou continue working Henry's presenting challenges.

Henry describes previous sexual abuse by an Uncle at an early age. After a few more weeks of counseling, Lou is out with a few friends at the local Applebee's having a few drinks and eating some appetizers. They are waiting for their friend to arrive. After 20 minutes, the friend arrives but brings Henry (Lou's client). Avoiding the awkwardness and attempting to maintain confidentiality, Lou pretends that he does not know Henry and they continue hanging out as a group. A few more hangout sessions occur and Lou starts realizing that he is becoming attracted to Henry.

During a counseling session, Henry tells Lou that he is attracted to him and wants to go on a date. Lou informed Henry that he has similar feelings but they would have to keep the dating relationship secretive because he could get in trouble for dating a client. Henry reminds Lou that their counseling relationship will be ending soon because he has been feeling great, with no anxiety. Lou suggested they meet a few more times and then they can go on a date. During the next few sessions, Lou asks Henry to describe his sexual relation with his past romantic relationships because perhaps there is a reason why the relationships are not working out. Henry describes his sexual relationships in complete detail for Lou. After another month of counseling, Henry is terminated from counseling services due to completion of his counseling goal. Henry and Lou decided to go on a date and engage in a sexual relationship that is similar to Henry's description during the counseling session. Soon after dating (two months), Lou ends the relationship with Henry and tells him that it just is not working out.

CASE STUDY DISCUSSION

The counselor in the above scenario should have weighed many of the ethical sub-standards of Section A.5., roles and relationships with clients. The section is related to the development of professional boundaries with clients so that the therapeutic relationship can be maintained. First, Lou should have taken Rosemary's advice and sought professional counseling services to work on his relationship "break-up," prior to continuing to provide counseling services to his clients. One of the reasons that Henry asked Lou out on a date could be due to a perceived power-differential. If they start dating exclusively, they will be on the same level. Another possibility is that Henry feels alone and is comforted by Lou when engaging in non-professional interactions. It is essential that Lou recognize the potential risk of dating Henry because clients may have difficulties maintaining health boundaries.

The CRCC ethical standard clearly states that sexual or romantic relationships must be avoided for at least five years since the last day of services. Henry violated Sexual or romantic relationship associated with current clients (Standard A.5.a.), and former clients (Standard A.5.b.). Due to the previous sexual abuse that Henry experienced when he was younger, it appears that the counselor also violated the standard of sexual or romantic relationships with vulnerable former clients (A.5.c.). It is not apparent whether Lou wanted Henry to describe his past sexual relationships to help in a therapeutic way or Lou was asking in a personal way. In order to prevent these types of relationships, rehabilitation counselors should examine the research studies conducted by Pope[41] to learn the potential issues of engaging in sexual relationships with clients that have a history of abuse or sexual assault (e.g., hospitalization, suicidal attempts). Furthermore, the client may feel hostility towards counseling and may refuse to seek services in the future.

A.6. MULTIPLE CLIENTS

When rehabilitation counselors agree to provide services to two or more persons who have a relationship (e.g., husband/wife; parent/child), rehabilitation counselors clarify at the outset which person is, or which persons are, to be served and the nature of the relationship with each involved person. If it becomes apparent that rehabilitation counselors may be called upon to perform potentially conflicting roles, rehabilitation counselors clarify, adjust, or withdraw from roles appropriately.[10,p.9]

There are many obstacles that could create ethical issues when engaging in counseling more than one client at a time. Examples of when a rehabilitation counselor may work with more than one individual in a clinical counseling setting include, but are not limited to, couples counseling and/or family counseling. One potential issue is related to the responsibility to the client.

Often times, the counselor may view the family or unit as one client; however, the relationship often includes multiple clients within the counseling relationship.[21] The CRCC code of ethics describes that rehabilitation counselors must clarify at the outset who is the client(s) and what the counseling relationship will consist of (Standard A.6.). For example, the rehabilitation counselor should describe the responsibility they have to each client (also included in the informed consent) and how the rehabilitation counselor will maintain confidentiality when meeting the multiple clients as a group and individually. Gehart[21] suggested that family counselors or those counseling multiple clients should continue to self-reflect to avoid "taking sides" and to remain objective. Often times, one of the clients in the counseling relationship may feel the rehabilitation counselor is taking the side of the other client, and this may diminish the therapeutic bond between each client.

A.7. GROUP WORK

A.7.a. SCREENING
Rehabilitation counselors screen prospective group counseling/therapy participants. To the extent possible, rehabilitation counselors select members whose needs and goals are compatible with goals of the group, who do not impede the group process, and whose well-being is not jeopardized by the group experience.[10,p.9]

The CRCC code of ethics specifically states that rehabilitation counselors must screen participants to determine their appropriateness in being a member within a group counseling framework. Rehabilitation counselors must become knowledgeable of the pre-group screening process. Delucia-Waack[14] suggested two key aspects important to group member selection, including:

1. providing information to potential group members about details of the group (e.g., goals, topics, typical interventions) so that they are truly giving informed consent when they agree to participate, and

2. gathering information to decide whether potential group members would benefit from participation based on their goals, willingness to participate, and interpersonal skills.[p.49]

Corey[11] recommended that pre-group selection should include the counselor:

➢   identifying the needs, expectations, and commitment of the potential participant,

➢   the participant's myths and misconceptions should be challenged,

> information should be conveyed in a manner that the participant understands (e.g., confidentiality, roles), and

> a standardized screening protocol should be established.

Likewise, rehabilitation counselors should develop the overall goal of the group (inter-group goals will be developed once the group members are formulated), and then select members who would benefit the group. Rehabilitation counselors should exclude individuals that are:

> hostile, angry, or aggressive,

> unable to empathize with others,

> extremely sensitive to criticism, and

> participants who are in crisis or suicidal.

The rehabilitation counselor should also consider the diversity and multicultural competence of group members and may consider incorporating social justice principles, such as becoming "self-aware and sensitive to broad areas of race, ethnicity, socioeconomic class, age, gender identity and expression, sexual orientation, religion, and spirituality.[14,p.8] When rehabilitation counselors are conducting group counseling with children and adolescents, Delucia-Waack[14] recommends that all group members be within two years of each other because of emotional development; siblings should not be in the same group; the group should be a mixture of family situations or barriers among the children to promote peer role models, generate alternative solutions to problem, and to instill hope.[14, p. 51] As with all clients, individual goals should be consistent with group goals. If these goals are inconsistent, it will be beneficial to exclude the individual from the group. Delucia-Waack[14] recommended utilizing specific tests to assess an individual's appropriateness for a group counseling session. The Group Therapy Survey[44] has been revised and assessed for validity and reliability in later studies[8] and measures the domains of efficacy, myths, and vulnerability. Other assessments include:

1. Expectations about Counseling,[52]

2. The Group Assessment Form,[34]

3. Readiness for Group.[14]

A.7.b. PROTECTING CLIENTS
In a group setting, rehabilitation counselors take reasonable precautions to protect clients from harm or trauma.[10,p.9]

Rehabilitation counselors should take all precautions to protect the client from harm and trauma in all capacities. Corey[11] suggested that within a group counseling relationship, the therapist should make regular appointment times that are specified in advance, enforce set starting time and ending times for each session, decline to provide client personal information to other clients, refuse to include a client under the influence of alcohol or other drug, avoid sexual or personal contact with group members and prevent sexual or personal relationships between group members, and terminate counseling sessions if threats are made or acts of violence are committed against the counselor or a group member.[48,49] As related to the screening standard aforementioned, excluding group members that are not appropriate for the counseling group may reduce potential harm or trauma to other group members. Within the group counseling session, the rehabilitation counselor should continue to monitor and facilitate the group to determine if immediate intervention is needed (e.g., a client is confrontational to another group member that is not therapeutic) to prevent harm or further harm to the group members.

The rehabilitation counselor should also provide an informed consent and disclosure form to the client that discloses to group members that they:

1. have the right to leave the group if it is not what they expected or wanted,

2. if the group counseling sessions will be recorded,

3. how information will be processed (confidentiality),

4. expectations of the group,

5. if research will be involved, and

6. freedom from group pressure.[11]

Protecting clients may also involve the rehabilitation counselor's reaction to the group members. Rehabilitation counselors should continue to self-reflect and remain alert in determining how their reaction impacts the group process (e.g., countertransference), and rehabilitation counselors should refrain from using the group as a platform to address their own personal problems.

CASE STUDY

Lilly graduated with her master's degree in rehabilitation counseling approximately five years ago and works in her private practice providing outpatient substance abuse counseling services. She is currently a certified rehabilitation counselor, licensed clinical professional counselor, and licensed addiction counselor. As a part of her employment, she provides DUI evaluations and education courses, individual counseling services, and group counseling services. Throughout the past few years, Lilly's practice has been growing tremendously and she has had difficulty working with each client individually. She contacted her former classmate Billy to ask how he manages such a large caseload in his private business. Billy informed Lilly that instead of providing individual counseling services, he has the clients meet as a group and perform group counseling services. Billy stated that he can make more money this way because he is collecting money from 10 clients for two hours of work in a group counseling session, rather than only collecting money from two clients in an individual counseling capacity. Lilly asked what Billy does if a client would benefit more from an individual session and Billy stated that he informs the client that he primarily does group counseling and the client would have to adjust.

Lilly decided to attempt this approach and started having group counseling sessions. She was excited because she was making more money and devoting less time to individual counseling sessions. However, one of her new clients suggested that he had been diagnosed with social anxiety and was not comfortable engaging in group counseling but would prefer individual counseling. After reading the client's personal records, he did have a diagnosis of social anxiety and the treating psychologist wrote a note indicating that the client has an extreme fear of social situations. The note continued to describe that the client may become violent when faced with social situations. The psychologist stated that he and the client had made great progress at reducing the outbursts and violent behavior but they were still working on it and recommended that counseling be completed on an individual basis. Lilly decided that since she is well experienced in de-escalation techniques and is competent in facilitating a group counseling session, she would have the client "try out" group counseling.

CASE STUDY DISCUSSION

In the case study aforementioned, it appears the counselors are engaging in some questionable practices. First, ethical Standard A.7.a., clearly states that rehabilitation counselors must screen prospective clients to determine if they are suitable for the group and whether the group would be therapeutic to the client. Furthermore, the client's well-being (principle of beneficence) needs to be considered. The psychologist stated that this specific client who was diagnosed with social anxiety has emotional and violent outbursts in social situations. Although the client has not displayed this behavior, previous reports from the client's psychologist stated that this behavior would arise when involved in a group setting. Therefore, Lilly should have considered the potential pitfalls of forcing her client to participate in the group. It also appears that the rehabilitation counselor may be violating Standard A.7.b in that the counselor is responsible for protecting clients and taking reasonable precautions to protect clients from harm or trauma (Standard A.7.b). The specific violation is the protection of other clients within the group. By having a client who has these barriers, she is risking the safety of the other clients within the group because they could become a victim to the client's emotional and behavioral response to being in the group counseling session. Delucia-Waack[14] states that clients should be excluded from group counseling when the client presents hostility, anger, or aggressiveness.

A.8. TERMINATION AND REFERRAL

A.8.a. COMPETENCE WITHIN TERMINATION AND REFERRAL

If rehabilitation counselors determine they lack the competence to be of professional assistance to clients, they avoid entering or continuing professional relationships. Rehabilitation counselors are knowledgeable about culturally and clinically appropriate referral resources and suggest these alternatives. If clients decline the suggested referrals, rehabilitation counselors discontinue the relationship.[10,p.9]

Rehabilitation counselors have an ethical obligation to avoid entering counseling relationships when they are unable to provide effective services to clients. This standard not only reflects counselor competence in the counseling session, but also reflects an ability to refer clients to professionals that will be of assistance.[11] Suppose a client requests help from their rehabilitation counselor to treat their substance-related barriers. The rehabilitation counselor may not be familiar with this specific area (e.g., substance-related disorders) and has limited knowledge to assess the severity of the disability. Therefore, the rehabilitation counselor should discuss their limitations in this area and provide a referral to a professional who may be better equipped to assess the severity and work with this client. Essentially, a rehabilitation counselor should be familiar with their knowledge, skills, and abilities and should avoid entering professional counseling relationships that are beyond their scope of practice and knowledge.[43]

A.8.b. VALUES WITHIN TERMINATION AND REFERRAL

Rehabilitation counselors refrain from referring prospective and current clients based solely on the rehabilitation counselor's personally held values, attitudes, beliefs, and behaviors. Rehabilitation counselors respect the diversity of clients and seek training in areas in which they are at risk of imposing their values onto clients, especially when the rehabilitation counselor's values are inconsistent with the client's goals or are discriminatory in nature.[10,p.9]

Rehabilitation counselors do not always need to agree with their clients, but it is important to put the client first by providing them respect and autonomy. Rehabilitation counselors are trained to work with clients from a wide variety of backgrounds (e.g., ethnic backgrounds, religions, sexual orientations, and gender identities), disabilities, and settings. However, there are some circumstances where a client needs more specialized trainer or a higher level of care to meet their treatment goals. Rehabilitation counselors need to assess whether they can provide the appropriate services or whether a referral is appropriate in order to meet the client's needs.[57] Counselors do not refer or terminate clients based on the counselor's values, but rather if the client issue falls outside of their scope of practice. It is important to note that counselors that live in highly densely populated areas can provide referrals easier than counselors in rural areas. Sprong, et al.,[45] indicated that biases could affect rehabilitation counselors' judgement and ability to utilize professional values when interacting with clients, and therefore should engage in self-reflection to raise awareness and self-efficacy to make sure that these biases do not interfere in the delivery of services. Given that it is not uncommon for rehabilitation counselors to have clients that may have an issue that conflicts with the rehabilitation counselor's personal values, it is essential to identify this conflict and take the necessary steps to resolve the conflict so that appropriate services can be provided. Oftentimes, rehabilitation counselors are told to leave their biases at the door, which seems like an impossible task. Rather, rehabilitation counselor should evaluate their biases, and develop a plan that prevents the imposition of these values onto the services that are being provided.

A.8.c. APPROPRIATE TERMINATION AND REFERRAL

Rehabilitation counselors terminate counseling relationships when it becomes reasonably apparent that clients no longer need assistance, are not likely to benefit, or are being harmed by continued services. Rehabilitation counselors may terminate services when in jeopardy of harm by clients or other persons with whom clients have a relationship. Rehabilitation counselors may terminate services: (1) if a client is determined no longer eligible for services; (2) when agreed-upon time limits are reached; or (3) when clients or funding sources do not pay agreed-upon fees or will not pay for further services. Rehabilitation counselors are aware of alternate resources in the communities in which they practice. They provide pre-termination counseling and recommend other clinically and culturally appropriate and accessible service sources when necessary. Rehabilitation counselors make reasonable efforts to assure clients are eligible for the services from the service provider to which they are making a referral.[10,p.10]

The CRCC code of ethics states that when counseling is no longer likely to benefit the client, will create harm to the client by continued use, or the client no longer needs assistance, the counseling relationship should be terminated. Vasquez, et al.,[57] stated that termination occurs when the client has reached their maximum potential for achieving the mutually agreed counseling goals, and/or for other reasons. Vasquez, et al.,[57] recommended that counseling professionals use 12 practice recommendations to ensure the client is appropriately and effectively terminated from services. For example, rehabilitation counselors should help clients develop health and referral plans for post-termination life (e.g., support system, self-care plan, other counseling services).[57] The primary purpose of termination is not to stop services but to determine how to end services so that the therapeutic process within the client continues to prosper.[57] Therefore, rehabilitation counselors should emphasize the client's gains (note: can be accomplished by comparing individual gains against original treatment plan), develop a maintenance plan, and validating the client's growth, strengths, and resilience.[40,57] Finally, the rehabilitation counselor can help the client understand the counseling process and inform them that counseling services can be continued in the future if these services are needed.

A.8.d. APPROPRIATE TRANSFER OF SERVICES

When rehabilitation counselors transfer or refer clients to other practitioners, they make reasonable efforts to ensure that appropriate counseling, services, and administrative processes are completed in a timely manner and that appropriate information and records are communicated and/or transferred to the referral source to facilitate a smooth transition.[10,p.10]

In some cases, rehabilitation counselors may need to transfer services to another professional. When these instances occur, rehabilitation counselors must "ensure appropriate counseling and administrative processes are completed in a timely manner," and use appropriate communication strategies to keep the client updated with the transfer of services process. Corey[11] suggested that when it is necessary to transfer services, clients must be made aware of the reason for transferring services, the strengths, and limitations of the new professional in assisting the client, any unforeseen consequences that may occur, and an anticipated timeline for the services to be transferred. Likewise, rehabilitation counselors should continue working with the client until the transfer of services is completed. The rehabilitation counselor must make the client aware of what information will transfer to the new professional, and if any communications will occur between the current rehabilitation counselor and new professional who is receiving the transfer, while providing details of the information that will be exchanged. Rehabilitation counselors must also develop a plan to prepare for instances of incapacitation, death, or termination of practice. One way to assist the professional who will be replacing the rehabilitation counselor is by maintaining good documentation so that another professional can determine the rehabilitation goals that have been met and rehabilitation goals that are currently being worked on.

CASE STUDY

Mike is a rehabilitation counselor at a community-based rehabilitation program that is grant funded by the state vocational rehabilitation program. Mike has been employed by his agency for 8 years and usually has a caseload of 20 clients concurrently. In the past, Mike has received scrutiny for being unavailable to clients and failing to return phone calls in a timely manner. For instance, one of Mike's clients has recently contacted the agency to report that Mike has been absent during their counseling sessions and whenever they try to contact Mike, they do not hear from him for weeks. The agency's supervisor, Michele, has confronted Mike about his lack of communication with clients and suggested that Mike reduce his caseload to 10. Specifically, Michele stated that rehabilitation counselors generally have a caseload of 10 so that they can provide effective and efficient services to their clients, rather than being spread thin. Mike told Michele that he knew he would struggle maintaining a caseload of 20 but wanted to receive the small bonus and award that he has become accustomed to every year for working with so many clients. Michele stated that the clients should be the first priority. Mike assured Michele that he would practice some self-reflection during his vacation next week to determine what he should do with his caseload.

During Mike's vacation, Michele received numerous calls from clients stating that they are unable to get in touch with Mike. One caller specifically stated that Mike and he were supposed to practice interviewing skills as he has a job interview on Monday. Michele asked if he tried contacting the replacement rehabilitation counselor that will handle Mike's caseload while he is on vacation. The client stated that he was unaware that Mike was going on vacation and he was not informed that he would be working with another rehabilitation counselor this week.

CASE STUDY DISCUSSION

In this case study, it appears that there are certain ethical standards that Mike needs to consider in his service delivery. The ethical principle of fidelity "keeping promises" may have been violated as Mike stated that he would work with the client on interviewing skills prior to the client's interview the following Monday. Mike failed to inform his client that he would be on vacation and to find a rehabilitation counselor to manage his caseload while unavailable. This behavior conflicts with ethical Standard A.8.a which states that "rehabilitation counselors do not abandon or neglect clients in counseling...and make appropriate arrangements when absent."[10,p.10] It also appears that Mike has difficulty assisting his clients and may be in violation of Standard A.8.b. Mike has 20 clients on his caseload and clients have complained about the lack of Mike's presence in the counseling relationship. Mike was aware that he would struggle while working with a large caseload and should have considered:

a. values within termination and referral (Standard A.8.b.), or

b. transferring the client(s) to another rehabilitation counselor (Standard A.8.d).

Michele's assertion that the clients need to be the primary priority is referring to the ethical principle of beneficence (having the welfare of the client in mind). Mike is obviously concerned with receiving the bonus and award he has become accustomed to, but Mike should reflect to determine if this award and bonus are coming at the result of providing ineffective services to his clients, as is apparent in the above scenario.

A.8.e. ABANDONMENT PROHIBITED

Rehabilitation counselors do not abandon or neglect clients. Rehabilitation counselors assist in making appropriate arrangements for the continuation of services when necessary during extended absences and following termination.[10,p.10]

It is essential for rehabilitation counselors to avoid abandoning or neglecting clients in counseling. Although there is not a clear definition of abandonment, which has led to the removal of specific standards in other professional counseling code of ethics,[57] abandonment generally refers to unanticipated or unwanted termination from treatment when the client still needs care.[53] This may include failing to provide a reliable replacement when the rehabilitation counselor is absent (e.g., vacations, illness). If the rehabilitation counselor will be absent for a period of time, they should provide the client with the contact information of another professional to communicate with in the case of a crisis or establish a replacement rehabilitation counselor for the duration of the absence. Abandonment may also include terminating services when the funding is no longer available, and the rehabilitation counselor terminates service regardless of the client still needing service. Despite the discrepancy in what constitutes abandonment, rehabilitation counselors should strive to reduce abandonment (unanticipated or unwanted termination of services) by providing a process of continuation of services when the counselor is unavailable.

A.9. END-OF-LIFE CARE FOR TERMINALLY ILL CLIENTS

The CRCC code of professional ethical standards provides guidance in three key areas related to rehabilitation counselors working with clients who are making end-of-life decisions:

1. counselor competency for working with end-of-life clients;

2. counselor scope of practice regarding end-of-life clients; and

3. counselor choices pertaining to confidentiality in cases where terminally ill clients are considering hastening their own deaths.

However, it should be noted that the primary challenges rehabilitation counselors face when working with clients making these types of decisions is not imposing their values within the decision-making process. Despite this difficulty, rehabilitation counselors must obtain competency when working with clients in this capacity. Wadsworth, et al.,[58] asserted, rehabilitation counselors may be the initial point of contact and may find themselves involved with end-of-life issues through participation in case management, ethics, research, and administrative committees in which decisions regarding end-of-life practices can occur. The American Counseling Association[1] removed the End-of-Life standards from their newest version of the code of ethics because there was a feeling that end-of-life referral was value-based and the Ethics Revision Task Force was interested in eliminating personal value in the new code of ethics.[28,9] Therefore, a rehabilitation counselor should take careful consideration of the following standards when working in this capacity.

A.9.a. QUALITY OF CARE

When the need arises, rehabilitation counselors advocate for services that enable clients to: (1) obtain high quality end-of-life care for their physical, emotional, social, and spiritual needs; (2) exercise the highest degree of self-determination possible; (3) be given every opportunity possible to engage in informed decision-making regarding their end-of-life care; and (4) receive complete and adequate assessment regarding their ability to make competent, rational decisions on their own behalf from mental health professionals who are experienced in end-of-life care practice.[10, p.10]

The purpose of the quality-of-care standard is to emphasize that rehabilitation counselors who are working with a client in the final stages of life should try to maximize the client's perceived quality of life. Less education, unemployment, low income, higher levels of poverty, increased need for support from family or service agencies, higher medical costs, and costs associated with accessibility and assistive technology are all factors that should be considered by rehabilitation counselors when developing an end-of-life rehabilitation plan.[37] Therefore, when working with clients to develop an end-of-life care plan, rehabilitation counselors should carefully develop the plan so that the formation of the plan is client-centered, meaning that self-determination and informed decision-making are always desired. Furthermore, the goal of the rehabilitation counselor is to act as an audience to the client's decision-making process and assist the client by bringing up common issues involved in the end-of-life plan that the client may have missed. Upholding self-determination and informed decision-making, the rehabilitation counselor never initiates action, but rather assists and acts as a sounding board to the client.

The only precedent for action initiated by the rehabilitation counselor is in the event that the client is determined not able to make competent and rational decisions. In this case, the rehabilitation counselor takes the appropriate steps to protect the client and seeks supervision and guidance in order to act in the best interest of the client. In these specific circumstances, it may be beneficial for the rehabilitation counselor to suggest a team approach, consisting of health care and mental health professionals, family, friends, or other support system members, and spiritual advisors.[3,30]

A.9.b. CONFIDENTIALITY

Rehabilitation counselors who provide services to terminally ill individuals who are considering hastening their own deaths through such mechanisms as assisted suicide or refusing life-sustaining treatments have the option of maintaining confidentiality on this matter, depending on applicable laws, the specific circumstances of the situation, and after seeking consultation or supervision from appropriate professional and legal parties.[10,pg.10]

The concept of confidentiality is vital to maintaining a trustworthy counseling relationship. Generally, the information provided by the client is never disclosed unless certain circumstances arise. For example, if a client is threatening to harm themself or someone else, records are subpoenaed by a court of law (note: only release the related information requested), among others (e.g., child abuse, child sexual assault, elder abuse).[11] In some instances, clients in the end stages of life may consider P-AS. In the states of Oregon, Washington, and Montana, counselors are legally permitted to counsel in a confidential manner terminally ill clients who are considering hastening their death. However, California, Colorado, District of Columbia, Hawaii, Maine, New Jersey, Oregon, Vermont, and Washington are the only states legalizing P-AS, and Montana allows P-AS via court ruling. It must be noted that in circumstances pertaining to P-AS, one who considers hastening their own death does not necessarily constitute "serious and foreseeable harm" and, therefore, is not subject to mandatory reporting.[31] Rehabilitation counselors should evaluate state legislation to determine specific laws related to P-AS and confidentiality.

CASE STUDY

Rhonda is currently 55 years of age and works as a construction foreman at a striving construction business. She was recently having some medical problems and scheduled an appointment with her family physician. Rhonda told her family physician that she has been experiencing abnormal vaginal bleeding and pain during sex. Rhonda informed the doctor that her mother died of cervical cancer and had similar symptoms. The physician referred Rhonda for some exams and informed Rhonda that the results indicated that she has cervical cancer at stage 4 (spread to distant organs/bladder or bowel). The physician informed Rhonda that approximately 5% would survive for 5 years or more after being diagnosed with Stage 4 cervical cancer. Rhonda told the physician that she has always determined that if she is ever diagnosed with cervical cancer, she will consider legally hastening her own death. The physician suggested she talk it over with her family prior to making a decision since she will most likely need their support throughout the coming processes, depending on her decision. After speaking with her family, Rhonda decided it might be best to speak with a counselor. Therefore, Rhonda scheduled an appointment with a counselor in her hometown.

During the initial appointment, Rhonda discussed with her new counselor that she was diagnosed with stage 4 cervical cancer and only has a 5% chance of living more than 5 years. She informed the counselor that she is interested in P-AS because she does not want to let the cancer "take her." The counselor informed Rhonda that he does not believe in P-AS and does not think she should consider hastening her death but will still work with her throughout this process. Rhonda asked her counselor if her state allowed P-AS and the counselor responded with an immediate response of "no." However, after conducting some research on her own, Rhonda discovered that the state of Oregon does allow P-AS.

After bringing this information to her counselor's attention, her counselor stated that she needed to have a court order to proceed. After consulting a local attorney, she discovered that she does not need a court order and that the counselor is providing misinformation. After discussing the information, she obtained with her counselor, the counselor confesses that he does not believe in this action and will not support it. Furthermore, the counselor stated that he is not familiar with the laws related to P-AS. However, the counselor stated that he would disclose her desire to hasten her death and report this to the authorities.

CASE STUDY DISCUSSION

There are many ethical-related issues to consider within the aforementioned scenario. As rehabilitation counselors, we have a duty to our clients to be competent in the services we provide. As stated by the counselor, he was not familiar with laws related to P-AS and, therefore, was providing false information to his client (violated the ethical principle of Veracity). As mentioned earlier, Veracity is the principle of truth telling, and lying on purpose or omitting information are two forms of violating this principle.[59] Likewise, the counselor was violating the Standard A.9.a., " *of Care,*" by providing information related to state legislation and then attesting that he does not have knowledge of the laws. This may lead to the client mistrusting the counselor and to the client making the decision on her own, without consulting a counselor who can help her make an informed decision. This lack of trust in the relationship is a direct violation of the ethical principle of Fidelity, which refers to the rehabilitation counselor establishing a therapeutic relationship with the client that is based on trust and non-judgment.[6] It appears that the counselor in the aforementioned scenario was about to violate confidentiality (Standard A.9.b.). The counselor, admitting that he is not familiar with legislation, should have consulted the laws governing P-AS for the terminally ill prior to suggesting that he will take this course of action. Finally, it appears that the quality of care (Standard A.9.a.) may have been violated as the counselor is doing all but support the autonomy of his client and helping her improve her quality of life. Rather than exploring this decision with his client, he is imposing his personal values onto the client. AUTONOMY refers to the individual's freedom to choose the best course of action with respect to their rehabilitation plan. Within this ethical principle, rehabilitation counselors respect the individual's ability to make decisions free from the constraint of others.[11]

REFERENCES

[1]American Counseling Association (2005). *ACA code of ethics.* https://www.counseling.org/docs/default-source/default-document-library/2014-code-of-ethics-finaladdress.pdf?sfvrsn=96b532c_2

[2]Badgett, L., Burns, C., Hunter, N. D., Krehely, J., Mallory, C., & Sears, B. (2013). *An executive order to prevent discrimination against LGBT workers.* https://www.americanprogress.org/issues/lgbt/report/2013/02/19/53931/an-executive-order-to-prevent-discrimination-against-lgbt-workers/

[3]Barnett, J. E., & Johnson, W. B. (2014). *Ethics desk reference for counselors* (2nd ed.).Wiley.

[4]Benjamin, A. (1981). *The helping interview.* Houghton Mifflin.

[5]Bersoff, D. N. (2008). *Ethical conflicts in psychology* (4th ed.). American Psychological Association.

[6]Bosede, A. F. (2010). Ethical principles of guidance and counselling. *International Journal of Tropical Medicine, 5*(2), 50-53. https://doi.org/10.3923/ijtmed.2010.50.53

[7]Braun, S. A., & Cox, J. A. (2011). Managed mental health care: Intentional misdiagnosis of mental disorders. *Journal of Counseling & Development, 83*(4), 425-433. https://doi.org/10.1002/j.1556-6678.2005.tb00364.x

[8]Carter, E. F., Mitchell, S. L., & Krautheim, M. D. (2001). Understanding and addressing clients' resistance to group counseling. *Journal for Specialists in Group Work, 26*(1), 66-80. https://doi.org/10.1080/01933920108413778

[9]Case, J. C., Blackwell, T. L., & Sprong, M. E. (2016). Counselor ethical considerations for end-of-life care. *Journal of Rehabilitation, 82*(1), 48-58.

[10]Commission on Rehabilitation Counselor Certification (2017). *Code of professional ethics for rehabilitation counselors.* . Schaumburg, IL: Author. https://www.crccertification.com/filebin/Ethics_Resources/CRCC_Code_E ff_20170101.pdf

[11]Corey, G. (2013). *Theory and practice of counseling and psychotherapy* (9th ed.). Cengage Learning.

[12]Cottone, R. R., Tarvydas, V., & Claus, R. E. (2007). Ethical decision-making processes. In R. R. Cottone & V. M. Tarvydas (Eds.), *Ethical and professional issues in counseling (3rd ed., pp. 85–113).* Pearson Education.

[13]Crtalic, A. K., Gibbs, R. L., Sprong, M. E., & Dell, T. F. (2015). Boundaries with social media: Ethical considerations for rehabilitation professionals. *Journal of Applied Rehabilitation Counseling, 46*(3), 44-50.

[14]DeLucia-Waack, J. L. (2006). *Leading psychoeducational groups for children and adolescents.* Sage Publications.

[15]Drew, J., Stoeckle, J. D., & Billings, J. A. (1983). Tips, status, and sacrifice: Gift-giving in the doctor-patient relationship. *Social Science and Medicine, 17*(7), 399-404. https://doi.org/10.1016/0277-9536(83)90343-X

[16]Fleming, A. R., Fairweather, J. S., & Leahy, M. J. (2013). Quality of life as a potential rehabilitation service outcome: The relationship between employment, quality of life, and other life areas. *Rehabilitation Counseling Bulletin, 57*(1), 9-22. https://doi.org/10.1177/0034355213485992

[17]Fortuna, L. R., Alegria, M., & Gao, S. (2010). Retention in depression treatment among ethnic and racial minority groups in the United States. *Depression and Anxiety, 27*(5), 485-494. https://doi.org/10.1002/da.20685

[18]Francis, P. C., & Dugger, S. M. (2014). Professionalism, ethics, and value-based conflicts in counseling: An introduction the special section. *Journal of Counseling & Development, 92*(2), 131-134. https://doi.org/10.1002/j.1556-6676.2014.00138.x

[19]Garber, B. D. (2004). Therapist alienation: Foreseeing and forestalling third-party dynamics undermining psychotherapy with children of conflicted caregivers. *Professional Psychology: Research and Practice, 35*(4), 357-363. https:/doi.org/10.1037/0735-7028.35.4.357

[20]Garwick, A. G., & Auger, S. (2000). What do providers need to know about American Indian culture? Recommendations from urban Indian family caregivers. *Families, Systems, & Health, 18*(2), 177-190. https://doi.org/10.1037/h0091845

[21]Gehart, D. (2014). *Mastering competencies in family therapy.* Brooks/Cole.

[22]Gerig, M. S. (2004). Receiving gifts from clients: Ethical and therapeutic issues. *Journal of Mental Health Counseling, 26*(3), 199-210. https://doi.org/10.17744/mehc.26.3.vwb3lfh68c7p7f4b

[23]Herlihy, B. J., Hermann, M. A., & Greden, L. R. (2014). Legal and ethical implications of using religious believes as the basis for refusing to counsel certain clients. *Journal of Counseling and Development, 92*(2), 148-153. https://doi.org/10.1002/j.1556-6676.2014.00142.x

[24]Hovarth, A. O., Del Re, A. C., Fluckiger, C., & Symonds, D. (2011). Alliance in individual psychotherapy. *Psychotherapy, 48*(1), 9-16. https://doi.org/10.1037/a0022186

[25]Ivey, A. E., Ivey, M. B., & Zalaquett, C. P. (2014). *Intentional interviewing and counseling: Facilitating client development in a multicultural society* (8th ed.). Cengage Learning.

[26]Kadushin, C. (1972). Who are the elite intellectuals? *The Public Interest, 29*, 109-125.

[27]Kaplan, D. (2008). Counseling today ethics update: End-of-life care for terminally ill clients. http://ct.counseling.org/2008/06/ct-online-ethics-update-3/

[28]Kaplan, D. M. (2014). Ethical implications of a critical legal case for the counseling profession: Ward v. Wilbanks. *Journal of Counseling & Development, 92*(2), 142-146. https://doi.org/10.1002/j.1556-6676.2014.00140.x

[29]Katz, J. (1985). The sociopolitical nature of counseling. *Counseling Psychologist, 13,* 615-624. https://doi.org/10.1177/0011000085134005

[30]Kaut, K. P. (2006). End-of-Life assessment within a holistic bio-psycho-social-spiritual framework. In Werth, J. L. & Blevins, D. (APA), *Psychosocial issues near the end of life: A resource for professional care providers* (1st ed., pp. 111-132). American Psychological Association.

[31]Kocet, M. M. (2006). Ethical challenges in a complex world: Highlights of the 2005 ACA Code of Ethics. *Journal of Counseling & Development, 84*(2), 228-234. https://doi.org/10.1002/j.1556-6678.2006.tb00400.x

[32]Kolmes, K. (2010). My private practice social media policy. http://www.drkkolmes.com/docs/socmed.pdf

[33]Kottler, J., & Shepard, D. (2015). *Introduction to counseling: Voices from the field.* Cengage Learning.

[34]Lynn, G. L. (1994). The GAF: The group assessment form: A screening instrument for adolescent group therapy. *Journal of Child and Adolescent Group Therapy, 4*(3), 135-146. https://doi.org/10.1007/BF02548459

[35]National Council on Interpreting in Health Care. (2005). *National standards of practice for interpreters in health care.* http://www.ncihc.org/ethics-and-standards-of-practice

[36]Norcross, J. C. (2011). *Psychotherapy relationships that work: Evidence-based responsiveness* (2nd ed.). Oxford University.

[37]Olkin, R. (1999). *What psychotherapists should know about disability?* The Guilford Press.

[38]Pare, D. (2012). *The practice of collaborative counseling & psychotherapy: Developing skills in culturally mindful helping.* SAGE Publications, Inc.

[39]Pedersen, P. B., Lonner, W. J., & Draguns, J. G. (Eds.). (1976). *Counseling across cultures.* University Press of Hawaii.

[40]Pipes, R. B., & Davenport, D. S. (1999). *Introduction to psychotherapy: Common clinical wisdom* (2nd ed.). Allyn & Bacon.

[41]Pope, K. (2002). Sex between therapist and clients. *In the Encyclopedia of women and gender: Sex similarities and the differences and the impact of society on gender.* Academic Press.

[42]Pope, K. S., & Vasquez, M. J. T. (2011). *Ethics in psychotherapy and counseling: A practical guide (4th ed.).* John Wiley & Sons.

[43]Roessler, R. & Rubin, S. (2006). *Case management and rehabilitation counseling.* PRO-ED.

[44]Slocum, Y. S. (1987). A survey of expectations about group therapy among clinical and non-clinical populations. *International Journal of Group Psychotherapy, 37*(1), 39-54. https://doi.org/10.1080/00207284.1987.11491040

[45]Sprong, M. E., Currier, K., Hollender, H., Cerrito, B., & Buono, F. D. (2020). The influence of gender and sexism on the recommendation of certificate programs and consumer autonomy in vocational rehabilitation. *Journal of Rehabilitation 86*(1), 4-11.

[46]Stancliffe, R. J., Lakin, K. C., Larson, S., Engler, J., Taub, S., & Fortune, J. (2011). Choice of living arrangements. *Journal of Intellectual Disability Research, 55*(8), 746-762. https://doi.org/10.1111/j.1365-2788.2010.01336.x

[47]Stewart, C. J., & Cash, W. B. Jr. (2011). *Interviewing: Principles and practice* (13th ed.). McGraw-Hill.

[48]Substance Abuse Mental Health Services Administration [SAMHSA]. (2000). *Substance abuse treatment for persons with child abuse and neglect issues: Treatment improvement protocol series No. 36.* Center for Substance Abuse Treatment. https://store.samhsa.gov/product/tip-36-substance-abuse-treatment-for-persons-with-child-abuse-and-neglect-issues/SMA12-3923

[49]Substance Abuse Mental Health Services Administration [SAMHSA]. (2005). *Substance abuse treatment for persons with co-occurring disorders: Treatment improvement protocol series No. 42.* Center for Substance Abuse Treatment. https://store.samhsa.gov/product/tip-42-substance-use-treatment-persons-co-occurring-disorders/PEP20-02-01-004

[50]Sue, D. & Sue, D. (2013). *Counseling the culturally diverse: Theory and practice* (6th ed.). Wiley.

[51]Thurston, I. B., & Phares, V. (2008). Mental health utilization among African American and Caucasian mothers and fathers. *Journal of Consulting and Clinical Psychology, 76*(6), 1058-1067. https://doi.org/10.1037/a0014007

[52]Tinsley, H. E. A., Workman, A. M., & Kass, R. A. (1980). Factor analysis of the domain of client expectations about counseling. *Journal of Counseling Psychology, 27,* 561-570. https://doi.org/10.1037/0022-0167.27.6.561

[53]Treloar, H. R. (2010). Financial and ethical considerations for professionals in Psychology. *Ethics & Behavior, 20*(6), 454-465. https://10.1080/10508422.2010.521447

[54]Triffleman, E. G., & Pole, N. (2010). Future directions in studies of trauma among ethnoracial and sexual minority samples: Commentary. *Journal of Consulting and Clinical Psychology, 78*(4), 490-497. https://doi.org/10.1037/a0020225

[55]Üstün TB, Kostanjsek N, Chatterji S, Rehm J (2010): Measuring Health and Disability: Manual for WHO Disability Assessment Schedule: WHODAS 2.0, World Health Organization.

[56]Utsey, S. O., Grange, C., & Allyne, R. (2006). Guidelines for evaluating the racial and cultural environment of graduate training programs in professional psychology. In M. G. Constantine & D. W. Sue (Eds.), *Addressing racism* (pp.247-268). Wiley.

[57]Vasquez, M. J. T., Bingham, R. P., & Barnett, J. E. (2008). Psychotherapy termination: Clinical and ethical responsibilities. *Journal of Clinical Psychology, 64*(5), 653-665. https://doi.org/10.1002/jclp.20478

[58]Vespa, J., Medina, L., & Armstrong, D. (2020). Demographic turning points for the united states: Population project for 2020 to 2060. *United States Census Bureau, Current Population Report, February 2020,* 3-4. https://www.census.gov/library/publications/2020/demo/p25-1144.html

[59]Ward v. Wilbanks, No. 10-2100, Doc. 006110869854 (6th Cir. Court of Appeals, Feb. 11, 2011). http://www.counseling.org/resources/pdfs/EMUamicusbrief.pdf

[60]Younggren, J. N., & Gottlieb, M. C. (2008). Managing risk when contemplating multiple relationships. *Research and Practice, 35*(3), 253-261. https://doi.org/10.1037/0735-7028.35.3.255

CHAPTER 5

CONFIDENTIALITY, PRIVILEGED COMMUNICATION, AND PRIVACY

Lindsey Fullmer

Allison Fleming

Daniel L. Boutin

Michael P. Accordino

Alison Baranauskas

SECTION B: CONFIDENTIALITY, PRIVILEGED COMMUNICATION, AND PRIVACY

Confidentiality, privileged communication, and privacy of the Commission on Rehabilitation Counselor Certification (CRCC) Code of Ethics covers an area of great importance to rehabilitation counseling. Confidentiality is the underpinning of the counseling relationship. Without it, rapport cannot develop and the therapeutic relationship will fail to exist. Yet, there are instances where confidentiality can be broken and deeply shared personal information can be made public.

Privileged communication, or a client's right to have their information kept confidential, is a choice that rests with the client.[13] Since there are instances where confidentiality must be broken, often due to legal requirements, adequate planning on the part of the rehabilitation counselor is recommended. In order to plan for times when breaking a client's privileged communication, rehabilitation counselors should openly discuss these reasons with a client at intake. However, some counselors are hesitant to have such discussions for fear that they will inhibit client disclosure. This omission can cause greater damage to the counseling relationship if confidentiality is broken for legal reasons due to the counselor violating the promise to protect the client's privacy.

In developing the current code of ethics, which was completed in 2016 and went into effect on January 1, 2017, new terms and considerations were evident, especially those pertaining to private rehabilitation, technology, and their implications for confidentiality.[5,13,23] Confidentiality violations are among some of the more prevalent complaints that state licensure boards investigate.[29] This demonstrates how essential yet controversial that confidentiality can be. For example, there is an area that has been highlighted in research as a significant threat to confidentiality–the workplace. The shifting methodology of service delivery is a concern for maintaining confidentiality. Rehabilitation Counselors in both the public and private sectors tend to work in close quarters with coworkers in cubicles and other office configurations that are vulnerable for personal information being overheard by others or files being left in open view.[17] This situation is often the product of combining two or more area offices in a downsizing effort. In such instances, these threats to confidentiality are often not addressed due to the limitations of the physical environment or the feelings of helplessness on the part of the counselor.

It is clear that confidentiality is a concept that, although recognized as pivotal in rehabilitation counseling as well as other counseling providers, is an area that is at risk for being breached in many aspects of rehabilitation counselor delivery.[3] An overview of section B of the (CRCC) Code of Ethics is presented in the following sections, along with illustrative vignettes.

B.1 RESPECTING CLIENT RIGHTS

An effective client-counselor relationship is one that is established on the foundation of trust. According to Wheeler and Bertram[29] trust is established when clients believe their information is protected by their counselors. Clients have the right to ensure that any written documentation and/or verbal communication is protected.[7] These rights not only extend to current clients but prospective clients as well.[2] Clients also have the right to give permission to the nature in which their information can be shared. Even when subpoenaed by the courts, counselors must carefully consider the extent that client records (if any) will be released. Counselors must work with presiding legal professionals to limit any disclosures being requested in order to protect their clients.

B.1.a. RESPECT FOR PRIVACY
Rehabilitation counselors respect the privacy rights of clients. Rehabilitation counselors solicit private information from clients only when it is beneficial to the rehabilitation counseling process. Rehabilitation counselors make reasonable efforts to ensure that methods of sharing or transmitting information are secure.

The term *privacy* is often used interchangeably with the term *confidentiality*; however, both terms have distinct meanings.[29] Cottone and Tarvydas[7] define privacy as "a broad encompassing standard that protects the client by preventing revelation of the counseling relationship without the client's knowledge or approval."[p.145] Accordingly, counselors must ensure privacy concerning clients seeking services as well as what is communicated during sessions. This may include scheduling methods to avoid client-to-client interactions in waiting rooms, billing and administration procedures of client records, and the use of discrete contact through telecommunication (e.g., voicemail, e-mail).

CASE STUDY

Rose works for the student disability resource office at a private college. She has been assisting her client, Damian, with securing reasonable accommodations for his classes. One night after work, Rose attends a showing at a local movie theater with her friend. She crosses paths with Damian, who purchased tickets for the same movie. Damian cheerfully greets Rose and exchanges general pleasantries before heading to the concession stand. On the way into the theater, Rose's friend asks how she knows Damian. Rose explained that she was unable to discuss her relationship with Damian and redirected the conversation to another topic.

ETHICAL IMPLICATIONS:

In this vignette, Rose did everything correctly. Rose respected Damian's privacy by not disclosing he is a client. Chance encounters with clients are inevitable, especially when working in college or university settings, or in small communities. In this case, it is good practice to have conversations with clients about their preferences for handling such encounters. This can be done when reviewing informed consent paperwork.

B.1.b. PERMISSION TO RECORD

Rehabilitation counselors obtain permission from clients prior to recording sessions through electronic or other means.

B.1.c. PERMISSION TO OBSERVE

Rehabilitation counselors obtain permission from clients prior to observing sessions, reviewing session transcripts, and/or listening to or viewing recordings of sessions with supervisors, faculty, peers, or others within the training environment.

Clinical supervision is a process that occurs during the fieldwork experience within counselor training programs.[14] Fieldwork supervisors have an inherent responsibility to ensure counselors in training adhere to the professional and ethical standards of their field's practice to protect client welfare. Evaluation of counselors in training may include direct methods (e.g., watching a video recording of a previous session, live observation) or indirect methods (e.g., discussing client cases). In accordance with the Council for Accreditation of Counseling and Related Educational Programs (CACREP),[8] practicum and internship supervision must include the use of audio/video recordings and/or live observations of students' work with clients.[8] Barnett and Johnson[2] note that while these training procedures are used to benefit the client, counselors are not absolved from obtaining their clients' written consent.

CASE STUDY

Juan, a rehabilitation counseling student, is completing his internship at a state vocational rehabilitation agency. As part of his training requirements, Juan must have his sessions recorded and undergo weekly supervision with his field supervisor and group supervision with his faculty supervisor and peers. Examples of Juan's supervision may include direct observation of his sessions with clients, review of recorded sessions, and approval of case notes. During an intake with his first client, Juan begins to video record the session. When the client asks, "What are you doing?" Juan responds that he is required to record the session so his supervisor can watch.

ETHICAL IMPLICATIONS:

In this vignette, Juan failed to ask the client for permission to record the intake session. He also did not review his role as a rehabilitation counselor in training, which would further explain the need to have his sessions recorded as part of his supervision. Although this information is likely disclosed in the consent form that Juan would review with the client, it is necessary to first obtain verbal consent before moving forward. It is not only helpful for clients to understand what that will mean for the intake and future services but is also imperative for establishing rapport.

B.1.d. CULTURAL DIVERSITY CONSIDERATIONS

Rehabilitation counselors work to develop and maintain awareness of the cultural meanings of confidentiality and privacy. Rehabilitation counselors hold ongoing discussions with clients as to how, when, and with whom information is to be shared.

According to Meer and VandeCreek,[21] "the concept of confidentiality lends itself well to the Western value of individual rights to privacy and autonomy."[p.144] Counselors must be aware of how clients' culture may influence their perspectives on confidentiality.[2] This is especially important when working with children, adult clients that lack the capacity to provide consent, parents/legal guardians, or even clients from collectivist cultures that place minimal value on individual confidentiality. Culturally competent counselors should make every effort to understand their clients' understanding and perception of confidentiality and determine which parties will be privy to their information.[29] They should also discuss confidentiality from a professional and legal perspective with their clients.

CASE STUDY

Raven, a newly certified rehabilitation counselor, is conducting an intake with an adult client, Sanjay, who has sought rehabilitation services for a job accommodation after recently recovering from a traumatic brain injury stemming from a car accident. Sanjay was born in the United States to parents that emigrated from India. He discloses that his parents will want to be informed of his services moving forward but expresses some concern with this. Raven explores Sanjay's expectations for confidentiality from a cultural perspective, but also her professional and legal responsibilities as a rehabilitation counselor. Sanjay discusses which aspects of his services would be appropriate for Raven to disclose to his parents.

ETHICAL IMPLICATIONS:
In this vignette, Raven demonstrates cultural competence by recognizing the importance of family in Sanjay's case. While she has an ethical and legal responsibility to safeguard Sanjay's information, she understands the role of collectivist values within his culture. Raven balances her responsibilities as a rehabilitation counselor by first exploring Sanjay's understanding of confidentiality and expectations of this from a cultural perspective, and then discussing what this means within her clinical role. She then processes with Sanjay what aspects of his services he would feel comfortable with Raven disclosing so that the parents can still be involved while also instilling boundaries to protect Sanjay from anything he is uncomfortable disclosing.

B.1.e. RESPECT FOR CONFIDENTIALITY
Rehabilitation counselors do not share confidential information without consent from clients or without sound legal or ethical justification. Rehabilitation counselors do not release confidential records without a signed authorization to release information, except allowed by law or required by court order.

Confidentiality is the responsibility of counselors to protect the content disclosed within the therapeutic process.[7] This includes both verbal communication and written records (e.g., case notes, test results). Given the nature of counselors' legal responsibilities, Wheeler and Bertram[29] note it is possible to be sued for failure to protect client information without consent to do so (i.e., written permission from the client) or other exceptions under the law (i.e., mandated reporter responsibilities). If confidentiality must be broken, it is good practice for counselors to inform clients of this and include them in the process.[6]

CASE STUDY

Christie, a rehabilitation counselor, works in a school system for children with developmental disabilities. She also works outside of the school system for one of her students in his home. At school, she frequently discusses the child's home life. Conversations mainly entail the child's progress in his after-school work, which has nothing to do with his at school work. Christie also discloses the family's financial struggles and uses the student's and family members' names. She is also heard by her coworkers discussing minor, private family issues that occur at the child's home.

ETHICAL IMPLICATIONS
In this vignette, although the child attends the school that she works at, Christie should not be discussing the work that she does at home. She is

working for two separate agencies in which she is obligated to confidentiality in both settings. She should not be discussing home at school or school at home. Discussing family issues, financial struggles, and especially using family members' names is unnecessary and breaking confidentiality. Confidentiality should only be broken if someone is in danger or if there is a court order.

B.1.f. EXPLANATION OF LIMITATIONS

At initiation and as needed throughout the counseling process, rehabilitation counselors inform clients of the limitations of confidentiality and seek to identify foreseeable situations in which confidentiality must be breached.

Limitations to confidentiality exist and must be clearly communicated to clients.[6] This is typically reviewed during the informed consent process so that clients can decide whether they will proceed with treatment. While there are general limitations often discussed in counselor training programs, these may vary in certain settings and/or agencies, or even by state law. As such, it is crucial for counselors to be aware of these variations in their practice. Barnett and Johnson[2] note three common limits to confidentiality include when clients are a risk to themselves, other people, and/or groups, and when there is suspicion of abuse towards a child or other protected population (e.g., elderly, individuals with disabilities). Rehabilitation counselors often work with multidisciplinary teams to provide services to clients, which can complicate the safeguarding of client information.[7] As such, clients must be aware of and agree to the aspects of their information that will be transferred to team members.

CASE STUDY

Today was Dan's first meeting with his new client. He greeted her in the waiting room and welcomed her into his office. He informed the client of his qualifications, experiences, and nature of counseling. Dan also discussed client rights and expectations. Dan then began to explain confidentiality to the client. He stated that whatever was said during their counseling sessions was to be kept between the two of them; however, exceptions to confidentiality do exist. Dan explained his role as a mandated reporter and provided the client with a list of exceptions to confidentiality in the signed informed consent. The counselor also reviewed the exceptions verbally with the client.

ETHICAL IMPLICATIONS

In this vignette, Dan did everything correctly. It is essential to discuss client rights, expectations, and confidentiality with the client. He gave the client the informed consent and had her sign it. This is necessary for documentation and evidence that the client was aware of these guidelines. It was also good practice that Dan reviewed the information on the form with his client to ensure she understood everything she was agreeing to. This helps to build rapport and trust, which is vital in the early stages of the counseling process. Additional mandated reporter responsibilities may vary depending on the state where the rehabilitation counselor practices, so it is important to regularly review laws and regulations that pertain to this.

B.2. EXCEPTIONS

Confidentiality, privileged communication, and privacy are aspirational concepts in rehabilitation counseling practice but are not guaranteed for clients of rehabilitation programs. Information may still be shared with others depending on its nature or through legal processes. Rehabilitation counselors must consider the extent to which a client's disclosed information reflects endangerment to the client or others. Fortunately, measures can be taken to support client welfare despite compromising confidentiality. Clinical supervision may help service providers to manage ethical dilemmas associated with sharing client information.[16]

B.2.a. SERIOUS OR FORESEEABLE HARM AND LEGAL REQUIREMENTS
The general requirement that rehabilitation counselors keep information confidential does not apply when disclosure is required to protect clients or identified others from serious and foreseeable harm, or when legal requirements demand that confidential information must be revealed. Rehabilitation counselors must be aware of and adhere to standards and laws that govern confidentiality. Rehabilitation counselors consult with other professionals when in doubt as to the validity of an exception.

CASE STUDY

Yoseline is a certified rehabilitation counselor and licensed clinical professional counselor employed at an Illinois inpatient mental health facility where she has a caseload of young adults with serious mental illness. Her newest client is Paul, a 21-year-old male diagnosed with schizophrenia, including symptoms of persistent delusions and disorganized behavior. Paul's goal is to improve his social skills by better understanding his emotions associated with his personal relationships. Yoseline has met with Paul for several counseling sessions where he exhibited unpredictable agitation and extreme emotional reactions toward a family member.

In the most recent session, Paul laughed almost uncontrollably about his father's heart attack. Yoseline suspected that Paul had a false belief that his mother was physically abused and that his father was to blame for this situation. Paul stated, "The only way to help my mom is to get him out of the way. Tonight, I'm going to finish what the heart attack could not do – I'm going to kill my father!" Before Yoseline could respond to Paul's shocking statement, he darted out of the room and managed to get past security at the front doors. Paul had escaped the facility and was out of sight within seconds. Yoseline called the police department, informing them of details associated with Paul to protect his father from harm.

ETHICAL IMPLICATIONS

In this vignette, Yoseline is justified in disclosing her client's information for two reasons. First, she is ethically obligated to protect an identified person from harm as a certified rehabilitation counselor (Standard B.2.a.). According to Illinois law, a rehabilitation counselor, "in his or her sole discretion, [may determine] that disclosure [of client records and communications] is necessary to... protect the... other person against a clear, imminent risk of serious physical or mental injury... or death being inflicted upon...another."[22] Her client explicitly identified the person he intended to harm and was no longer constrained by safeguards of the inpatient facility.

Second, the Mental Health and Developmental Disabilities Confidentiality Act authorizes disclosure of limited client records and communications when that client, without approval, leaves a mental health facility. Therefore, the rehabilitation counselor demonstrated awareness of ethical standards and state law associated with confidentiality. Yoseline would also be acting responsibly to consult with her supervisor about the client's situation.

B.2.b. CONTAGIOUS, LIFE-THREATENING DISEASES

When clients disclose that they have a disease commonly known to be both communicable and life-threatening, rehabilitation counselors may be justified in disclosing information to identifiable third parties if they are known to be at demonstrable and high risk of contracting the disease. Prior to making a disclosure, rehabilitation counselors confirm the diagnosis and assess the intent of clients to inform the third parties about the disease or to engage in any behaviors that may be harmful to identifiable third parties. Rehabilitation counselors must be aware of and adhere to standards and laws concerning disclosure about disease status.

CASE STUDY

Steven is a state vocational rehabilitation counselor working primarily from home during the coronavirus disease 2019 (COVID-19) pandemic. His client, Faith, is a 36-year-old female and uses a wheelchair for mobility at the grocery store where she was recently hired as a part-time customer-service specialist. Steven received an email from Faith stating that she has not been feeling well in recent days and tested positive for COVID-19. She is currently experiencing severe fatigue but is otherwise asymptomatic. Faith said she plans to remain alone at home until cleared by her local public health department.

Faith did not mention her work in the email, and Steven had to assume that she notified her supervisor of the diagnosis and that coverage for Faith's shifts was secured. Steven was relieved that the client is not a threat to her coworkers because they are physically separated. He responded to Faith by wishing her a speedy recovery and asked her to notify him once she is cleared to return to work.

ETHICAL IMPLICATIONS

In this vignette, Steven chose to not disclose client information to her supervisor despite the client's statement that she tested positive for a life-threatening disease. The rehabilitation counselor came to this conclusion because of the physical distance amongst the people involved. However, he failed to verify the diagnosis and whether the client was indeed refraning from working. What remains plausible is that the client does have the disease but did not self-disclose to her supervisor and has continued to work her shifts. Therefore, Steven's actions are inadequate given the circumstances, and the ethical dilemma about whether to disclose client information to the supervisor remains unresolved. Rehabilitation counselors should use a deliberate and reflective process to properly interpret situations in which dilemmas are present.[25] In addition, Steven has an obligation to include relevant laws into his ethical decision-making process.

B.2.c. COURT-ORDERED DISCLOSURE

When subpoenaed to release confidential or privileged information without permission from clients or their legal representatives, rehabilitation counselors obtain written informed consent from clients, take steps to prohibit the disclosure, or have it limited as narrowly as possible due to potential harm to clients or the counseling relationship. Whenever reasonable, rehabilitation counselors obtain a court directive to clarify the nature and extent of the response to a subpoena. When release of raw assessment data is requested, refer to Standard G.2.b.

B.2.d. MINIMAL DISCLOSURE

When circumstances require the disclosure of confidential information, rehabilitation counselors clarify the nature of information being requested and make reasonable efforts to ensure only necessary information is revealed.

CASE STUDY

Jacey has been providing weekly substance use counseling with her client, Fernanda, for approximately six months because Fernanda struggles to control her use of alcohol. Fernanda has been mostly sober since she entered counseling but experienced a couple of "setbacks." During one of these occasions, Fernanda made the poor decision to consume a large quantity of alcohol while operating a motor vehicle. Fernanda lost control of her vehicle and drove down an embankment on the side of a rural road before hitting a tree. Fortunately, Fernanda was uninjured, but she fled the scene before the police arrived. Eventually, Fernanda was arrested and released pending a court hearing.

Not long after the accident, Jacey received a court-ordered subpoena for all records associated with Fernanda. At the next counseling session, Jacey and Fernanda discussed the facts associated with the accident and expectations for complying with a subpoena. Both client and counselor agreed that submitting all available records would be painful for Fernanda. Therefore, Jacey submitted a request to the court that she provide a written summary of Fernanda's treatment in lieu of other documents such as case notes, medical reports, school transcripts, and vocational evaluation reports. Soon after the court agreed with the request, Jacey discussed the process with her client, and Fernanda then signed a written consent for the court to receive only a summary of her treatment.

ETHICAL IMPLICATIONS

In this vignette, Jacey experienced an ethical dilemma about whether to submit to the courts all available client records. Doing so would comply with the legal process but jeopardize the client's health. Consequently, withholding records from the courts would reduce the chance of harming the client but would clearly violate the parameters of the subpoena. Standards B.2.c. and B.2.d. are informative to Jacey in this situation. Jacey rightfully attempts to negotiate a solution that would balance the right of the courts to obtain relevant information while minimizing the disclosure to protect the client from harm. She is successful at limiting the disclosure to only essential information. Rehabilitation counselors are advised to consult with other informative sources such as clinical supervision and decision-making models when experiencing ethical dilemmas.[16,25]

B.3. INFORMATION SHARED WITH OTHERS

B.3.a. WORK ENVIRONMENT

Rehabilitation counselors avoid casual conversation about clients in the work environment and make reasonable efforts to ensure that privacy and confidentiality of clients' information and records are maintained by employees, supervisees, students, clerical assistants, and volunteers.

Maintaining confidentiality is the responsibility of all employees of agencies providing counseling and human services and respecting this mandate within the workplace is critical. The maintenance of client privacy and confidentiality is required regardless of the setting, for example, offices of state vocational rehabilitation, community rehabilitation programs, hospitals, k-12 schools, postsecondary environments, insurance rehabilitation, corrections, independent living centers, corporations, or private rehabilitation companies. Various personnel work in close proximity to rehabilitation counselors across all of these settings. Therefore, the rehabilitation counselor must carefully consider the extent that each person within the work environment may have access to client information. The rehabilitation counselor must also monitor their own speech, handling of records, and selection of meeting spaces to minimize the risk of an information breach. Furthermore, the implications of other individuals in the workplace having access to client information should be determined.

CASE STUDY

Sasha is a rehabilitation counselor and works at a large public vocational rehabilitation agency providing services to state residents with disabilities. Sasha manages a general caseload but serves several deaf customers because she is the only person in the office fluent in sign language and knowledge of Deaf Culture. Angel is a 25-year old customer of vocational rehabilitation services with severe hearing loss and has worked with Sasha for several months. His rehabilitation plan includes educational training at a 4-year college for completing a degree in nutrition. Sasha met with Angel to briefly review his college transcripts. Because the meeting was scheduled for only 15 minutes, Sasha left the door to her office open as well as the window blinds facing inside the agency. Besides, she knew that Angel communicated visually and others would not understand sign language.

ETHICAL IMPLICATIONS

Sarah took a risk with Angel's privacy in this scenario. She assumed that others would not be able to understand sign language and therefore would not know what the conversation was about, but she does not know this for a fact. Angel should always maintain client conversations in a secure location where others do not have the opportunity to gain access to any information.

B.3.b. INTERDISCIPLINARY TEAMS

When services provided to clients involve the sharing of their information among team members, clients are advised of this fact during the professional disclosure process and are informed of the team's existence and composition.

According to Maki,[20] rehabilitation counselors provide a set of comprehensive services for individuals with disabilities, often involving interdisciplinary teams representing medicine, psychology, education, religion, or employment. Each team member plays a role in helping clients achieve their independent living and employment goals. The rehabilitation counselor is not only a member of these teams but often is central to its development and management.[15,19,20] The holistic approach to the rehabilitation of people with disabilities, therefore, may present a need to inform other professionals of sensitive client information. As a result, rehabilitation counselors must maintain transparency with their clients to address any potential rewards and risks to collaborating with outside professionals. This should be part of the professional disclosure process and include specific information about the individual members of the team who will have access to client information and under what circumstances.

CASE STUDY

Tyler is a rehabilitation counselor who manages a caseload of transition youth with disabilities and needs to prepare Lauren, a 17-year old customer with Down Syndrome, for a team meeting as part of her Individualized Education Program (IEP). Tyler explains to Lauren that the purpose of the meeting is to identify possible volunteer work opportunities based on her expressed interest in computers and the Internet. Lauren is informed that, besides herself and the counselor, attending today's meeting will be her mother, two of her high school teachers, and a vocational evaluator. During the meeting, Lauren mentioned a few businesses that might have computers and Internet access and are in close proximity to her home. Tyler applauded Lauren for her considerations but suggested to the group that Lauren should avoid working with men because of physical abuse she experienced years ago by a male family member.

ETHICAL IMPLICATIONS

While Tyler provided important information to Lauren about the nature of the meeting, and that other professionals would be present as part of the multidisciplinary team, he may have violated Lauren's privacy by discussing her trauma history. Tyler should not have disclosed this information in the group in this way, but rather have sought specific permission from Lauren on what personal information of hers he could share and under what circumstances.

B.3.c. OTHER SERVICE PROVIDERS

When rehabilitation counselors learn that clients have an ongoing professional relationship with another rehabilitation counselor or treating professional, they obtain a signed authorization prior to releasing information to other professionals. File review, second-opinion services, and other indirect services are not considered an ongoing professional relationship.

Rehabilitation counselors must respect client autonomy to receive care within medical, nursing, pharmacy, and allied health disciplines. Interventions such as physical therapy, occupational therapy, or osteopathic medicine are complementary to rehabilitation counseling services and can enhance the likelihood that clients secure employment. Although discouraged across many environments, being a client under multiple rehabilitation counselors in the absence of full disclosure and the relative ease of relocating in the 21st century is possible. Formal and collaborative relationships between professionals help to ensure efficient and thorough person-centered interventions. When a counselor recognizes that other professionals are serving a client, if information is to be shared, it must be done after a release of information is signed.

CASE STUDY

Andrea is a rehabilitation counselor at a state vocational rehabilitation agency. She was finishing her intake interview with Michael, a new customer with a physical disability, when he informed her that he recently began marriage and family counseling because he has been arguing with his spouse about their economic problems. After further inquiry, Andrea considered Michael's reasons for seeking counseling unrelated to his job goal or functional limitations and decided not to contact the counselor. Andrea's initial impression was that Michael might need minimal vocational rehabilitation services to become employable because of his outstanding educational background and work history.

ETHICAL IMPLICATIONS

In this instance, Andrea did the right thing by evaluating whether information from other treating professionals was relevant before asking the client if they will permit the exchange of treatment information. Andrea concluded that the information from the marriage and family therapist was not relevant, and therefore, not necessary, or helpful to her work with Michael.

B.3.d. CLIENTS ASSISTANTS

Clients have the right to decide who can be present as client assistants (e.g., interpreter, personal care assistant, advocates). When clients choose to have assistants present, clients are informed that rehabilitation counselors cannot guarantee that assistants will maintain confidentiality. Rehabilitation counselors impress upon assistants the importance of maintaining confidentiality. If the presence of a client assistant is detrimental to services, the rehabilitation counselor discusses the concern with the client. If the concern is not resolved, the rehabilitation counselor may consider termination and referral.

Persons with disabilities may use assistants to complete a broad range of tasks such as activities of daily living, educational training, essential job functions, or communication.[9,24] Clients have the right to choose whether assistants are present during rehabilitation counseling sessions. However, assistants are not infallible human beings, and no assumptions can be made on whether they fully understand confidentiality and the consequences of violating this ethical concept. Assistants are typically trained regarding their obligation to maintain confidentiality. Clients and counselors should be informed of their assistants' ethical guidelines.[12] If confidentiality is a concern, the counselor should discuss it with the client directly.

CASE STUDY

Megan is 20 years old with prelingual deafness and lives in a rural environment with her 17-year old sister and parents. A rehabilitation counselor is helping Megan to find a job stocking shelves at a local grocery store, but Megan becomes frustrated when trying to communicate with the store's manager. Only one certified sign language interpreter is located within 30 miles of Megan's home, but he is frequently on other assignments. Megan requests that her sister serves as the interpreter, but the rehabilitation counselor recognizes the potential problems associated with her sister's competency and ability to maintain confidentiality. Instead, the rehabilitation counselor plans to hire the certified interpreter for whenever he becomes available to assist Megan. The counselor discusses this with Megan.

ETHICAL IMPLICATIONS

Megan has the right to be assisted by her sister if she chooses. If the rehabilitation counselor has concerns with the assistants' ability to maintain confidentiality, they should address this with the client directly. In this instance, the counselor does so appropriately. Megan may decide that her sister is not a good person to serve as an assistant for this reason, or she may decide that she still would like her sister to help her communicate in this setting.

B.3.e. CONFIDENTIAL SETTINGS

Rehabilitation counselors are attentive to the type of service they are providing and whether confidential information is typically discussed. If confidential information is likely to be discussed, rehabilitation counselors choose settings in which they can reasonably ensure the privacy of clients. Prior to providing services in community or other settings where confidentiality cannot be maintained, rehabilitation counselors discuss with clients the risk to maintaining confidentiality.

Rehabilitation counseling is a profession where counselors actively assist persons with disabilities to reach their employment or independent living goals.[20] For instance, rehabilitation counselors might leave their offices to consult with employers, visit postsecondary environments, analyze jobs, collaborate with other providers, or provide expert testimony.[18] Discussion with and about clients most likely occurs across each of these locations. Therefore, rehabilitation counselors must recognize that client privacy is a concept that is mobile and not restricted to the physical location of the vocational rehabilitation agency. If services provided in the community carry the risk of a breach of confidentiality, this possibility should be discussed with the client.

CASE STUDY

Nicolas is a private-sector practitioner responsible for assisting injured workers across a large geographical area to return to employment. Although he completes most of his administrative tasks in his home office, Nicolas often travels to meet his clients face-to-face for intake interviews and other services such as job placement activities. Recently, a client expressed concern with having Nicolas in her apartment and suggested they meet at a local coffee shop. For the meeting, he selected a remote area where no one was sitting to enhance the confidentiality of the discussion. During the meeting, Nicolas could not help but notice that an employee infrequently walked past them to retrieve cleaning supplies.

ETHICAL IMPLICATIONS

In this scenario, the client has requested to meet in a public place. As part of arranging the meeting, Nicolas should have directly addressed the potential breach of confidentiality associated with the public meeting with the client. The client can then make an informed decision about the location within the context of privacy concerns.

B.3.f. THIRD-PARTY PAYERS

Rehabilitation counselors disclose information to third-party payers only when clients have authorized such disclosure, unless otherwise required by law.

Health care in the United States recently underwent a significant overhaul when the Affordable Care Act (ACA) was passed into law. Some of the critical health care reforms mandated by the ACA include additional consumer protections, increased access to care, and reduced costs.[26] Many third parties remain liable to pay for the health care services received by individuals regardless of the presence of disability.[4] Examples of third-party payers include managed care organizations, Medicare, court-ordered health coverage, workers compensation, and long-term care insurance. This substandard allows rehabilitation counselors to correspond to third-party payers only with prior approval from clients unless otherwise required by law.

CASE STUDY

Shelia's first client as a vocational counselor at a rehabilitation hospital is Joycelyn, a 54-year old female who experienced second-degree thermal burns across 18% of her body surface, including her entire head, neck, and anterior chest areas. Shelia knew to bill Joycelyn's insurance company for services rendered, but Joycelyn was not able to provide verbal authorization because of limitations from her burn injuries. Shelia assumed that Joycelyn must have previously approved disclosing her personal information to the insurance company when she was in the Intensive Care Unit and proceeded to fax the documents as required for reimbursement.

ETHICAL IMPLICATIONS

Shelia should not have assumed Joycelyn authorized this information sharing. Shelia is responsible for knowing the laws concerning third-party reimbursement seeking explicit authorization for information sharing unless the law dictates otherwise.

B.3.g. DECEASED CLIENTS

Rehabilitation counselors protect the confidentiality of deceased clients, consistent with laws, organizational policies, and documented preferences of clients.

Consistent with other privacy regulations (i.e., HIPAA), protection of confidentiality for rehabilitation counseling clients extends beyond death. Regulations over information sharing, records, and discussion of client information are still intact even after a client has died. In some instances, clients may have expressed preferences on how records or other information should be handled in the event of death, and these should be followed to the extent they are documented.

CASE STUDY

A couple of state vocational rehabilitation employees were talking during a break in the workday. John, a support staff member, informed Martin, a rehabilitation counselor, that he received a call earlier in the day from a family member who said the customer, Donna, passed away the night before. Martin was shocked at the sudden passing stating, "I was just on the phone with her last week!" Martin shared several examples with John about how great a customer Donna had been and the kinds of activities she enjoyed. In fact, one person in the waiting room had overheard Martin and commented on how she hoped that she could live as Donna lived. Martin ended his workweek with a smile knowing that Donna's story had inspired another person.

ETHICAL IMPLICATIONS

John and Martin should have been more careful about the setting and the possibility of others hearing when they discussed Donna and her story. Even though the information shared was positive, and her full identity may not have been revealed, John and Martin violated Donna's confidentiality with this conversation.

B.4. GROUPS AND FAMILIES

B.4.a. GROUP WORK

In group work, whether in-person or using electronic formats, rehabilitation counselors clearly explain the role and responsibility of each participant. Rehabilitation counselors state their expectation that all members maintain confidentiality for each individual and the group as a whole. Rehabilitation counselors also advise group members of

*the limitations of confidentiality and that confidentiality by other
group members cannot be guaranteed.*

Group work is a social intervention. Yalom and Leszcz[30] liken groups to a miniature social microcosm for each member, and that personal growth occurs as a result of regular interpersonal interactions with other group members. Rehabilitation counselors are not only obligated to protect the privacy of each group member but must strive to build a safe environment for the group to perform its work. For example, Yalom and Leszcz[30] prepare their groups by establishing the expectation of confidentiality as one of the ground rules for therapy. Together, the rehabilitation counselor and the group adhere to the ground rules to ensure that members speak freely and with confidence that their personal information stays within the group. However, even confidentiality has limits, such as when a group member or someone else is exposed to a high risk of serious harm.[30]

CASE STUDY

*Emily is a rehabilitation counselor who leads a therapy group for
people who have had a myocardial infarction. Two of the group
members include a self-described practical joker named John, and
Patrick, a reserved individual who lives alone. Following one of their
sessions, John informed Emily that he is planning to "trick" Patrick on
Halloween by scaring him with realistic blood and a knife seemingly
impaled in his body. Emily knew that Patrick was under medical care
for stress, and she became gravely concerned that John's "trick"
might trigger another heart attack for Patrick. Fearing for Patrick's
safety, Emily informed John of Patrick's health status and strongly
advised him to reconsider his plans.*

ETHICAL IMPLICATIONS

There was no need for Emily to disclose Patrick's personal healthcare information and violate his confidentiality. She could have referenced the fact that most people who take part in the group most likely have cardiovascular problems, and startling anyone in that condition could be dangerous. Emily could have explored John's feelings toward Patrick and helped him find a better way to have a light-hearted moment with Patrick.

B.4.b. COUPLES AND FAMILY COUNSELING

*In couples and family counseling, rehabilitation counselors clearly
define who the clients are and discuss expectations and limitations of
confidentiality. Rehabilitation counselors seek agreement concerning
each individual's right to confidentiality and document in writing such
agreement among all involved parties having the capacity to give
consent. Rehabilitation counselors clearly define whether they share*

or do not share information with family members that is privately,
individually communicated to rehabilitation counselors.

Counseling couples and families is akin to working through competing interests.[28] A parent or spouse is most likely managing their own distress and unable to recognize how their behaviors negatively impact others. Similarly, various people such as parents, school personnel, or lawyers may have an interest in a child receiving counseling with their own perspectives on the goals of therapy. Rehabilitation counselors should acknowledge the roles of others (e.g., parenting, educating, paying for treatment) but within the context of agreeing to primarily address the child's needs. Counselors must come to a mutual understanding with all couples and family members that some "family secrets" will be shared privately and are helpful to the therapeutic process. However, it is essential to clarify that not all information will remain private such as when threats of harm to self or others are made.[28] Rehabilitation counselors are to differentiate when facing these two extremes that information disclosed by others (e.g., parents, spouse) will be shared for the progression of therapy.

CASE STUDY

Aubrey is a rehabilitation counselor who conducts family therapy when at least one family member has a disability. Tonya is a 13-year old female with an eating disorder and attends Aubrey's family therapy sessions with her parents and older sister. Tonya likes Aubrey and feels comfortable sharing with Aubrey her deepest thoughts and feelings. During an individual session, Tonya told Aubrey that she has been using drugs as a way to decrease her appetite. She said that she occasionally takes Ecstasy (Methylenedioxymethamphetamine) to fight hunger but recently tried "Meth" (methamphetamine). Tonya is scared that her parents will discover her drug use. Aubrey immediately knew these drugs have a high potential for abuse and that Tonya could develop psychoses or even cerebral hemorrhage with the possibility of death. Aubrey considered sharing this information with her parents but did not in order to preserve the rapport she has with Tonya.

ETHICAL IMPLICATIONS
The rehabilitation counselor must show objectivity and not take sides of any one family member or a family dyad. Given that Tonya is experimenting with two recreational drugs that could lead to addiction and possibly death, the ethical implication of breaking confidentiality is a serious consideration. The best first step would be for Aubrey to work with Tonya, explore the danger inherent to using these two substances, and support Tonya in the process of disclosing this information to her parents. If Tonya is not willing to disclose

this information, Aubrey will have to consider breaking Tonya's confidentiality. Before doing so, it is important for Aubrey to consult with another rehabilitation counselor who has dealt with similar situations.

B.5 RESPONSIBILITY TO CLIENTS LACKING CAPACITY TO CONSENT

This sub-standard provides guidance on how to work with clients when they are not their own guardian. A client might have a guardian because of age (minors) or because a court has determined that this individual requires assistance with issues of personal care such as healthcare, safe housing, and taking care of their own basic needs. Guardianship laws vary by state[1] and the rehabilitation counselor is responsible for knowing and understanding the laws regarding guardianship in the state where they practice. Some states have different types or levels of guardianship. For example, a full guardian may have a more central role in decision making that spans life areas and activities, while a property guardian may only make only decisions regarding property and assets, and a healthcare proxy may only provide input on medical decisions and care[1] and The Arc, 2016. When clients have a legal guardian, this person is an integral part of the counseling process and must be included in decisions regarding the release of confidential information, communication of privileged information, and privacy. Discussions regarding privacy and information sharing should be structured so that the individual is an active part of the decision-making process and has an opportunity to share their preferences for consideration in decisions.

B.5.a. RESPONSIBILITY TO CLIENTS
When counseling minors or persons who are unable to give voluntary consent, rehabilitation counselors protect the confidentiality of information received in the counseling relationship, in any format, as specified by law, written policies, and applicable ethical standards.

Rehabilitation counselors working with minors or clients who lack the capacity to give voluntary informed consent are responsible for maintaining the confidentiality of client information shared in the counseling context, as consistent with laws, policies, and applicable ethical standards. The counselor should inform the client of any limits to confidentiality in a way that matches their cultural expectations or conventions and learning style. Rehabilitation counselors should be prepared to check for understanding of confidentiality and remind clients of the limits of confidentiality at regular intervals.

CASE STUDY

Lorenzo is a rehabilitation counselor working in a mental health agency. He recently started meeting with Carlos, who is 17 years old. Carlos brought his mother to the first meeting to sign the initial paperwork and releases, go over the counseling process and expectations, and review Lorenzo's scope of practice and areas of competence. At this first meeting, Lorenzo explained to Carlos and his mother the meaning of confidentiality and discussed what information would be kept between Lorenzo and Carlos and what had to be shared with Carlos' mother or others. Lorenzo included examples that were relevant to someone of Carlos' age and asked him to explain in his own words what confidentiality meant. From then on, Lorenzo reminded Carlos of the limits of confidentiality every few sessions to make sure that he remembered and understood when Lorenzo would need to tell his mother something that Carlos said in the session.

ETHICAL IMPLICATIONS

In this case, Lorenzo acted within the guidelines. He used a few strategies to ensure that Carlos understood confidentiality and the limits, including what would need to be shared with his mother for legal reasons. Using age-appropriate examples that a client is likely to relate to and asking the client to explain the concept in their own words are two useful approaches to ensure client understanding. In addition, Lorenzo reinforced these concepts during the ongoing sessions.

3.5.b. RESPONSIBILITY TO LEGAL GUARDIANS AND PARENTS

Rehabilitation counselors inform legal guardians, including parents who are legal guardians, about the role of rehabilitation counselors and the confidential nature of the services provided. Rehabilitation counselors are sensitive to the cultural diversity of families and work to establish, as appropriate, collaborative relationships with legal guardians to best serve clients.

When rehabilitation counselors work with clients who lack the capacity to provide voluntary informed consent, they are also responsible to the parent and/or legal guardians. Counselors must explain how they will be working with the client, and the nature, and limits, of confidentiality.[1] This includes any information that must be shared with the parent/guardian regarding the welfare of the client. The rehabilitation counselor and client and parents/guardians ought to discuss the cultural meanings of privacy and confidentiality, as well as any instances that information must be shared. This should minimally include a detailed discussion of the information that will be shared, including the methods of sharing and who will be included.

CASE STUDY

John works with the local high school to assist students with disabilities in the special education program and decide what to do for work or further education once they graduate. While many of the students he visits during the school day are 18, some of them are 16 and 17 years old. When John first meets with students, he asks the parents to attend as well so that they can sign the required forms (if they are guardians), and he can explain to them what a rehabilitation counselor does, and how he will be involved with their son or daughter. Typically, he will discuss the families' preferences for communication, and whether or not they feel comfortable with John meeting with the student without their parents present. He will also explain to the student what kind of information he must share with their parents.

ETHICAL IMPLICATIONS

John is following good practices for working with families. He is doing some key things to try to make sure that he is fulfilling his responsibility to the client and the parents and guardians. He includes parents in the meeting so that they can hear and understand the same things that the client does and makes sure that they are the ones signing the forms while the client is still a minor. John considers the families' preferences, including their cultural norms and expectations, regarding communication and meetings. He also explains aspects of the limits of confidentiality to all parties at once to make sure that the message is consistent and understood by everyone.

B.5.c. RELEASE OF CONFIDENTIAL INFORMATION

When working with minors or persons who lack the capacity to give voluntary informed consent to the release of confidential information, rehabilitation counselors obtain written permission from legal guardians or legal power of attorney to disclose the information. In cases where there is no legal guardian or legal power of attorney, rehabilitation counselors engage in an ethical decision-making process to determine appropriate action. In such instances, rehabilitation counselors inform clients consistent with their level of understanding and take culturally appropriate measures to safeguard client confidentiality.

Oftentimes, rehabilitation counselors will need to seek permission to gain access to confidential information or share confidential information with other professionals (e.g., health professionals, evaluators, other vocational programs). When this is necessary, and the client lacks the capacity to give voluntary consent, the legal guardian must be consulted and agree to the information release before the counselor can proceed. However, the client should also be informed that the information will be shared and how confidentiality will be maintained, in a way that is consistent with the client's cultural norms and comprehension ability.

CASE STUDY

Vanessa is working with a new client, Jeannette. Jeannette is 36 years old and has an intellectual disability. Jeannette's sister, Mia, is her legal guardian. Mia came to the first meeting and said that Jeannette really does not need a guardian, but their parents insisted. Mia says that whatever Jeannette wants is fine and to just go ahead without her input. Mia has her own family and a demanding job, so she does not have much time to help Jeannette or get involved with her decisions. Vanessa would like to have Jeannette evaluated to get a recent assessment of her skills, mental status, and functioning, but forgot to have Mia sign the release of information to send the referral to the psychologist. Jeannette agreed to have her information shared with the psychologist for the purpose of the evaluation. Mia has not returned Vanessa's calls about signing the release form.

ETHICAL IMPLICATIONS

Vanessa is in a difficult position here. She would like to provide services in a timely manner, and Mia, the client's legal guardian, has indicated that she does not have much time to be involved with Jeanette's case. However, she does have a legal and ethical responsibility to seek Mia's permission in order to release information about Jeanette. It would be best if she was able to connect with Mia, perhaps with Jeanette's help, so that she can sign the official forms granting the release of information.

B.6. RECORDS AND DOCUMENTATION

Maintaining client records and documentation is an essential aspect of the counseling process.[2] All records must be kept accurate and updated to reflect the most current client information. This is not only important for counseling and treatment planning but also when making referrals. Counselors must also ensure their records are accurate in the event they are subpoenaed for legal proceedings. Storage of clients' hard records (i.e., paper documentation) should be kept in a safe and locked space, while electronic records should be stored on a password-protected computer.[7] These records may include extremely personal information about an individual's physical and mental health, instances of abuse or trauma, academic reports, the results of psychological assessments (e.g., interviews, intelligence scores), and clinical notes taken by various medical, psychological, and rehabilitation professionals.

B.6.a. REQUIREMENT OF RECORDS AND DOCUMENTATION
Rehabilitation counselors include sufficient and timely documentation in the records of their clients to facilitate the delivery and continuity of needed services. Rehabilitation counselors make reasonable efforts to ensure that documentation in records accurately reflects progress and services provided to clients. If errors are made in records, rehabilitation counselors take steps to properly note the correction of such errors according to organizational policies.

Keeping records that are accurate, up to date, and provide sufficient detail is an important responsibility of counselors.[6] Case records are live documents that should be updated each time there is client contact. Information may vary depending on the work setting but will often include information pertaining to the services provided, client and counselor's responsibilities, client progress, counselor recommendations, and clinical rationale for treatment decisions.[2] Keeping records updated is essential for many reasons, including the ability to minimize interruption in services should the client begin to work with another counselor, accuracy in the event that the case records are requested by another professional, or subpoenaed for legal proceedings. If an error is made in documentation, counselors take appropriate steps to make addendums to correct the inaccuracies. This includes notation of the date and rationale for change; however, it is recommended that rehabilitation counselors further consult with their agencies and/or institution's policies for specific procedures on this.

CASE STUDY

Monica is a rehabilitation counselor working for a public agency. Typically, Monica sets aside 10 minutes following each meeting or contact with a client to update her case notes. Unfortunately, yesterday was a busy workday for Monica. She had three clients drop in to meet with her on top of the three clients she already had scheduled. Today, she realizes that she made an error in one of her notes and goes into the case management system to update it. She notices that her supervisor already approved the last note, so she cannot edit it. Monica considers whether this error is significant enough to correct or if she should just leave it.

ETHICAL IMPLICATIONS
In this vignette, it would appear that Monica's error may have been minor; however, she should still take the necessary steps to correct it so that the record

is accurate. Even the most careful counselor can make errors now and then, and even if the error is not of any consequence, steps should be taken to correct it. In this case, Monica should make a new note to reflect the updated information and then pass it along to her supervisor for approval.

B.6.b. CONFIDENTIALITY OF RECORDS AND DOCUMENTATION

Rehabilitation counselors make reasonable efforts to ensure that records and documentation, in any format, are kept in a secure location and that only authorized persons have access to records.

As we have discussed, client records include information that is personal and private in nature and must be protected.[6] Records might include medical documentation, clinical notes, psychological assessments, and educational information. Clients' hard records should be kept in a safe and locked space, while electronic records should be stored on a password-protected computer or removable device (i.e., flash drive, hard drive).[7] Case files should only be shared with individuals who have a direct interest in a case, typically for the purposes of treatment, consultation, or at the request of the client. Agencies should also adopt policies concerning the removal of confidential files from the office. It is unethical for counselors to remove confidential files from secured spaces without compelling reasons for doing so, given the risk that files could be lost, stolen, and/or accessed by unauthorized individuals. These regulations are in place because of the importance of keeping client records confidential.

CASE STUDY

Ann-Marie is working as a counselor for a mental health agency. She has been seeing clients steadily all day, so she needs to devote the last few hours of the workday to update case files and send out documentation in response to official requests and insurance companies. Ann-Marie needs to make copies of large portions of several clients' files to fill the requests. As Ann-Marie gets to the copier, she realizes that she has forgotten a file. She puts the cases that are in her arms down and goes back to her office to retrieve the file. While she is gone, several other office staff, counselors, and clients walk by the copier where she left the cases.

ETHICAL IMPLICATIONS

In this vignette, Ann-Marie has made a significant error in judgment. Although it is unlikely that anyone in the office would disturb her files or look at them, Ann-Marie failed to secure her clients' sensitive information. In this case, Ann-Marie should have taken all of the files back to her office while she retrieved the one that she forgot.

B.6.c. CLIENT ACCESS

Rehabilitation counselors provide reasonable access to records and copies of records when requested by clients or their legal representatives, unless prohibited by law. In situations involving multiple clients, rehabilitation counselors provide individual clients with only those parts of records that relate directly to them and do not include confidential information related to any other client. When records may be sensitive, confusing, or detrimental to clients, rehabilitation counselors have a responsibility to exercise judgment regarding the timing and manner in which the information is shared and educate clients regarding such information. When rehabilitation counselors are in possession of records from other sources, they refer clients back to the original sources to obtain copies of those records.

Historically, paternalistic attitudes towards persons with disabilities and mental health conditions prevented clients from having access to their records.[11] Clients may request to review or retain copies of their case records and have every right to do so.[2] Prior to releasing records, counselors should consider whether any information may be sensitive, detrimental, or difficult to understand. For clients with disabilities, it is important that records are accessible, including documentation that is concise and easy to understand.[27] Clients may benefit from having their information thoroughly explained or reviewed with them. In rare cases, information may be withheld for the client's benefit.[2] It is good practice for the counselor to document their rationale for doing so and support clients to avoid any misunderstandings. If case records contain information about other clients, confidential information about other people should be withheld. If the case record contains information from other sources, the client must go to the original source to request the information. Rehabilitation counselors should not release records from third parties, instead directing the client to the source.

CASE STUDY

Miguel has been working with Sarah in a counseling capacity for nearly eight months. Recently, Sarah asked to see her case record. Miguel reviewed her record and noticed that one of the documents in Sarah's file included a psychological assessment by a third party that provided a clinical opinion of Sarah that she may have found upsetting. Miguel decided to provide Sarah with his own notes and documentation from her case and refer her to the professional who did the assessment to provide her with the results. Miguel reviewed Sarah's file with her and answered her questions regarding documentation.

ETHICAL IMPLICATIONS

Miguel is balancing two ethical responsibilities here: autonomy and nonmaleficence. On the one hand, Sarah has a right to see her records. On the other, if Miguel knows that she may be upset or harmed by what she reads, he should take action. In this case, the potentially upsetting information was not his report but was from another professional. Miguel's resolution of reviewing Sarah's file with her and then facilitating a meeting between Sarah and the third party to review the report that she may have found upsetting was a good solution. The evaluator who produced that documentation should be equipped to review it with her and explain what the information means. This way, Miguel is respecting Sarah's right to review her own records but is taking steps to reduce the risk of harm related to potentially upsetting information.

B.6.d. DISCLOSURE OR TRANSFER

Unless exceptions to confidentiality exist, rehabilitation counselors obtain written permission from clients to disclose or transfer records to legitimate third parties. Rehabilitation counselors make reasonable efforts to ensure that recipients of counseling records are sensitive to their confidential nature.

Sometimes it is necessary for rehabilitation counselors to disclose or transfer client records to another professional or person for legitimate reasons. Under the Health Insurance Portability and Accountability Act of 1996 (HIPAA), counselors identified as covered entities must adhere to provisions concerning client privacy, informed consent, and the disclosure or transfer of records.[10] If deemed necessary to release client information, counselors must obtain written permission from their clients, typically in the form of a release of information form, to allow access to records. Written permission should include a description of the information being released, the purpose and use for the information being released, identified persons that may access the released information, an expiration date for the release of information form, and required signatures (i.e., the counselor, client, and/or legal guardian as appropriate).

Sharing records may also be requested by clients and is often for their benefit. For example, a client may want to send a copy of a recent assessment to another service provider to prevent having to undergo multiple assessments that are similar in a short period of time. Although they requested the record to be shared, the client (or their legal guardian as appropriate) must still grant written permission. When any confidential information is released, it should adhere to relevant privacy legislation, ethical guidelines, and agency policy. The recipient must understand that the records in question are confidential and should treat them accordingly.

CASE STUDY

Lewis is working with Jonathan in a public rehabilitation agency. Lewis is referring Jonathan for a comprehensive vocational assessment and would like to include some of Jonathan's records with the referral. Jonathan wants to have the vocational assessment and agrees to sign a written release of information for parts of his records that will help inform the evaluation. As part of the release, Lewis explains to Jonathan what records are being shared and how they will be sent. The records go to the evaluator with instructions that the contents are confidential and only the evaluator may open the packet. The evaluator is asked to destroy the records once the evaluation has been completed and the report accepted.

ETHICAL IMPLICATIONS:

In this vignette, Lewis has taken two important steps to ensure that he is following this ethical guideline. First, he spends the time explaining to Jonathan what records are being shared for the assessment and how they will be sent. This way, Jonathan is informed of what information the evaluator knows about him and that it has been sent in a secure manner to protect his privacy. Also, Lewis clearly marks the information confidential. This should direct others to protect the information and not open it as other mail or messages are opened in an office. Finally, he asks the evaluator to destroy the information once it is no longer needed. This will ensure that others do not access the information once the evaluation is complete.

B.6.e. STORAGE AND DISPOSAL AFTER TERMINATION

Rehabilitation counselors store records of their clients following termination of services to ensure reasonable future access. Rehabilitation counselors maintain records in accordance with organizational policies and laws, including licensure laws and policies governing records. Rehabilitation counselors dispose of records and other sensitive materials in a manner that protects client confidentiality. Rehabilitation counselors apply careful discretion and deliberation before destroying records that may be needed by a court of law (e.g., notes on child abuse, suicide, sexual harassment, or violence).

Once a case has been closed, counselors and/or their agencies must securely store clients' information in case it is needed for future use. Many reasons for accessing closed cases exist, including instances where clients re-open their services, or applicability to legal proceedings. State and local statutes, as well as agency policy, will guide the length of time that records must be preserved.[29] This applies to both a paper and electronic case record. During this time, the security of the stored files is a concern. Just like active case files, closed records should be stored in a secure manner (i.e., locked, password-protected, encrypted) with restricted access. Stored case files should also be reviewed to ensure that documents are destroyed once the appropriate length of time has passed.[7] Destruction does not just mean discarded; it means shredded, burned, or otherwise destroyed so that no one will be able to recover the information.

CASE STUDY

Frank is the supervisor in an office of a rehabilitation agency. Part of his responsibility is to maintain the closed case paper files. When a counselor closes a case, they send the paper file to Frank to be sent to the locked office where the inactive cases are stored. Frank and one other person in the office have a key to the room and each of the locked file cabinets. Occasionally a case file will be needed for something after the case is closed. When this happens, the policy states that a written request is to be made to Frank with signatures from the appropriate persons. Case records are to be stored for five years before being destroyed. A new office manager has started leaving these keys out during the day because Frank is not always available when someone needs to access that room.

ETHICAL IMPLICATIONS

In this vignette, Frank and the office manager have failed in their responsibilities to safeguard client information. While it seems unlikely that an unauthorized person would take the key and access the closed records, it is still a risk that the key is left out. The office manager may not have realized that leaving the key out is a problem. Frank, as the responsible supervisor in this situation, should have made sure the key was secured and that policies were followed to protect client records.

B.6.f. REASONABLE PRECAUTIONS.

Rehabilitation counselors take reasonable precautions to protect the confidentiality of clients in the event of disaster or termination of practice, incapacity, or death of the rehabilitation counselor. Rehabilitation counselors appoint a records custodian when appropriate.

While not an everyday occurrence, rehabilitation counselors must take precautionary measures to protect the confidentiality of clients in the event that something unforeseen happens to the practice and/or the counselor.[2] The majority of events falling under these areas are well out of our control, but "reasonable" precautions, as stipulated in the code, means that rehabilitation counselors should habitually maintain the security and privacy of records. For example, counselors should keep identifying information in a secured area rather than on a desk and ensure that all clinical notes are safely stored prior to ending the day. Depending on the setting, it may be essential to store documents separately (e.g., billing information and clinical documents). Other examples might include signing out of a secure case management system and computer before stepping away or leaving for the day.

Appointing a records custodian to take custody of clients' records is necessary in the event of the rehabilitation counselor's death or disability that will prevent returning to work.[29] Rehabilitation counselors who work for agencies or large practices are typically not concerned with this. The agency or practice is always appointed as the records custodian; however, those working in private practice should appoint a records custodian early in their work. The records custodian should be a trusted, credentialed colleague who will not only take custody of clients' records, but also notify clients of their rehabilitation counselor's death or inability to work and provide them with referral assistance. It is also suggested that the records custodian be someone that will still be able to carry out their responsibilities despite any distressing news regarding their colleague.

CASE STUDY

Brian works at a community rehabilitation program. His office is in the middle of a busy floor, with many people going by each day. He is currently providing counseling to several consumers concerning a variety of personal issues, including worry and concern about work, adjustment to disability, stress management, and working on becoming more assertive. He keeps notes from sessions and has files for each person. He keeps these in a locked cabinet and does not leave any identifying information unlocked when he goes out during the day or home at night. His supervisor has a copy of his keys and is aware of the clinical notes he has stored. He has labeled the folders with a first name and last initial, and they are all labeled "confidential." If Brian did not come back to work for any reason, only individuals with proper access to his records would be able to get the files.

ETHICAL IMPLICATIONS

In this vignette, Brian has taken measures to protect his clients' information in the event that something unforeseen happens to him. This includes Brian's habitual storage precautions, particularly not leaving information out and locking his file cabinets when he is not in the office. Brian has also taken measures to ensure that others realize the information is confidential, which is necessary to avoid incidental breaches of information. These measures are shared with Brian's supervisor, who is also the records custodian, in the event that his files need to be accessed.

B.7. CONSULTATION

B.7.a. DISCLOSURE OF CONFIDENTIAL INFORMATION.

When consulting with colleagues, rehabilitation counselors do not disclose confidential information that reasonably could lead to the identification of clients or other persons or organizations with whom they have a confidential relationship, unless they have obtained the prior written consent of the persons or organizations or when the disclosure cannot be avoided. They disclose information only to the extent necessary to achieve the purpose of the consultation.

Some rehabilitation counselors seek consultation regarding an individual consumer (i.e., case-basis) or an agency or program. In the process of seeking consultation, it is often necessary to share confidential information in order to inform a professional opinion or judgment. However, counselors are still obligated to ensure confidentiality of the information when appropriate and seek to maintain the privacy of individuals and organizations. Counselors seeking consultation must be prudent about the information shared, ensuring that only pertinent details are included to reduce the risk of identifying any individuals discussed. If identifying information is an essential part of the consultation, permission must be obtained.

CASE STUDY

Cassandra has been asked to consult on some cases with a group of newly hired rehabilitation counselors for an agency that she used to work for. She will come in to do group meetings with four counselors and work with them in an advisory capacity to help them with clients. During the first meeting, Cassandra and the counselors discuss their roles and responsibilities related to protecting confidential information. The counselors agree to describe clients with minimal identifying details, and Cassandra agrees to keep the information that she learns about the clients privileged. Cassandra clearly outlines information she would not be able to keep confidential.

ETHICAL IMPLICATIONS

In this case, Cassandra is following some good practices in her consultant role. She has reviewed the precautions that will be taken to protect client information. Both Cassandra, and the counselors she will be working with, have agreed to take identified precautions. Cassandra has also explained the limits to confidentiality that she is held to; similar to the way a counselor would with a client. By having this important discussion and creating an agreement before any information is shared, Cassandra is likely to avoid trouble in this area.

B.7.b. RESPECT FOR PRIVACY

Rehabilitation counselors share information in a consulting relationship for professional purposes only with persons directly involved with the case. Written and oral reports presented by rehabilitation counselors contain only data germane to the purpose of the consultation, and every effort is made to protect the identity of clients and to avoid undue invasion of privacy.

When serving in a consultant role, rehabilitation counselors must strive to protect clients' identity and privacy. Any client information, particularly data that might identify a client, should be treated with particular care. When providing consultation, rehabilitation counselors must limit their discussion of clients to those who are involved with the case. The counselor serving as a consultant is not free to disclose confidential information. Another ethical consideration in the consultation process is related to the kind of information presented about clients. While some personal or identifying information is relevant and thus can be discussed, the presenting counselor, as well as the consultant, should work to minimize the potential for invasions of client privacy. After completing the consultation arrangement, handling of written reports should follow standards for storing and destroying records.

CASE STUDY

Ana is visiting a community rehabilitation program to consult with some of the job developers. She asks each of them to present a consumer that has been job seeking without success for a long time. When she outlines what kind of information would be helpful to know, she reminds them not to tell a real name and to change or disguise non-pertinent details about the person in order to protect client identity. Ana does not keep any of the materials presented; she returns all of the documents to the job developers to be returned to cases or destroyed.

ETHICAL IMPLICATIONS
Ana has taken some critical steps to protect clients' privacy while she serves as a consultant. Since her job is to assist the job developers with their client services, she may become privy to certain private information. However, this does not mean that she has to know everything about the clients presented. As the responsible CRC in this scenario, Ana has explained what information is necessary and what should not be shared. As another protective measure, Ana is not going to retain any information that she reviews; she plans to destroy or

return documents and other materials once they are no longer required for the purpose of her consultation. By taking these steps, Ana is less likely to violate the privacy of the clients.

B.7.c. CONFIDENTIALITY IN CONSULTATION

Rehabilitation counselors seeking consultation obtain agreement among the parties involved concerning each individual's right to confidentiality, the obligation of each individual to preserve confidential information, and the limits of confidentiality of information shared by others.

Rehabilitation counselors seeking consultation do not disclose information that could identify a client or an organization unless there has been previous written permission. Any information disclosed must be related to the goal of consultation. As part of the initial consultation meeting and agreement, it is essential to discuss and come to agreement on confidentiality rights and expectations, the obligation of all parties to protect information, and any limits of confidentiality that may exist. This is particularly important in a local geographic area where people may know each other, or of each other, within a particular community. For example, if a rehabilitation counselor provides consultation at two agencies in the same area, they must be careful not to discuss issues within one organization with the other. If disclosure seems like it may occur, or would be beneficial, the rehabilitation counselor should seek permission prior to sharing any information.

CASE STUDY

Zack is working as a consultant and has been hired by two rehabilitation service providers in the same town. He is aware that some of the counseling and service staff have worked for both organizations and know each other. Some spend time together socially or may see each other at community events. Prior to starting his work with each, he discloses his professional relationship with both providers and talks about what kind of confidential or identifying information about clients and the agency may and may not be shared. He creates written agreements with each provider.

ETHICAL IMPLICATIONS

Zack is in a difficult position here. He is working with two groups of people who have some social and professional overlap. It is possible that disclosure of information could lead to greater disclosure of private information, especially in a case where people know each other. Therefore, his steps of openly discussing his relationship with each organization and identifying the need to keep information confidential are both critical. Finally, his written agreement with each provider outlining what can and cannot be shared is a key precaution against a violation through his consultation with each organization.

REFERENCES

[1]American Association on Intellectual and Developmental Disabilities, & The Arc. (2016, March 16). *Autonomy, decision-making supports, and guardianship*. https://www.aaidd.org/news-policy/policy/position-statements/autonomy-decision-making-supports-and-guardianship

[2]Barnett, J. E., & Johnson, W. B., (2015). *Ethics desk reference for counselors* (2nd ed.). American Counseling Association.

[3]Beveridge, S., DiNardo, J., France, K., Chan, C. D., & Glickman, C. (2019). Ethical concerns and clinical judgments related to the use of psychometric assessments for rehabilitation counselors. *Journal of Applied Rehabilitation Counseling, 50*(4), 268–285. https://doi-org.springfieldcollege.idm.oclc.org/10.1891/0047-2220.50.4.268

[4]Centers for Medicare and Medicaid Services. (2014). *Coordination of Benefits & Third Party Liability*. https://www.medicaid.gov/medicaid/eligibility/coordination-of-benefits-third-party-liability/index.html.

[5]Commission on Rehabilitation Counselor Certification. (2020). *Advisory opinions from the ethics committee minutes 1996-2020.* https://www.crccertification.com/filebin/pdf/AdvisoryOpinions_2020-08.pdf

[6]Corey, G., Schneider Corey, M., & Corey, C. (2019). *Issues and ethics in the helping professions* (10th ed.). Cengage.

[7]Cottone, R. R. & Tarvydas, V. (2016). *Ethics and decision making in counseling and psychotherapy* (4th ed.). Springer.

[8]Council for Accreditation of Counseling and Related Educational Programs. (2015). *2016 CACREP standards*. http://www.cacrep.org/wp-content/uploads/2017/08/2016-Standards-with-citations.pdf

[9]Falvo, D. R. (2014). *Medical and psychosocial aspects of chronic illness and disability* (5th ed.). Jones & Bartlett.

[10]Fisher, C. B., (2017). *Decoding the ethics code: A practical guide for psychologists* (4th ed.). Sage.

[11]Ford, G. G. (2006). *Ethical reasoning for mental health professionals.* Sage.

[12]Hamerdinger, S., & Karlin, B. (2019). Therapy using interpreters: Questions on the use of interpreters in therapeutic settings for monolingual therapists. *JADARA, 36*(3), 12-30.. https://repository.wcsu.edu/jadara/vol36/iss3/5

[13]Hartley, M. T., & Bourgeois, P. J. (2020). The commission on rehabilitation counselor certification code of ethics: An emerging approach to digital technology. *Rehabilitation Research, Policy and Education, 34*(2), 73–85. https://doi-org.springfieldcollege.idm.oclc.org/10.1891/RE-19-04

[14]Herbert, J. T. (2018). Rehabilitation counselor supervision. In V. M. Tarvydas & M. T. Hartley (Eds.), *The professional practice of rehabilitation counseling* (2nd ed., pp. 419-435). Springer.

[15]Koch, M. C., Vajda, A. J., & Koch, L. C. (2020). Trauma-informed rehabilitation counseling. *Journal of Applied Rehabilitation Counseling, 51*(3), 192–207. https://doi-org.springfieldcollege.idm.oclc.org/10.1891/JARC-D-19-00025

[16]Landon, T. J., & Schultz, J. C. (2018). Exploring rehabilitation counseling supervisors' role in promoting counselor development of ethical fluency. *Rehabilitation Counseling Bulletin, 62*(1), 18-29. https://doi.org/10.1177/0034355217728912

[17]Lane, F. J., Shaw, L. R., Young, M. E., & Bourgeois, P. J. (2012). Rehabilitation counselors' perceptions of ethical workplace culture and the influence on ethical behavior. *Rehabilitation Counseling Bulletin, 55*(4), 219–231. https://doi.org/10.1177/0034355212439235

[18]Leahy, M. J., Chan, F., Sung, C., & Kim, M. (2013). Empirically derived test specifications for the rehabilitation counselor examination. *Rehabilitation Counseling Bulletin, 56*(4), 199-214.

[19]Leahy, M. J., Muenzen, P., Saunders, J. L., & Strauser, D. (2009). Essential knowledge domains underlying effective rehabilitation counseling practice. *Rehabilitation Counseling Bulletin, 52*(2), 95-106. https://doi.org/10.1177/0034355208323646

[20]Maki, D. R. (2012). Concepts and paradigms in rehabilitation counseling. In D. R. Maki & V. M. Tarvydas (Eds.), *The professional practice of rehabilitation*

[21]Meer, D., & VandeCreek, L. (2002). Cultural considerations in release of information. *Ethics & Behavior, 12*(2), 143–156. https://doi-org.springfieldcollege.idm.oclc.org/10.1207/S15327019EB1202_2

[22]Mental Health and Developmental Disabilities Confidentiality Act, 740 ILCS 110 § 11 (2008). https://www.ilga.gov/legislation/ilcs/ilcs3.asp?ActID=2043&ChapterID=57

[23]Robinson, R., & Watson, E. (2019). Private sector rehabilitation counseling ethics: Evolution of the 2017 CRCC code. *Rehabilitation Professional, 27*(1), 23–33.

[24]Rubin, S. E., Roessler, R., & Rumrill, P. D. (2016). *Foundations of the vocational rehabilitation process* (7th ed.). PRO-ED.

[25]Tarvydas, V. M., & Johnston, S. P. (2018). Ethics and ethical decision making. In V. M. Tarvydas & M. T. Hartley (Eds.), *The professional practice of rehabilitation counseling* (2nd ed., pp. 313-342). Springer.

[26]U.S. Department of Health and Human Services. (2014). *Healthcare.* http://www.hhs.gov/healthcare/

[27]van Dooren, K., Lennox, N., & Stewart, M. (2013). Improving access to electronic health records for people with intellectual disability: a qualitative study. *Australian Journal of Primary Health, 19*(4), 336-342. https://doi.org/10.1071/PY13042

[28]Watts, R. E., Bruhn, R., Nichter, M., & Nelson, J. (2018). Marriage, couples, and family counseling. In S. C. Nassar & S. G. Niles (Eds.), *Orientation to professional counseling: Past, present, and future trends*. (pp. 251–283). American Counseling Association.

[29]Wheeler, A. M., & Bertram, B. (2015). *The counselor and the law. A guide to legal and ethical practice* (7th ed.). American Counseling Association.

[30]Yalom, I. D., & Leszcz, M. (2020). *The theory and practice of group psychology* (6th ed.). Basic Books.

CHAPTER 6

ETHICS IN REHABILITATION COUNSELING:

A CASE STUDY APPROACH
ADVOCACY AND ACCESSIBILITY

ROXANNA N. PEBDANI

SECTION C: ADVOCACY AND ACCESSIBILITY

C.1 ADVOCACY

Section C of the Code of Professional Ethics for Rehabilitation Counselors (Code) [1] presents ethical principles related to advocacy and accessibility. When working with clients, rehabilitation counselors should be aware of and able to address barriers such as discrimination or stereotyping against people with disabilities and should also be aware of their own biases relating to disability (C.1.a.). Rehabilitation counselors should also be prepared to help clients advocate for themselves, and to advocate for clients when necessary (C.1.b.). Advocacy on behalf of clients can occur within one's own agency or with other service providers (C.1.c.), but rehabilitation counselors must always have consent from the client prior to advocating on their behalf (C.1.d.). Similarly, rehabilitation counselors should have enough knowledge regarding laws and national systems to be able to explain benefits and rights to clients (C.1.f., C.1.g.). Finally, rehabilitation counsellors who are advocating on behalf of their clients should adhere to principles of confidentiality unless they have received consent to disclose information about a client (C.1.e.).

C.1.a. ATTITUDINAL BARRIERS
Rehabilitation counselors address attitudinal barriers that inhibit the growth and development of their clients, including stereotyping and discrimination.

Rehabilitation counselors address their own biases against people with disabilities (or members of any other minority group) and are continually working to become more aware of these biases in themselves and in our culture as a whole. Similarly, rehabilitation counselors must be aware of the attitudinal barriers of others in society, and must remain aware of the stereotyping and discrimination against people with disabilities that occurs in society.

CASE STUDY

Sarah is a first year master's student in rehabilitation counseling. She shares a picture on Instagram that shows a young boy with two prosthetic legs running on a track. The picture has the caption "your excuse is invalid." One of Sarah's classmates, Kate, responds to the post explaining that she finds this picture to be offensive. Kate explains that the use of images of people with disabilities doing everyday things with inspirational captions is something that many in the disability

*community find to be offensive. Kate also explains that these photos
are often made to make people without disabilities feel better about
themselves and feel bad for people with disabilities. Sarah responds
that she was just sharing a picture that made her feel good, and that as
a rehabilitation counselor, she knows how people with disabilities feel.
Sarah thinks Kate is just being oversensitive.*

ETHICAL CONSIDERATIONS

1.   Which ethical standards apply in this case?

2.   How would you handle this if you were in Sarah's place?

3.   How would you handle this if you were in Kate's place?

C.1.b. EMPOWERMENT

*Rehabilitation counselors empower clients, parents, or legal
guardians by providing appropriate information to facilitate their self-
advocacy actions whenever possible. Rehabilitation counselors work to
help clients, parents, or legal guardians understand their rights and
responsibilities, speak for themselves, and make informed decisions.
When appropriate and with the consent of a client, parent, or legal
guardian, rehabilitation counselors act as advocates on behalf of that
client at the local, regional, and/or national levels.*

Many clients will have access to the information they need in order to
advocate for themselves. However, some clients will not have these tools.
When working with clients who need help with advocacy, it is important that
rehabilitation counselors assist them in obtaining the information they need to
advocate for themselves. This ensures autonomy in that it allows clients to
make their own advocacy decisions and speak for themselves. Rather than
speaking for clients, when possible, rehabilitation counselors facilitate
situations where clients can speak for themselves. However, there are instances
where rehabilitation counselor advocacy is important. Rehabilitation counselors
should be prepared to advocate with and for clients at the local, state, and
national level.

CASE STUDY

*Chantal is a rehabilitation counselor who works with clients who
have physical disabilities that impact their mobility. She learns that a
law is being considered at the state level that would reduce funding for
personal assistant services. In response to this, the advocacy group
ADAPT! is organizing a protest outside the state capitol. Chantal
learns about the protest and attends as a way to show support and*

advocate for her clients but does not share any information about the protest with them.

CASE STUDY DISCUSSION

1. Which ethical principles apply in this case?

2. What could Chantal have done differently to support her clients?

3. How would you handle this if you were in Chantal's place?

C.1.c. ORGANIZATIONAL ADVOCACY

Rehabilitation counselors remain aware of actions taken by their own and cooperating organizations on behalf of clients. When possible, to ensure effective service delivery, rehabilitation counselors act as advocates for clients who cannot advocate for themselves.

Rehabilitation counselors should be aware of current events within their own agencies and agencies with which they are affiliated to ensure that their client's needs are being considered. When a rehabilitation counselor comes across a situation in these settings that necessitates advocacy, they advocate on behalf of their clients to ensure that clients have access to the services they need.

CASE STUDY

Ned is a rehabilitation counselor who does vocational evaluations in a state agency. Part of his job is to explain the evaluations to his clients, after completion. Ned takes a one-hour session with each client to explain the specific results of each client's evaluation to the client and anyone else the client wants present (family members, case managers, job coaches, etc.). Ned has recently been told that he is no longer allowed to have these debrief and explanation sessions with clients, and instead is to solely submit his vocational evaluation report to others in the agency. Ned believes that this is a disservice to his clients but does nothing.

CASE STUDY DISCUSSION

1. Which ethical principles apply in this case?

2. What could Ned have done differently to support his clients?

3. How would you handle this if you were in Ned's place?

C.1.d ADVOCACY AND CONSENT

Rehabilitation counsellors obtain client consent prior to engaging in advocacy efforts on behalf of an identifiable client to improve the provision of services and to work toward removal of systemic barriers or obstacles that inhibit client access, growth, and development.

Though ultimately, the best situation is for clients to have the opportunity to advocate for themselves, there may be situations in which a rehabilitation counselor must advocate on behalf of a client. If a rehabilitation counselor is advocating on behalf of a client, they must either ensure that their advocacy efforts protect the anonymity of the client or they must first obtain consent from the client to share identifying information.

CASE STUDY

Ebony is a rehabilitation counsellor who works as district administrator in the California Department of Rehabilitation. She recently won an award for her hard work and advocacy on disability issues outside of her role in vocational rehabilitation. As part of her award, she will be given an opportunity to spend 30 minutes with the Governor of California. She would like to use her time to address some concerns she has with how the state manages access to home health services for individuals with disabilities. She seeks examples of poorly managed home health care access from the counselors she works with at the state Department of Rehabilitation who share examples of things their clients have experienced regarding home health care. She then takes that information to her meeting with the governor and shares.

CASE STUDY CONSIDERATIONS

1. What ethical principles apply in this case?

2. What should Ebony do to ensure she acts ethically?

3. What should her counsellors do to ensure they act ethically?

C.1.e. ADVOCACY AND CONFIDENTIALITY

When engaging in advocacy on behalf of clients, should circumstances require the disclosure of confidential information, rehabilitation counselors obtain and document consent from the client and disclose only minimal information.

Rehabilitation counselors will encounter barriers that have a negative impact on the lives of their client. These barriers can have a detrimental effect on an individual's life, and rehabilitation counselors should advocate on behalf of their clients in these situations. However, when advocating on behalf of clients, rehabilitation counselors must obtain consent from clients before advocating on their behalf. Unless they have permission, rehabilitation counselors should keep the names and information of clients they are advocating for confidential, unless they have explicit permission to identify the clients.

CASE STUDY

Neha is a rehabilitation counselor who works in a vocational rehabilitation setting. Her client, Jacob, has both cerebral palsy and a co-occurring alcohol use disorder. Jacob is currently in recovery and is abstaining from alcohol. Neha decides that Jacob would benefit from a referral to a service provider who works specifically with individuals who have cerebral palsy, but then learns that this agency with which her agency is related does not accept clients who have substance use disorders, even those in recovery. Neha recognizes this as discriminatory and contacts the agency on Jacob's behalf, without telling him she is doing so. She tells them that they are being discriminatory and that they should change their policies and uses Jacob as an example of why they should change their policy.

CASE STUDY DISCUSSION

1. Which ethical standards apply in this situation?

2. What could Neha have done differently to support her client?

3. How would you handle this if you were in Neha's place?

C.3.f. AREAS OF KNOWLEDGE AND COMPETENCY
Rehabilitation counsellors are knowledgeable about systems and laws, as well as organizational policies, and how they affect access to employment, education, transportation, housing, civil rights, financial benefits, medical services, and mental health services for individuals with disabilities. They keep current with changes in these areas to advocate effectively for clients and/or to facilitate self-advocacy of clients in these areas.

Rehabilitation counselors should be knowledgeable about issues that affect people with disabilities. This means that rehabilitation counselors should know about both systems and laws that affect people with disabilities at the local level, the regional or state level, and the national level. Rehabilitation counselors should pay attention to these systems and laws as they affect individuals with disabilities, especially those systems and laws that affect employment, education, transportation, housing, financial benefits, and medical services. In order to remain aware and current on these topics, rehabilitation counselors obtain training in these systems and laws where possible, and they advocate with and, where necessary, for their clients on these topics.

CASE STUDY

Amira has been working clients with intellectual disabilities in a school to work transition program for approximately three months. Through her graduate training, she has become knowledgeable about the ADA and other laws that apply to people with disabilities who are over the age of 18. However, she is less confident with laws that apply to youth with disabilities. One day, the father of one of her clients contacts her asking about his rights as a parent in an Individualized Education Program (IEP) meeting. He then asks about his child's Individualized Plan for Employment (IPE), and whether his child's transition and career goals are specified in his child's IEP. Amira has not seen the student's IEP and is unaware of whether or not the student's IPE should be specified in the IEP.

CASE STUDY DISCUSSION

1. Which ethical principles apply in this case?

2. What could Amira have done differently to support her client?

3. How would you handle this if you were in Amira place?

C.1.g. KNOWLEDGE OF BENEFIT SYSTEMS

Rehabilitation counselors are aware that disability benefit systems directly affect the quality of life of clients. They provide accurate and timely information or appropriate resources and referrals to individuals knowledgeable about benefits.

Rehabilitation counselors must understand the importance of disability benefit systems, in that they are closely intertwined with quality of life for many clients. Change in or loss of benefits can lead to major difficulties in an individual's life, and rehabilitation counselors should ensure that clients have access to information about these benefits and/or access to the resources they need to utilize these benefits.

CASE STUDY

Daniel is a vocational rehabilitation counselor who works with clients who receive Social Security Disability Insurance (SSDI) cash payments. His job is to provide his clients with the supports they need to return to work to the level at which they are able. His clients rely on both their cash benefits and their health insurance: Medicare. Daniel is somewhat aware of how SSDI cash benefits and Medicare work post-job acquisition, however he does not understand the nuances of cash benefits and how they are paid out once a client is working. Daniel has a client who has obtained a flexible job that she can do from her home and has returned to work. She is still receiving cash benefits, at a reduced rate calculated by Social Security. However, after four months of work, they find out that Social Security has been overpaying her. Social Security requires her to pay this money back, though she has already spent it. Because of this, she is unable to pay rent and loses her home. Because she works from home, this makes her unable to work and she loses her job.

CASE STUDY DISCUSSION

1. Which ethical principles apply in this case?

2. What could Daniel have done differently to support her client?

3. How would you handle this if you were in Daniel's place?

C.2. ACCESSIBILITY

Subsection two of the Advocacy and Accessibility section of the Code [1] pertains to accessibility (C.2.). Rehabilitation counsellors should help their clients access accommodations they need – including not just technology but also accommodations to access services, as necessary (C.2.a.). They should also ensure that when they refer clients to another service, that those services are both accessible and non-discriminatory (C.2.b.). Finally, rehabilitation counsellors should ensure that their own services are accessible (C.2.c.). Though brief, this section on accessibility is important to access for clients with disabilities.

C.2.a. ACCOMMODATIONS

Rehabilitation counselors facilitate the provision of necessary, appropriate, and reasonable accommodations in accordance with the law, including physically and programmatically accessible facilities, services, and technology to address the barriers encountered by individuals with disabilities.

Rehabilitation counselors recognize the importance of reasonable accommodations and supporting clients in obtaining reasonable accommodations as needed. This refers not only to physical accommodations and technology, but also to access to facilities and services.

CASE STUDY

Liz is a rehabilitation counsellor who works with clients who are Deaf or hard of hearing. At the start of the Covid-19 Pandemic she realized that her state's daily press conferences on the pandemic were not accessible–they were done live and the captioning was sometimes very wrong. Liz reached out to a friend at the Department of Health and relayed her concern that individuals who were Deaf or hard of hearing were not able to access the information provided in the press conferences in real time. A few days later, the Department of Health began including a sign language interpreter in each press conference.

CASE STUDY DISCUSSION

1. Which ethical principles are at play in this situation?

2. Should Liz have done anything differently?

C.2.b. REFERRAL ACCESSIBILITY
Rehabilitation counselors make reasonable efforts to refer clients only to programs, facilities, or employment settings that are appropriately accessible and that do not condone or engage in the prejudicial treatment of an individual or group based on their actual or perceived membership in a particular group, class, or category.

Rehabilitation counsellors should be knowledgeable about the agencies to which they refer clients. When referring clients to another program or facility, rehabilitation counselors should ensure that these facilities and agencies are accessible. This means physically accessible, but also accessible in terms of content and provision of accommodations for clients. Lastly, rehabilitation counselors should ensure that these agencies or programs do not discriminate on the basis of any protected class (age, race, gender, ethnicity, national origin, disability, religion, and beyond) or any other perceived difference (culture, gender identity, sexual orientation, marital status, language preference, and beyond).

CASE STUDY

Jungnam works as a vocational rehabilitation counselor in a state setting. Her office is currently undergoing renovations and she has been moved to an office on the first floor of her building. To enter, clients have to climb two small steps to enter the office. She knows that this may be a problem for some of her clients, but because it is temporary, she decides that it does not matter. Instead, when she is meeting with a client who has a mobility disability that makes it difficult to enter her office, she instead meets with them in the conference room.

Her clients are displeased with this and express their unhappiness. They also take this time to explain to Jungnam that this happens to them often. Some of them report experiencing these physical barriers at the offices of service providers where Jungnam has referred them. Jungnam says that she is busy and it would be impossible for her to assess the physical accessibility of every agency where she refers clients, but that her clients are welcome to advocate for those agencies to improve their physical accessibility.

CASE STUDY DISCUSSION

1. Which ethical principles apply in this situation?

2. What could Jungnam have done differently to support her client?

3. How would you handle this if you were in Jungnam's place?

C.2.c. BARRIERS TO SERVICES

Rehabilitation counselors collaborate with clients and/or others to identify and develop a plan to address physical or programmatic barriers to services.

Rehabilitation counselors should be aware of barriers that affect their client's access to their services. These barriers should be identified through collaborative work with clients and other professionals or stakeholders who are familiar with the functional limitations of clients, and the resulting barriers that they encounter. As these barriers are identified, rehabilitation counselors should be prepared to share this information with those in power in order to work to remove the barriers.

CASE STUDY

Juan is a bilingual counselor who speaks both English and American Sign Language (ASL) and works in a major metropolitan area. He works with clients with dual diagnoses, clients who are Deaf or Hard of Hearing and have a co-occurring physical disability. Juan's clients are happy with the services he provides and are pleased to have access to a counselor who is fluent in ASL. However, Juan's office is difficult for clients to get to. His office is not on a major train or bus line, and many of his clients have to take paratransit to access his office. Unfortunately, the paratransit system is notoriously difficult for people to use, and often causes users to arrive late or to miss appointments. Juan has a cancelation policy that states that if a client misses more than two sessions without notifying him 24 hours in advance, he will no longer see them. Juan's policy also states that being more than 10 minutes late to an appointment counts as a no-show. Many of Juan's clients are being dropped for being "no-shows" because the paratransit system picked them up late and therefore they were late to their appointments.

Juan speaks with a few clients about the paratransit services in their city and realizes that it is unreliable and causes problems for his clients. Not only does paratransit often make his clients late to their counseling sessions, but it also causes them to be late to work and late to other social events. Because of this, Juan decides to amend his cancelation policy due to its harmful effect on his clients. However, this is the extent of his advocacy on paratransit.

CASE STUDY DISCUSSION

1. Which ethical principles apply in this case?

2. What could Juan have done differently to support his clients?

3. How would you handle this if you were in Juan's place?

CONCLUSION

It is especially important that rehabilitation counselors be aware of how attitudes affect individuals with disabilities. This includes their own attitudes as well as the attitudes of others. Similarly, rehabilitation counselors must be prepared to be advocates with and for their clients, while ensuring that their clients have autonomy in the advocacy process. Rehabilitation counselors also ensure that their clients have access to appropriate and accessible services.

Advocacy and accessibility are essential parts of rehabilitation counseling, and an important part of our code of ethics.

DISCUSSION QUESTIONS

1. How do you ensure that you are helping to empower your clients in advocacy (C.1.b.) without taking over?

2. Disability benefit systems can be extremely complicated (C.1.g.), how can you ensure you are familiar with these systems and that you maintain that familiarity with them as they change?

3. How can you ensure that the services you provide are physically and programmatically accessible (C.2.c.)?

REFERENCE

Commission on Rehabilitation Counselor Certification, (2017). *Code of professional ethics for rehabilitation counselors.*, Schaumburg, IL: Author.

CHAPTER 7

PROFESSIONAL RESPONSIBILITY

JAMES L. SOLDNER

MATTHEW E. SPRONG

MICHELE DENT

SUBSTANDARD D: PROFESSIONAL RESPONSIBILITY

This section of the Commission on Rehabilitation Counselor Certification (CRCC) Code of Professional Ethics[6] (the Code) is related to the professional responsibility of practicing Rehabilitation Counselors and rehabilitation counseling service delivery. The encompassing goal of *Section D, Professional Responsibility,* of the Code is to assure professional, ethical, and culturally competent rehabilitation counseling practice, as well as to continue to demonstrate Rehabilitation Counseling as a legitimate profession. Furthermore, it is essential for all rehabilitation counselors to practice thorough self-assessment on a continuous basis to determine if they are providing competent services to their clients.

Section D of the Code is comprised of six primary Standards, including: (D.1.) professional competence, (D.2.) cultural competence and diversity, (D.3.) functional competence, (D.4.) professional credentials, (D.5.) responsibility to the public and other professionals, and (D.6.) scientific bases for interventions. The Ethics Task Force for the Code has determined that these six principles are essential to demonstrating and maintaining Professional Responsibility as part of rehabilitation counseling service delivery and the profession. If service delivery is being diminished due to lack of competence (i.e., professional, cultural, and functional), rehabilitation counselors should seek guidance through clinical supervision to identify ways to increase competence in the areas that are deficient. The subsequent Section D and its six standards also include a corresponding case study and case study discussion.

D.1. PROFESSIONAL COMPETENCE

D.1.a. BOUNDARIES OF COMPETENCE
Rehabilitation counselors practice only within the boundaries of their competence, based on their education, training, supervised experience, professional credentials, and appropriate professional experience. Rehabilitation counselors do not misrepresent their competence to clients or others.

D.1.b. NEW SPECIALTY AREAS OF PRACTICE
Rehabilitation counselors transitioning into specialty areas requiring new core competencies begin practicing only after having obtained appropriate consultation, education, training, and/or supervised experience. While developing skills in new specialty areas, rehabilitation counselors make reasonable efforts to ensure the competence of their work and to protect clients from possible harm.

D.1.c. EMPLOYMENT QUALIFICATIONS

Rehabilitation counselors accept employment for positions for which they are qualified by education, training, supervised experience, professional credentials, and appropriate professional experience. Rehabilitation counselors hire individuals for rehabilitation counseling positions who are qualified and competent for those positions.

D.1.d. AVOIDING HARM

Rehabilitation counselors act to avoid harming clients, students, employees, supervisees, and research participants and to minimize or to remedy unavoidable or unanticipated harm.

D.1.e. MONITOR EFFECTIVENESS

Rehabilitation counselors continually monitor their effectiveness as professionals and take steps to improve when necessary. Rehabilitation counselors take reasonable steps to seek peer supervision as needed to evaluate their efficacy as rehabilitation counselors.

D.1.f. CONTINUING EDUCATION

Rehabilitation counselors recognize the need for continuing education to acquire and maintain a reasonable level of awareness of current scientific and professional information in their fields of activity. They maintain their competence in the skills they use, are open to new procedures, and keep current with professional and community resources for diverse and specific populations with which they work.

The ethical standard related to *Boundaries of Competence* refers to rehabilitation counselors practicing within the scope of their education, training, supervised experience, professional credentials, and professional experience. Although competence can be defined as the ability to perform a task at an acceptable level[8] it should be noted that counselors are unable to be competent in offering *all* services they provide.[20] For example, an individual who primarily works in a Substance Abuse setting may be very competent in applying the evidence-based practices and understanding case management principles related to this specific population. Although the rehabilitation counselor may be competent in this context, they may struggle if they are introduced into a new employment setting, such as Forensic Rehabilitation.

The reason that a rehabilitation counselor may struggle with being competent in all contexts is due to the fact that there are specialties within rehabilitation counseling (e.g., substance abuse counseling, public vocational rehabilitation, forensic rehabilitation). The ethical standard of *New Specialty Areas of Practice* refers to the notion that rehabilitation counselors should

145

obtain specialized training prior to providing services in these areas or have supervision throughout the service delivery process. This can be accomplished by attending workshops, conferences, and/or educational courses to obtain the necessary competencies to work in the specialty area. In addition, rehabilitation counselors should become familiar with the literature related to these specialty areas. If a rehabilitation counselor is not "qualified for employment," the counselor should seek supervision and additional education and training prior to accepting the position. Of course, sometimes, specialized skills and competencies are learned while working in the new position. In this instance, it may be difficult for rehabilitation counselors to understand their boundaries of competence and, therefore, should rely on other professionals to assist them in pursuing the necessary knowledge and skills needed to provide competent service delivery.

Rehabilitation counselors should continue to self-reflect and assess in order to determine if they are providing highly competent services. Having other professionals who are competent in the specific employment context and conducting self-reflection and assessment techniques will assist the rehabilitation counselor in abiding by the ethical standard related to *Monitoring Effectiveness.* As with all of the four aforementioned sub-standards that relate to professional competence, rehabilitation counselors should seek supervision and other training opportunities (e.g., continuing education) to increase competency.

Continuing Education is vital to fostering professional development and growth as a Rehabilitation Counselor. The CRCC has established requirements for a minimum of 10-hours of continued education related to ethics prior to having the CRC renewed [note: renewal is every 5 years and requires 100 CEUs] (see www.crccertification.com). As evidence-based practices evolve, it is essential for rehabilitation counselors to learn these new techniques when assisting persons with disabilities. For instance, early rehabilitation counseling practices involved helping individuals find employment.[26] Yet, researchers have discovered that if a person is a good match for the environment, and the environment is a good match for the person, then the likelihood of the person having meaningful employment is greater (see Super's Person-Environment Fit Theory).[26] As new discoveries are made, it is sometimes difficult to have this research translate into practice (e.g., rehabilitation counselors have large caseloads and may have difficulty finding time to read the research). The use of continuing education can help ensure that rehabilitation counselors are learning what the research is finding so that they can implement this into practice. Obtaining the necessary amount of CEUs will help ensure that Rehabilitation Counselors are maintaining their competence and evolving with the profession. It is essential to remember that learning is a continuing process and does not end once a rehabilitation counselor completes a master's degree program. Although many practicing rehabilitation counselors do not wish to pursue a doctoral program, there are other ways for them to continue the learning process, e.g., continuing education.

CASE STUDY

Monica is a doctoral student in a rehabilitation counseling training program. She has recently graduated from the master's degree program in Rehabilitation Counseling and has limited experience working in the profession. She realizes that in order to obtain employment as a faculty member in a university, she needs to obtain professional experience. Monica decided to obtain this experience by starting her own practice and providing Forensic Rehabilitation Services. This appears to be the best option, since she can arrange her work schedule to accommodate her class schedule and teaching assistantship. Although she has never worked in the private sector and has never conducted labor market surveys or job analyses other than an assignment in class, she feels confident that she will be able to figure it out.

Monica followed the procedures necessary to opening her practice and has been able to register as a vocational expert with the Social Security Administration's Office of Disability Adjudication and Review. She informed the office that she has a master's degree in Rehabilitation Counseling and is currently a Certified Rehabilitation Counselor. She was scheduled with the regional office to provide vocational expert (VE) testimony for a hearing in two weeks, as the vocational expert who was expected to testify had an emergency and was no longer available. Monica has never observed a hearing, but felt she was prepared enough in her courses to "figure it out." She was sent a CD to review the exhibits for her upcoming cases and classified each claimant's previous work (i.e., Dictionary of Occupational Titles [DOT] Job title and associated code number, specific vocational preparation, strength needed to perform the job as indicated in the DOT and actually performed by the claimant).

During the hearing, the judge asked Monica some basic questions (e.g., is the résumé in the file a true and accurate description of your professional qualifications and experience?). The Judge then asked the claimant's representative if they opposed or objected to using Monica as a vocational witness. The claimant's representative requested that they have the opportunity to ask the VE some questions about her experience. The judge agreed and the representative asked Monica if she has ever conducted a labor market survey or job analysis. She stated she has performed these as part of her classroom assignments and has performed a few during her clinical training. The representative then asked if she has any experience providing job placement services to persons with disabilities. Monica indicated that she had some experience providing job placement services to clients with disabilities during her clinical training. The representative asked how many clients she worked with and Monica said two. The representative asked what kind of services she provided, and Monica indicated that it was individuals with severe impairments, and she was mainly working on job skills such as interviewing, résumé development, how to complete an application, etc.

The representative stated that they objected to Monica serving as a vocational witness based on limited experience. The Judge indicated they would note the objection but would proceed with Monica as the vocational witness. The judge asked Monica to classify the claimant's previous work. The Judge then provided Monica the first few hypothetical questions, in which Monica was asked to indicate how many jobs there are both nationally and regionally. Afterwards, the claimant's representative asked Monica to indicate how much off task behavior is tolerated within unskilled work, how many absences are allowable in unskilled work, and where this information comes from. Monica said she was unable to answer, since she has not performed enough labor market surveys to have a reasonable representation of what employers tolerate.

Case Study Discussion

There are many issues that Monica should consider before considering providing forensic rehabilitation services and serving as a vocational expert. First, the CRCC code of professional ethics clearly states that Rehabilitation Counselors understand their boundaries of competence. Monica has limited experience working in the profession and has only completed a labor market survey and job analysis for a class assignment. Additionally, Monica has limited experience in providing job placement services and speaking to employers to gain an understanding of what is tolerated in employment (e.g., off-task behavior, absenteeism). Even though Monica received training within her educational program, prior to serving as a vocational expert, she should obtain appropriate professional experience and seek a mentor who can guide her in Forensic Rehabilitation.

Often times, vocational experts must rely on their professional experience since the DOT, Selected Characteristics of Occupations, and Handbook of Analyzing Jobs do not discuss some limitations such as off-task behavior. If an individual does not have professional experience, it is difficult for Monica to serve as an expert witness because she lacks the professional experience required. Monica did respond appropriately, when she said she was unable to answer the questions from the Claimant's representative because she has not performed enough labor market surveys. However, Monica should have also considered the standards related to *New Specialty Areas of Practice* and

Qualified for Employment as these standards describe that a rehabilitation counselor must have professional experience in addition to educational training when engaging in areas that are new to the rehabilitation counselor.

The repercussions following a Rehabilitation Counselor who engages in a specialty that they are not familiar with may include a claimant losing a social security case due to the counselor's limited competence as a Vocational Expert. Although not indicated within the case study, hopefully, Monica realizes her limited competence within Forensic Rehabilitation and honors the standard related to *Monitoring Effectiveness* by seeking supervision and a possible mentor-mentee relationship with another professional who has been working in this capacity for a substantial amount of time. Of course, even though someone may have worked in Forensic Rehabilitation for a substantial period of time, they themselves may not be providing competent services, and Monica should consult other Rehabilitation Professionals prior to agreeing to be mentored by a specific Forensic Rehabilitation Counselor. It is hoped that Monica recognizes that having a master's degree and the CRC credential do not automatically make her qualified to serve as a Vocational Expert.

D.2. CULTURAL COMPETENCE/DIVERSITY

D.2.a. CULTURAL COMPETENCE

Rehabilitation counselors develop and maintain knowledge, personal awareness, sensitivity, and skills and demonstrate a disposition reflective of a culturally competent rehabilitation counselor working with diverse populations.

D.2.b. INTERVENTIONS

Rehabilitation counselors develop and adapt interventions and services to incorporate consideration of cultural perspective of clients and recognition of barriers external to clients that may interfere with achieving effective rehabilitation outcomes.

Effective rehabilitation counseling rests on the foundation of an effective working relationship between counselor and client. This relationship is built on the belief of the client and the truthfulness, and faithfulness of the counselor, as well as the ability of the counselor to be open to interacting with the client in an accepting, and welcoming manner. The counseling relationship must always be supportive between the counselor and the client, and at times, the client's family. This is an important distinction to recognize, many people from various cultural groups, including the family in important decision-making is expected. The counselor learning if this is an important expectation for a particular client may be the difference between successfully navigating the process together, or losing the client.[33] This is only one characteristic that may influence the design and implementation of an intervention and lead to either success or a lack thereof.[1] Although it is important to utilize evidence-based interventions when working with clients, rehabilitation counselors should also consider if these are culturally-appropriate.[25]

D.2.c. NONDISCRIMINATION

Rehabilitation counselors do not condone or engage in the prejudicial treatment of an individual or group on their actual or perceived membership in a particular group, class, or category.

Discrimination is the practice of treating a person or a group of people unfairly based on characteristics such as age, gender, ethnicity, marital status, race, national origin, or disability.[36] In order to refrain from discriminating against anyone with whom a rehabilitation counselor would come into contact with as a function of the profession, it is imperative to begin with awareness. Corrigan[7] stated that public stigma is comprised of three stages, including stereotypes, prejudice, and discrimination. *Stereotypes* can be described as a negative belief about an individual or a group. *Prejudice* is agreement with the belief and/or a negative emotional reaction. *Discrimination* is a behavioral response to prejudice. Rehabilitation counselors should practice self-assessment techniques to determine if they are holding stereotypes and prejudices about certain clients and determine if these stereotypes and prejudices are leading to negative consequences in the services being provided. Wilson and Gines[39] found that race is the second most powerful predictor of VR acceptance after controlling for 15 other independent variables (e.g., gender). Although the exact determination of why clients of a different racial category are not being accepted to services is not known. Rehabilitation counselors need to reflect to determine if their stereotypes and prejudices are leading to these discrepancies. Like other services that may be provided, rehabilitation counselors should determine if their personal values and beliefs are influencing the services being provided. For example, rehabilitation counselors who hold traditional values related to gender roles may unconsciously be transferring their personal beliefs to what services they provide to a client. If a client wishes to develop a specific rehabilitation goal, and the counselor has personal reasons why this should not be explored, this could lead to discrimination.

CASE STUDY

Mary, a rehabilitation counselor, is sitting at her desk, reviewing the preliminary notes she made for her next appointment with a young woman who is a U.S. citizen, with a last name that looks Chinese. Mary noticed that her client is in her early twenties and still living at home with her family but doesn't yet have a driver's license. This could be a barrier to accessing services and employment. Getting a driver's license would support the client becoming independent. Mary adds it to her notes of items to cover during the initial meeting and plans for it to be something that will need to be included as one of the preliminary goals for the client.

Mary's new client arrives on time and signs in. She is also accompanied by five family members. When Mary walks out to greet her new client, all five family members stand up and introduce themselves. As Mary asks her new client to walk down the hall to her office, all five family members begin to follow along. Mary is perplexed by this and tells the client and her family that only the client needs to accompany her for the appointment. The client looks back and forth between her family and the counselor, with obvious confusion and reluctance. Mary again insists that the organization's policy requires that only the client accompany her to her office. She suggests that her family members may remain in the waiting room until the appointment concludes. The family members have a brief discussion in a language that Mary is not familiar with, and then politely make their farewells and thank Mary for her time. The family leaves the office, taking the new client with them.

CASE STUDY DISCUSSION

Mary was focused on the client as the only person to whom she was providing services and thus, the only person who should be considered as necessary for the appointment. In this situation that approach was inappropriate. The client was from a culture that expects the family to participate in all-important decision-making. This expectation was outside of Mary's cultural expectation that a woman in her twenties should be able to "stand on her own two feet." From Mary's cultural perspective, an adult should be able to make her own decisions about her life.

Awareness of different cultural expectations regarding what it means to be an adult would have given Mary a better chance at forming a working relationship with her new client and her client's family. Coming into contact with different perspectives on family provides an opportunity to gain insight into how to interact with clients from cultures that have other ways of supporting family members making important decisions. Recognizing the different views as valid is an important factor in creating an environment of trust that leads to a counseling relationship.[33]

D.3. FUNCTIONAL COMPETENCE

D.3.a. IMPAIRMENT

Rehabilitation counselors are alert to the signs of impairment due to their own health issues or personal circumstances and refrain from offering or providing professional services when such impairment is likely to harm clients or others. They seek assistance for problems that

*reach the level of professional impairment, and if necessary, they limit,
suspend, or terminate their professional responsibilities until it is
determined they may safely resume their work. Rehabilitation
counselors assist colleagues or supervisors in recognizing their own
professional impairment, provide consultation and assistance when
colleagues or supervisors show signs of impairment, and intervene as
appropriate to prevent harm to clients.*

The standard of counselor impairment refers to the notion that rehabilitation
counselors must refrain from providing services when physical, emotional,
psychological, or other limitations are preventing the counselor from being
competent in relevant service delivery responsibilities. The American
Counseling Association recognized counselor impairment as an issue in the
1980s due to litigation involving mental health professionals who were not
addressing their problems or colleagues problems associated with counselor
impairment, which was leading to ineffective services being provided.[32] The
litigation has prompted counseling organizations to initiate protocols for
counselor impairment that include rehabilitation counselors recognizing
colleagues that are impaired and providing necessary interventions to prevent
harm to the client.

Counselor impairment is the inability to deliver competent client care[32] and
may compromise or reduce the quality of services being rendered.[30] Counselor
impairment could be the result of situational factors, such as
countertransference (psychological tendency to catch the pathologies of clients
with whom they work with closely and empathically);[12] or the death of a loved
one. Counselor impairment may also include, but is not limited to, the result of
alcohol abuse or being under the influence of other substances, symptom
exacerbation as a result of a mental illness, disability-related barriers, or
"burnout or the sense of emotional depletion which comes from stress."[32, pg.258]
All of these factors may also lead to countertransference. Counselors may also
have difficulty remaining objective and neutral when a client is disclosing
personal information that is similar to the issues the counselors are trying to
deal with themselves. Additionally, the counselor may unconsciously impose
their values onto their client.

The current standard suggests that rehabilitation counselors should limit,
suspend, or terminate services until they are safely able to continue work.
However, rehabilitation counselors should first seek clinical supervision to
discuss the best courses of action. Additionally, rehabilitation counselors
should conduct a self-assessment to determine if they are providing effective
services to the consumers they serve, or if personal impairment is limiting their
ability to assist their clients. This involves determining if they are using the
counseling session as a personal therapy session, imposing their current
challenges onto the client, if their barriers are preventing them from being
active listeners, or if they are unable to continue to be objective and provide a

safe and non-judgmental environment. As aforementioned, when a rehabilitation counselor recognizes they are experiencing counselor impairment and are inadequately serving their client, they should seek immediate supervision and refrain from continuing to provide services.

CASE STUDY

Andre has been employed for the past 8 years as a substance abuse counseling supervisor at a residential treatment facility. He has been well trained in providing clinical supervision to the other substance abuse counselors and technicians and has used his skills to help counselors who have been working in the field, as well as new counselors who do not have much experience working as professional counselors. Andre is considered a seasoned counselor at the agency, with only one other counselor, "Melissa" being employed longer.

Melissa has been an excellent counselor throughout her employment at the agency. She provided guidance to Andre throughout his master's program, since she graduated one year prior to Andre receiving his master's degree and helped him get a job at the agency where they are currently employed. Melissa and Andre have maintained a professional relationship and have continuously attended professional conferences and have taken additional addiction-related courses to improve the service delivery they provide.

Recently, Andre noticed that Melissa has not been acting like herself. She has been losing her attentiveness that clients appreciate. In fact, a few fellow counselors informed Andre that they have been noticing behaviors similar to individuals experiencing addiction, such as coming in late, appearing extremely stressed, and occasionally finding Melissa crying in her office. Andre was aware that Melissa had a history of abusing drugs and alcohol but has been "clean" for nearly 20 years. Andre was also aware that Melissa has been working closely with a young client, aged 15 who had a diagnosis of a substance related disorder (i.e., heroin), and had a co-existing diagnosis of borderline personality disorder. She started working with this client approximately 2 months ago and has been working non-stop to help the child be a "success story." Usually, Melissa's approach has been that clients need to take ownership of their recovery. Because she usually works with adults, Melissa's approach has been different with this client.

The next day, Andre requested to speak to Melissa to see what was troubling her. She informed Andre that she feels it is her personal mission to help this client because the client reminds Melissa of her younger sister who died from a heroin overdose when she was about the same age. Melissa stated that she has worked so hard with this client and has not seen any improvement and is afraid the client is going down a similar path. Moreover, Melissa mentioned that next week is the anniversary of her sister's death. She said she was using drugs with her sister when her sister overdosed and is having many psychological-related challenges as of late. Melissa stated that she has been unable to focus during her counseling sessions and thinks that her clients are suffering since she is unable to be a counselor. She also says she is overwhelmed that she has not had many success stories lately, with many of her clients leaving treatment early, or relapsing immediately after completion of treatment.

CASE STUDY DISCUSSION

There are many different challenges that Melissa is facing within this case study. It appears that Melissa may not be experiencing burnout. She has not indicated a lack of desire to discuss work with friends or family and has not displayed being displeased when clients cancel appointments. However, she has been displaying emotional and physical exhaustion and appears to be somewhat displeased with her inability to help the client who is 15 years of age. Melissa may be experiencing *countertransference*, since she is working in a field that oftentimes shows little improvement. She has indicated that her only focus has been on helping this one client, which is consistent with the concept of countertransference.[12]

Regardless of the exact cause that is leading Melissa to have limitations in the services she is providing, it is evident that there is some counselor impairment present. Andre and other staff need to meet with Melissa to determine the best course of action to prevent Melissa's clients from feeling the effects of her impairment, while allowing Melissa the opportunity to work on the challenges with which she is presented. It would be a direct violation of Standard D.3.a to allow Melissa the opportunity to continue working with her clients, because she has indicated she is unable to provide competent services.

D.3.b. DISASTER PREPARATION AND RESPONSE

Rehabilitation counselors make reasonable efforts to plan for continued client services in the event that rehabilitation counseling services are interrupted by disaster, such as acts of violence, terrorism, or a natural disaster.

Disaster preparation and response has been a novel area of exploration within the rehabilitation discipline. The most recent version of the CRCC code of professional ethics has incorporated a standard that assists rehabilitation counselors in understanding what their responsibilities are when services are interrupted by disasters. This specific standard was in response to the limited preparedness of persons with and without disabilities during the Hurricane

Katrina disaster. This hurricane impacted many of the southern states, but New Orleans received the most impact. During Hurricane Katrina, research literature indicated that trauma-related psychological symptoms increased,[22] as well as generalized anxiety disorder.[37]

Prior to Hurricane Katrina, the "Harris Survey"[13] was distributed to persons with disabilities and found that 24% of people with disabilities have not made comprehensive emergency preparedness plans, 61% of persons with disabilities did not have plans developed to quickly and safely evacuate their homes, and 32% of persons with disabilities suggested their workplaces did not have emergency response plans or that these plans did not incorporate them.[24] These results led to the Emergency Preparedness initiative, which has two goals, including (1) individuals with functional or special needs are addressed prior to an emergency, and (2) to ensure that persons with disabilities are included in the emergency planning process.[31] With the release of this initiative, and Standard D.3.b. of the CRCC code of professional ethics, it is essential for rehabilitation counselors to consider receiving training related to how to effectively plan for disasters or emergency situations while considering the needs of persons with disabilities. Sprong, et al.,[31] recommended that agencies consider incorporating three functions to address preparedness, response to and recovery from disasters, and mitigation, including: 1) strategic plans, 2) operational plans, and 3) tactical plans (see Sprong, et al.,[31] for more detailed information). Incorporating these three functions within an agency's emergency preparedness plan will help ensure where and how services will be provided in the event that a location is compromised (e.g., debris or other hazardous materials prohibiting use of facility). Rehabilitation counselors should consider receiving additional training in psychological first aid and disaster-related crisis intervention,[2] and training related to helping persons with disabilities develop individualized preparedness plans that provide general knowledge on how to maintain independence, how to shelter-in-place, receive emergency related communications, and access medical care, among others.[35]

D.4. PROFESSIONAL CREDENTIALS

D.4.a. ACCURATE REPRESENTATION

Rehabilitation counselors claim or imply only professional qualifications actually completed and correct any known misrepresentations of their qualifications by others. They truthfully represent the qualifications of their professional colleagues. Rehabilitation counselors accurately represent the accreditations of their academic programs and accurately describe their continuing education and specialized training.

D.4.b. CREDENTIALS

Rehabilitation counselors claim only licenses or certifications that are current and in good standing.

D.4.c. EDUCATIONAL DEGREES

Rehabilitation counselors clearly differentiate between earned and honorary degrees.

D.4.d. IMPLYING DOCTORAL-LEVEL COMPETENCE

Rehabilitation counselors refer to themselves as "doctor" in a counseling context only when their doctorate is in rehabilitation counseling or a closely related field from an accredited university. If rehabilitation counselors have a doctoral-level degree in an unrelated field, they clearly state the field in which the doctoral degree was earned. Rehabilitation counselors do not use any abbreviation or statement to imply the attainment of a credential.

Accurate representation of professional credentials delineates the boundaries within which each rehabilitation counselor practices. This is sometimes referred to as scope of practice.[19] When practicing in the field, it is critical for each rehabilitation counselor to recognize the limits of their own scope of practice, as determined by formal education, clinical experience, and professional development. Clients often times seek services from those with specific credentials (e.g., the CRC) because the credential generally translates that the counselor has demonstrated the necessary competencies needed to be effective in the services they provide. If an individual failed the CRC examination, but continued to inform the public that they are certified, this could have unforeseen consequences (e.g., the rehabilitation counselor may not be aware of evidence-based practices and interventions, resulting in inadequate service delivery). The accurate representation of professional credentials standard is important when discussing the ethical standard of *credentials.*

Each profession develops a standard that must continually be met by those within the profession, as well as those who wish to join that profession. This can be considered from a pre-service standpoint, when one is participating in a formal educational setting, as well as ongoing professional development after beginning to practice. For rehabilitation counselors, credentials are bestowed upon meeting specific criteria for coursework completed, as well as supervised clinical experience, and successfully passing a rigorous examination. In order to maintain the credential, ongoing professional development must be completed through approved providers and within a given time frame.

In maintaining accurate representation of professional credentials, rehabilitation counselors must also become aware of the distinction between *educational degrees* (i.e., earned vs. honorary degrees). Earned degrees are bestowed upon completion of specific required coursework, supervised clinical experience, and formal evaluation. This is not the case for honorary degrees, which do not imply any education or specialized training. Educational degrees are important because it implies that rehabilitation counselors have received rigorous training to provide competent services. Credentialing serves as a gate-keeping mechanism to make sure rehabilitation counselors meet these competencies on a continuous basis and continue to develop professionally through continuing education requirements. Those with honorary degrees may not necessarily have the knowledge, skills, and abilities needed to provide competent services. Rehabilitation counselors should be aware of the difference between these degrees, especially when referring clients for other services. Rehabilitation counselors are expected to be experts and protect the client from misleading services.

Rehabilitation counselors also must have an awareness of the influence of the counselor on the client/consumer, to guard against undue influence, and safeguard autonomy. Within the counseling relationship, using the title "doctor" may have a strong influence on the client/consumer's process. This can be especially critical to balancing the power dynamic at place in any counseling relationship.

CASE STUDY

Bryan is starting a new job at a local community clinic that offers a variety of services to clients. He has several years of experience working in the human services field, and he is working towards completing his master's degree in Rehabilitation Counseling. He has been reviewing files of the clients he will be working with and to introduce himself, he has been making phone calls to the clients. As he is speaking on the phone with one of his new clients, she calls him "doctor"—Bryan corrects her, and explains that he is not a physician, and that he is working towards completing his training in rehabilitation counseling. The client expresses confusion and asks if she can see someone with a "real degree." Bryan attempts to reassure the client, explaining that the type of work he will be doing, case management, is within his set of skills. The client again asks to speak to someone with a "real counseling degree." Bryan promises to speak with his supervisor to share the request of the client.

CASE STUDY DISCUSSION

It is never an easy thing to have someone question professional competence. For Bryan, as a newly hired case manager, this was a difficult reaction to deal with from a prospective new client. Although it was an unpleasant conversation to have, Bryan handled it well, explaining why he was able to provide services, as well as his current level of education. While an awkward situation to deal with, Bryan made a good decision, offering to contact his supervisor and share the concerns of the client. By listening to the client's concerns and being honest, Bryan's interaction with the client corresponded to the requirements of D.4 of the code.

D.5. RESPONSIBILITY TO THE PUBLIC AND OTHER PROFESSIONALS

D.5.a. HARASSMENT
Rehabilitation counselors do not condone or participate in any form of harassment, including sexual harassment.

Sexual harassment can have a variety of negative consequences for all persons involved. Schneider, et al.,[48] stated that sexual harassment can have psychological implications (e.g., depression, anxiety, denial, fear, anger, insecurity, shame, self-blame, isolation), physiological implications (e.g., headaches, lethargy, weight fluctuations, phobias, sleep disturbances), and career-related implications (e.g., decreased job satisfaction, absenteeism, withdrawal from work or school, unfavorable performance evaluations) on the individual being harassed. The United States Equal Employment Opportunity Commission (EEOC)[36] is a government organization that was established in 1989. Part of this organization's responsibility is to "enforce laws that prohibit discrimination based on race, color, religion, sex, nationality, disability, age in hiring, promoting, firing, setting wages, testing, training, apprenticeship, and all other terms and conditions of employment."[36]

The EEOC describes sexual harassment as "unwelcome sexual advances, requests for sexual favors, and other verbal or physical conduct of a sexual nature constitute sexual harassment" when this is explicitly or implicitly a term of an individual's employment; submission to or rejection of this conduct is used as a basis for employment-related decisions; or these behaviors interfere with an individual's work performance or creates an intimidating, hostile work environment."[28, pg.401] The CRCC professional code of ethics related to sexual harassment specifically states that rehabilitation counselors will not participate or condone others who engage in sexual harassing behaviors. This is not only applicable within an employment-related setting as sexual harassment is inappropriate in all settings. If a rehabilitation counselor observes this behavior occurring from another professional, they should confront the individual to explain why this is inappropriate behavior, notify the supervisor (if in an employment setting, educational setting, or other setting that has some type of similar infrastructure), and report the offense to the certification/licensing board (if the individual is certified and/or licensed).

CASE STUDY

Forrest is employed at a state vocational rehabilitation (VR) agency as a rehabilitation counselor. He was hired 2 months ago to fill the vacancy of a recently retired rehabilitation counselor. His supervisor, Jenny has been truly kind in helping Forrest acclimate to his new position, since he is a recent graduate with limited experience working as a rehabilitation counselor in public VR. Forrest has been somewhat confused as he has feelings that Jenny has been somewhat flirtatious with him but is not sure if this is her intent or is just trying to be nice. One afternoon, Jenny called Forrest into her office and asked if he wanted to grab dinner after work. She informed him that she is very attracted to him and that she would like to get to know one another on a personal level. She informed Forrest that if he did not want a "dating" relationship, they could keep it purely sexual. Forrest indicated that he is happily married and is uncomfortable with such interaction both at work and after work. A few days later, Forrest received a note stating that he must agree to the romantic relationship if he wanted to stay employed at the agency.

CASE STUDY DISCUSSION

It is apparent that Forrest is being threatened and intimidated to engage in an unwanted romantic relationship by his supervisor. Sexual harassment alone may create psychological challenges, as well as other difficulties concentrating at work. However, now Forrest is being sexually harassed by his superior, who is threatening his employment. This issue needs to be reported immediately, as Forrest may continuously be threatened, which could impact the effectiveness of the services he is providing. Likewise, there could be extreme consequences that manifest from the continuous sexual harassment from his supervisor.

D.5.b. REPORTS TO THIRD PARTIES

Rehabilitation counselors are accurate, honest, and objective in reporting their professional activities and judgments to appropriate third parties (e.g., courts, health insurance companies, recipients of evaluation reports).

Sprong, et al.,[30] states that we have certain duties as rehabilitation professionals. For example, we have a duty to persons with disabilities, society, students, colleagues, and a duty to our profession. In addition to these duties, we also have a duty to warn or protect third parties from harm. The CRCC code of professional ethics standard *Reports to Third Parties,* describes that third parties may include courts, health insurance companies, those who are the recipients of evaluation reports (e.g., public vocational rehabilitation agencies), and others. In many instances, there may be an opportunity to provide false information on reports in order to cause a client to obtain services or to lose services. The ethical standard mandates that rehabilitation counselors provide accurate, honest, and objective information in their reports. Providing false information cannot only hurt the profession of rehabilitation, but also have negative consequences on the clients being served. For example, if a client is referred for a comprehensive vocational evaluation, the findings from the tests administered will be used to determine vocational ability, and incorrect information may preclude certain opportunities or be a reason clients receive services that are inconsistent with their abilities (may cause potential harm). It is essential for rehabilitation counselors to maintain their credibility because providing falsified information can have legal implications as well as professional.

CASE STUDY

Lilly is a mental health counselor and is currently working with her client named Barney. Barney was involved in a motor-vehicle accident approximately 1.5 years ago, which resulted in a spinal cord injury at the T-5 level. Barney has sought services from Lilly because he wanted to receive counseling to work on some of his stressors related to the accident and his inability to go back to his current job. Barney only has transportation to Lilly's office every two weeks. After meeting with Barney for a few months, Barney informed Lilly that they would need to stop meeting because Barney still has not received social security and would not be able to continue until he has his hearing next month. Lilly suggested that she serve as an expert witness in his case.

After a month passes by, Lilly is at the hearing in order to discuss Barney's mental health symptoms. The Judge begins questioning Lilly about the counseling services she has provided, with respect to frequency of contact and duration. Lilly stated that she has met with Barney on a weekly basis for approximately a year. The Judge asked what psychological impairments and related symptoms she observed throughout their interactions. Lilly stated she saw symptoms related to post-traumatic stress disorder and depression. The Judge then asks Lilly if she is telling the truth, as she is under oath. Lilly states yes and the judge questions her credibility. Judge: "There is documentation that Barney only meets with you every other week and has been seeing you for only a few months...I have asked Barney if he is experiencing the symptoms indicated in your report and he stated he has never indicated such symptoms." Lilly quickly states that she has made up some information, as she believes Barney deserves disability benefits.

160

She then requests to obtain an attorney before making any more claims.

CASE STUDY DISCUSSION

In this instance, Lilly has lied under oath, fabricated reports and symptoms related to her client, Barney, and not only has to deal with some legal implications as a result of her lying under oath but has made many ethical violations. First, she has fabricated her reports and testimony to the social security administration (violation of D.5.b.). This can be a huge barrier that Barney needs to overcome, as once someone is diagnosed with a mental disorder; it generally follows them for the rest of their lives. Although her intentions are to help him receive disability benefits, Barney may have to deal with the stigma attached to a mental diagnosis when seeking other services. Furthermore, services (e.g., psychological) may be developed based on these falsified reports. The Judge may report Lilly to the certification and licensing boards, which will start its own investigation. However, all reports sent to third parties are now in question as to the credibility of these reports. Depending upon how many clients were served and whom these reports were sent to, it may result in opening up old cases. For example, Lilly could have testified in another person's case and benefits may have been awarded. The testimony on these previous cases may be jeopardized and re-examined.

D.5.c. PRESENTATIONS

When rehabilitation counselors provide advice or commentary by means of public lectures, demonstrations, radio or television program, recordings, technology-based applications, printed articles, mailed material, or other media, they make reasonable efforts to ensure that: (1) the statements are based on appropriate professional literature and practice; (2) the statements are otherwise consistent with the Code; and (3) it is clear that a professional counseling relationship does not exist.

Connecting members of the community to resources is one of the responsibilities of rehabilitation counselors. Dispersing information through various media can be an efficient approach to fulfilling this obligation. Making sure that what is provided is understood as a route to information for the larger community is critical in order to ensure that the sharing of information is seen as only that, rather than as a counseling relationship. Using social media to disperse information may be mistaken as a relationship; this misinterpretation must be avoided, in order to protect the public, as well as the profession.[17]

CASE STUDY

Megan was feeling conflicted about how things were going at the center. She had been taking on additional responsibilities for the

*counseling center, including getting the word out to the community
about new programs and services with the use of social media outlets
(e.g., Facebook, Twitter, etc.). This was fine with her since she enjoyed
using various types of social media. For the center, she had developed
pages that clients and potential clients could access and gain
information and contact the center. At first, it really seemed to be
working well, with contacts about services and programs doubling
over the last few months. Then something that she had not expected
happened with a former client. Megan was receiving repeated contacts
from one former client about current difficulties. The client described
what was going on in specific terms, and Megan did not know how to
respond–or whether to respond at all.*

CASE STUDY DISCUSSION

Sharing information with the larger community about the programs and
services available is one of the obligations of professionals in the human
services field, particularly in rehabilitation counseling.[19] As social media has
become an increasingly more utilized manner of sharing information with the
world community, using good judgment has become imperative.[17] For Megan,
the intention of sharing information was obvious, but for her former client it
was not. In order to deal with the current situation and to avoid further issues
going forward, Megan needs to include a description of the purpose of the
information posted, and to delineate the limitations of how the social media
pages may be used, by clients, potential clients, and staff at the organization.
Simply not responding will not be sufficient to meet the requirements of D.5 of
the Code.

D.5.d. PROFESSIONAL STATEMENTS

*When making professional statements in a public context,
regardless of media or forum, rehabilitation counselors clearly identify
whether the statements represent individual perspectives or the
position of the profession or any professional organizations with which
they may be affiliated.*

Often times, rehabilitation counselors may have the opportunity to make
personal statements in a public context (i.e., academic conference). It is
important that rehabilitation counselors understand that their statements in a
public context, although personal, may be taken as all rehabilitation counselors
have the same or similar personal beliefs. Rehabilitation counselors should
determine if their remarks can be construed in this manner, and if so, they
should avoid making such statements. If rehabilitation counselors do wish to
make personal statements in a public context, they should clarify that they are
not speaking for their colleagues, the profession, and/or a specific professional
organization.

For example, suppose a rehabilitation counselor was speaking to a local news organization about a particular political party and their stance on an important disability-related issue. The rehabilitation counselor may be asked what particular political figure(s) they would endorse and their personal stance on the issue at hand. In this situation, it is important to clarify that their personal statements on a political issue are not necessarily a reflection of how the rehabilitation counseling profession, a particular professional organization, or other rehabilitation counselors endorse and align with the statement.

D.5.e. Exploitation of Others
Rehabilitation counselors do not exploit others in their professional relationships to seek or receive unjustified personal gains, sexual favors, unfair advantages, or unearned goods or services.

It is essential to be aware of the influence the counselor has over the client and its presence in any counseling relationship. This awareness enables the counselor to avoid creating an environment that would support any form of exploitation. This is another aspect of the power dynamic of the counseling relationship, in which the counselor must safeguard the autonomy of the client.[10] Hetherington[15] suggested that exploitation in counseling occurs minimally. However, sexual exploitation is the most common form. This form of exploitation occurs because the counselor is perceived as an authority figure and in a position of power.

D.5.f. Conflict of Interest
Rehabilitation counselors recognize that their own personal or professional relationships may interfere with their ability to practice ethically and professional. Under such circumstances, rehabilitation counselors are obligated to decline participation or to limit their assistance in a manner consistent with professional obligations. Rehabilitation counselors identify, make known, and address real or apparent conflicts of interest in an attempt to maintain the public confidence and trust, discharge professional obligations, and maintain responsibility, impartiality, and accountability.

The conflict of interest standard is usually described as the counselor having a "special interest that has potential for adversely affecting professional judgment on behalf of a client."[9, pp.160-161] This can be described as a dual-relationship where the counselor occupies two or more different personal or professional roles with the same client. It should be noted that not all dual relationships are inappropriate or avoidable if handled appropriately and ethically (e.g., a rehabilitation counselor educator is a teacher in many courses and the academic advisor to the same student). This type of relationship between an educator and student where the educator is also the academic advisor is not necessarily a conflict of interest, even though the faculty member has two separate roles with the student. This could become an issue if grades are increased in return for special favors from the student (e.g., sexual).

When rehabilitation counselors are providing services to clients, they should be aware of the issues that can arise when there is a conflict of interest. For example, suppose a rehabilitation counselor is serving a client in a public VR agency and is teaching a graduate-level rehabilitation counseling course at a university in which the client is enrolled. The rehabilitation counselor is aware that the client needs to obtain a passing grade in order to continue receiving funding through their agency. In this instance, the rehabilitation counselor could have a conflict of interest because they serve the client in two separate capacities. The specific issue is that the rehabilitation counselor may provide a passing grade to their client but fail to serve in their capacity as an educator by not holding the student accountable and serving as a Gatekeeper to the profession. There are many different examples of dual relationships, and rehabilitation counselors need to become educated on the different types and consider the strengths and limitations of each of these relationships.

CASE STUDY

Natalie is a certified rehabilitation counselor and a licensed clinical professional counselor. She received her bachelor's degree in the late 1990s and has a great deal of experience in the public and private rehabilitation sectors. She opened her private counseling practice in the early 2000s and she has sought other employment opportunities to supplement her private employment. She obtained a position at the local university as an instructor. This opportunity was beneficial for Natalie because she was now receiving health insurance coverage from the university and could practice part-time in her counseling practice. She began teaching undergraduate level courses and quickly developed a rapport with students since they were interested in learning from someone with such great experience in the field. One day, she met with the graduate school faculty during a meeting where they were deciding who would be accepted into the graduate program. She started advocating for one student named Tiffany, who wanted to pursue an advanced degree. It was determined that this student should be accepted on provisional status. Natalie began to push strongly for full acceptance. She stated that she is counseling Tiffany in her private practice and knows that graduate school will help with her counseling goals. Furthermore, Natalie stated that Tiffany has had a lot of trouble related to abuse and she began to describe very pertinent details related to her counseling treatment and clinical issues. Natalie stated that she is also Tiffany's academic advisor and believes she will make it through the graduate program. The other faculty stated that Tiffany scored in the 1 percentile on all of her GRE scores (i.e., quantitative, verbal, analytic writing), has an undergraduate GPA of 2.7, and stated that she has had many personal issues that have caused extreme absenteeism from other classes due to employment related responsibilities. The other undergraduate instructor indicated that he had to provide Tiffany with a medical incomplete, even though he expects her to fail his class since she requested the incomplete with only one assignment left. He stated that Tiffany has stated numerous times that education is not her priority at this time. The other faculty stated that during the graduate school application process, they interviewed Tiffany and she stated she did not want to be a counselor but did not know what other direction to take.

CASE STUDY DISCUSSION

It is apparent that a potential conflict of interest may be present within the case study. Natalie is not only serving as Tiffany's personal counselor, but she is also her undergraduate academic advisor and instructor in many courses. Even though graduate school may be the best fit for the treatment goals that Tiffany and Natalie developed in individual counseling, Natalie should refrain from being a part of the graduate school decision-making process since she has two duties that are conflicting (counselor and academic advisor). It may not be in the best interest of the profession to allow Tiffany into the program at this time, because she has demonstrated strong academic deficiency, absenteeism, and has stated that she is not interested in counseling. Rehabilitation educators must serve as gatekeepers and protect the profession.

D.5.g. VERACITY

Rehabilitation counselors do not engage in any act or omission of a dishonest, deceitful, or fraudulent nature in the conduct of their professional activities.

The development of ethical standards within a profession are intended to protect the public and the corresponding accountability to maintain and promote those standards.[27] Specifically, Standard D.5 of the *Code of Professional Ethics for Rehabilitation Counselors (*CRCC,[6] the *Code)* is intended for the profession of rehabilitation counseling to promote ethical practice and professional responsibility to the public and other professionals. Standard D.5.f. Veracity is the principle of truth telling, which is essential to honor the person's autonomy.[38] Truth telling is violated by the act of lying or providing erroneous information to the client, as well as, by omitting all or some portions of the truth. Therefore, violating this ethical principle by withholding or providing false information to the client can eliminate or reduce a client's right to make decisions related to the rehabilitation plan.

D.5.h. DISPARAGING REMARKS

Rehabilitation counselors do not disparage individuals or groups of individuals.

Standard D.5.h., *Disparaging Remarks* can be described as derogatory statements made by the counselor directly to a client. If a rehabilitation counselor makes derogatory remarks, this can reduce the therapeutic alliance between the counselor and client. To maintain a healthy counseling relationship, the counselor must be supportive, empathetic, and set clear boundaries.[16] Mozdzierz, et al.,[23] stated that clients in the pre-contemplation stage of substance abuse treatment are one example of when counselors could potentially make derogatory statements and/or mock the client. Specifically, the client who is mandated to treatment is extremely upset with being forced into treatment when he or she does not believe they have an alcohol or drug problem. Often times, the client will be very confrontational with the counselor, especially when the counselor attempts to confront the client on their drug or alcohol use. The counselor may become frustrated with the lack of insight from the client, and intentionally or unintentionally use disparaging remarks. Although disparaging remarks may occur frequently, a study conducted by Hartley and Cartwright[14] revealed that four ethical citations were reported to the CRCC [year(s) 2006–2013] regarding counselors who were involved in making disparaging comments to individuals or groups during the provision of services.

Mozdzierz, et al.,[23] recommended that counselors receive training in how to handle situations that are heavily confrontational, which should reduce the use of disparaging remarks. Specifically, they recommended following four steps, including:

1. neutralizing the derogatory statements to the client even when the client is making disparaging remarks directed at the counselor,

2. tranquilizing the situation (i.e., help calm the clients who are upset and overwhelmed with emotion,

3. energize and positively mobilize client resources in more useful rather than useless directions, and

4. challenge client behaviors that are disruptive to client functioning and/or well-being.[p.63]

When counselors are engaging in the last step of challenging client behaviors that are disruptive, motivational interviewing techniques may be more useful in evoking client behavior change in a non-confrontational manner.[21]

CASE STUDY

James is a rehabilitation counselor at the vocational rehabilitation (VR) office and currently has a caseload of 100 clients. James recently attended the American Rehabilitation Counseling Association's conference to receive his Rehabilitation Counselor of the Year award. The local news station asked to interview James on his award and wants to ask him how societal and vocational barriers limit the inclusion of people with disabilities. The news organization is also interested in understanding how James helps his clients overcome these obstacles.

During the interview, James describes how he contacts employers to advocate for his clients. He states that employers are usually willing to hire employees with disabilities but are often unfamiliar with how to make an accommodation. After discussing the vocational challenges that people with disabilities face, the interviewer asks what his position is in relation to substance related disorders. James provided the following response: "I think individuals who use drugs or alcohol should not receive any public funding…they are choosing to use the substance and are burdens to society…." The next day, one of James's clients requests a meeting with James and a supervisor. Upon arriving at the meeting, the client angrily starts telling James that he disagrees with how he views individuals with drug or alcohol barriers. James informs the client that he thinks clients with disabilities who are drug addicts should not receive VR services, because they are a waste of taxpayer's money. The client asks if James has always felt this way and James stated: "Yes, this is why I do not allow you to receive specific services, because you probably will not show up…the job opportunity at the local distribution center was looking for persons with disabilities to hire; however, I did not inform you of this position because I knew you would be unable to continuously go to work because of your drug problem." The client stated that it is her choice if she chooses to apply for the job.

CASE STUDY DISCUSSION

It is apparent that there are three primary ethical standards that James needs to consider prior to engaging in the interview with the local news reporter, and before meeting with his client. First, he needs to consider how his personal views will impact the clients he serves. He was being interviewed for his professional accomplishments but provided a personal response when being asked about his stance on substance related disorders. He failed to clarify that this is his personal opinion. Next, James made disparaging remarks to his client, calling her a drug addict and scum of the earth. It is apparent that James has some personal resentment towards individuals who use drugs or alcohol, and this is limiting his ability to assist his client properly in obtaining employment. For example, James indicated that he is not being truthful with the client about job opportunities because he feels she will mess it up because of her drug addiction. This violates the ethical principle related to veracity because James is withholding vital job-related information, which is not allowing his client to make informed decisions.

D.6. SCIENTIFIC BASES FOR INTERVENTIONS

D.6.a. ACCEPTABLE TECHNIQUES/PROCEDURES/MODALITIES
Rehabilitation counselors use techniques/procedures/modalities that are grounded in theory and/or have an empirical or scientific foundation.

D.6.b. NEW OR NOVEL PRACTICES
When rehabilitation counselors use new or novel techniques/procedures/modalities, they explain any related potential risks, benefits, and ethical considerations. Rehabilitation counselors work to minimize any potential risks or harm when using these techniques/procedures/modalities.

D.6.c. HARMFUL PRACTICES
Rehabilitation counselors do not use techniques/procedures/modalities when evidence suggests the likelihood of harm, even if such services are requested.

D.6.d. CREDIBLE RESOURCES
Rehabilitation counselors ensure that the resources used or accessed in counseling are credible and valid (e.g., Internet sites, mobile applications, books).

In recent years there has been a growing interest and movement towards the concept of evidence-based practice (EBP) within allied health professions, including rehabilitation counseling.[18] This shift towards EBP in the field of rehabilitation counseling has largely been the result of an increased need for outcome based and cost-effective rehabilitation counseling service delivery.[3] Although many definitions exist, EBP has been described simply as the process of applying research to practice.[5] Additionally, EBP is intended to establish a professional practice that is based on theoretical knowledge and the use of the best scientific evidence available for clinical and organizational decision-making.

To adopt an EBP approach in the field of rehabilitation counseling, Dunn and Elliot[11] highlight the need to:

1. utilize a comprehensive theory-driven research agenda,

2. validate effective interventions based on this research agenda, and

3. assure the provision of empirically supported interventions based on the research evidence.

At the individual level, the process and use of EBP for rehabilitation counselors must begin by first generating clinical questions to ask, then determining the best evidence available, and finally critically appraising the evidence for validity and applicability to the particular situation.[4] Although successfully utilizing EBP in rehabilitation counseling has been met with a number of challenges, including:

1. the scope of rehabilitation services,

2. lack of scientific rigor and sophistication of rehabilitation counseling research, and

3. concern regarding rehabilitation counselors' skills to evaluate and incorporate research findings into practice.[4]

Moreover, the challenge for rehabilitation counselors to be knowledgeable of and utilize EBP in their daily practice also has important ethical implications.

According to Burker and Kazukauskas,[3] the words, "evidence-based practice" are not explicitly used in the Code of Professional Ethics for Rehabilitation Counselors (CRCC),[6] although it is implicitly woven throughout the Code. Although, from an ethical perspective, the need for all rehabilitation counseling practice to be evidence-based is apparent throughout many sections of the Code. For example, Section D.6.a states that "Rehabilitation counselors use techniques/procedures/modalities that are grounded in theory and have an empirical or scientific foundation."[6, p.13] Additionally, Section D.6.b, states that "Rehabilitation counselors ensure that the resources used or accessed in counseling are credible and valid (e.g., Internet link, books used in bibliotherapy)."[6, p.13] Burker and Kazukauskas[3] highlight the need for rehabilitation counselors to provide services that have a scientific foundation and to ensure that resources are valid. In addition, rehabilitation counselors need to access the rehabilitation literature, assess its scientific rigor, and implement it in practice. As a result, it is the ethical responsibility of all rehabilitation professionals, including rehabilitation counselors, to utilize EBP throughout all relevant aspects of their professional work. As a result, the knowledge and use of EBP among rehabilitation counselors should enhance a counselor's ability to develop high quality rehabilitation plans most effective with clients in specific situations, as well as to improve overall consumer services and outcomes.[34]

CASE STUDY

Thomas is a new rehabilitation counselor at a state vocational rehabilitation agency with a mission of providing innovative rehabilitation counseling services to a broad spectrum of individuals with disabilities. As part of his employment, Thomas is expected to be primarily involved with the initial intake interview portion of service delivery. In this role, Thomas is expected to initially meet with each consumer and provide each consumer with an overview of the services provided, obtain personal and vocational relevant information, and generally establish a strong working alliance between counselor and consumer. Before facilitating the initial intake interview on his own, Thomas is expected to observe and learn the intake interview process from a senior rehabilitation counselor, Tracey, who has over 30 years of experience in the rehabilitation counseling field facilitating the initial intake interview process with consumers. During their first meeting together, Thomas asked his fellow rehabilitation counselor colleague what particular theoretical approach and scientific foundation her intake interview approach was grounded in. The counselor responded, "Ah, none, other than the approach that seems to work for me and the client." The senior rehabilitation counselor went on to say that she used an interview approach that she was trained to use by another senior rehabilitation counselor over 30 years ago.

Around the same time that Thomas has been observing Tracey facilitate intake interviews, he has been participating in an initial employment orientation. As part of this orientation process, Thomas is introduced to motivational interviewing (MI), an emerging and evidence-based approach grounded in theory and with a growing body of empirically supported literature showing its effectiveness with varied consumers of rehabilitation counseling services. As part of the orientation, the training team provided Thomas and other trainees with relevant and current literature devoted to MI, including published journal articles and a textbook devoted to the topic. Thomas is excited to use the MI approach as part of the intake interview, once he has reviewed the relevant literature and had a chance to practice and receive feedback on the effectiveness of his use of MI techniques.

At the completion of the most recent MI training, Thomas informs Tracey of his excitement and interest in using MI techniques as part of the intake interview process. Tracey informs Thomas that she has not yet heard of MI and was therefore skeptical of its efficacy with consumers of rehabilitation counseling services. Instead, Tracey encourages Thomas to do it her way, besides, it has worked for her over the past 30 years, therefore, it should work for Thomas as well. Thomas does not want to appear to oppose Tracey, especially since he just started employment at the agency and because of her 30 years of experience in the field, although, he feels that he has an ethical obligation to use evidence-based approaches, such as MI, when conducting intake interviews present and future.

CASE STUDY DISCUSSION

Thomas is experiencing a number of challenges with regard to being exposed to and utilizing evidence-based practices as part of his initial employment at the agency. In particular, the intake interview approach that Thomas is being trained to utilize and has been used by the senior rehabilitation counselor, Tracey, appears to be in violation of both Standards D.6.a. and D.6.b. As evidence, the intake interview approach that Tracey is using appears not to be grounded in theory and/or have an empirical or scientific foundation, which is in direct violation of Standard D.6.a. Additionally, the intake interview approach that Tracey has been using has not been derived from credible and valid resources (e.g., professional, peer-reviewed journal publications) and is in direct violation of Standard D.6.b. As a result, Thomas is unsure of how to proceed with an intake interview approach, based on the mixed messages he has received from Tracey and the training team.

In conclusion, it is essential that Thomas be exposed to and encouraged to utilize evidence-based practices in all aspects of his rehabilitation counseling practice and work with consumers. In doing so, effective consumer services and successful outcomes will be strengthened. In turn, it is important that all personnel (i.e., practitioners, trainers, administrators, etc.) within the agency also utilize and advocate for the use of EBPs as an ethical mandate at their respective agency.

REFERENCES

[1]Ahmed, S. Wilson, K. B., Henriksen, R. C., & WindWalker Jones, J. (2011). What does it mean to be a culturally competent counselor? *Journal for Social Action in Counseling and Psychology, 3,* 17- 28.

[2]Baker, L. R., & Cormier, L. A. (2015). *Disasters and vulnerable populations: Evidence-based practice for the helping professions.* New York, NY: Springer Publishing Company.

[3]Burker, E. J., & Kazukauskas, K. A. (2010). Code of ethics for rehabilitation educators and counselors: A call for evidence-based practice. *Rehabilitation Education, 24*(3&4), 101-112.

[4]Chan, F., Bezyak, J., Romero Ramirez, M., Chiu, C. Y., Sung, C., & Fujikawa, M. (2010). Concepts, challenges, barriers, and opportunities related to evidence-based practice in rehabilitation counseling. *Rehabilitation Education, 24*(3&4), 179-190.

[5]Chronister, J. A., Fang, F., da Silva Cardosa, E., Lynch, R. T., & Rosenthal, D. A. (2008). The evidence-based practice movement in healthcare: Implications for rehabilitation. *Journal of Rehabilitation, 74*(2), 6-15.

[6]Commission on Rehabilitation Counselor Certification (2017). *Code of professional ethics for rehabilitation counselors.* Schaumburg, IL: Author.

[7]Corrigan, P. W. (2002). *On the stigma of mental illness: Practical strategies for research and social change.* Washington, D.C.: American Psychological Association.

[8]Cramton, R. C. (1981). Incompetence: The North American Experience. In L. E., Trakman & D. Watters (Eds.). *Professional competence and the law* (pp. 158-163). Halifax, Nova Scotia, Canada: Dalhousie University.

[9]Davis, M., & Stark, A. (2001). *Practical and professional ethics: Conflict of interest in the professions.* New York, NY: Oxford University Press.

[10]Day, A. (2010). Psychotherapists' experience of power in the psychotherapy relationship. Middlesex University's Research Repository. Retrieved from: http://eprints.mdx.ac.uk/13049/

[11]Dunn, D. S., & Elliot, T. R. (2008). The place and promise of theory in rehabilitation psychology. *Rehabilitation Psychology*, 53(3), 254-267.

[12]Emerson, S., Markos, P. A. (1996). Signs and symptoms of the impaired counselor. *Journal of Humanistic Education & Development, 34* (3), 28-37.

[13]Harris Interactive and National Organization on Disability. (2005). *Emergency preparedness topline results.* Study number 26441. Retrieved August 28, 2015, from http://www.nod.org/Resources/PDFs/episurvey05.pdf.

[14]Hartley, M. T., & Cartwright, B. Y. (2015). Analysis of the reported ethical complaints and violations to the Commission on Rehabilitation Counselor Certification, 2006-2013. *Rehabilitation Counseling Bulletin, 58*(3), 154-164.

[15]Heatherington, A. (2010). Exploitation in therapy and counseling: A breach of professional standards. *British Journal of Guidance & Counseling, 28*(1), 11-22.

[16]Ivey, A. E., Ivey, M. B., & Zalaquett, C. P. (2013). *Intentional interviewing & counseling: Facilitating client development in a multicultural society* (8th ed.). Independence, KY: Cengage Learning.

[17]Jain, S. H. (2009). Practicing medicine in the age of Facebook. *New England Journal of Medicine, 361,* 649-651.

[18]Leahy, M. J., & Arokiasamy, C. V. (2010). Prologue: Evidence-based practice research and knowledge translation in rehabilitation counseling. *Rehabilitation Education, 24*(3&4), 173-176.

[19]Leahy, M. J., Chan, F., & Saunders, J. L. (2003). Job functions and knowledge requirements of certified rehabilitation counselors in the 21st century. *Rehabilitation counseling bulletin, 46,* 266-281.

[20]Locke, D. C., Myers, J. E., & Herr, E. L. (2001). *The handbook of counseling.* Thousand Oaks, CA: Sage Publications Inc.

[21]Miller, W. R., & Rollnick, S. (2012). *Motivational interviewing: Helping people change* (3rd ed.). New York, NY: Guilford Press.

[22]Mills, M. A., Edmondson, D., & Park, C. L. (2007). Trauma and stress response among Hurricane Katrina evacuees. *American Journal of Public Health, 97*(1), 116-123.

[23]Mozdzierz, G. J., Peluso, P. R., & Lisiecki, J. (2014). *Advanced principles of counseling and psychotherapy: Learning, integrating, and consolidating the nonlinear thinking of master practitioners.* New York, NY: Routledge.

[24]National Organization on Disability (2001). *Guide on the special needs of people with disabilities: For emergency managers, planners & responders.* Retrieved from http://dola.colorado.gov/dem/publications/ Guide_on_special_needs_people.pdf

[25]Pedersen, P. B., Lonner, W. J., & Draguns, J. G. (Eds.). (1976). *Counseling across cultures.* Honolulu: University Press of Hawaii.

[26]Rubin, S. E., & Roessler, R. T. (2008). *Foundations of the vocational rehabilitation process* (6th ed.). Austin, TX: Pro-ed.

[27]Saunders, J. L., Barros-Bailey, M., Rudmand, R., Dew, D. W., Garcia, J. (2007). Ethical complaints and violations in rehabilitation counseling: An analysis of commission on rehabilitation counselor certification data. *Rehabilitation Counseling Bulletin, 51*(1), 7-13.

[28]Schneider, K. T., Swan, S., & Fitzgerald, L. F. (1997). Job-related and psychological effects of sexual harassment in the workplace: Empirical evidence from two organizations. *Journal of Applied Psychology, 82*(3), 401-415.

[29]Sheffield, D. S. (1998). Counselor impairment: Moving toward a concise definition and protocol. *Journal of Humanistic Counselling, Education & Development, 33*(22), 96–106.

[30]Sprong, M. E., Lewis, T. A., Soldner, J. L., & Koch, D. S. (2011). Emergency preparedness for persons with disabilities: Implications for rehabilitation administrators. *Journal of Rehabilitation Administration, 35*(1), 27-38.

[31]Sprong, M. E., Cioe, N., Yalamanchili, P., & McDermott, A. (2015). Principles of Ethics. In J. Stano (Eds.), Ethics in Rehabilitation Counseling: A Case Study Approach. Osage Beech, MO: Aspen Professional Services.

[32]Stadler, H. A., Willing, K. L., Eberhage, M. G., & Ward, W. H. (1988). Impairment: Implications for the counseling profession. *Journal of Counseling & Development, 66*(6), 258.

[33]Sue, S., Zane, N., Nagayama Hall, G. C., & Berger, L. K. (2009). The Case for Cultural Competency in Psychotherapeutic Interventions. *Annual Review of Psychology, 60*, 525–548. doi:10.1146/annurev.psych.60.110707.163651

[34]Tarvydas, V., Addy, A., & Fleming, A. (2010). Reconciling evidenced-based research practice with rehabilitation philosophy, ethics, and practice: From dichotomy to dialetic. *Rehabilitation Education, 24*(3), 191-204.

[35]U.S. Department of Homeland Security: Federal Emergency Management Agency. (2010). *Emergency planning for special needs communities: Participant Guide.* Morgantown, WV: Homeland Security Programs.

[36]U.S. Equal Employment Opportunity Commission (EEOC). (2012). Federal Equal Employment Opportunity (EEO) Laws. Retrieved from http://www.eeoc.gov/facts/qanda.html

[37]Weems, C. F., Pina, A. A., Costa, N. M., Watts, S. E., Taylor, L. K., & Cannon, M. F. (2007). Predisaster trait anxiety and negative affect predict posttraumatic stress in youths after Hurricane Katrina. *Journal of Consulting and Clinical Psychology, 75,* 154-159.

[38]Welfel, E. R. (2012). *Ethics in counseling & psychotherapy: Standards, research, and emerging issues.* Belmont, CA: Brooks/Cole.

[39]Wilson, K. B., & Gines, J. E. (2009). A national reassessment: Exploring variable that predispose people with disabilities to vocational rehabilitation acceptance. *Rehabilitation Education, 2,* 159-170.

CHAPTER 8

RELATIONSHIPS WITH OTHER PROFESSIONALS AND EMPLOYERS

CINDY ZABINSKI

BRANDON HUNT

SECTION E: RELATIONSHIPS WITH OTHER PROFESSIONALS AND EMPLOYERS

E.1 RELATIONSHIPS WITH COLLEAGUES, EMPLOYERS, AND EMPLOYEES

E.1.a. DIFFERENT PROFESSIONAL APPROACHES

Rehabilitation counselors are respectful of approaches that are grounded in theory and/or have an empirical or scientific foundation but may differ from their own. Rehabilitation counselors acknowledge the expertise of other professional groups and are respectful of their practices.

To provide effective and ethical services, rehabilitation counselors need to be aware of counseling approaches and interventions that are grounded in research and stay current on the emerging rehabilitation counseling literature. They also need to be aware of their own cultural beliefs and attitudes and how their life experiences might affect their work in addition to being aware of their clients' cultural backgrounds. This awareness includes openness to learning about new cultures, including discussing clients' beliefs and how those beliefs or cultural practices might affect their working together. Awareness also includes receiving supervision to ensure the counselor is not inadvertently showing bias.

CASE STUDY

Tammy is a Certified Rehabilitation Counselor working as a vocational counselor in a community mental health agency. She was recently referred a 25-year old Catholic male client who has a diagnosis of bipolar disorder by his private counselor, who is a faith-based counselor in the Catholic community. The client arrived for the appointment, and suggested Tammy join him in a prayer as they began their work, similar to how he begins sessions with his private counselor.

Tammy was surprised by this. However, she supported the client in his prayer. As Tammy continued the vocational intake with the client, he often brought up his faith and the role his religion plays in him choosing a career path. This felt uncomfortable to Tammy, as her religious views were different and she had never had a client bring their religion into vocational work before.

After the session, Tammy realized she needed to learn more about faith-based counseling and practices, so she reached out to the client's personal counselor (with consent from the client) and asked about the client's work in counseling. During that meeting and with additional research she learned more about the way in which religion can play a role in a person's career search, coping with the vocational process, and life in general. She also learned more about faith-based counseling and the experience the client had in working with his counselor.

The client returned for his second appointment, and Tammy felt much more comfortable working with him. The client appeared more at ease with Tammy, knowing she took the time to reach out to his counselor and learn about her work with him. They continued working together in a way that respected his religious beliefs and his work with his private counselor, while also providing the services he needed to attain stable gainful employment.

E.1.b. NEGATIVE EMPLOYMENT CONDITIONS

The acceptance of employment in an organization implies that rehabilitation counselors are in agreement with its general policies and principles. Rehabilitation counselors alert their employers of unethical policies and practices. They attempt to effect changes in such policies or procedures through constructive action within the organization. When such policies are inconsistent with the Code, potentially disruptive or damaging to clients, and/or limit the effectiveness of services provided, rehabilitation counselors take necessary action if change cannot be affected. Such action may include referral to appropriate certification, accreditation, or licensure organizations. Ultimately, voluntary termination of employment may be the necessary action.

Rehabilitation counselors have a responsibility to be engaged members of their agency, and that includes working to make sure the agency is running as effectively and efficiently as possible. In cases where agency practice or policy might create an unethical and even potentially harmful situation or prevent counselors from doing their work as well as possible, rehabilitation counselors have a responsibility to make suggestions for ways to improve the situation. Rather than just being frustrated about the problem, rehabilitation counselors must take steps to resolve the problem.

CASE STUDY

Marcus has worked at the same proprietary rehabilitation counseling agency for 10 years. He has primarily worked with clients who have work-related injuries. The agency employs 24 other rehabilitation counselors. A year ago, the company came under new management and they implemented a policy about how insurance paperwork was handled. Previously counselors submitted their own paperwork to the insurance company, but the new policy required that counselors submit the paperwork to an accounting clerk who then submitted the reimbursement paperwork.

It is important that reimbursement paperwork be submitted in a timely manner so clients can receive services and they can return to work. Marcus noticed it was taking longer and longer to get approval from the insurance company to provide services to his clients and after some exploration he learned that the insurance company was now receiving the reimbursement forms in batches three times a month, rather than on a daily basis like before.

He met with the accounting clerk, who explained she was submitting the paperwork according to the agency policy. Marcus met with his supervisor and outlined how the new policy was having a negative effect on clients in terms of receiving services in a timely manner. Marcus provided an alternative plan for submitting paperwork. His supervisor took this plan to her supervisors and the company revised the policy so the accounting clerk could submit reimbursement paperwork two times a week. Clients were then able to receive services in a timely manner.

E.1.c. PROTECTION FROM PUNITIVE ACTION AND RETALIATION
Rehabilitation counselors, whether in an employee or supervisory role, take care not to dismiss, threaten, or otherwise retaliate against employees who have acted in a responsible and

ethical manner to expose inappropriate employer policies or practices, Code violations, or suspected Code violations.

Part of the ethical responsibility of rehabilitation counselors is to ensure their colleagues are also acting in an ethical and responsible manner. The intent of this standard is to provide protection for rehabilitation counselors who raise concerns about how agency policies and procedures are put into practice. It is similar to whistleblower laws that protect people who report negative or inappropriate behavior or actions in the workplace. This substandard provides support for rehabilitation counselors to come forward when they have concerns about agency policies and practices, including behavior of supervisory and administrative staff.

CASE STUDY

Margaret learned her supervisor was submitting insurance paperwork for clients who were no longer receiving services. When she raised her concern with Sylvia, her supervisor, Sylvia said the agency was reimbursed for service on a quarterly basis so it was acceptable to submit paperwork for the remainder of the quarter even if the client was no longer receiving services. Margaret met with Sylvia's supervisor, who then met with Sylvia and told her to stop the practice of billing for clients who were no longer receiving services.

A month before she met with her supervisor to discuss her billing concerns, Margaret submitted a request to attend an all-day training conference and Sylvia verbally approved her request. Two weeks after the billing incident was resolved, Margaret received an email from Sylvia stating there was no funding for Margaret to go to the training. The next day Margaret learned her supervisor granted approval for four rehabilitation counselors in her division to attend an all-day training on crisis intervention.

Due to her previous positive experience with Sylvia's supervisor, Margaret returned to him to discuss this concern, and a meeting between Margaret, Sylvia, and Sylvia's supervisor helped all of them to discuss their concerns and move forward in working together cooperatively.

E.1.d. PERSONNEL SELECTION AND ASSIGNMENT

Rehabilitation counselors select competent and appropriately credentialed staff and assign responsibilities compatible with their education, skills, and experiences.

Rehabilitation counselors who are in a position to hire new staff are not only responsible for ensuring the new staff have the necessary education and credentials for the position, but they should also ensure the staff have the necessary experience and counseling skills to provide effective and appropriate services to clients. Depending upon the rehabilitation counselors' role, they should provide supervision or arrange for the new hire to receive supervision, particularly early in the new hire's employment. It is the responsibility of the employer to provide staff with any additional training required to fulfill responsibilities for their role if they do not have the previous experience or skills needed.

CASE STUDY

Angelique was recently promoted to supervisor at a community mental health agency and she just hired a new counselor, Samantha. Because this was the first staff person she was responsible for hiring, Angelique interviewed the top three applicants twice and personally called all of their references. Angelique felt confident about her choice but thought it would be good to schedule weekly meetings for the first two months of Samantha's employment and to co-sign all of her case notes. While there was no agency policy about this Angelique's supervisor supported her decision.

After the three weeks, Angelique was impressed with the quality of work Samantha was providing her clients, but she noticed Samantha's case notes did not reflect individual client differences and read more like a template that she used for all clients. Angelique met with Samantha to review her case notes and learned her previous agency required staff use the same template for all case notes. They discussed the importance of why case notes should be individualized, and Samantha agreed to change her note writing style.

After two weeks, Angelique realized the notes were still not client specific enough, so she met with Samantha to review specific notes and discuss ways to revise them. After this meeting, Samantha's notes became more informative and Samantha said she found the new method helpful for her as a counselor. As a result, Angelique talked with her supervisor and arranged to have a note writing training session for all the counselors since they had not received agency training on this topic for a number of years.

E.1.e. EMPLOYMENT PRACTICES

Rehabilitation counselors, as either employers or employees, engage in fair employment practices with regard to hiring, promoting, and training.

Hiring, promoting, and training decisions should be equal and fair for all rehabilitation counselors. Decisions should not be made about who to hire, promote, or train that could be based on bias or favoritism for one counselor over another, but instead should be based on experience and merit.

CASE STUDY

Darcy has been working as a rehabilitation counselor at a non-profit agency for 9 years. Darcy has received numerous letters of recognition for her work with her clients and she consistently receives positive annual reviews. She has worked under the same supervisor for two years, and twice in the past year, she has applied for a promotion to clinical supervisor. Another counselor was selected both times.

During a conversation at lunch with a colleague, Darcy learned that her current supervisor told another supervisor she would not promote Darcy because she needed her to continue to work with her caseload, which is one of the more challenging caseloads in the agency. Darcy chose not to approach her supervisor about what she heard since her supervisor was the person who did not select her for the promotion. Instead, she applied for other jobs and within six weeks Darcy was hired as a clinical supervisor at another agency. She was happy to have her hard work and dedication to the field recognized and continued her efforts in supervising ten counselors at this new agency.

E.2 ORGANIZATION AND TEAM RELATIONSHIPS

E.2.a. TEAMWORK

Rehabilitation counselors who are members of interdisciplinary teams delivering multifaceted services to clients must keep the focus on how to serve clients best. They participate in and contribute to decisions that affect the well-being of clients by drawing on the perspectives, values, and experiences of their profession and those of colleagues from other disciplines. Rehabilitation counselors promote mutual understanding of rehabilitation plans by all team members cooperating in the rehabilitation of clients.

The focus of rehabilitation counselors is to assist clients in achieving their rehabilitation goals. Interventions used by rehabilitation counselors are best determined by examining what the rehabilitation counselor and other members of the treatment team have observed as effective in the past, and by using evidence-based treatment approaches that exist within the counseling profession and other helping professions.

Each professional focuses on different aspects of clients depending on the nature of their work. It is important that all professionals collaborate on client treatment plans since a collaborative approach within an interdisciplinary treatment team allows the strengths of each professional to be maximized when working with clients. It also helps ensure no two professionals negate the work of the other by promoting a goal that does not match the goals that are being worked on with other professionals and enables the team to create treatment plans together with clients that will promote wellness and attainment of client goals.

CASE STUDY

Matthew, a rehabilitation counselor who works in a sober house, meets weekly with Richard to discuss the possibility of employment and what types of jobs may be best for him at this point in his sobriety. Matthew notices Richard has difficulty being alert at the morning house meetings. Matthew, from his past work with other sober house residents, knows clients have benefitted from focusing on increasing the amount of exercise they engage in and decreasing the naps they take during the day. Richard reports a change in these behaviors, but still appears sluggish at their meetings. Matthew, unsure of what else to do, begins to focus with Richard on looking for job opportunities that require him to work in the afternoon, so his morning sluggishness will not affect his job performance.

Richard may become employed, and in a job that he enjoys very much, however, his issue of being tired in the mornings has not been addressed. Matthew would have benefitted from bringing this concern to the treatment team meeting or collaborating with professionals from other disciplines within the agency. Matthew could have spoken with the agency psychiatrist, Dr. Smith, who may have suggested a psychiatric consultation to discuss the possibility of Richard having depression, which can be treated with psychotropic medication and counseling. Dr. Smith may also suggest Richard be evaluated by his primary care physician to be prescribed a non-addictive sleep medication. These suggestions may not be apparent to Matthew due to his training and experiences so far in his job. Having professionals from different disciplines within the agency could help Matthew obtain various perspectives about client situations and possible solutions to concerns that clients have.

E.2.b. TEAM DECISION-MAKING

Rehabilitation counselors implement team decisions in rehabilitation plans and procedures, even when not personally agreeing with such decisions, unless these decisions breach the Code. When team decisions raise ethical concerns, rehabilitation counselors first attempt to resolve the concerns within the team. If they cannot reach resolution among team members, rehabilitation counselors recuse themselves and consider other approaches to address their concerns consistent with the well-being of clients.

Rehabilitation counselors abide by the ethical code of their profession, the Code of Professional Ethics for Rehabilitation Counselors. Likewise, other professionals who they may work with on a treatment team are to abide by the ethical codes of their professions. In working together as a team, it is important for rehabilitation counselors to voice any concerns when making team decisions if any suggestions appear to be unethical within the Code. Rehabilitation counselors must also respect the ethical codes of other professionals. This may result in helping implement decisions they may not fully support, but that adhere to professional codes of all team members.

When rehabilitation counselors believe a decision being made within the interdisciplinary team violates the Code of Professional Ethics for Rehabilitation Counselors, it is best to discuss the concern first with the members of the team. Rehabilitation counselors may bring their copy of the Code to the meeting, and read aloud the standard/substandard they believe would be violated. The counselors may also suggest alternative decisions that would abide by the Code. If the team disagrees with the rehabilitation counselors, the counselors may choose to seek supervision from their superior regarding their concern. If rehabilitation counselors continue to feel decisions being made within the agency are unethical, they may choose to contact the CRCC ethical board and/or may seek employment at an agency that abides by the Code of Professional Ethics for Rehabilitation Counselors.

CASE STUDY

Ed is a rehabilitation counselor at an outpatient substance abuse clinic. He works with many other types of professionals, including psychiatrists, psychologists, certified substance abuse counselors, social workers, and professional counselors. He is the only rehabilitation counselor at the clinic. At a team meeting, a coworker, Ann, brings up an adult client they are working with who has a sister who calls Ann frequently. Ann reports that there is no release of information signed by the client, but she became so frustrated with the constant phone calls that she gave in to discussing the client's treatment with the sister. Ed does not agree with this, but since he knows that he is the only rehabilitation counselor at the clinic, and his Code may be different from the ethical code of other professionals, he remains quiet and allows the meeting to continue.

The ethical code of all professionals involved in a treatment team must be considered when working with a client. Ed could best handle the situation by raising a concern during the treatment team meeting, referencing the section of his Code that he believes is being violated within the agency. Through discussion, the team will decide if the decision is indeed unethical, and if so, will consider alternative options. If the majority of the team decides the original decision is the best option, does not pose harm to the client, and is ethical under their respective Codes, then Ed should schedule a meeting with his supervisor to discuss his concern.

E.2.C. DOCUMENTATION

Rehabilitation counselors attempt to obtain from other specialists appropriate reports and evaluations when such reports are essential for rehabilitation planning and/or service delivery.

All professionals have their specialty areas and may work within different aspects of each client's life. Therefore, communication between all professionals is important. When rehabilitation counselors sit down with clients, clients will focus on facts and descriptions of areas that they feel are important for the counselor to know. If clients do not feel certain things are important to share even if it would be important for the counselors to know, they may not disclose much detail about that area.

Rehabilitation counselors would benefit from requesting a release of information for all other professionals working with clients in order to receive reports about the services being provided about a client's progress. This helps rehabilitation counselors understand current conditions affecting clients to assist them in creating attainable goals and overcoming obstacles.

CASE STUDY

Lindsay, a rehabilitation counselor working in an outpatient psychiatric rehabilitation program, is assigned a new client who was referred by a nearby psychiatric hospital. During the evaluation process, Lindsay is informed the client was diagnosed with Type II diabetes and has a monthly appointment with a diabetes specialist. The client recently relapsed in the use of cocaine and alcohol, and the client attends an outpatient substance abuse program down the street. The client assures Lindsay that she takes care of her diabetes and has been abstinent from drugs and alcohol for some time now. Lindsay accepts the client's reports as fact and works with the client on her treatment plan for the psychiatric program.

In this situation, it is not to say that Lindsay should not believe what the client is reporting. Rather, it is important for Lindsay to confirm the information with the other specialists the client is working with and become aware of details the client may not have thought important to disclose. Lindsay should obtain informed consent from the client and contact the client's diabetes physician, psychiatric hospital, and substance abuse program for reports, which will help Lindsay understand the client's history, current condition, and help her in developing the client's rehabilitation plan with the client. Lindsay could learn from the reports of other specialists that the client complies with the medication prescribed to help manage her diabetes but has not yet made necessary changes to her lifestyle (i.e., food intake and exercise) that her physician has recommended. Lindsay may also become aware of more details about the client's history of substance use, rather than only relying on the verbal report the client provided. Having this additional information could help Lindsay ensure she is effectively and ethically meeting the comprehensive needs of her client.

E.2.d. CLIENTS AS TEAM MEMBERS

Rehabilitation counselors make reasonable efforts to ensure that clients and/or their legally authorized representatives are afforded the opportunity for full participation in decisions related to the services they receive. Only those with a need to know are allowed access to the information of clients, and only then upon a properly executed release of information request or receipt of a court order.

All services rehabilitation counselors provide to clients are meant to benefit the clients. Since no one knows clients better than they know themselves, it is crucial that clients are actively involved in any decisions made. In the event clients are incapable of representing themselves, their legally recognized representatives should be involved. Clients and/or their legally recognized representatives have a right to decide who is permitted to be aware of the services they are receiving and the progress they are making within those services. Informed consent is needed regarding the nature of the information to be released, and should be outlined in a manner that both parties clearly understand. It is also important for rehabilitation counselors to explain the information that may be released if a court order is received.

CASE STUDY

Kimberly is a rehabilitation counselor who works with clients who have developmental disabilities. She is working with Denise, who is currently living in a house with five other adult females who also have developmental disabilities. Denise has been doing very well, taking care of herself physically, attending all programming events, completing all assigned chores, and socializing with her fellow housemates. Kimberly has worked with many clients within the program who have moved into their own apartment after successfully living in a house for a period of one year and have done very well. Kimberly thinks Denise will benefit from a similar experience and begins to provide information about Denise to other housing programs that offer individual apartment-style housing options for clients with developmental disabilities. She has several phone conversations with counselors in these programs about Denise's progress, and is excited to tell Denise that she is accepted into a nearby apartment. Denise immediately becomes upset.

Kimberly may know a great deal about Denise from working with her for a period of time, however, even though other clients have had success in entering individual housing options, this does not mean that changing Denise's housing is in her best interest. It would be best for Kimberly to sit down with Denise first and discuss the options she has regarding her housing. Kimberly may find out Denise prefers to live with other people for social reasons or that she has anxieties about living alone that must be processed before taking further action.

Since Denise is the person receiving services, she also has the right to decide who is permitted to receive information about her involvement and progress in services. Denise may not want to have her information sent to certain housing agencies if she has family or friends who work there that she does not want to have contact with. Without having these important discussions with Denise, Kimberly will not be acting in the best interest of the client.

E.3. PROVISION OF CONSULTATION SERVICES

E.3.a. CONSULTATION

As consultants, rehabilitation counselors only discuss information necessary to achieve the purpose of the consultation. When engaging in formal and informal consultation, rehabilitation counselors refrain from discussing confidential information that reasonably could lead to the identification of a client unless client consent has been obtained or the disclosure cannot be avoided. Rehabilitation counselors refrain from providing consultation when they are engaged in a personal or professional role that compromises their ability to provide effective assistance to clients.

Rehabilitation counselors work with a variety of clients and at some point will work with clients who have certain concerns or issues with which the counselor does not feel competent. In these situations, it is appropriate and ethical for the rehabilitation counselor to seek assistance from a consultant or a person who is knowledgeable about the topic. Often, rehabilitation counselors may turn to people within their own agency who have training in areas in which they may not be trained. If the appropriate consultant is not present at the agency, rehabilitation counselors may seek consultation from other professionals in the field.

CASE STUDY

Joe is a rehabilitation counselor working in a vocational program who specializes in working with clients who have psychiatric disorders. He is assigned a new client, Mary, who expresses during her first session that she has an extensive legal history and is unsure how that will affect her ability to obtain stable gainful employment. Joe recalls talking about legal history in his classes 15 years ago but does not remember much about the topic. He is new to the agency, however, and does not want his new coworkers to think he is not fit for the job. Mary also appears sad about having such a history and Joe wants to give her hope. Joe assures Mary that her ability to become employed will not be affected by her legal history.

Due to Joe's lack of knowledge in this area, it is unethical for him to provide information about which he is unsure. He would benefit from consulting with another counselor on his treatment team who specializes in working with people who have legal histories. Joe and the consultant can discuss Mary's concerns and resources that she may benefit from using. Treatment teams are best formed with rehabilitation counselors who specialize in different areas, as consultation can regularly occur when situations like these arise. The treatment team should be understanding of Joe seeking assistance, as all treatment team members use consultation at some point in their careers.

E.3.b. CONSULTANT COMPETENCY

Rehabilitation counselors provide consultation only in areas in which they are competent. They make reasonable efforts to ensure they have the appropriate resources and competencies. Rehabilitation counselors provide appropriate referral resources when requested or needed.

Rehabilitation counselors may serve as consultants, whether it is within their agency as part of a treatment team or as a fee for service self-employment opportunity. By accepting work as consultants with other professionals, it is expected that rehabilitation counselors are competent in the areas of concern that consultees present and have a wealth of resources available to offer.

When rehabilitation counselors are approached for consultation purposes and they do not have adequate training in the area of concern it is unethical for them to serve as a consultant. The rehabilitation counselors must instead refer consultees to professionals who have the necessary training. Likewise, if consultants become aware of concerns regarding their competencies during the consultation process, they must explain this to consultees and refer them to professionals who are competent in that area.

CASE STUDY

Beth, who supervises a Veterans Administration outpatient rehabilitation clinic, was approached by Ted, one of the clinic's counselors. Ted reported one of his clients is prescribed an antidepressant; however, Ted is concerned the antidepressant is not effective because the client has not shown any improvement in symptoms in the past three months. Ted also reported the client has been complaining of sexual side effects that Ted believes may be due to the antidepressant. Beth has little knowledge about this medication, so she looks it up online, and notices on a website that sexual side effects are common for people prescribed this medication. She also noticed that a person made a comment on the website saying that there was a different antidepressant that worked better. Beth tells Ted to inform the client to stop taking the medication, and the next time the client sees the psychiatrist they can discuss the alternative medication.

Rehabilitation counselors, like all other professionals, have training within a specific realm. Beth, as a rehabilitation counselor, is not trained as a medical doctor, and therefore it is unethical for her to make decisions about a client's medication. Using websites for information is also problematic, as the validity of the information on the website is questionable. Even though Beth is the supervisor of the clinic, it would be ethical for her to refer Ted to the treatment team's psychiatrist to discuss this concern. The psychiatrist is more knowledgeable about the antidepressant that the client is currently taking and alternatives that have a basis in medical research on the treatment of depression. Beth can explain to Ted she appreciates him approaching her to discuss this and provide Ted with the best way to get in contact with the team's psychiatrist so the issue can be discussed in a timely manner.

E.3.c. Informed Consent in Consultation

When providing consultation, rehabilitation counselors have an obligation to review, in writing and verbally, the rights, responsibilities, and roles of both rehabilitation counselors and consultees. Rehabilitation counselors use clear and understandable language to inform all parties involved about the purpose of the

*services to be provided, relevant costs, potential risks and benefits,
and the limits of confidentiality. Working in conjunction with the
consultees, rehabilitation counselors attempt to develop a clear
definition of the problem, goals for change, and predicted
consequences of interventions that are culturally responsive and
appropriate to the needs of consultees.*

In the event rehabilitation counselors are approached to be consultants, it is important not to provide clinical recommendations immediately. First, rehabilitation counselors must establish the appropriate relationship with consultees through discussion of the roles the consultant and consultee will serve in the relationship, as well as all expectations of services that will be provided. This information should also exist in written form and be signed by both parties, and both parties should have a copy of the agreement.

Beyond discussion and agreement regarding the terms of the relationship, it is also important for rehabilitation counselors to understand the problem presented by the consultees. In any consultation work, rehabilitation counselors must consider cultural aspects of the problem and the people involved in order to provide possible goals and interventions that meet the needs of the consultees.

CASE STUDY

*Erica, a rehabilitation counselor who works in a state
vocational program, is contacted for consultation via phone by
Brian, a schoolteacher. Brian is working with a student who has an
IEP, but Brian is concerned the IEP is not appropriate for the
student based on his behavior in the classroom. Erica immediately
agrees to assist Brian and listens to Brian's concerns for about ten
minutes on the same phone call. Erica informs Brian she will call
him back the following day with recommendations. The next day,
Erica leaves a voicemail for Brian with a few ideas regarding
working with this student and sends a bill to him for the consultation
services. Brian, after listening to the voicemail, begins using the
ideas presented, which are not culturally appropriate for the child,
and is surprised and perplexed upon receiving a bill in the mail.*

*The initial phone call would have best been used to determine if
Erica was competent to assist Brian with his concerns, and to set up*

a meeting between the two professionals. At the meeting, Erica and Brian could discuss details of the work Erica would be doing, and establish guidelines for the services Erica would provide, the cost, the possible risks and benefits, and possible limitations to confidentiality. Once this is agreed upon, Brian could explain his concerns in more detail, and Erica could ask questions necessary to understand the problem, including possible cultural aspects, prior to presenting any possible goals and interventions. This would ensure both parties fully understood the consultation relationship, and that the goals and interventions provided would be appropriate and beneficial to the student.

DISCUSSION QUESTIONS

1. You are a supervisor in a vocational rehabilitation program looking to hire a rehabilitation counselor. You have received five resumes: two are from friends of people who currently work in the program, one is from an old colleague of yours, and two are from other professionals who have worked in the field. How would you go about the hiring process?

2. You are working with a client in an inpatient psychiatric program to identify possible vocational options. You notice the client is having difficulty focusing on tasks and staying on topic in conversations with you, and you begin to consider ways in which this may affect her vocational options. What other types of clinicians employed in the program would you want to consult with before completing your assessment? Explain why.

3. A client moves into the community residence where you are a rehabilitation counselor. This client is from a culture unfamiliar to you. What steps do you take to ensure the client receives culturally appropriate services?

4. You are working in an outpatient psychiatric day program. In meeting with a client being admitted to the program, he tells you he has been in ten inpatient psychiatric programs, the latest of which he completed one week ago. He also has a private psychiatrist and private counselor he has been seeing on and off for the past three

years. What reports/evaluations are important for you to request? How would you go about requesting them?

5. You have been working for 15 years with clients who have addictions. A colleague contacts you because she does not have any experience working with clients who have addiction issues, and one of her new clients is diagnosed with Alcohol Use Disorder, Severe in addition to mental health issues. What steps would you want to take before agreeing to enter into a consultation relationship with your colleague?

CHAPTER 9

FORENSIC SERVICES

CHERIE L. KING

SECTION F. FORENSIC SERVICES

The Rehabilitation Counseling profession has seen an expansion of roles and functions over the last few decades. Beginning in the 1970s, many rehabilitation counselors made a shift from the public or non-profit sector to start careers in the private sector.[6] Private rehabilitation firms, insurance carriers, corporations, and those self-employed created new employment settings for the rehabilitation counselor, expanding beyond traditional vocational rehabilitation into other areas, (e.g., insurance rehabilitation, case management, employer-based disability management, and forensic rehabilitation). This expansion created a shift in service focus and clearly altered the traditional purpose of rehabilitation counseling and the role of the rehabilitation counselor by mediating the traditional client-centered outcomes with an increased emphasis on utilizing rehabilitation counseling competences for cost containment and in the legal realms.[9]

Forensic rehabilitation services evolved and were refined to address the differences in roles and functions of the rehabilitation counselor. Forensic rehabilitation services are defined by the CRC Code as "providing expertise involving the application of professional knowledge and the use of scientific, technical, or other specific knowledge for the resolution of legal or administrative issues, proceedings, or decision" (glossary). Specifically, forensic rehabilitation practice utilizes rehabilitation counseling expertise in legal settings, (e.g., Workers' Compensation, Social Security, personal injury, medical malpractice, product liability, and divorce). Many forensic rehabilitation counselors function as vocational expert (VE) witnesses and forensic consultants in these settings.[7] For example, attorneys often hire VEs to provide opinions regarding the vocational and economic impact of disabilities on an individual's employability and earning capacity. In the Social Security Disability (SSDI) and Supplemental Security Income (SSI) systems, VEs are utilized at the administrative law hearing to provide opinions on a claimant's vocational potential and employability in the labor market.

In these contexts, forensic rehabilitation counselors function as vocational experts and do not provide direct services to individuals with disabilities. The differentiating context is that no counseling relationship is created between the evaluee and rehabilitation counselor.[1] Hence the label of "evaluee" replaces "client." The relationship between a rehabilitation counselor and evaluee is complicated in the forensic context by involvement of third parties, (e.g., attorneys, insurance carriers, the government, and employers) thus creating complex and potentially conflicting roles.

F.1. EVALUEE RIGHTS

F.1.a. PRIMARY OBLIGATIONS

Forensic rehabilitation counselors produce unbiased, objective opinions and findings that can be substantiated by information and methodologies appropriate to the service being provided, which may include evaluation, research, and/or review of records. Forensic rehabilitation counselors form opinions based on their professional knowledge and expertise, which are supported by the data. Forensic rehabilitation counselors define the limits of their opinions or testimony, especially when there is no direct contact with an evaluee. Forensic rehabilitation counselors acting as consultants or expert witnesses may or may not generate written documentation regarding involvement in a case.

This sub-standard relates to the professional obligation of the forensic rehabilitation counselor to strive for objectivity in providing professional forensic services. Rehabilitation counselors are expected to provide balanced and impartial expert opinions grounded in accepted methodology by utilizing accepted sources and appropriate documentation. Forensic rehabilitation counselors must define the confines of professional judgments and findings. When in the role, they must maintain accepted records that include case notes and reports related to their work with an evaluee and referral sources.

CASE STUDY

John is referred to a Worker's Compensation case to conduct a vocational assessment regarding an injured worker. He is provided with medical records from the Workers' Compensation insurance adjuster. The injured worker is represented by an attorney who does not give John permission to conduct a vocational interview or meet with the injured worker. John performs a hypothetical vocational assessment based upon the record he is provided which is missing information. John does not have complete information regarding the injured worker's employment and educational background, functional work capacity, or medical information. Due to an impending hearing, John is under a tight deadline to produce a report. He submits the report based upon the information he has without noting the limitations to his vocational opinion.

ETHICAL CONSIDERATIONS

1. Did John violate this standard?

2. What do you think are the limitations of a "hypothetical vocational evaluation?"

3. How might John have better served the needs of this injured worker?

F.1.b. INFORMED CONSENT

When an evaluation is conducted, the evaluee is informed in writing that the relationship is for the purpose of an evaluation and that a report of findings may or may not be produced. Written consent for an evaluation is obtained from the evaluee or the evaluee's legally authorized representative unless a court or legal jurisdiction orders an evaluation to be conducted without the written consent of the evaluee or when an evaluee is deceased. If written consent is not obtained, forensic rehabilitation counselors document verbal consent and the reasons why obtaining written consent was not possible. When a minor or person unable to give voluntary consent is evaluated, informed consent is obtained from the evaluee's legally authorized representative.

Informed consent is embedded in the philosophy of rehabilitation counseling. One aspect of informed consent is the autonomy of evaluees and the ability to make decision for themselves.[5] In cases where there is a question of autonomy, forensic rehabilitation counselors must secure appropriate documentation as to the ability of the evaluee to give consent. In cases where this is in question, the forensic rehabilitation counselor must be able to secure alternative consent from parents, guardians, or conservator.

CASE STUDY

Susan is hired by an insurance company to perform a vocational assessment of a 25-year-old male who sustained a traumatic brain injury due to a car accident. As Susan is preparing for the assessment interview, she reviews all of the medical and psychological records on the evaluee since the injury. She finds two neuropsychological evaluations conducted within 6 months of each other. One evaluation indicates that the evaluee has permanent functional limitations related to executive processing, memory, and judgment. The other evaluation and records do not mention this information.

The insurance company indicates that the evaluee has an attorney and that the evaluee is living at home with his parents and not

*working. He is able to perform his own activities of daily living but has
an Independent Living Skills Trainer (ILST) who comes to the home
every day to assist with cognitive rehabilitation and living skills. When
Sally is preparing for the assessment, she is unable to determine if the
evaluee will be able to fully understand the purpose of assessment and
provide written consent.*

ETHICAL CONSIDERATIONS
1.   How should Susan proceed in the context of informed consent?

F.1.c. ROLE CHANGES
*Forensic rehabilitation counselors carefully evaluate and
document the risks and benefits to evaluees before initiating role
changes. When forensic rehabilitation counselors change roles from
the original or most recent contracted relationship, they discuss the
implications of the role change with the evaluee, including possible
risks and benefits (e.g., financial, legal, personal, or therapeutic). They
complete a new professional disclosure form with the evaluee and
explain the right to refuse services related to the change, as well as the
availability of alternate service providers. Forensic rehabilitation
counselors refrain from frequent and/or indiscriminate role changes.
When changing roles more than one time, forensic rehabilitation
counselors evaluate and document the risks and benefits of multiple
changes.*

The Code requires that forensic rehabilitation counselors do not mingle
roles that can create significant objectivity concerns. Risks and benefits of role
changes need to be reviewed and if deemed appropriate, then new professional
disclosure which defines the new role be explicit. The purpose of this is to keep
the role of the forensic rehabilitation counselor and the rehabilitation counselor
as clear as possible.

CASE STUDY

*Sam worked for many years as a vocational rehabilitation
counselor in the state vocational rehabilitation agency. He then left
this job to begin his own forensic rehabilitation practice. After a year
in practice, he received a referral from a local attorney to conduct a
forensic vocational assessment on a 50-year-old woman who, due to a
back injury, had been unable to work for the last 8 years. In addition,
she experienced chronic pain that impacted her psychologically and
had been in treatment for many years for depression since the injury.
Sam reviewed the referral records in the case and realized that he
had worked for one year with the evaluee while he was a state VR*

*counselor. He had determined that she was an excellent candidate for
VR services and had developed an employment plan in collaboration
with the evaluee. She had returned to a new job for only 6 weeks and
then was unable to continue due to her chronic pain and depression.
After many months of follow up, Sam closed her case because she was
unable to return to work. Due to his past counselor-client relationship
and vocational rehabilitation work with the evaluee, Sam feels he is
able to provide a strong opinion for the forensic assessment.*

ETHICAL CONSIDERATIONS

1. Would his past exposure to this client be a help or hindrance to
   Sam?

2. What are the risks and/or benefits to changing his role and the
   impact on the evaluee?

3. How should Sam proceed?

F.1.d. CONSULTATION

*Forensic rehabilitation counselors may act as case consultants.
The role as a case consultant may or may not be disclosed to other
involved parties. When there is no intent to meet directly with an
evaluee, whether in person or using any other form of communication,
professional disclosure by the forensic rehabilitation counselor is not
required.*

The recent revision of the CRCC Code clarified the ethical question of
"who is the client" in forensic rehabilitation contexts. Vocational evaluation in
forensic rehabilitation requires forensic rehabilitation counselors to conduct
vocational evaluations to assess the employability and earning capacity of an
individual with a disability for insurance or legal purposes. The forensic
rehabilitation professional who is engaged as the evaluator does not have a
client. Rather, the evaluee is the subject of an objective and unbiased evaluation
and not a recipient of rehabilitation counseling services.[3] Although the evaluee
is not the rehabilitation counselor's "client," there remains a question regarding
the ethical responsibility to disclose the nature of the relationship and the
services provided when there is no face to face contact with the evaluee.
Professional disclosure is the act of sharing information with the evaluee that is
necessary in order to clarify the role and nature of the rehabilitation process and
services.[8] The code specifically says that a forensic rehabilitation counselor
who does not have contact with evaluee does not require professional
disclosure.

CASE STUDY

Andrea is a rehabilitation counselor who is retained by an insurance company to perform a forensic vocational evaluation on a claimant receiving Long Term Disability (LTD) benefits. Andrea is unable to contact the claimant to schedule a face to face evaluation as instructed by the LTD carrier. After a review of the records, Andrea performs a transferable skills analysis and labor market survey to document the claimant's employability. Andrea submits her report to the LTD carrier. Based on Andrea's vocational opinion that the claimant was capable of working in any occupation, the claimant's LTD benefit is terminated. The claimant appeals the termination decision.

ETHICAL CONSIDERATIONS

1. What were Andrea's obligations for disclosure in this scenario?

2. Do you think the claimant is justified in her appeal?

F.2. FORENSIC COMPETENCY AND CONDUCT

F.2.a. OBJECTIVITY

Forensic rehabilitation counselors are aware of the standards governing their roles in performing forensic services. Forensic rehabilitation counselors are aware of the occasionally competing demands placed upon them by these standards and the requirements of the legal system. They attempt to resolve these conflicts by making known their commitment to this Code and taking steps to resolve conflicts in a responsible manner.

Forensic rehabilitation counselors working as Vocational Experts are often asked to provide vocational opinions in legal settings in which competing interests may influence the rehabilitation counselor's objectivity. In Workers' Compensation settings, forensic rehabilitation counselors are often retained to perform assessments on injured workers who are represented by attorneys. Depending on the state Workers' Compensation laws, attorneys and injured workers have the right to refuse to meet with a forensic rehabilitation counselor for the purposes of a forensic vocational assessment.

Conflict can result in discord concerning professional ethics and accountability, how to balance the evaluee needs, demands of third parties, and referral sources.[2] In these situations, forensic rehabilitation counselors can conduct an assessment without face-to-face contact with the evaluee and rely on the medical, functional, and vocational records provided to perform the assessment. They may also be asked to testify regarding the results of their assessment. Forensic rehabilitation counselors must be aware of the ethical implications of providing a vocational opinion in writing or through testimony without the benefit of a face-to-face examination of the evaluee.

CASE STUDY

Amy received a referral from a Workers' Compensation carrier to perform a forensic assessment. The Workers' Compensation claim adjuster provides her with the most recent medical records and vocational information on the injured worker. The records show that the independent medical examination (IME) determined that the injured worker has a functional capacity of light work. There is also some information from the injured worker's treating physician that indicates the worker does not have a work capacity.

Amy talks with the claim adjuster about the discrepancy and asks for additional information on the injured worker's capacity. The claim adjuster indicates that the treating physician never provides work capacities and requests that Amy conduct the assessment based on the IME results. Amy is not given permission to meet with the injured worker and conducts the assessment based on the records. Based on the information she has been given, Amy determines that the injured worker is employable in several light work jobs.

Amy is asked to testify in a deposition on the results of her assessment. In the deposition, Amy testifies that the injured worker is employable but does not disclose that she did not have face-to-face contact with the injured worker for the assessment. The injured worker's attorney cross-examines Amy and provides new work capacity information that was not provided to her by the Workers' Compensation claim adjuster. The injured worker's attorney shows Amy a recent Functional Capacity Evaluation (FCE) report and the treating physician's report that determine that the injured worker does not have a work capacity at this time. Amy is asked to provide her opinion of the injured workers employability given the new functional capacity and medical information.

ETHICAL CONSIDERATIONS

1. Did Amy's failure to disclose the fact that she had no face-to face contact with the injured worker "set her up" for the situation she finds herself in?

2. How should Amy respond to the attorney's request to give her opinion of the injured worker's employability given the new information?

F.2.b. QUALIFICATION TO PROVIDE EXPERT TESTIMONY
Forensic rehabilitation counselors have an obligation to present to finders of fact the boundaries of their competence, the factual bases (knowledge, skill, experience, training, and education) for their qualifications as experts, and the relevance of those factual bases to their qualifications as experts on the specific matters at issue.

To perform the roles and functions of a forensic rehabilitation counselor, it is necessary to prepare professionally beyond the bounds of their rehabilitation counseling education and work experience. In cases requiring forensic assessment in which a forensic rehabilitation counselor is to qualify as a vocational expert witness for hearings, deposition, and/or trials, the rehabilitation counselor must have the necessary certifications, additional training, and educational requirements necessary to be considered an "expert."

CASE STUDY

Edward is a rehabilitation counselor for a non-profit agency serving adults with developmental disabilities. Edward has a master's degree in Rehabilitation Services and is CRC credentialed. His job history involves working with both youth and adults with intellectual and co-occurring disabilities by providing job skills training and job placement. Edward is interested in expanding his career opportunities and takes part in an on-line webinar called "Forensic Rehabilitation 101." Based on his assessment of his work experience and educational background, he decides to start marketing himself as a Vocational Expert to area Workers' Compensation and Social Security Disability attorneys. He is able to get a few vocational assessment referrals.
He is asked to testify in a deposition regarding one of his reports. In qualifying as an expert, he is asked about his experience and training working with injured workers, work injury cases, and understanding of medical and functional information, and the labor market. Edward testifies he completed an online training program.

ETHICAL CONSIDERATIONS

1. Does Edward qualify as an expert? Why or why not?

F.2.c. AVOIDING POTENTIALLY HARMFUL RELATIONSHIPS
Forensic rehabilitation counselors who provide forensic evaluations do not enter into potentially harmful professional or personal relationships with current evaluees or their family members, romantic partners, and close friends. Rehabilitation counselors give careful consideration to the potential for sexual or romantic

*relationships to cause harm to former evaluees. In cases where the
former evaluee is at risk of potential exploitation and/or harm,
rehabilitation counselors avoid entering into such interactions or
relationships.*

Conducting assessments or providing forensic evaluations for individuals
who have a relationship with the rehabilitation counselor is a challenging
situation. For example, many rural areas or small communities have limited
resources and professionals to provide such services. Forensic rehabilitation
counselors can potentially be in situations where they are the only qualified
professional to conduct a forensic assessment on someone they know, have a
close personal relationship with (relatives, partners), or a close connection
through others (friend of a friend). Forensic rehabilitation counselors must
carefully evaluate the risk of providing or not providing forensic services to
such individuals and need to use an ethical decision-making model or process
to assess fully the potential for harm.

CASE STUDY

*Alex is a private rehabilitation consultant who practices in a rural
area in the Northwest. She is the only forensic rehabilitation counselor
within 8 hours of her community. Alex's sister-in-law has been
receiving LTD benefits from a disability insurance carrier for many
years. Alex's sister-in-law calls to ask for her help as her LTD benefits
have been terminated. The LTD insurance carrier states that the sister-
in-law is employable and able to work, thus no longer is disabled by
the contract definition.*

*Alex's sister-in-law asks Alex to assist her in getting her benefits
reinstated by helping her prove she is still too disabled to work. Alex
spends a lot of time with her sister-in-law and sees first-hand the
struggles she has in functioning in everyday activities. Alex has also
worked for many LTD insurance carriers as a rehabilitation
consultant. As a result, she understands the claim and appeal process.
Alex is certain her sister-in-law cannot work but is reluctant to enter
into a "professional" relationship with her sister-in-law.*

ETHICAL CONSIDERATIONS

1. What are the pros and cons of Alex entering a "professional
   relationship" with her sister-in-law?

2. Should the fact that Alex believes her sister-in-law cannot work
   have any bearing on her decision?

F.2.d. CONFLICT OF INTEREST

Forensic rehabilitation counselors recognize their own personal or professional relationships with parties to a legal proceeding may interfere with their ability to practice ethically and professionally. Under such circumstances, forensic rehabilitation counselors are obligated to decline participation or to limit their assistance in a manner consistent with professional obligations. Forensic rehabilitation counselors identify, make known, and address real or apparent conflicts of interest in an attempt to maintain public confidence and trust, fulfill professional obligations, and maintain objectivity, impartiality, and accountability

A conflict of interest is when a forensic rehabilitation counselor is involved in numerous interests, which could potentially influence their motives and professional judgment. In the forensic services context, primary attention to conflict of interest is focused on the protection of evaluees. In addition, consideration of other conflicts such as financial gain ahead of evaluee interests is also a concern. Forensic rehabilitation counselors need to be clear about their own values, beliefs, and relationships that may influence or interfere with objective practice.

CASE STUDY

Frank is a forensic rehabilitation counselor who is well known and utilized frequently by attorneys as the best in the city. He has received many referrals from a local attorney and over the years has become friendly with the attorney. They socialize frequently by playing golf or having dinner and eventually become close friends. The attorney asks Frank to be the Godfather to his new child. Due to the positive references and use of professional referrals, the referring attorney is the main reason Frank's practice has grown and he has been able to take on several employees. Frank receives a new referral from this attorney that could mean a lot of work and income for Frank. He is concerned about the potential conflict he may have given his relationship with the attorney but is also concerned about the success of his business.

ETHICAL CONSIDERATIONS

1. How might Frank deal with this conflict of interest?

2. Would using an employee to serve this referral source resolve this conflict? Why or why not?

F.2.e. VALIDITY OF RESOURCES CONSULTED
Forensic rehabilitation counselors make reasonable efforts to ensure the resources used or accessed in supporting opinions are credible and valid.

Forensic rehabilitation counselors use many professional resources and validated data when conducting assessments and labor market surveys in order to provide forensic opinions. Resources such as transferable skills analysis software and methodologies, current state and government occupational data, and employment statistics are used to help a forensic rehabilitation counselor provide accurate information to support their employability and rehabilitation assessment of an individual with a disability. It is important that forensic rehabilitation counselors utilize the most accurate, up to date, and accepted data standards in order to form and maintain the credibility of their opinions.

CASE STUDY

Shannon is a vocational expert (VE) for the Social Security Administration. She is asked to testify in a hearing regarding the vocational and employability aspects of a case for Social Security Disability Insurance (SSDI) benefits. Mary reviews the case in preparation for the hearing. In the hearing, she is able to gather additional information regarding the applicant's current status.

The Administrative Law Judge presiding over the hearing poses several hypothetical situations in which Shannon must provide her opinion regarding the applicant's employability, types of occupations the applicant could perform, and the number of these jobs within the state and nationally. Shannon identifies three occupations from the Dictionary of Occupational Titles (DOT) and uses state and national occupational statistical data published several years ago. Shannon states that these occupations are in abundance in the local and national labor market.

ETHICAL CONSIDERATIONS

1. The DOT is no longer maintained by the federal Department of Labor. How can Shannon justify using this resource to make recommendations for a claimant?

2. What other resources could Shannon use that would help her better comply with this ethical standard?

F.2.f. FOUNDATION OF KNOWLEDGE

Forensic rehabilitation counselors have an obligation to maintain current knowledge of scientific, professional, and legal developments within their area of competence. They use knowledge, consistent with accepted clinical and scientific standards, and accepted data collection methods and procedures for evaluation, treatment, consultation, or scholarly/empirical investigations.

In their role as a forensic rehabilitation counselor, it is important to maintain the highest level of knowledge and skill in order to stay current in the field. Forensic rehabilitation professionals who do not integrate and seek new knowledge and stay abreast of new developments in the field are at risk of making decisions and providing opinions regarding evaluees that may be harmful. Ethical practice as a forensic rehabilitation counselor includes continued education through many avenues such as attending training workshops, conferences, reading current professional literature and research, and learning new methodology and resources in the field. Part of this maintenance of professional knowledge is to understand, utilize, and explain how data and resources (clinical and scientific) are accepted within the profession of forensic rehabilitation services. Without an on-going plan and process for maintaining current practice, the forensic rehabilitation counselor is at risk of reducing professional credibility and harming the evaluee.

CASE STUDY

Adam has been a forensic rehabilitation counselor in private practice for 15 years. At the time he was entering the practice of forensic rehabilitation, he was faithful in attending local and national forensic rehabilitation conferences and workshops to build his skills and learn new approaches and methodology. He was also very active in a professional association and maintained additional certifications beyond the CRC. Adam's practice was incredibly busy and he was receiving more referrals than he could handle. As Adam accepted more and more referrals and cases, he gradually stopped his involvement in the professional association and his attendance at workshops and conferences decreased. He also did not have time to read any of the professional literature related to forensic rehabilitation practice and research. His business was booming, but he was producing work that was based on his knowledge and practice standards from 15 years ago. In several cases, he based vocational opinions on dated occupational analysis methodology and determined that the evaluees were employable and there was no loss of earning capacity. This resulted in evaluee benefits being terminated.

ETHICAL CONSIDERATIONS

1. Adam is clearly in violation of this standard. What things can he do to bring his practice into compliance with this standard?

2. Is this problem serious enough that he should suspend his practice until he has dealt with this issue? Why or why not?

F.2.g. DUTY TO CONFIRM INFORMATION

Where circumstances reasonably permit, forensic rehabilitation counselors seek to obtain independent verification of data relied upon as part of their professional services to the court or to parties to the legal proceedings.

Reliable information and data are the most important part of the forensic rehabilitation professional's role in forensic cases. It is important that forensic rehabilitation counselors are knowledgeable and up to date on the admissibility of information and data depending on the systems they are providing forensic services. For example, an evaluee's legal status is an important piece of data in some legal systems and in others can be considered prejudicial. Forensic rehabilitation counselors need to know what data is permitted and how they independently verify the data.

CASE STUDY

Mary is a VR counselor who has received a case from a carrier for Workers' Compensation. She is asked to perform forensic assessment and loss of wage earning capacity on an injured worker who may be an undocumented worker. There is no documentation if this is true and through her interview with the injured worker, he denies he is undocumented but does not have appropriate paperwork. The injured worker's employer has been uncooperative about providing any verification. In her state of practice, the undocumented nature of the injured worker is considered an important piece of information in the Workers' Compensation system. This is Mary's first Workers' Compensation case and is concerned about the status of the injured worker.

ETHICAL CONSIDERATION

1. How should Mary proceed?

F.2.h. REVIEW/CRITIQUE OF OPPOSING WORK PRODUCT

When evaluating or commenting upon the work or qualifications of other professionals involved in legal proceedings, forensic rehabilitation counselors seek to represent their differences of opinion in a professional and respectful tone and base their opinions on an objective examination of the data, theories, standards, and opinions of the other experts or professionals.

In some cases, forensic rehabilitation counselors are asked to review other expert's work and to provide their own opinions regarding the work product or the expert's credentials. In these cases, forensic rehabilitation counselors may opine that the opposing expert's work is flawed in terms of methodology, accepted criterion, and conclusions. It is important for the forensic rehabilitation counselor to be fair and balanced in providing the review and opinion based upon the objective facts and data of the case. Providing discrediting or inaccurate opinions of other experts and their work product is a violation of the intent of this sub-standard in the Code.

CASE STUDY

Ellen is a forensic rehabilitation counselor for Workers' Compensation. She is asked by a plaintiff attorney to review the credentials and a report prepared by another expert. Ellen has a master's degree in Rehabilitation Counseling and has been a CRC for 20 years. She also obtained additional credentials through the American Board of Vocational Experts (ABVE) and has been practicing as a forensic rehabilitation expert for 10 years.

The opposing expert works for a small case management firm. The expert has a master's degree in Mental Health Counseling and is not a CRC. In reviewing the report, Mary finds many gaps in information, inaccuracies related to the medical information, incorrect transferable skills analyses, and inappropriate use of labor market data. In sum, Mary completely disagrees with the opposing expert's opinion and questions the credibility and credentials of the opposing expert to be considered an expert in the case. Mary is asked to create a report and also testify as to her findings related to the opposing expert's work and credentials. Mary writes and testifies that based on her experience and training, the opposing expert is not an expert and discredits the opposing report as unprofessional and amateurish.

ETHICAL CONSIDERATION

1. How can Mary handled this situation without violating the ethical standard?

F.3. FORENSIC PRACTICES

F.3.a. CASE ACCEPTANCE AND INDEPENDENT OPINION

Forensic rehabilitation counselors have the right to accept any referral within their area(s) of expertise. They decline involvement in cases when asked to support predetermined positions, assume invalid representation of facts, alter their methodology or process without foundation or compelling reasons, or when they have ethical concerns about the nature of the requested assignments.

Due to the nature of forensic rehabilitation work, many third parties such as insurance carriers, attorneys, or employers are involved with disability cases. For example, a Long Term Disability carrier is providing a disability benefit to an individual who meets the policy definition of what is disability and inability to work. Many policies are limited to two years of disability benefits if an employee is disabled from their own occupation. After two years, the definition of disability within the policy changes to disability and inability to work in any occupation based on transferable skills, education, and work experience. As a cost containment effort, it is in the interest of the LTD carrier to determine that an employee is not disabled after the two-year period.

A forensic rehabilitation counselor is used frequently to review these cases and determine employability based on the record. It is important that the forensic rehabilitation counselor utilize objectivity in reviewing all records and data without influence from the referral source (i.e., LTD carrier or attorney). If a forensic rehabilitation counselor is asked to only review records and render an opinion based on what benefits the carrier, it is important that the Forensic rehabilitation counselor understand their ethical right to decline a case.

CASE STUDY

John is a forensic rehabilitation counselor and is retained by a plaintiff attorney to dispute a vocational assessment and labor market survey prepared by an opposing expert for a Workers' Compensation carrier. The plaintiff attorney indicates to John that his opinion is that his evaluee (the injured worker) is totally disabled and unable to work ever again. He also feels that any vocational rehabilitation services would not be beneficial to his client. He provides John with only the opposing report and selected records. He also sits in on the vocational interview with the evaluee and interjects throughout the interview. He answers many questions for the evaluee and coaches the evaluee on how to respond. John has difficulty communicating to the attorney that objectivity and gathering information from the evaluee without influence is critical. The attorney indicates to John that his client is uneducated and does not understand the process and says that he has many similar client cases. He also indicates that if this case settles positively and he is able to settle the case for a large amount of money, John will definitely get additional referrals that would be lucrative for the attorney and John. John is in private practice and depends on consistent referrals for income.

ETHICAL CONSIDERATIONS

1. Do you believe John can have an ethical relationship with this attorney?
2. How should John proceed?

F.3.b. TERMINATION AND ASSIGNMENT TRANSFER
If it is necessary to withdraw from a case after having been retained, forensic rehabilitation counselors make reasonable efforts to assist evaluees and/or referral sources in locating another forensic rehabilitation counselor to accept the assignment.

Occasionally, due to personal or professional reasons, a forensic rehabilitation counselor must withdraw or terminate work on a case. It is their ethical responsibility to assist the referring sources in locating another forensic rehabilitation counselor to handle the case. In addition, they must be prepared to fairly resolve any financial remuneration as a result of being retained.

CASE STUDY

Kevin has been given a retainer of $5000 to provide forensic services in a medical malpractice case. The evaluee has permanent functional limitations resulting from a back surgery. Kevin begins work on the case and the referring attorney asks him to put it on-hold for several months. In the meantime, Kevin decides to close his practice and change careers. He informs the referring attorney who then asks Kevin to help find a new forensic rehabilitation counselor to work on the case. Kevin agrees to provide the attorney with other names but never follows through.

ETHICAL CONSIDERATION

1. Kevin has violated this standard in two ways. What are they?

F.4. FORENSIC BUSINESS PRACTICES

F.4.a. PAYMENTS AND OUTCOME

Forensic rehabilitation counselors do not enter into financial agreements that may compromise the quality of their services or otherwise raise questions as to their credibility. Forensic rehabilitation counselors neither give nor receive commissions, rebates, contingency or referral fees, gifts, or any other form of remuneration when accepting cases or referring evaluees for professional services. Payment for services is never contingent on an outcome of a case or award

Due to the legal and business context of forensic cases, forensic rehabilitation counselors are hired by plaintiff and defense attorneys, employers, insurance carriers, and government entities to assess, evaluate, analyze, and opine regarding disability, employability, and loss of earnings. In order to be retained and paid to provide these services, forensic rehabilitation counselors must be clear regarding financial arrangements for retainers and payments.

Standardized retainer and payment agreements between forensic rehabilitation counselors and referral sources are common and must unambiguously delineate the responsibilities of the forensic rehabilitation counselor's scope of services and the payment obligations of the referral party. The CRC Code states that rehabilitation counselors must be cognizant of "entering into financial agreements that could compromise the quality of their services or raise questions as to their credibility."F.4.a. The results of assessments, findings, opinions, and report outcomes are not to be connected to any payment for services. Rehabilitation counselors working in forensic settings are not to accept cases and payments for services based on contingencies.

CASE STUDY

Larry has been marketing his services to a Long Term Disability (LTD) insurance company. He has been seeking referrals from this carrier since he has seen a decrease in referrals from his Workers Compensation customers. He is interested in performing employability evaluations and Labor Market Surveys to determine if claimants with disabilities are able to work and the availability of job openings in their area. Larry is told by the LTD carrier that in order to receive referrals, he must agree to their pre-determined payments for initial vocational evaluations and Labor Market Surveys. He is also told that in order to receive additional referrals in the future, he must agree to their payment structure.

ETHICAL CONSIDERATION

1. Would Larry be in violation of this standard if he agreed to the insurance company's payment structure? Why or why not?

F.4.b. FEE DISPUTES

Should fee disputes arise during the course of evaluating cases, forensic rehabilitation counselors have the right to discontinue their involvement.

A forensic rehabilitation counselors has the right to dispute fee and payment disagreements as they are evaluating cases and prior to legal proceedings such as trials. Fee disputes can include lack of payment for work performed in preparation for trial or deposition. If the forensic rehabilitation counselor is not satisfied with the status of fee disagreements, they can discontinue involvement in cases.

CASE STUDY

Steve, a forensic rehabilitation counselor, was retained by an attorney representing an injured worker in a Workers' Compensation case. The agreement between the attorney and Steve was that he was to be paid an initial retainer fee of $2000 to perform the vocational evaluation and records review to prepare a report for a hearing. Any additional services beyond the initial assessment and report (i.e., preparation for deposition/testimony, actual deposition or hearing testimony, or additional research or reports) would be billed as services were completed. The agreement stated that payments for services billed must be current if Steve was to continue work on the case. The attorney requested that Steve prepare additional labor market and wage earning information after the submission of the initial report. Steve completed the work and provided an invoice for his time to the attorney. After 30 days, Steve had not received payment for the additional services. He was contacted by the attorney to testify at a Workers' Compensation hearing the next week. Steve inquired about the outstanding bill and he was told by the attorney that he could not pay Steve until the case was settled.

ETHICAL CONSIDERATION

1. Is Steve obligated to show up at the hearing and testify?

REFERENCES

[1]Barros-Bailey, M., Carlisle, J., & Blackwell, T. L. (2010). Forensic ethics and indirect practice for the rehabilitation counselor. Rehabilitation Counseling Bulletin, 53(4), 237-242. doi:10.1177/0034355210368728

[2]Blackwell, T. L., Strohmer, D. C., Belcas, E. M., & Burton, E. K. (2002). Ethics in rehabilitation counselor supervision. Rehabilitation Counseling Bulletin, 45(4), 240-247.

[3]King, C. L. (2011). Rehabilitation counselor supervision in the private sector: A qualitative examination of long-term disability. The Rehabilitation Professional, 19(3), 83-92.

[4]Kontosh, L. G. (2000). Ethical rehabilitation counseling in a managed care environment. Journal of Rehabilitation, 66(3), 9-13.

[5]Maki, D. R, & Tarvydas, V. M. (2012). The professional practice of rehabilitation counseling. New York; Springer.

[6]Matkin, R., & Riggar, T. (1986). The rise of private sector rehabilitation and its effects on training programs. Journal of Rehabilitation, 52(2), 50-58.

[7]Shaw, L. R., Fong, C., Lam, C. S., & McDougall, A. (2004). Professional Disclosure Practices of Rehabilitation Counselors. Rehabilitation Counseling Bulletin, 48(1), 38-50.

[8]Shaw, L. R., & Tarvydas, V. M. (2001). Ethical practice and rehabilitation counselor education. Journal of Applied Rehabilitation Counseling, 32(4), 10-19.

[9]Vaughn, B. T., Taylor, D. W., & Wright, W. R. (1998). Ethical dilemmas encountered by private sector rehabilitation practitioners. Journal of Rehabilitation, 64(4), 47-52.

CHAPTER 10

ETHICS IN ASSESSMENT

ANDREA PERKINS NERLICH

SANG QIN

AMANDA BOYD

SECTION G: EVALUATION, ASSESSMENT, AND INTERPRETATION

Assessment and evaluation–or more generally, information gathering–is the first phase in the rehabilitation process, although it permeates all phases of the process.[18] It promotes consumer self-awareness, provides insight into one's potential, and guides the plan development process.[19] Assessment is a major job function and knowledge domain within rehabilitation counseling (RC) service provision, including testing and evaluation techniques, transferable skills analysis, and interpretation of results for rehabilitation planning purposes.[11] Accredited rehabilitation counseling graduate program curricula all address the principles, purposes, and techniques of assessment,[7] but the extent to which that knowledge gets put into practice in a competent manner beyond graduation varies from professional to professional. Those who do engage in assessment service delivery need to learn techniques through a reputable, supervised process and remain up-to-date with their knowledge and skills, as well as trends in the field. Regardless of whether or not assessment and evaluation is a primary job function for an individual counselor, all rehabilitation counselors need to be competent consumers of assessment services and information to translate it into meaningful and attainable goals for consumers.

The principles of informed consent, confidentiality, and cultural competence pervade the CRCC ethical standards related to evaluation, assessment, and interpretation. Accountability for upholding these principles not only dictates the conduct of the rehabilitation counselor, but it is also the ethical responsibility of the counselor to oversee that these standards are maintained in third party relationships (i.e., contracted evaluation services). Rehabilitation counselors are charged with the ethical tasks of ensuring the safety, comfort, and understanding of consumers and their families; facilitating the provision of culturally-sensitive, individualized assessment techniques; and safeguarding the integrity of assessment instruments and the evaluation process. As such, the following provides interpretation and elucidation of the substandard governing ethical assessment practices.

G.1. INFORMED CONSENT

G.1.a. EXPLANATION TO CLIENTS

Rehabilitation counselors explain the nature and purpose of the assessment or evaluation process, and the potential use of the results, prior to initiating the process. The explanation is given in the language and cognitive level of clients (or other legally authorized persons on behalf of clients) unless an explicit exception has been agreed upon in advance. Rehabilitation counselors consider the personal or cultural context of clients and the impact of the results on clients. Regardless of whether scoring and interpretation are completed by rehabilitation counselors, by assistants, or by computer or other outside services, rehabilitation counselors make reasonable efforts to ensure that appropriate explanations are given to clients.

At the heart of this substandard is the value of empowerment, which is the core to the rehabilitation counseling profession. In order for a person to become empowered, they must have clear information to drive the process; this leads to consumer direction, or the philosophy that an informed consumer has more control over the actions in their life. Kosciulek's[10] Consumer-Directed Theory of Empowerment outlines that increased consumer direction within the rehabilitation service delivery system allows for greater community integration, empowerment, and quality of life among people with disabilities. Here, knowledge truly *is* power.

Within the provision of assessment services, there are typically many professionals involved, but the ultimate ethical responsibility falls to the rehabilitation counselor to ensure a consumer is comfortable and informed along the way. Consumers often do not have the technical skills to interpret scores and reports on their own, relying on the counselor to allay concerns and present results in plain and practical language. Counselors, however, should not only be concerned with assuring consumers understand the *outcomes* of the assessment process; the substandard also reflects that information regarding assessment should be provided *before* an evaluation begins–including what will occur, why it is happening, and how the results will affect them. With the goal of any evaluation being to optimize a consumer's performance,[14] a clear orientation and dialogue about expectations set the stage for this to occur.

CASE STUDY

Mauricio primarily works with youth transitioning from high school to adult roles. To facilitate the planning process for the final year of school and post-graduation, he typically has students complete a comprehensive vocational evaluation the summer before at a local non-profit agency. At the completion of the evaluation, Mauricio either meets with each student and their family at the evaluation site, where the evaluator discusses the results; or, when this is not possible, schedules an assessment results meeting at his office. He prefers to do this within 30 days of the end of the evaluation, so the experience is "fresh" in the students' minds. Mauricio has attempted to set a date with his student, Sal, and his family three times, but family vacations, car trouble, and other conflicts have kept this from happening. He is

worried that summer is ending and he will not have a chance to meet
with them before the beginning of the school year, in advance of the
annual IEP meeting. Mauricio decides to mail the report home to Sal.
The following week, he receives a frantic, sobbing phone message from
Sal: "Mauricio, this is hopeless! I guess I'm stupid. I scored in the 50's
and 60's [percentile scores] on all of these tests. I failed! No one will
ever hire me."

G.1.b. RECIPIENTS OF RESULTS

Rehabilitation counselors consider the welfare of clients, explicit
understandings, and prior agreements in determining who receives the
assessment or evaluation results. Rehabilitation counselors include
accurate and appropriate interpretations with any release of individual
or group assessment or evaluation results. Issues of cultural diversity,
when present, are taken into consideration when providing
interpretations and releasing information.

Both legal and ethical mandates guide rehabilitation counselors in decisions
regarding the dissemination and release of assessment results.[17] Typically,
agency policy will dictate the need for a signed, current release of information
on the part of the consumer, or their guardian, before information can be
provided to a third party. Those individuals who have reached the age of
majority have access to their own records and have control over who should
receive results; even in circumstances where assessment has been mandated.
The spirit of this substandard would be to inform consumers at the outset of the
evaluation as to who would be receiving the results and how it would impact
them.[5] Even when a consumer grants permission for the release of assessment
information, the rehabilitation counselor should be accurate, but still prudent in
the extent of information provided to a third party. Over the course of
interviewing and evaluation, a consumer may reveal personal information
above and beyond the scope of the evaluation. Counselors may also face
situations where the consumer requests to withhold information from certain
parties or omit information from the report. Counselors should consider the
overall welfare of the consumer, purpose of the evaluation, and nature of the
request when determining the breadth of information to be shared where legally
allowable, erring on the side of discretion to maintain the working alliance.

CASE STUDY

Joe works at a community agency that provides counseling for
people who are blind or have low vision. Their services include
vocational evaluations, support and advocacy, counseling services,
and linkages to other community supports. Joe met with Sophia, a 19-
year-old high school student who is legally blind. She reported the

*need for documentation regarding the extent to which her disability
impacts her and recommendations for appropriate accommodations to
send to the colleges to which she has applied. Sophia's motivation to
advocate for herself and go away to college impressed Joe. He was
discouraged to hear her parents do not support her goals and believe
her disability will prevent her from being successful on a college
campus. Joe completed a series of tests with Sophia and compiled the
necessary report. Shortly after, he received a voicemail from Sophia's
mother, who expressed concern about her daughter applying to
colleges. Joe wished her parents could focus more on Sophia's abilities
rather than her limitations. He hoped he could influence this
perspective and shared with her mother the positive results of the
evaluation. Shortly after doing so, he received a voicemail from Sophia
expressing her anger that he spoke to her mother without her consent.*

G.2. RELEASE OF ASSESSMENT OF EVALUATION INFORMATION

G.2.a. MISUSE OF RESULTS
*Rehabilitation counselors do not misuse assessment or evaluation
results, including test results and interpretations, and take reasonable
steps to prevent the misuse of such by others.*

The misuse of test results can generally be avoided by counselors if they:

1. have acquired a proper level of training and competency to
    interpret the results, and

2. do not make assertions or assumptions outside their scope of
    practice.

However, inadvertent misuse of results could be a byproduct of a counselor not
being tuned into their own biases, resulting in the use of data to confirm ill-
formed, early assumptions about a consumer.[20] Rehabilitation counselors also
bear the onus of responsibility as the gatekeeper of assessment results, ensuring
that those provided with assessment data have the qualifications to understand
and apply the results appropriately. This also applies to safeguarding the
welfare of consumers by determining how a third party intends to use
information and representing results in a way the other party comprehends. If
another clinician misuses results due to their own lack of knowledge, the ethical
violation still falls squarely with the rehabilitation counselor who released the
information.

CASE STUDY

Sara is a transition-aged youth entering her junior year of high school. She has been involved in special education for her entire school life, as she has a learning disability and mild cerebral palsy. At her end-of-year meeting, she discussed wanting to do an internship in the community during her junior year. Sara's family privately pays to have a vocational evaluation done over the summer at a local community-based agency and requests that the results of the evaluation be released to the school. At the conclusion of the evaluation, the rehabilitation counselor sends the report to Sara's special education resource teacher. The results are indicative of Sara's difficulty with remembering verbal instructions, motor coordination, and spatial and clerical perception. The counselor suggested accommodations be made to overcome these deficits, like visual prompts and working in a hazard-free environment. When her teacher receives the report in the fall, since she is not familiar with the tests used or how to implement the results and accommodations into a vocational goal, she tells Sara the team cannot support her desire to work in an internship, and suggests she continue with the Life Skills classes she has been taking.

G.2.b. RELEASE OF RAW DATA TO QUALIFIED PROFESSIONALS

Rehabilitation counselors release raw data in which clients are identified only with the consent of clients or their legal representatives, or by court order. Such raw data is released only to professionals recognized as qualified to interpret the data.

This substandard again falls within the "gatekeeping" function when disseminating assessment information. Even more so than with completed reports, raw data requires a higher degree of knowledge and competence to interpret properly, especially absent the context of observations and the testing environment. Rehabilitation counselors must be judicious when deciding who is qualified to receive and interpret raw assessment data. Knowledge of assessment principles and practices is standard within accredited rehabilitation counseling programs;[7] however, it cannot be assumed this content was part of the professional training of related practitioners, such as educators/school personnel, attorneys, and social workers, particularly for vocational and psychological assessments and their impact on career or psychosocial planning. Even if a consumer consents to data being sent, the RC professional should counsel them on the appropriateness of that decision, if the intended recipient does not have the qualifications to understand the information. Blackwell, et al.,[2] provide guidance to counselors who are court ordered to submit assessment data, urging they seek the court's help to resolve ethical and legal conflicts by narrowing the scope of the subpoena, limiting the use of test data, or permitting the counselor to submit the materials only to a competent, qualified professional for interpretation.

CASE STUDY

Martin works for a private rehabilitation company that often provides evaluations for both plaintiff and defense cases. He had recently completed an evaluation of a claimant who was injured and now has an active Workers' Compensation case. Martin's company had been providing vocational rehabilitation services to this person with the hopes of returning him to employment with a different employer within the same industry. However, after several months of attempting a job placement, the claimant decided he would rather reach a settlement with his former employer. Martin had never worked with a person who wanted to settle rather than find a new job, but he wanted to respect his decision and autonomy. The attorney contacted Martin for assessment results to be used in the settlement. Given he had a release on file, he forwarded a copy of his evaluation report. The attorney called the next day and demanded to see copies of all the test protocols used to review himself, stating that a courier would be by the office to collect them. Martin had never been asked that before, but as he packaged up the test blanks and raw data he questioned the need for that level of information.

G.3. PROPER DIAGNOSIS OF MENTAL DISORDERS

G.3.a. PROPER DIAGNOSIS

If it is within their professional and individual scope of practice, rehabilitation counselors take special care to provide proper diagnosis of mental disorders using the most current diagnostic criteria. Assessment techniques (including personal interviews) used to determine care of clients (e.g., focus of treatment, types of treatment, or recommended follow-up) are selected carefully and used appropriately.

To arrive at a diagnosis of a psychiatric disability, rehabilitation counselors use the most current criteria for diagnoses and empirically-sound diagnostic assessment methods.[16] Proper diagnosis of a mental health condition is necessary for a rehabilitation counselor to select an appropriate, evidence-based treatment protocol and facilitate a consumer's growth. The goal is to choose the treatment that best aligns with the consumer's needs and desires, and the counselor's level of competence and scope of practice.

The reality of service delivery and managed care systems, though, is that constraints may be placed on entrance criteria, or the diagnostic codes and types of services eligible for insurance reimbursement. These scenarios create an ethical dilemma as a counselor struggles between beneficence/autonomy for the consumer and the requirements of the service system. In the best interest of their consumer, counselors may provide an inaccurate diagnosis in order to obtain necessary services and insurance coverage/reimbursement. However well-meaning, intentional misdiagnosis carries with it legal and ethical prohibitions, and may in turn hurt the consumer, if they are denied future benefits because of the diagnosis.[3] A mental health diagnosis carries with it stigma and other disadvantages, including discriminatory treatment and negative prognosis for goal attainment.[6] Rehabilitation counselors should strive to work within the system and the economic capabilities of the consumer to provide the best possible diagnosis and treatment.

CASE STUDY

Finley has always had difficulty in school, and high school was no exception. He has had a diagnosis of attention deficit disorder and learning disabilities for much of his school career. He is entering his junior year and his mother, Stephanie, thinks his needs are more involved–that he deserves a higher level of service. He is due for a triennial evaluation and she decides to pay for an independent evaluation, as she feels the school "doesn't get it." At Finley's school, most of the intensive services and vocational programming options are geared toward students with autism spectrum disorder (ASD); in fact, the only students who have been allowed to remain in school past the age of 18 have been those on the autism spectrum. The school has recently begun a vocational program for students with ASD ages 18-21 under a new state grant. Stephanie contacts Roger, a rehabilitation counselor in private practice, to conduct the evaluation. He evaluates Finley and reviews his history. He concludes that Finley does present with a number of the symptoms of ASD but is just short of the criteria for a diagnosis under the DSM-5 guidelines. He knows Finley will greatly benefit from a higher level of service and would thrive in the extended vocational program, but only those with an ASD diagnosis meet the eligibility requirements. "I'm really on the fence about what to do," Roger thinks.

G.3.b. CULTURAL SENSITIVITY

Rehabilitation counselors recognize that culture affects the manner in which a client's symptoms are defined and experienced. A client's socioeconomic and cultural experiences are considered when diagnosing mental disorders.

This substandard, along with others in the code, recognizes the impact of working in a country whose population is richly diverse and inclusive. Given this diversity, understandings of disability and the expression of mental health disorders by cultural or immigrant groups may not be consistent with a Western conceptualization.[9] For example, although science and technology are used to determine disability in first world countries, many societies and cultures still attribute disability to spiritual causes or fate/punishment because of family misdeeds. Some cultures may be avoidant of people with disabilities–or fear exposure; while others lack a word for "disability" in their language, as it is not seen as an impediment to contributing to society.[12] Gender role performance, such as whether contributing to the economic welfare of the family or caring for the others within the home is valued, will also dictate the impact or perception of the disability. However, counselors must also consider the effects of acculturation and avoid making stereotypical assumptions based on the consumer's culture of origin. Culture and other representational identities, as well as the perspectives of valued family members, should be incorporated into the assessment process to be sure a proper diagnosis is made, one that will be accepted by the consumer and their family. To assist in this process, the *Diagnostic and Statistical Manual of Mental Disorders, 5th Edition* (DSM-5) has provided additional guidance on how to incorporate cultural presentations and descriptions of symptoms when making diagnoses, including a cultural formulation interview guide to facilitate better decision making for counselors.[1]

CASE STUDY

Meiying, a 44-year-old Chinese-American immigrant woman, has been referred by the state vocational rehabilitation agency for a comprehensive evaluation, which includes a vocational evaluation and psychological assessment. The referring counselor listed a number of areas to be addressed by the evaluation, adding: "Family members have expressed concern about her behavior at home, which suggests she may be despondent, and it's possible she has a depressive disorder. Please assess." The rehabilitation counselor, John, conducts the vocational component of the evaluation and works in conjunction with the clinical psychologist to provide behavioral observations and complete various psychometric tests for use in the psychological evaluation. When the psychologist, Fran, arrives to meet with Meiying,

John shares his observations and findings. He does not believe Meiying is depressed, explaining, "I think her problem is something more physical in nature that needs to be ruled out. She has had various kinds of complaints every day during the evaluation–headaches mostly, and sometimes an upset stomach." Thinking for a moment, he adds, "If there is a mental disorder, maybe it's some type of somatic symptom disorder." Fran nods and says, "I'll take that into consideration, but I'd be hesitant to jump to conclusions about that until I have a better understanding of her cultural background and influences. For women from Asian cultures, it's not uncommon for depression to be expressed as some form of physical symptoms. I'll explore this in more depth when I meet with her."

G.3.c. HISTORICAL AND SOCIAL PREJUDICES IN THE DIAGNOSIS OF PATHOLOGY

Rehabilitation counselors recognize historical and social prejudices in the misdiagnosis and pathologizing of certain individuals and groups and strive to become aware of and address such biases in themselves or others.

This substandard addresses some of the historical shortcomings of assessment methods, such as underrepresentation of individuals of diverse backgrounds in standardization groups, disparate impact of certain test instruments on minority groups,[17] and the overrepresentation of male and African American youth in special education services.[4] As such, these historical and social issues may subtlety impact the observations, inferences, and judgments a counselor makes when working with individuals; or conversely, a counselor may discount the impact of a consumer's background, as though irrelevant to the assessment process.[6] Rehabilitation counselors are cautioned to be aware of their use of stereotypes, heuristics, illusory correlations, and confirmatory bias when processing information about and observations of consumers,[8] to be sure they are not perpetuating the practice of unequal outcomes. Awareness of one's own perceptions and personal experiences will allow counselors to interpret assessment results, make interpretations, and render diagnoses that are neutral and fair. Selection of tests should also be made with caution, as most psychological tests are developed using a Western framework and normed on a mainstream population, creating an unintended disadvantage to people of color, those with immigrant status, and consumers with various disabilities (i.e., physical disabilities).[9]

CASE STUDY

As part of its quality assurance (QA) program, an assessment center is collecting data on its services, which include follow-up

studies on the diagnoses and recommendations from assessment
reports. Preliminary findings suggest that one of the newer evaluators,
Marcia, has made an unusually high number of recommendations for
special education services in the last couple of years. In an effort to
better understand and explain these findings, the QA coordinator,
Betty, meets with Marcia to review the reports. Betty explains, "You
know, one thing that might help us identify any patterns or reasons for
this spike in special education recommendations would be if we had
some important background information about these kids, such as their
race/ethnicity or socioeconomic status, for example. But, as I look at
these reports, I do not see any reference to that, and we know that
there's a history of kids from minority backgrounds often being
referred for special ed when it wasn't needed. So it would help if that
information were in these reports." Marcia frowns and says, "I know
we used to put that in reports, but I decided it wasn't relevant
anymore. I mean, what difference does it make what color or ethnicity
someone is? Even though I am White, I consider myself to be totally
'color blind'. It really does not matter to me, so why put this kind of
information in a report? If anything, I think it could bias people who
are reading it."

G.3.d. REFRAINING FROM DIAGNOSIS

Rehabilitation counselors may refrain from making and/or
reporting a diagnosis if they believe that it would cause harm to the
client or others. Rehabilitation counselors carefully consider both the
positive and negative implications of a diagnosis.

This substandard demands rehabilitation counselors be aware of the
potential risks in making a premature diagnosis or over-pathologizing
consumers. Rehabilitation counselors may be conditioned by the extensive
training and practical experience to quickly identify indications and symptoms
of a mental disorder, which could lead to incorrect treatment planning. A
counselor should employ an inclusive approach to view consumers' thoughts
and behaviors through a multicultural lens, avoiding pathologizing culturally-
appropriate or contextually-specific behaviors. To ensure the welfare of the
consumer, a counselor should recognize the bias embedded in the traditional
medical model and promote a recovery-oriented practice.[6] In some cases, a
consumer may come to the evaluation with expectations of certain diagnoses to
qualify for services and/or insurance policies. A counselor should elucidate
both positive and negative consequences of a diagnosis, as well as its
implications on treatments.

CASE STUDY

Robert is a veteran returning from Afghanistan. He expressed interest in vocational services and was referred to a vocational rehabilitation counselor, Dennis, to undergo comprehensive vocational and clinical assessments. During the initial meeting, Robert disclosed he was physically and sexually assaulted in the military for being a sexual minority, but he did not readily associate those experiences with trauma. He also shared he did not believe in mental illness and thought those were excuses for "weak people."

Dennis is a recent graduate from a Master's-level rehabilitation counseling program. He also identifies as a member of the LGBTQ+ community and shared a similar experience to Robert's while an undergraduate student. While listening to Robert in the interview, Dennis recalled a recent workshop where he learned individuals with LGBTQ+ identity are at higher risk of developing depressive symptoms and substance use disorders; he shared some of this data as he moved to the psychosocial section of the interview. He took additional time to inquire about feelings, behaviors, social interactions, and coping skills. Robert reported he felt unmotivated every day and wanted to find a job quickly to kill time. He also shared that he reconnected with old friends and spent a lot of time hanging out with them at the local bar. Recently, Robert's family expressed concerns to him about his drinking and encouraged him to get some professional help before proceeding with his vocational plan.

To ensure Robert qualified immediately for needed services, Dennis diagnosed him with PTSD, alcohol dependence, and depression. Robert strongly disagreed with the results and was afraid those diagnoses might hurt his chance of getting a job. He insisted all his issues were related to "missing structure in life" and accused Dennis of applying stereotypes about LGBTQ+ people.

G.4. COMPETENCE TO USE AND INTERPRET TESTS/INSTRUMENTS

G.4.a. LIMITS OF COMPETENCE

Rehabilitation counselors utilize only those tests/instruments they are qualified and competent to administer. Rehabilitation counselors make reasonable efforts to ensure the proper use of assessment techniques by persons under their supervision. The requirement to develop this competency applies regardless of the manner of administration.

Although graduates of accredited programs take one or more courses specific to assessment and evaluation, this alone does not make a rehabilitation counselor proficient in administering and interpreting assessments. On-the-job training under supervision, work experience, training provided by assessment publishers, and professional continuing education workshops are all proper methods for gaining and improving proficiency with psychological and vocational assessments. Rehabilitation counselors should also be aware of the requirements for the administration of specific assessments and be sure they meet the educational and/or credentialing qualifications provided by the test publishers for the use of such assessments.[17] In cases where rehabilitation counselors are overseeing other counselors or assistants conducting assessments, it is their responsibility to provide proper orientation, instruction, and supervision for these staff.

CASE STUDY

Jessica recently graduated with her Master's in rehabilitation counseling and passed her certification exam. During her fieldwork experiences, she completed a practicum at a university disability access services office and her internships at an outpatient alcohol treatment center and the local office of the state vocational rehabilitation agency. For her first job, she applied to a community-based vocational program as a case manager and was hired! The duties of the job include counseling individual clients, securing training services, conducting job readiness groups, and providing job placement. Jessica feels she is well prepared for this position because the majority of her fieldwork was geared toward counseling and case management; she has been researching vocational group topics in anticipation of her first day on the job. The first week of her job was fairly uneventful–reading policies, shadowing coworkers, and observing groups. She feels ready to take on a limited caseload at the end of her second week. When Jessica arrives to work the following Monday, she learns that one of the evaluators broke her leg and will be out for the week. Marjorie, the assistant director, approaches her and asks if she can fill in with the evaluation unit for the week until she gets her caseload. Although Jessica received an "A" in her first-year assessment class, she did not administer assessments in her fieldwork beyond observations and does not feel entirely comfortable with conducting evaluations; however, she is too scared to look incompetent during her probationary period. "Sure thing, Marjorie. Wherever you need me."

G.4.b. APPROPRIATE USE

Rehabilitation counselors are responsible for the appropriate applications, scoring, interpretations, and use of tests/instruments relevant to the needs of clients, whether they score and interpret the tests/instruments themselves or use technology or other services. Generally, new tests/instruments are used within one year of publication, unless rehabilitation counselors document a valid reason why the previous versions are more applicable to their clients.

Understanding and integrating salient characteristics of a consumer (e.g., gender, disability, ethnicity) should occur throughout all phases of the evaluation process, from test selection through report writing and dissemination.[9] As the consumer population becomes more diverse and intersectional, rehabilitation counselors should exercise caution and document any concerns they have with the use of a test with a specific individual, as the validity of the test is constrained by its applicability to and suitability for that consumer. Some instruments available to counselors may not incorporate cultural, disability, sexual orientation, or gender identity characteristics within their sample population, limiting the utility of the inferences made. If the purpose of the evaluation is not diagnostic, and only meant to develop a case conceptualization or develop a plan, then using informal measures, ecological assessment, or inadequately normed instruments (with reservations noted) would be sufficient.[8] Although budget limitations are often cited for out-of-date materials, rehabilitation counselors should advocate for the purchase of new assessment materials, as they become available in the field.

CASE STUDY

Henry was just assigned a new consumer for evaluation. Faisal is an immigrant from Iran who has an intellectual disability as a result of scarlet fever when he was a young boy; he only speaks Farsi and needs a translator to complete all assessments. Henry arranges for a Farsi translator to be available for the duration of the evaluation, but given Faisal's cognitive limitations, limited education, and cultural differences, he does not feel that most of the assessments available at the agency will be appropriate for him–even with a translator. Henry consults with his assistant director about the limited resources for use in an evaluation of this consumer. His assistant director says, "We have a referral for a three-week evaluation. We have dozens of tests in the evaluation room. You mean to tell me you cannot find more for him to do? We need to fill those three weeks to get paid the full amount." Henry decides he can use some of the standardized work samples, a reading-free interest test, and a picture vocabulary test, but opts to fill the rest of the evaluation time with hands-on situational tasks. He does not feel comfortable using assessments that are not culturally relevant or lack norm groups that do not more closely relate to Faisal.

G.4.c. DECISIONS BASED ON RESULTS
Rehabilitation counselors responsible for recommendations that are based on test results have a thorough understanding of psychometrics.

Evaluation is a holistic process, and as such, the results of the assessment data must be considered in light of the person's cultural, physical, cognitive, and psychosocial characteristics. This substandard guides rehabilitation counselors to apply sound logic when transforming results into recommendations. This relies on foundational knowledge of psychometrics–the theories and techniques of measurement. Reliability, validity, standard scores, and norm group referencing allow a counselor to make inferences about a person in comparison to the performance of others.

However, the results of a specific test must be considered through a real world lens. Even when sound psychometric measures are used, the rehabilitation counselor must still interpret the findings with respect to the individual experience of the client. This is especially true for counselors who utilize computer-based assessments that produce a score report with recommendations. The computer will produce quality vocational and training recommendations based on the person's score and profile data, but it is up to the RC professional to tailor the utility and applicability of those findings to the person and their unique situation. While a recommendation may "match" based on the empirical data, it might not make practical sense if it violates a person's cultural norms, would cause complications to one's health or disability, or if the costs far outweigh the benefits.

CASE STUDY

Denise recently completed an evaluation and her counselor, Trevor, feels she has many vocational options. Although Denise has low vision, he feels that, with accommodations, she would be able to parlay her interests in science and personal service into a career in nutrition. Her local community has nursing homes, hospitals, schools, and other industries that utilize this degree, and it is a growing field. Her academic aptitudes were good and he feels she should be able to receive proper accommodations in the classroom to complete an associate degree program. Trevor knows he should be able to get approval for funding for her to attend the community college in her county. Excited to meet to discuss her options, Trevor lays out what he perceives to be a two-year plan of study, with job placement services to follow. Denise, disheartened at this recommendation, says, "I'm sure that would be a great option, but I don't drive and the commute to and from the school from where I live on a daily basis would be at least four hours round-trip on a good day. I don't think I can do that for two years."

G.4.d. ACCURATE INFORMATION

Rehabilitation counselors provide accurate information and avoid false claims or misrepresentation when making statements about tests/instruments or testing techniques.

This substandard relies on two premises:

1. the counselor will remain within their scope of practice, and

2. the counselor is perceived to have authority as a result of one's expertise, and as such, could unwittingly influence a consumer.

The first of these is more straightforward. Rehabilitation counselors should remain within their professional scope of practice, understand the limits and utility of their assessment techniques, and perform according to their personal level of competence. Even in passing, a counselor should not be tempted to speculate on matters best handled by a more specialized professional, as it could cause confusion to the consumer. It is sensible to provide a referral in these instances. In relation to the second matter, while an RC professional could provide a sound opinion on many issues–such as potential to complete a physical task, likelihood of a consumer completing an apprenticeship, or the prospect of being accepted into an academic program–many of these outcomes are outside the control of the counselor; to offer such an opinion might be taken out of context by the consumer as an absolute. A consumer may foreclose on viable options or cling to a single, potentially barrier-laden choice because of how they interpreted a counselor's opinion. It is best to provide all information in an objective and practical manner.

CASE STUDY

Rehabilitation counselor Lloyd and vocational evaluator Christina are all around the table with their consumer, Abby, to review the results of her evaluation. Christina summarizes, "I think Abby's strengths are her analytical abilities, her work ethic and determination, and her spatial abilities. She demonstrated average to slightly above average ability when it came to general academics, so I believe she would be able to pursue any of the associate degree programs you suggested at referral. In terms of limitations, she did have some difficulties with a few fine motor and manual dexterity activities, but she noted these activities did make her anxious because

229

of the time limits. Again, I don't think these limitations are going to pose a problem in either the academic programs or in future employment." Lloyd responded, "This is all good news. But I do need an answer from you on something. The guidelines of the occupational therapy assistant program require that students be able to drive in order to attend their internships. Is she going to be able to drive?" Christina replies, "While spatial ability and coordination are assessed in this evaluation, I don't think that I would be able to make that determination based on this assessment." Lloyd continues to press, "Yeah, but if you HAD to make an opinion, what would you say? I need this information before I can write the IPE." Christina holds her ground, "Lloyd, if you need that answer, then you are going to have to contact the agency that provides driver's evaluations. Would you like me to get that number for you?"

G.5. TEST/INSTRUMENT SELECTION

G.5.a. APPROPRIATENESS OF INSTRUMENTS

When selecting tests/instruments, rehabilitation counselors carefully consider their appropriateness, validity, reliability, and psychometric limitations. When possible, multiple sources of data are used in forming conclusions, diagnoses, and/or recommendations.

Adequate levels of reliability and validity are the gold standard within the field of evaluation. Ultimately, these speak to the usefulness of a test for making predictions about a person's future performance or treatment needs; instruments need to be sensitive and specific to provide this utility.[8] Rehabilitation counselors should be cautioned about overreliance on internet-based assessments that lack psychometric information, in an effort to contain cost. The utilization of these instruments is not forbidden, although they should be complementary to established, validated assessment techniques, and interpretation should still be provided by the counselor. In general, when providing interpretation and recommendations based on test results, it is preferred that multiple sources of data collection are used. No single test score should be the basis of major decisions; data should be corroborated and triangulated to form a more accurate and justifiable conclusion.

The appropriateness of any instrument, however, relates to the test's utility with a specific test taker, or group of consumers. If an instrument presents a content bias (i.e., consumer will be disadvantaged because of lack of exposure to/experience with the content) or a format bias (i.e., consumer cannot perform optimally because the manner in which the test is presented/performed creates a disadvantage), this will limit the appropriateness of that instrument; the assessment should be measuring a target skill (i.e., skill measured by the test), not an access skill (i.e., how the person demonstrates the skill).[13]

Accommodations can be provided to overcome many instances of format bias, such as presenting material verbally rather than visually to someone with a visual impairment, without altering the purpose and validity of the test. Some accommodations, such as additional time, can be provided to those with cognitive impairments or disorders that limit attention and concentration; although, this manner of accommodation will impact the reliability and validity of the results gained. Timed and extended time scores should both be reported to demonstrate the influence of the accommodation on performance. Some test manuals provide instructions for making specific accommodations, which are then accounted for in the psychometric properties of the test. For example, the WAIS-IV offers specific guidance on which subtests to omit for consumers with physical limitations and/or language difficulties.[9]

CASE STUDY

Felicity and Dylan are preparing for the upcoming group of consumers in the evaluation unit. Felicity, the evaluation supervisor, is providing details on the consumers and working with Dylan to formulate a plan and select appropriate initial assessments for each person. "So, I am going to assign this first one, Jackson, to you. He is a 19-year-old recent high school graduate with attention deficit, inattentive type, and generalized anxiety disorder. Jackson says he utilized a number of accommodations in school including a scribe, extra time, and a quiet testing location, what are your thoughts with him?" Felicity asks. "Well, I think in the first week, I'll use one of the computer-based assessments, probably CareerScope, since the younger guys seem to like the computer. Then I would like to use an achievement test, another aptitude test, and a few work samples before we move into the situational assessments next week. Since it says he might want to consider an auto body career, I can probably speak with Tom down at the garage to do something for next week." Felicity pauses to think, "While I think that those are some great assessments to use, we might want to rethink the approach with Jackson. With his profile, I think that too many timed tests are going to be a bit overwhelming. We want to make sure that we can get the best performance possible, so how can we rework this?"

G.5.b. REFERRAL INFORMATION

If clients are referred to a third party for evaluation, rehabilitation counselors provide specific referral questions, furnish sufficient objective client data, and make reasonable efforts to ensure that appropriate tests/instruments are utilized.

When referring for evaluation services, rehabilitation counselors use their knowledge of a consumer to provide detailed referral questions and background information. This practice leads to a more consumer-centered assessment process and yields specific information to complete the holistic picture of the individual.[14] Moreover, it provides the basis from which evaluators can determine the need for accommodations and alternative assessment methods. Any skilled evaluator will not limit their assessment to the single list of referral questions, but it does provide guidance to them regarding the information already known versus what answers still need to be discovered. Lack of referral information, or more commonly "boilerplate" referrals, place the responsibility on the evaluator to determine the purpose of the evaluation; this is neither cost nor time efficient. With dwindling time afforded for evaluations in current service delivery models, providing accurate and pointed referral information allows an evaluator to home in on techniques that produce the most robust, individualized data.[19]

CASE STUDY

Beth was recently hired as the director of a state agency that provides vocational counseling to people with disabilities. She tries to quickly learn the policies and procedures of the agency, which are quite different from her previous non-profit setting. She spends a great deal of time sitting in with members of her team and shadowing their roles, with the goal of understanding how the operation runs. She observes the referral process counselors utilize when sending consumers for vocational evaluations at a nearby center. The counselor hands the consumer a voucher, and the consumer calls to schedule an appointment for the evaluation. Beth notices that the voucher includes only the consumer's name, date of birth, and diagnosis, but no other information. She also meets with consumers who have completed an evaluation, and, overall, they express a wish that the evaluation had been more specific to their vocational goal and personal needs. She reviews the reports received from the evaluation center and notices most are similar to one another, often not depicting the goals specifically mentioned by the consumer in their vocational counseling intake interview. Beth believes this is not in the consumers' best interest and develops a new referral process that requires the vocational counselor to complete a referral packet and set up the consumer's initial appointment for the evaluation. The packet contains a sheet with referral questions jointly created by the counselor and consumer to guide the evaluation. The consumers respond positively to the changes, as they feel their needs are being better met, and counselors state the report has more utility in counseling and plan development.

G.5.c. CULTURALLY DIVERSE POPULATIONS

Rehabilitation counselors use caution when selecting tests/instruments for use with a client from a culturally diverse population, avoiding tests/instruments that lack appropriate psychometric properties for the client's population.

As discussed earlier, the utility of a test for consumers from a culturally diverse background will be limited if the demographics of the standardization sample do not represent them. Rehabilitation counselors, however, also need to consider the applicability and relevance of assessment *in general* to diverse populations; especially immigrant populations.[12] One assumption in the field of testing is that a test holds similar meaning for all people–that their experiences are common to the majority culture. Another is that a test measures what it is supposed to measure. In the area of psychological testing, this measure of validity is construct validity, meaning that there is an agreed upon definition and presentation of the phenomenon being measured;[17] most, if not all, of these definitions are based on Western culture and values. Therefore, traditional assessments might not be appropriate for use with cultures that value collectivism over individualism, consensus-seeking over independence, or quality over efficiency. To determine the utility of certain measures with diverse consumers, rehabilitation counselors must first understand the general values that define the consumer's culture, decipher *that person's* adherence to the traditional values of the culture of origin (or conversely, the person's level of acculturation to the dominant culture), and then select appropriate assessment tools based on this profile to avoid disadvantaging or misdiagnosing the individual.

CASE STUDY

Gail is perplexed. She has been working with her consumer, Idi, for a week now. Idi is originally from Nigeria, but she has received all of her education since high school in the United States and attained average to above average grades. Despite having a lower limb amputation, she has been active within her community and church. However, after a week of assessments, the results are very incongruent with her past performance, showing low scores in several areas. Gail slumps onto the couch in her colleague's office to seek some advice. "Terrence, I just don't get it. Here you have a bright girl, who has an associate degree in business administration, volunteers at her church, and has worked for three summers in the business office at a children's camp. Now I am looking at her performance scores and there are highs and lows all over the place. I think that she might have a processing issue, or maybe she is just distractible. She said that she did not receive any accommodations in school, but when I give her a timed test, she barely gets through any of the questions. I mean, what she does is always right, but her work speed is SLOW." Terrence chuckled a little and sat up in his chair. "Have you ever worked with someone from an African country?" he asked. Gail shook her head. "What's likely going on has less to do with processing speed and more to do with a cultural difference. You are coming at this with our typical East Coast mentality. Some cultures are a lot less 'time focused' than we are, which might be what is going on in her case."

G.6. TEST/INSTRUMENT ADMINISTRATION CONDITIONS

G.6.a. STANDARD CONDITIONS

Rehabilitation counselors administer tests/instruments according to the parameters described in the publishers' manuals. When tests/instruments are not administered under standard conditions, as may be necessary to accommodate clients with disabilities or when unusual behavior or irregularities occur during the administration, those conditions are noted in interpretation, and the results may be designated as invalid or of questionable validity.

The reliability and validity of a test are preserved when the instrument is administered using the standardized instructions in the test manual. When working with individuals with disabilities or linguistic differences, it may be necessary to make accommodations to this process to optimize performance. Care should be taken by the evaluator/counselor to provide accommodations, not *modifications*, to the assessment process. The difference in these approaches is an accommodation change to way the test is administered or responded to by the individual, whereas a modification alters the content (and ultimately the validity) of the test.[13] For example, when administering a vocabulary test to a consumer with Parkinson's disease who may have limitations in writing, it would be appropriate to read items and record answers; however, it would be invalid to restate one of the items using a less difficult synonym if the person is uncertain. This modification changes the complexity of the content, which is the purpose for the test. All variations from the standardized process must be noted in the evaluation report.

An additional caution to rehabilitation counselors is to not "over-accommodate" the testing process, such as to create conditions that might not be mirrored in the workplace. The application of excessive accommodations might result in a performance profile that is not indicative of the person's actual potential. For example, it would be reasonable, in a testing situation, to allow for five minutes of additional time on a subtest that is typically allotted ten minutes (reporting both the performance of the person under timed *and* extended time conditions), as an employer might make a reasonable accommodation of time and a half in a work setting. However, allowing unlimited additional time to complete an instrument might not simulate the performance expectations of the workplace and would limit the RC professional's ability to make inferences about that person's potential for success.

CASE STUDY

Oscar is visiting with his rehabilitation counselor, Franklin, to review the results of his vocational evaluation. Franklin says happily, "Oscar, you really did great, man. I think you took my advice and focused. It says here that you did average across all of your academic subjects and scored at the 9th grade level in math. We only needed you to score at the 8th grade level to meet the entrance criteria for the plumbing training program! How did you feel?" Relieved, Oscar says, "Well, I was super nervous, but the evaluator, Ms. Johnson, let me use a calculator and said not to worry about the time because she was going to give me ten extra minutes. That really took the pressure off." Franklin thumbs quickly through the report and sees no mention of accommodations used. "Oh no, Oscar, I have to give Ms. Johnson a call. You are not allowed to use a calculator for that test and she didn't report what your score was without additional time. We may have to do a different test because I won't be able to use this for the entrance score on your application."

G.6.b. TECHNOLOGICAL ADMINISTRATION

Rehabilitation counselors make reasonable efforts to ensure that technologically administered tests/instruments are accessible, function properly, and provide accurate results.

Although technology has enhanced the provision of assessment services, slow computer processing speeds, spotty internet connections, and faulty hardware create a host of issues for an evaluator. Agencies and rehabilitation counselors who use computer-based assessments should routinely inspect and upgrade their technology. Prior to starting an evaluation, counselors should also gauge a consumer's familiarity and ease of use with a computer, as lack of experience with technology can impact performance. While younger participants may be more comfortable with assessments using technology, older consumers, those who have had long incarcerations, and immigrants from developing countries might not demonstrate the same comfort level. Limitations from a disability, such as vision and motor control impairments, should be considered prior to deciding to use computer-based assessments, as well.

CASE STUDY

Jen is in charge of the evaluation room at a community agency that performs vocational evaluations. The agency has recently transitioned to using almost all computer-based assessments rather than the traditional paper-and-pencil instruments, which has been an exciting, yet stressful time for her. She becomes familiar with the assessments and finally begins to feel comfortable with the new system, despite not being very experienced with computers in her personal life. Jen sees the benefits of the changes; she does not have to spend hours scoring the assessments! The first few weeks pass smoothly, and consumers express satisfaction with the change. Jen receives praise from her administrators, as consumers are able to move more swiftly through the evaluation process since her attention can be more focused on report writing and case conferences.

On Tuesday, Jen is at maximum capacity, and begins to work with a new consumer, Esmerelda, who is young and appears competent in her use of computers. However, as Jen is compiling results and writing reports, Esmerelda approaches her several times, stating that the computer screen is flickering as she tries to complete the assessments. Jen instructs her to try turning the monitor off and back on again, but Esmerelda returns to report no improvements. Jen tells her to do the best that she can. Esmerelda completes the evaluation process, and when Jen sits down with her on the last day of her evaluation to review, she is surprised by the lower scores on some of the assessments. As she shares them with her consumer, Esmerelda begins to cry. She sobs, "I really tried, but it was so hard to concentrate with the flickering of the computer screen." Jen feels guilty, wishing she had paid more attention to Esmerelda's concerns during the evaluation process.

G.6.c. UNSUPERVISED ADMINISTRATION

Rehabilitation counselors do not permit unsupervised or inadequately supervised use of tests/instruments unless they are designed, intended, and validated for self-administration and/or scoring.

The purpose of consumer supervision in evaluation is:

1. to develop rapport that makes the consumer more comfortable with the process;

2. to make observations of the person that contribute to interpretations;

3. to safeguard the assessment is performed in a standardized way, with no outside assistance or distractions; and

4. to be available to the consumer if questions arise or clarification is needed.

There are a number of self-administered and/or scored instruments that are completed without supervision or the assistance of an evaluator, unless requested. These tests are typically untimed, opinion-based inventories, meaning they are not vulnerable to cheating or completed under time constraints. When providing evaluations, rehabilitation counselors should structure the day and schedule activities so that adequate supervision is provided to all participants. Even when an accommodation of a limited-distraction environment is provided for testing, the counselor should be available and make observations.

CASE STUDY

Joshua was experiencing an unusually large volume of consumers in the assessment unit this week; cancellations from last week meant there were a number of people returning to finish while the typical group of "new starts" was arriving for their first day. He knew he was going to have to get some of the old people started on their final tasks while he conducted orientation with the new group. Joshua had a few people start the Self-Directed Search followed by some online vocational exploration. A few others were tasked with practicing job applications and writing samples. However, Bill still needed to complete his timed aptitude test. He had only missed one day and had just this test to finish. Joshua felt that Bill had been a "model consumer" throughout the evaluation–putting forth great effort, performing well, and demonstrating motivation to move onto vocational planning. With fifteen minutes before the start of orientation, Joshua got Bill set up in a private testing room. He explained the test and how each section of the test is five minutes in length. "So, normally, Bill, I would read the instructions out loud and time each of the sections for you, but you have been doing so great in the evaluation, I don't think you need me to read it all to you–I think you get it. Here is a stopwatch. Just click it here to start and stop the time, here to reset. At the end of each five minutes, move onto the next section and start the time again after you read those instructions. If I am not in the office when you are done, just grab a cup of coffee and we'll wrap things up when I get back and get you out of here."

G.7. TEST/INSTRUMENT SCORING AND INTERPRETATION

G.7.a. PSYCHOMETRIC LIMITATIONS

Rehabilitation counselors exercise caution and qualify any conclusions, diagnoses, or recommendations that are based on tests/instruments with questionable validity or reliability.

Even when standardized administration is followed, this substandard addresses a situation where a red flag is raised for the counselor regarding the overall applicability of an instrument, or even select items. Examples of this could include the relevance of asking a question on American history to a client from Zimbabwe; requesting a youth recently transplanted from the United Kingdom to show the correct coins for change; or providing a computer-based assessment to a person with hand tremors. Limited exposure to information and experiences, and lack of representativeness in norm groups can create variability within a person's results; counselors should note their reservations in these situations and describe the strengths and limitations of the interpretations.[9]

CASE STUDY

Eva is ready to get started with her second day evaluating Yasmin. Yasmin is a young woman with some physical limitations who emigrated from El Salvador about 3 months ago. Tino, a local Spanish translator, has been assisting with the assessments. Eva decides to use a picture vocabulary test to assess some of her academic skills. She explains the purpose and instructions for the test and Tino relays this to Yasmin in Spanish. The test appears to be going well as Eva reads off the next item, "Vacuum." Tino pauses and looks at her. "There's no Spanish word for 'vacuum'?" Eva asks. "Well, yes, of course there is," Tino says, "but she grew up in a rural village with dirt floors. I don't think this item is appropriate for her." Eva makes the decision to skip that item on the test, as well as another for the word 'snowman'. She makes comments in the report about the changes to the testing procedure and provides her rationale as to why she felt these items

*were unsuitable for her consumer, citing that the score is a good
estimate of her abilities, but might not fully represent them.*

G.7.b. DIVERSITY ISSUES IN ASSESSMENT
*Rehabilitation counselors use caution when interpreting results
normed on populations other than that of the client. Rehabilitation
counselors recognize the potential effects of disability, culture, or other
factors that may result in potential bias and/or misinterpretation of
data.*

The accuracy of interpretations is enhanced when a rehabilitation counselor
can compare the performance of one's consumer to a representative norm
group. The suitability of norm groups for comparison with a consumer should
be considered before a test is administered. While *all* of a person's diversity
characteristics might not be represented in the sample population, both primary
(e.g., gender, age) and secondary (e.g., marital status, religious beliefs)
dimensions of diversity need to be considered when selecting appropriate
assessments for a particular consumer.[19] Greater effort has been made to
incorporate factors like culture and disability into the demographic profiles of
standardization/norm groups, to be in line with the demographics of the
national population, although characteristics like sexual orientation and gender
identity are almost wholly omitted.[15]

CASE STUDY

*Jeff has been conducting career counseling groups for students at
the local university. As part of this, he administers an interest test and
discusses with the group how these interests relate to their desires,
values, and personality. This activity feeds into other exercises he does
with the group to help the students explore these constructs further as
they begin to develop their vocational self-concept and career profiles.
After the session, Jeff notices one of the students lingering behind. "Is
there something else that I can help you with?" he asks. The student,
Kris, states that, although presenting male at the college, she is really a
transgender female; she does not feel the results really work well for
her. Jeff nods, "Well, the results of this assessment are interpreted
using gender-based norms, and you were interpreting these using the
male norms. This could possibly be why you do not feel connected to
the results. There really are not tests yet, that I know of, that have
incorporated norm groups for sexual orientation and gender identity.
Why don't we make an appointment for you to come by my office
tomorrow and we can look at your results, look at your scores
interpreted using the female norms as well, and then just have a
discussion about what seems to make sense to you? Vocational*

decision-making is more about finding the fit for YOU, not just following what one test says. It's just a tool." Kris felt relieved with this solution.

G.7.c. REPORTING STANDARDIZED SCORES
Rehabilitation counselors include standard scores when reporting results of a specific instrument.

In order to maximize the transparency and objectiveness of assessment results, rehabilitation counselors should report the standardized scores of the testing instrument within their report. Depending on reporting style and the preferences of the report's author, this can be done in the narrative of the results section of the report, in tables throughout the report, or in a summary of scores attached as an appendix to the report. Inclusion of specific scores allows for meaningful interpretation of a client's performance in comparison to the norm group for that instrument. Intelligence and aptitude tests are often norm-referenced. In situations in which there is not an adequate norm group (e.g., lack of data for a specific disability population), the rehabilitation counselor should thoroughly highlight the intent and rationale for use of the instrument.

CASE STUDY

Dwayne is the lead evaluator for the agency contracted with providing vocational evaluations for transition students in the local school district. In his experience, the report and case consultation meetings can be overwhelming for students and their families, as many of the students will be first-generation high school graduates. For this reason, Dwayne presents the results in a narrative, qualitative manner in his reports, highlighting areas of low, average, and high performance rather than getting overly detailed about the specific scores. He also likes to use graphics and charts to represent this. At a recent consultation meeting for a rising junior Marco, one of the school counselors remarked, "This is great and all, but I can't use 'average in math' to qualify him for the automotive technician program at the vocational cooperative. He needs to be at least at the 60th percentile for entry-level candidates." Dwayne nods, "No worries. It is all in there. If you flip to the back of the report, you will see the chart with a breakdown of all the tests, norm groups, standard scores, and confidence intervals for the entire evaluation. I put that at the end for the professionals who can understand and need the details. What I have here is to make sure Marco and his mom get a better sense for where he's at."

G.7.d. INTERPRETING TEST/INSTRUMENT RESULTS TO CLIENTS

When interpreting test results to a client, rehabilitation counselors consider the client's personal and cultural background and the level of the client's understanding. Rehabilitation counselors are sensitive to the effect of the information on the client.

The assessment process can be stressful and intimidating for any client, especially in regard to anticipating the results; however, this can be heightened further based on personal characteristics and experiences. Rehabilitation counselors need to consider the client's background, culture, and disability when presenting results. While counselors and evaluators are often comfortable with the scoring, psychometrics, and assessment-reporting jargon, this cannot always be said of clients. Reports should be written in an approachable manner for other professionals, clients, and their support systems. Extra care should then be given in the consultation meeting following an evaluation to interpret the findings in plain language, especially in regard to how it relates to future goals and potential. Counselors should be prepared to restate the results in multiple ways and provide examples to enhance clarity. Literacy, education level, and cognitive ability should be taken into account in this process. To the greatest extent possible, the primary audience for understanding results should be the client themselves to facilitate the highest level of consumer direction and autonomy.

CASE STUDY

Vincent was assigned a new consumer, Christian, for an intake at his agency. Christian had been diagnosed with learning disability and ADHD since the age of 12. Despite support from the school's special education program, he struggled academically. As a result, he became withdrawn and avoided difficult classes. Christian recently graduated from high school and wanted to go to college. His mother, Martha, was concerned about this decision and thought he might need more time to be ready for college. Christian refused to take a gap year and believed "things will be different in college." He was accepted into an engineering program at a four-year university.

Although he was receiving accommodations, Christian had a difficult time meeting course expectations and could not deal with the rigors of his program. He felt overwhelmed with pressures and anxieties and reported experiencing reduced appetite and fatigue. At the end of the first semester, Christian failed multiple courses and decided to take a medical leave. He moved back in with his parents; at their urging, he sought services for the difficulties with which he was dealing.

During the intake and initial assessment period, Vincent conducted the typical psychosocial assessment, but decided to give a few more assessments to get a better understanding of Christian's strengths, needs, and barriers. These included the DSM-5 Level 1 Cross-Cutting Symptom Measure and the Level 2 Depression Measure, since he wanted to screen for the need for further mental health assessment. At the end of the first week, Vincent asked Christian to invite his support system to discuss and develop a service plan. During the meeting, he relayed what he learned about Christian, including his profile on the DSM-5 Level 1 and 2 Measures; these measures pointed to symptoms of depression. Martha exclaimed, "So he does have depression! I saw on the news that depression can be quite dangerous." She then turned to Christian, "I told you that you weren't ready for this. You should listen to me." Vincent tried to slow her down, "Actually, these instruments are considered 'emerging measures.' We cannot use them to make a diagnosis, but they can help us. I thought I told you this when you were taking them, Christian. You still would need a referral for a psychologist or psychiatrist to get a definitive diagnosis." Christian grumbled, "Great, more testing."

G.8. TEST/INSTRUMENT SECURITY

Rehabilitation counselors maintain the integrity and security of tests/instruments consistent with legal and contractual obligations. Rehabilitation counselors do not appropriate, reproduce, or modify published tests/instruments or parts thereof without acknowledgment and permission from the publisher.

The established reliability and validity of an instrument is predicated on the fact that the person taking the test does not have prior knowledge of test items and the person administering the assessment has the requisite competency and qualifications to do so. Rehabilitation counselors should maintain test manuals, scoring sheets, and completed assessments in a secure location. In accordance with copyright law, test booklets and scoring sheets should not be duplicated, unless expressly permitted by the publisher in writing. Professionals should reference this standard with their employing agency to avoid an ethical violation if this is common practice at their site. Counselors should also avoid citing actual test items in reports, as it can impact the integrity of the instrument. Two laws–the Health Insurance Portability and Accountability Act (HIPAA) and the Family Educational Rights and Privacy Act (FERPA)–were created with the intent to increase the rights of citizens to access their own medical and educational records but have actually created barriers to maintaining test security.[8] Under both of these laws, individuals and families are allowed access to personal records, which may include test blanks, scoring sheets, and raw data. Debate still looms on this issue; therefore, rehabilitation counselors should take all reasonable steps to maintain the integrity of tests, when possible.

CASE STUDY

Leslie is a counselor educator in the Rehabilitation Counseling program at the local university. As such, she is often asked by non-profit community rehabilitation programs to consult on how they can improve the quality of their services. Kevin, the assistant director of one local agency and a graduate of their program, contacted her to assist with updating their vocational evaluation and job placement services programs. On the day of the consult, Kevin starts by giving Leslie a tour of the building and programs. She meets with the staff and several participants in the evaluation unit. As the tour proceeds, she notices consumers are completing an aptitude test, but they are using a poorly-made photocopy of the answer sheet to record their responses. When asked by Leslie if this was standard practice, Kevin responds, "I know that we have the originals in one of our filing cabinets, but we go through so many evaluations here that we can't keep up with the demand for materials, especially with what the publishers are charging these days."

G.9. OBSOLETE TESTS/INSTRUMENTS AND OUTDATED RESULTS

Rehabilitation counselors do not rely on data or results from tests/instruments that are obsolete or outdated for the current purpose. Rehabilitation counselors may use an outdated version only when necessary due to specific, individual needs (e.g., updated version lacks appropriate norms for particular populations).

While the costs associated with obtaining and maintaining assessment materials can be high, rehabilitation counselors are ethically bound to begin using the most recent assessments soon after they become available. Newer iterations of instruments often offer updated, more inclusive norms and rectify shortcomings of previous editions. In some cases, the instrument itself may not change, but an evaluator can obtain the most recent scoring and interpretation manual with the contemporary norms. If a third party provides outdated results, the referring counselor should interpret the scores with caution and note reservations. In order to prevent the misuse of obsolete protocols, rehabilitation counselors should properly destroy these materials to maintain the integrity of current editions, as many items are typically retained in later editions. In the spirit of this standard, rehabilitation counselors providing assessment and evaluation services should make it an annual practice to research current instruments in use for updates and newer versions.

CASE STUDY

Veronica began working with Charles, a 26-year-old man with cerebral palsy. As a result of his condition, he has some limitations with fine and gross motor dexterity, as well as speech disarticulation and difficulties with concentration. Charles is a college graduate, although it took him six years to complete his baccalaureate program in philosophy because of his needs for accommodations and reduced coursework each semester. He indicated he would like to consider going to law school to specialize in special education and disability rights law. Knowing the expectations of law school will be more intense and perhaps less flexible than Charles experienced in his undergraduate program, Veronica decides to send him for a neuropsychological evaluation to determine the extent of his cognitive abilities and shed light on alternative accommodation techniques, assistive devices, and organizational strategies to best prepare him to pursue a degree in law. Veronica contracts with a local neuropsychologist to perform the evaluation and prepares Charles for what to expect out of the experience.

A few weeks later, she receives the report and is a little concerned with the results. The profile depicted Charles as a person with significant cognitive and social impairments, not someone her agency is likely to recommend for graduate school training. As she reads further, she realizes the evaluator used the WAIS-III to establish a measure of cognitive ability, rather than the WAIS-IV. Veronica assumed the most recent version of the intellectual test would be used, as the modern version corrected for barriers experienced by people with motor and speech-processing difficulties. She knows this is not the most accurate portrayal of Charles' abilities! She feels a bit hamstrung by the situation; on the one hand, she knows her supervisors are not going to authorize to support education for a person with limited potential, but they are also not likely to provide additional funding to reassess him. Although law school is likely to pose some challenges to Charles, with accommodations and advocacy, she felt he would be able to achieve his dream.

G.10 TEST/INSTRUMENT CONSTRUCTION

Rehabilitation counselors use established scientific procedures, relevant standards, and current professional knowledge of

244

test/instrument design in the development, publication, and utilization of testing techniques.

When creating new assessment materials, rehabilitation counselors should rely on the principles of test worthiness to guide them in their development.[8] Even when a newly developed protocol lacks empirical validation, like in the case of a behavior checklist or situational assessment developed at the agency-level, knowledge of workplace expectations, a task analysis, and psychological constructs should undergird the process. A properly developed protocol should include standard instructions to staff for:

1. orienting consumers to the task,

2. conducting the assessment,

3. making observations, and

4. recording data, to enhance the reliability of inferences made over time.

CASE STUDY

Wendy, an evaluator at a local rehabilitation service provider, is presenting at the state rehabilitation association's annual conference about the innovative assessment techniques she and her agency's staff have developed. Given that her agency serves mostly people with more significant disabilities, they found many of the standardized test measures were not adequate to assess their consumers' potential. She detailed how staff each submitted an idea for a simulated work task or job, procured materials to complete the tasks, and created checklists to evaluate a consumer's performance on the assessment. Audience members were impressed by the variety of tasks created, including library assistant, custodian, retail merchandising, and data entry. At the end of the session, when Wendy invited questions from the audience, one person stood up and asked what procedure was used for creating a standard instruction protocol for each of the assessments. Wendy stated, "Well, each staff member provided an overview of the assessment to the other staff and we all use the same checklist to record data and evaluations." The audience member added, "Yes, that is all good, but without a manual, how do you know you are all giving the assessment in the same way so that it's a reliable measure of ability across consumers?"

DISCUSSION QUESTIONS

1. Given that graduate programs prepare students with entry-level competency in evaluation, what is the ethical responsibility of practicing counselors to enhance these skills and knowledge once in the field? Describe strategies for becoming both competent consumers and practitioners of assessment and evaluation.

2. Even when sound methods of assessment and data collection are used, the results might lack practical utility to a consumer. Discuss the factors that can impact recommendations and interpretations made. Use the case of Denise as a first example.

3. The diverse background of a consumer can pose a number of challenges in terms of providing accurate and culturally-sensitive services, from test selection all the way to interpretation and dissemination of results. Discuss the impact of the following characteristics on the evaluation process and how you can ensure ethical practice in assessment planning:

    a. Gender

    b. Disability

    c. Culture of origin, race, and ethnicity

    d. Sexual orientation and gender identity

REFERENCES

[1]American Psychiatric Association. (2013). *Diagnostic and statistical manual of mental disorders* (5th ed.). Author.

[2]Blackwell, T. L., Autry, T. A., & Guglielmo, D. E. (2001). Ethical issues in disclosure of test data. *Rehabilitation Counseling Bulletin, 44*(3), 161-169. https://doi.org/10.1177/003435520104400306

[3]Braun, S. A., & Cox, J. A. (2005). Managed mental health care: Intentional misdiagnosis of mental disorders. *Journal of Counseling & Development, 83*(4), 425-433. https://doi.org/10.1002/j.1556-6678.2005.tb00364.x

[4]Burkhardt, S. (2014). Diversity and disability. In A. F. Rotatori, J. P. Bakken, S. Burkhardt, F. E. Obiakor, & U. Sharma (Eds.), *Special education international perspectives: Biopsychosocial, cultural, and disability aspects* (pp. 33-52). Emerald Group Publishing.

[5]Carlisle, J., & Nerlich, A. T. (2010). The necessity of professional disclosure and informed consent for rehabilitation counselors. *Rehabilitation Counseling Bulletin, 53*(4), 218-225. https://doi.org/10.1177/0034355210368567

[6]Corrigan, P., & Jones, N. (2015). Counseling interventions for people with psychiatric disabilities. In F. Chan, N. L. Berven, & Thomas, K. R. (Eds.), *Counseling theories and techniques for rehabilitation and mental health professionals* (2nd ed.) (pp. 399-416). Springer.

[7]Council on the Accreditation of Counseling and Related Educational Programs. (2015). *2016 CACREP standards.* Author. http://www.cacrep.org/wp-content/uploads/2018/05/2016-Standards-with-Glossary-5.3.2018.pdf

[8]Gersten, A. (2013). *Integrative assessment: A guide for counselors.* Pearson Education.

[9]Horin, E. V., Hernandez, B., & Donoso, O. A. (2012). Behind closed doors: Assessing individuals from diverse backgrounds. *Journal of Vocational Rehabilitation, 37*(2), 87-97.

[10]Kosciulek, J. F. (1999). The consumer-directed theory of empowerment. *Rehabilitation Counseling Bulletin, 42*(3), 196-213.

[11]Leahy, M. J., Chan, F., Iwanaga, K., Umucu, E., Sung, C., Bishop, M., & Strauser, D. (2019). Empirically derived test specifications for the certified rehabilitation counselor examination: Revisiting the essential competencies of rehabilitation counselors. *Rehabilitation Counseling Bulletin, 63*(1), 35-49. https://doi.org/10.1177/0034355218800842

[12]Mpofu, E., & Harley, D. A. (2015). Multicultural rehabilitation counseling: Optimizing success with diversity. In F. Chan, N. L. Berven, & Thomas, K. R. (Eds.), *Counseling theories and techniques for rehabilitation and mental health professionals* (2nd ed.) (pp. 417-441). Springer.

[13]Niebling, B. C., & Elliott, S. N. (2005). Testing accommodations and inclusive assessment practices. *Assessment for Effective Intervention, 31*(1), 1-6. https://doi.org/10.1177/073724770503100101

[14]Power, P. W. (2013). *A guide to vocational assessment* (5th ed.). Pro-Ed.

[15]Sangganjanavanich, V. F., & Headley, J. A. (2013). Facilitating the career development concerns of gender transitioning individuals: Professional standards and competencies. *Career Development Quarterly, 61*(4), 354-366. https://doi.org/10.1002/j.2161-0045.2013.00061.x

[16]Sánchez, J., Muller, V., Barnes, E. F., & Childs, J. R. (2019). Assessment of psychopathology. In D. R. Strauser, T. Tansey, & F. Chan (Eds.), *Assessment in rehabilitation and mental health counseling* (pp. 99-131). Springer.

[17]Sheperis, C. J., Drummond, R. J., & Jones, K. D. (2020). *Assessment procedures for counselors and helping professionals* (9th ed.). Pearson.

[18]Strauser, D. R., & Greco, C. E. (2019). Introduction to assessment in rehabilitation. In D. R. Strauser, T. Tansey, & F. Chan (Eds.), *Assessment in rehabilitation and mental health counseling* (pp. 3-13). Springer.

[19]Thirtieth Institute on Rehabilitation Issues. (2003). A *new paradigm for vocational evaluations: Empowering the VR consumer through vocational information* (30th Institute on Rehabilitation Issues). Rehabilitation Services Administration, US Department of Education. http://www.iriforum.org/download/IRI30.pdf

[20]Wright-McDougal, J. J., & Toriello, P. J. (2013). Ethical implications of confirmation bias in the rehabilitation counseling relationships. *Journal of Applied Rehabilitation Counseling, 44*(2), 3-10. https://doi.org/10.1891/0047-2220.44.2.3

CHAPTER 11

SUPERVISION, TRAINING, AND TEACHING

CHERIE L. KING

SECTION H: SUPERVISION, TEACHING, AND TRAINING

Many rehabilitation counselors find themselves in professional settings and various roles that require them to teach, supervise, and/or train other rehabilitation counselors. The role of teacher, supervisor, or trainer involves:

1. Instructing and monitoring standards that are specific to a particular setting or consumer population,

2. competencies of the rehabilitation counselors in providing services, and

3. client service outcomes.[20]

The demands of rehabilitation counseling employment settings are becoming more complicated with an increase in stakeholders' (e.g., consumers, employers, lawmakers, attorneys, and advocacy groups) involvement in the rehabilitation process.[15] The ability to effectively manage these varied interests and roles while remaining accountable to the ethical standards is crucial.

Teaching, supervision, and training functions are an important part of helping the rehabilitation counselor to manage and balance the needs of their consumers, the demands of external stakeholders, and their own needs. The tasks related to teaching, supervision, and training serve to ground and support rehabilitation counselors in their daily work by emphasizing ethical practice through the CRCC Code of Ethics and applying an appropriate decision-making model for carrying out job duties and being prepared to resolve ethical dilemmas.[14]

The roles and functions of a teacher, supervisor, or trainer are different from that of a rehabilitation counselor. These functions address the professional development of a rehabilitation counselor in order to cultivate personal and professional progression and provides valuable oversight and evaluation of the supervisee's work to ensure quality services to the public;[4] while conveying the skills, knowledge, standards of practice, and attitudes of the profession to the next generation of practitioners. These roles are the professional cornerstones of the rehabilitation counseling profession including pre-service training, pre and post educational supervision, training, certification, and licensure.[14]

Section H of the Code of Ethics acknowledges and delineates these roles, responsibilities, and functions as distinct from traditional rehabilitation counselor roles. Any CRC who has the responsibility of teaching, supervising, or training other rehabilitation counselors must consider the nuances of the specific ethical codes related to these roles and functions.

Supervision is one of the most important ingredients in the professionalization process for rehabilitation counselors. The goals and expected outcomes of supervision are to promote quality assurance, ethical practice, and in-service delivery to individuals with disabilities through clinical accountability.[14]

H.1. CLINICAL SUPERVISOR RESPONSIBILITIES

H.1.a. CLIENT WELFARE

A primary obligation of rehabilitation counselor supervisors is to monitor client welfare by overseeing supervisee performance and professional development. To fulfill these obligations, rehabilitation counselor supervisors meet or communicate regularly with supervisees to review the supervisee's work and help them become prepared to serve a diverse client population.

Supervision is infused in the foundations of Master's-level training and accreditation standards, certification, knowledge and skill competencies, and scope of practice. It also is a critical component in the workplace for continuing education, clinical accountability, professional counselor licensure, and professional identity. The ethical practices of supervision are to ensure that the client's welfare is in the forefront of the process. Regular supervision (i.e. weekly) to review cases, discuss problems, and oversee the performance of the rehabilitation counselor supervisee is carried out within administrative processes and procedures. Those in supervisory roles, there must be understanding and prioritization of time in order to provide appropriate and consistent clinical supervision to supervisees.

The rehabilitation counseling profession has incorporated the fundamental belief that development of counselor competence takes place in a supervised setting more readily than in an unsupervised setting.[6,7] Lack of attention to supervision time and quality with supervisees places supervisors at risk when client welfare issues become problematic. Ultimately, the supervisor is responsible for any action or in-action by a counselor under their supervisor.

CASE STUDY

Steve worked in state VR for many years and recently received a promotion to supervisor of his unit of seven counselors. In addition to his new role and supervisor tasks, he is also carrying a small caseload. Steve has had no training as a supervisor and he has been told that the best rehabilitation counselors always make good supervisors. He decides that his supervision approach is going to be casual because he knows over the years that as a counselor, he has had supervisors who were "too controlling" and he felt micromanaged. He does not want to supervise his unit in that way. He tells his staff his door is always open and to come and see him when they need him. A few of his supervisees stop in his office for quick questions, but see that Steve is extremely busy with his other job duties. Several months go by and Steve is alerted that a high profile case with one of his counselors is having significant problems and a complaint has been made by the consumer regarding the lack of professionalism by the rehabilitation counselor. Steve must respond to his Director and the Client Advocacy agency regarding the complaint. He has never reviewed this case nor discussed it with the rehabilitation counselor. He meets with the rehabilitation counselor and he is told that she did not seek help because Steve was not available and she was afraid she would look incompetent in his eyes.

ETHICAL CONSIDERATIONS

1. How could have Steve handled his supervision style and approach?

2. What ethical issues arise with Steve's approach and attention to the supervisor role?

H.1.b. REHABILITATION COUNSELOR CREDENTIALS
Rehabilitation counselor supervisors make reasonable efforts to ensure that supervisees communicate their qualification to render services to their clients.

H.1.c. CLIENT RIGHTS AND INFORMED CONSENT
Rehabilitation counselor supervisors make supervisees of policies and procedures to protect the rights of clients including right to privacy and confidentiality in the counseling relationship. They ensure that supervisees are advised of their ethical obligations under the code.

Qualifications of rehabilitation counselors are seen as a fundamental aspect of quality rehabilitation counseling services. The use of written professional disclosure serves the purpose of communicating to consumers the credentials of the counseling supervisee. Consumers need to understand what they are getting in the rehabilitation counseling process and who is providing the services. Many agencies have standard professional disclosure and informed consent forms that detail the rights of consumers during the rehabilitation process. However, rehabilitation counselor supervisors need to emphasize this important practice by providing examples of the forms and working with their supervisees in the development of a professional disclosure statement so that they can provide this information to consumers. The disclosure statement should also include details regarding the limits of confidentiality in supervision. Examples of professional disclosure statements can also be accessed on the CRCC website.

CASE STUDY

Working as a private rehabilitation counselor, John uses his own professional disclosure form that he provides and explains to his clients. The disclosure outlines his educational background, certifications, work experience as well as his service limits and funding authorizations. John hires a rehabilitation counseling intern to help with his growing caseload. Although John reviews cases with his intern on a weekly basis and provides good oversight in training and supervising his new intern, he is more focused on teaching the intern to efficiently perform intake assessment, develop jobs, place clients, and the appropriate billing of cases. His intern is independent and goes to see clients in the field. In his first meeting with a new client, the intern explains the reason for the referral and the vocational rehabilitation process but does not provide any information regarding her status as an intern. She also is remiss in providing the client with an informed consent form or the limits of confidentially. After working the case for 30 days, the client becomes frustrated with the intern's inability to provide clear information about what services he is entitled to and who has access to his information. He begins to doubt her competence and asks to speak with her supervisor, John.

John explains to the client in more detail about the process, services available, and how he is aware of the details of the client's case. The client becomes terribly angry and states that he did not know that his counselor was an intern and had not been informed of John's access to his information.

ETHICAL CONSIDERATIONS

1. What steps should John have taken to ensure appropriate ethical practices regarding client welfare, rehabilitation counselor credentials, informed consent, and client rights?

2. How could John integrate the aspects of this ethical code into supervision with his intern?

H.1.d. SUPERVISEE RIGHTS AND INFORMED CONSENT FOR SUPERVISION

Rehabilitation counselor supervisors have an obligation to review, in writing and verbally, the rights and responsibilities of both the supervisor and supervisee. Rehabilitation counselor supervisors disclose to supervisees organizational policies and procedures to which supervisors are to adhere and the mechanisms for due process appeal of individual supervisor actions. Issues unique to the use of distance supervision are included.

An important practice of a rehabilitation counselor supervisor is developing and consistently using a professional disclosure and informed consent document when working with supervisees. According to Campbell,[3] a professional disclosure and informed consent agreement plays a vital function in ethical supervisory practice. Development and use of such documents "informs and shapes the supervisory relationship."[p.126] According to the Code, the rehabilitation counselor supervisor must provide professional disclosure consistent with their practice jurisdiction. Examples of the necessary information to provide within a professional disclosure document can include the supervisor's professional, educational, and training background, credentials, their philosophy and understanding of the clinical supervision process, their practice model(s), and ethical standards for how they approach supervision. An informed consent is an ethical statement of the supervisor's practice of supervision. These documents are provided to the supervisee and signed by both parties. They can be revisited as often a necessary as it serves as a preventive framework of what to expect in the relationship and the mutual understanding between supervisor and supervisee. A Rehabilitation Counselor Supervisor can also include specific organizational policies and procedures in a separate documents as well as the use of distance supervision processes.

CASE STUDY

Bill is a CRC working within a Workers' Compensation carrier. He supervises one rehabilitation counselor. Within this fast-paced work setting, Bill finds it difficult to practice supervision as he was accustomed to in his master's program. There is little time in the day to meet with his supervisee and he finds himself doing mostly administrative supervision or supervision via the phone or video conferencing. He feels he has a good relationship with his supervisee and does not use a professional disclosure or informed consent agreement. He also has not disclosed or provided information to his supervisee regarding new organizational policies and procedures (he assumes the supervisee knows these).

ETHICAL CONSIDERATIONS

1. As a CRC, is Bill practicing ethically?

2. What steps does Bill need to take in order to develop and implement the use of such a disclosure and informed consent document?

3. How might Bill integrate the use of such a document in his role as supervisor?

4. What are the potential risks that a fast-paced private sector setting has on Bill's ethical obligation as a supervisor?

5. What are to nuances of providing supervision by phone and online ?

H.1.e. EMERGENCIES AND ABSENCES

Rehabilitation counselor supervisors establish and communicate to supervisees the procedures for contacting them or, in their absence, alternative on-call supervisor to assist in handling crises.

It is important for supervisors to provide a process and procedure for communication with supervisees. Supervisors need to establish a means and methods (e.g. phone calls, voicemail, email, texting) for contact. This can be accomplished in writing (within the professional disclosure and informed consent document) and/or verbally. Supervisees need to know how to contact the supervisor in case of a crisis and if the supervisor is not available, a back-up on-call resource.

CASE STUDY

Carrie is a clinical supervisor to a summer rehabilitation counseling practicum student. The course session is 10 weeks and one of her students needs a four-week extension to complete the required hours. Carrie has planned a month long international vacation after the completion of the summer session. She leaves for her vacation without providing contact information for her student nor does she arrange a backup supervisor for the student.

While in practicum, the student experiences a difficult interaction with a client in which she is verbally attacked. The student is worried and scared. The student tries to reach Carrie but does not receiving any return phone calls or emails.

ETHICAL CONSIDERATIONS

1. As a CRC, what is Carrie's responsibility to her supervisee in this situation?

2. What are the possible problems that arise if her supervisee is unable to contact her or does not have access to alternative supervisory support?

H.1.f. TERMINATION OF SUPERVISORY RELATIONSHIP

Supervisors or supervisees have the right to terminate the supervisor relationship with adequate notice. Reasons for considering termination are discussed, and both parties work to resolve differences. When termination is warranted, supervisors make appropriate referral to possible alternative supervisors.

There can be many sources of differences between supervisors and supervisees. Campbell[3] notes several examples:

- anxiety,

- transference and countertransference,

- difference in personality, style, or viewpoint,

- dual relationships,

- multicultural differences,

- environmental factors and organizational culture,

- stress, burnout, and compassion fatigue.

There needs to be attempts to resolving differences in supervisory relationships. It involves openness to engage in a challenging discussion. Supervisors and supervisees need to remember that the approach they take with each other should be based on seeking understanding rather than reacting or censorship. If termination is necessary, both parties have the right to discontinue the relationship.

CASE STUDY

As a supervisor in a community rehabilitation program, Lynn has three supervisees. Lynn meets with all of her supervisees once per week to discuss cases. One of her supervisees, Liz, is a person with a disability. In their session, an issue arises regarding Liz's work with a client who is experiencing the same disability as Liz. Liz is a strong advocate for her clients, but she has been struggling with this client. The themes in Liz's supervision involve her belief that the client is not trying hard enough, is lazy, and using his disability as an excuse.

Lynn has used many supervision techniques to help Liz process and work through her beliefs, but she is feeling frustrated with Liz's inflexibility. Liz is equally frustrated with Lynn. She does not feel supported by her supervisor and states that Lynn will never understand because she does not have a disability and does not know what it is like. Liz also says she thinks a supervisor with a disability might be a better match for her.

ETHICAL CONSIDERATIONS

1. In this scenario, what are the relevant ethical issues that arise for Lynn as a supervisor?

2. What steps can Lynn and Liz take to resolve these differences?

3. Should they terminate their supervisory relationship because of their differences?

H.2. CLINICAL SUPERVISOR COMPETENCE

H.2.a. SUPERVISOR PREPARATION
Prior to offering supervision services, rehabilitation counselor supervisors are trained in supervision methods and techniques. Rehabilitation counselor supervisors offer supervision services, regularly pursue continuing education activities, including both rehabilitation counseling and supervision topics and skills.

Supervision is a distinct practice beyond rehabilitation counselor preparation. The authors found that field-based CRCs acknowledge the importance of providing supervision in their work settings but recognize the limitations of their supervisory knowledge, skills, preparation, and current practices.[21] This is a significant omission in the preparation of rehabilitation counseling supervisors. Although CRCC has provided general guidelines in the Code of Ethics, most supervisors are uncertain about their roles as a supervisor and the attendant processes, models, or techniques.[8,13,19] Lack of supervisory training has been identified as one of the reasons for inconsistencies and barriers in the work setting.[9,18,21] Although the Council on the Accreditation of Counseling and Related Educational programs (CACREP) contains standards and student learning outcomes related to the supervisory roles, function, and models, there continues to be minimal formal preparation of supervisory roles and functions for Master's-level counselors. This can be attributed to a perception that supervision training is mostly a doctoral-level function. Supervisors need to understand the importance of continuing education and training related to skills and models for rehabilitation counseling supervision. Traditional rehabilitation counselor education will not be sufficient in the development of supervisory competencies. Supervisors need to seek out formal preparation through continuing education, workshops, or seminars to prepare rehabilitation counselors for supervisory roles. If formal coursework is not possible, Masters Level programs and continuing education programs should consider integrating introductory clinical supervision content (i.e., models, roles, and processes) into practicum and internship seminars. Consideration for supervision training could include didactic teaching and experiential learning of clinical supervision skills, models, roles, and practices for evaluation of skills through videotape review, presentation, and feedback.

CASE STUDY

Frank was recently promoted to supervisor within his agency. He is a master's level CRC and has been working in the field for 10 years. He had some introduction to clinical supervision training when he was in his master's program but has not needed to utilize any knowledge he retained from the course work. He has been given administrative supervision training by his agency but he is now responsible for 10 counselors and does not know where to start. He knows how he has been supervised over the years and he feels that what he has learned from his own supervisors is enough preparation for the role. He feels he does not have the time nor does his agency readily support outside education or training, so he does not pursue additional preparation.

ETHICAL CONSIDERATIONS

1. As a CRC, how may Frank's decision impact his ethical responsibilities regarding supervisory competence and preparation?

H.2.b. CULTURAL DIVERSITY IN REHABILITATION COUNSELOR SUPERVISION
Rehabilitation counselor supervisors are sensitive to the role of cultural diversity in their relationships with supervisees. Rehabilitation counselor supervisors understand and use culturally sensitive and competent supervision practices. They assist supervisees in gaining knowledge, personal awareness, sensitivity, dispositions, and skills necessary for becoming a culturally competent rehabilitation counselor working with a diverse client population.

Given the growing diversity within the population, it is critical that the rehabilitation counselor supervisor is aware and understands multicultural issues. Many times, both supervisors and supervisees feel uncomfortable in acknowledging and/or addressing cultural differences. The supervisor is responsible for raising cultural differences with their supervisees.[1] According to Campbell,[3] it is not a matter of raising the issues but the approach to the discussion of possible differences and their impact on the relationship. Rehabilitation counselor supervisors must seek out and explore their own feelings, beliefs, and biases regarding culture so that they are sufficiently prepared and grounded to talk with supervisees about potential issues. Supervisors also need a way to frame discussions regarding culture with supervisees by having specific questions or activities to facilitate the sharing of backgrounds, beliefs, and experiences. Some examples include facilitating conversations about what the supervisor and supervisee believe is important for others to know about their culture or dispelling stereotypical judgments about cultures. It is important for supervisors to know that these conversations are difficult and that they need to be prepared to work openly and objectively with a supervisee who may appear to be resistant or reluctant to engage in the discussion or disclosure. Building trust within the supervisory relationship takes time. Open and honest communication from the supervisor can help facilitate the discussion but also model professional behaviors when engaging in difficult content.

CASE STUDY

Liz is a professor in a graduate rehabilitation counseling program and is teaching and supervising an internship class. One of her students, Carl, is an African American man in his 20's who is the first in his family to seek an advanced degree. He is completing his internship within an urban community mental health agency. Carl has been an average student often missing classes and handing in assignments late. In their weekly internship seminar, Liz asks all of the students to be prepared to bring in a client case to discuss. Carl is ill prepared but responds to questions about his work with the particular client. Liz has a sense that Carl is committed to his clients, he understands their issues and culturally identifies with them, but Carl is not demonstrating other necessary academic requirements.

Liz asks Carl to see her after class to discuss his performance in class. Carl is defensive and is reluctant to discuss what is happening regarding the course requirements. He says that he is doing great on internship site, building counseling competencies, and his clients like him. Liz explains that there is more to evaluating his readiness for the profession. She explains that she is concerned about his lack of attention to class assignments, preparation, and attendance. Carl indicates that he is a good counselor and knows the lives of his clients because that is how and where he grew up. He feels that is more important than handing in papers on time and Liz is holding him to an unfair academic standard. He also says that because Liz is a white female, she does not understand how his background and race are needed in the counseling community. She is extremely uncomfortable with Carl's comment and does not understand what race has to do with their relationship. Liz is surprised and is unable to continue the conversation.

ETHICAL CONSIDERATIONS

1. What steps should Liz take to evaluate her own feelings and discomfort with Carl's comments?

2. As a faculty supervisor, how do you think Liz should approach this situation with Carl?

H.2.c. TECHNOLOGY-ASSISTED SUPERVISION

When using technology in supervision, rehabilitation counselor supervisors are competent in the use of technology. Rehabilitation counselor supervisors take necessary precautions to protect confidentiality of all information transmitted through any electronic means.

With the increased use of technology for clinical supervision, it is necessary that rehabilitation counselor supervisors become familiar with the challenges of supervision at a distance as opposed to face to face with supervisees. Rehabilitation counselor supervisors also need to become proficient in using difference modes of technology (such as phone, email, online platforms i.e. Zoom. WebEx, Skype) and the ethical and legal compliance of utilizing these modes regarding HIPAA. Specialized training in using different platforms and how to protect confidential information is necessary.

H.3. ROLES AND RELATIONSHIPS BETWEEN SUPERVISORS AND SUPERVISEES

H.3.a. RELATIONSHIP BOUNDARIES WITH SUPERVISEES

Rehabilitation counselor supervisors are aware of the power differential in their relationships with supervisees. They do not engage in electronic and/or in-person interactions or relationships that knowingly compromise the supervisory relationship. Rehabilitation counselor supervisors consider and clearly discuss the risks and benefits of extending boundaries with their supervisees and take appropriate professional precautions to minimize the risk of harm to supervisees.

A rehabilitation counseling supervisor holds multiple roles when working with supervisees. The roles in the supervisory relationship are inherent and for the most part can be handled as long as there is understanding regarding ethical boundaries between the supervisors and their supervisees. However, it can present challenges to professional, personal, and social boundaries and possible issues can arise when the supervisor's judgment is potentially impaired or that the supervisee is at risk of exploitation. The relationship between the supervisor and supervisee is an important relationship in which the supervisor serves as a role model, teacher, counselor, and mentor. These relationship issues cannot be avoided but can be managed by diligent communication and ethical behavior.

CASE STUDY

Carrie is a rehabilitation counselor educator and practicum/ internship supervisor in a small graduate program. Carrie has a great

*relationship with her supervisees and provides excellent clinical
supervision. She is careful to explain her role, what her responsibilities
are as a professor and supervisor, and her expectations for her
supervisees. Carrie understands that clinical fieldwork is a demanding
component of a supervisees' training and many issues can arise which
challenge the student personally during these experiences.*

*Carrie has one student, Andrew, who has been in a few of her courses
and now is in Carrie's internship class. Andrew, an experienced
professional in the field has been doing well in the graduate program.
During the internship, Andrew discloses that he is having significant
marital problems and is seeking a divorce from his wife. Carrie is
supportive and focuses her supervision on his awareness of the impact this
major life crisis may have on his performance in his internship and
requirements for class. He states that he is having a significant amount of
anxiety and is feeling depressed but feels this is not an issue that will
impact the internship. Carrie is concerned about his successful completion
of the internship and begins to counsel him regarding his divorce because
she feels he needs extra support.*

ETHICAL CONSIDERATIONS

1. What issues does Carrie need to be aware of in taking on this role with
   Andrew?

2. What potential behaviors might she be exhibiting that may have
   ethical implications?

H.3.b. SEXUAL OR ROMANTIC RELATIONSHIPS WITH CURRENT SUPERVISEES
*Rehabilitation counselors are prohibited from engaging in electronic
or in-person sexual or romantic interactions or relationships with their
current supervisees.*

H.3.c. EXPLOITATIVE RELATIONSHIPS
*Rehabilitation counselors do not engage in exploitative relationships
with their supervisees.*

Intimate or exploitative relationships between supervisors and supervisees are
never appropriate. Given the many roles and power differentials between
supervisors and supervisees, it is important to set clear boundaries and to have a
keen awareness of any interaction with a supervisee that may be sexual or have the
potential for exploitation.

A rehabilitation counselor's ability to examine their own needs if they are
sexually attracted to a supervisee is of the utmost importance. Seeking out their
own supervision or consultation regarding these feelings or potential exploitation
is necessary to set clear boundaries and ethical practice.

CASE STUDY

Erin is a supervisor in a vocational rehabilitation agency. She supervises five rehabilitation counselors. Her group works well together and she has worked hard to develop relationships with each of her supervisees and to facilitate a cohesive work unit. The group frequently has lunch together and occasionally will go out after work for drinks.

One of her supervisees, Megan, is a hard worker and a great employee. Erin finds herself becoming attracted to Megan beyond a working relationship and casual socialization outside of work. In their weekly supervision sessions, Erin finds herself preoccupied with Megan and finds reasons to seek Megan out in the office. She has asked Megan to have lunch to discuss her caseload without the rest of the team. Erin also assigns Megan to a special project with larger responsibilities. Erin feels she is an ethical practitioner and is aware of her ethical code but feels that she can manage a relationship with a supervisee by compartmentalizing her supervisory role and an intimate relationship.

ETHICAL CONSIDERATIONS

1. What issues do you feel Erin needs to address?

2. What problems are likely to occur if Erin continues to supervise Megan?

H.3.d. HARASSMENT
Rehabilitation counselor supervisors do not condone or participate in any form of harassment, including sexual harassment.

As with any relationships in the workplace, a social or professional situation that involves unwanted harassment or sexual advances or obscene remarks is outside the CRC ethical code. Rehabilitation counselor supervisors do not overlook or participate in any harassment of supervisees or trainees.

CASE STUDY

John is a senior rehabilitation counselor within an insurance company. He works with four other rehabilitation counselors who are assigned to different claim units. John is responsible for coaching and training the junior rehabilitation counselors. The rehabilitation counseling team works closely together and frequently has lunch together. One of the other senior rehabilitation counselors who John has known for 10 years, Jerry, has been working in the field for 30 years and calls himself "one of the boys." The rest of the team consists of female rehabilitation counselors. Jerry is frequently making off color jokes and sexual suggestive comments at lunch or in meetings. The female rehabilitation counselors usually laugh and change the subject.

One of the junior rehabilitation counselors that John coaches and trains announces her pregnancy. Through the pregnancy she continues to work on the claim unit and Jerry's jokes and comments begin to focus on her changing body. Jerry also sends this counselor emails asking how she is feeling. John is aware of Jerry's behavior and notices the co-worker's uncomfortable responses to Jerry's jokes and comments. John has been uncomfortable saying anything to Jerry or his female trainee.

ETHICAL CONSIDERATIONS

1.   What are John's ethical responsibilities in this type of situation?

H.3.e. RELATIONSHIPS WITH FORMER SUPERVISEES

Rehabilitation counselor supervisors or educators are aware of the power differential in their relationships with supervisees or trainees. Rehabilitation counselor supervisors discuss with former supervisees potential risks when they consider engaging in romantic, sexual, or other intimate relationships.

Herlinhy[11] states that "although it has been argued" once a client, always a client' that claim is not made about supervisees."[p.27] Many times supervisors and former supervisees develop and maintain professional and social relationships beyond their supervisory relationship. There is "relaxing" that occurs in maturing professional relationships.[12] In rehabilitation counseling, it is common for supervisees to become professional colleagues. Former supervisors need to understand that changes can be viewed as a progression to a developing professional relationship.[1] However, when these situations occur, it is important for the rehabilitation counselors to discuss the risks of the former relationship and its potential impact or influence changes in the current relationship.

H.3.f. SUPERVISION OF RELATIVES AND FRIENDS

Rehabilitation counselor supervisors make every effort to avoid accepting close relatives, romantic partners, or friends as supervisees. When such circumstances cannot be avoided, rehabilitation counselor supervisors utilize a formal review mechanism.

CASE STUDY

Steven, CRC, has his own private rehabilitation company in a small rural community. His daughter, Shannon, works as an administrative assistant for his practice. Shannon is also obtaining her master's degree

*in rehabilitation counseling and needs to complete her 600 hour
internship under a CRC. There are no other CRCs in their rural area.
Steven is happy to provide supervision to his daughter for her master's
degree but is struggling as a potential supervisor to assess fairly her
performance as a student.*

ETHICAL CONSIDERATIONS

1. What ethical issues arise in this scenario?

2. What are Steven's ethical responsibilities under the code?

3. What steps should he take to avoid risking or compromising Shannon's internship experience?

4. What would a formal review mechanism look like for this scenario?

H.4. REHABILITATION COUNSELOR SUPERVISOR EVALUATION, REMEDIATION, AND ENDORSEMENT

H.4.a. EVALUATION OF SUPERVISEES

*Rehabilitation counselor supervisors document and provide
supervisees with ongoing feedback regarding their performance and
schedule periodic formal evaluative sessions throughout the supervisory
relationship.*

Evaluation is a key element of supervision, a cornerstone of ethical and fair practice, and the one factor that sets supervision apart from counseling.[3] The role of evaluation in the supervisory relationship must be handled mindfully as it can create challenges to the working alliance. Clearly delineated expectations, time frames for evaluation, and documentation of evaluation is required whether supervising novice or an experienced rehabilitation counselors. Evaluation serves as an open process using developmental supervisory techniques. It is also used for the assessment of job performance goals. Supervisees need to know at the beginning of a supervisory relationship what is expected of them, what the evaluation process entails including criteria, what sources and tools are used in the evaluation process, and their responsibilities within the evaluation process. CRC supervisors need to balance both positive and corrective feedback to supervisees in a way that promotes learning and development of competence and confidence. A negative evaluation should never be a surprise to a supervisee if the supervisor has been consistent with expectations and corrective feedback.

H.4.b. GATEKEEPING AND REMEDIATION FOR SUPERVISEES

*Through initial and ongoing evaluation, rehabilitation counselor
supervisors are aware and address supervisee limitations that might*

impede performance. If remedial assistance does not resolve concerns regarding supervisees performance and supervisees are unable to demonstrate they can provide competent professional services to a range of diverse clients, rehabilitation counselor supervisors may recommend dismissal from training programs or supervision settings. Rehabilitation counselor supervisors seek consultation and document their decision to recommend dismissal. They make reasonable efforts to ensure that supervisees are aware of options available to them to address such decisions.

Honest and consistent evaluation of performance in the form of verbal and written feedback is an obligation for supervisors in order to address problems and concerns regarding rehabilitation counselor professional development and competence.[2] Supervision interventions, activities, behaviors, and processes that occur between a supervisor and supervisee are necessary in order to foster professional development of competence to assist the supervisee to work effectively with consumers with disabilities. However, in some cases, supervisors may become aware of deficiencies in their supervisee's development or loss of competence. As gatekeepers of the profession, CRC supervisors have an ethical responsibility to monitor and intervene (when necessary) when there are signs of impairment in professional functioning and behavior. Through initial and ongoing evaluation, faculty and supervisors are aware of student/supervisee limitations that might impede performance.

CRC supervisors need to be prepared to assist in identifying the areas of weakness or need for remediation. It is appropriate for supervisors to seek consultation with other CRCs in supervisory roles in order to assess fully the appropriate paths for addressing performance and competency while maintaining objectivity. If a supervisee is lacking in areas necessary for competent rehabilitation counseling practice, the CRC supervisor must assist in the development of a remediation plan to help the supervisee improve skills, gain additional knowledge, or address personal issues impacting competency. The plan needs to have specific goals, timelines for goals, and expected outcomes to improve supervisee capabilities. The supervisee needs to contribute to development of the plan in order to ensure commitment. If the plan or efforts toward remediation are unsuccessful, the supervisor must notify the supervisee of organizational or institutional due process. In some cases, this may mean supervisee termination or referral.

CASE STUDY

Jim is a rehabilitation counselor and supervises several rehabilitation counselors in his office. The rehabilitation counselors have weekly supervision with Jim and he focuses on helping some of his newer counselors on skills development. Jim provides feedback to his supervisees to improve their skills and to gain confidence.

One supervisee that Jim has been observing is Eric. Jim has become concerned about Eric because he is struggling with the demonstration of basic counseling skills such as active listening and empathy with his clients. Eric seems to focus on giving his clients advice and he is missing many cues in which his clients are talking about feelings. Throughout the course, Jim has been giving him constructive feedback about his observations, but Eric is defensive and resistant to integrating the feedback into practice. In a supervisory session, Jim was giving Eric feedback and examples of how to respond to a client and Eric becomes angry and leaves the office.

Afterward, Jim emailed Eric and asked to schedule a time to meet and discuss what transpired during their meeting. Eric was angry and accusatory toward Jim. Jim explained that effective counselors possess characteristics that include a willingness to use and accept feedback, ability to deal with conflict, ability to accept personal responsibility, and the ability to express feelings effectively and appropriately. Jim felt Eric was not adequately demonstrating these attributes. Jim offered assistance to develop a plan to remediate this challenging area for Eric.

ETHICAL CONSIDERATIONS

1. As a gatekeeper to the profession, what can Jim do to assist Eric?

2. What should he include in a remediation plan for Eric?

3. What are Eric's responsibilities in contributing and carrying out to the plan?

4. What can Jim do if the plan is not successful?

5. What issues arise for Jim and his ethical duties as a gatekeeper?

H.4.c. REFERRING SUPERVISEES FOR COUNSELING

If supervisees request counseling or if counseling services are suggested as part of remediation process, rehabilitation counselor supervisors assist supervisees in identifying appropriate services. Rehabilitation counselor supervisors do not provide counseling services to supervisees but may address interpersonal competencies in terms of impact of these issues on the supervisory relationships, professional functioning, and/or clients.

It is common for supervisees to experience difficulty in their personal or professional lives that may impact upon their functioning as a rehabilitation counselor. CRCs, as trained counselors are capable of addressing most issues presented in supervisory sessions and are inclined to offer assistance. However, as a supervisor, CRCs must be prepared to differentiate between appropriate supervisory interventions and counseling a supervisee. Awareness of how a supervisee's personal background, attitudes, biases, or coping skills impact their professional performance is critical. A supervisor must be prepared to refer the supervisee for assistance such as personal counseling as it is not appropriate to blur the supervisor and counselor roles.

CASE STUDY

In the earlier Jim and Eric case, they have met to develop a remediation plan to assist Eric in looking at some personal feelings and beliefs that are significantly impacting his professional development. During the remedial planning process, Eric discloses information about his own mental health struggles and how the expectations of the job and interaction with his clients have impacted his performance. Eric thought he could manage his issues and not let them effect his role as a rehabilitation counselor. As a CRC, Jim provides support to Eric. However, Eric asks Jim to provide counseling to him.

ETHICAL CONSIDERATIONS

1. How is Jim to handle Eric's request?

2. What are his ethical responsibilities in this situation?

H.4.d. ENDORSEMENT

Rehabilitation counselor supervisors endorse supervisees for certification, licensure, employment, or completion of academic or training programs based on satisfactory progress and observations while under supervision or training. Regardless of the qualifications, rehabilitation counselor supervisors do not endorse supervisees whom they believe to be impaired in any way that would interfere with the performance of the duties associated with the endorsement.

Supervisees frequently request endorsement from their supervisors for employment, credentialing, or seeking advanced education or training. Provided that the supervisor is confident about the supervisee's competency, it is appropriate for supervisors to sanction a supervisee. Only in cases in which in the CRC is concerned about supervisee deficiencies should a supervisor refuse endorsement.

CASE STUDY

Ralph supervises a newly graduated rehabilitation counselor. Sarah is preparing to take the CRC examination. She has struggled in her first months of employment and Ralph has spent a lot of time working with her to remediate counselor development issues such as the ability to work cooperatively with her supervisor and team, ability to deal with conflict, self-awareness, and accepting personal responsibility. Ralph seeks consultation with several other supervisors regarding Sarah's performance. Sarah comes to Ralph to sign her CRC exam application.

ETHICAL CONSIDERATIONS

1. What issues arise for Ralph in the request for endorsement?

2. What are the implications of endorsing or not endorsing Sarah to take the CRC exam?

H.5. REHABILITATION COUNSELOR EDUCATOR RESPONSIBILITIES

Rehabilitation counselor education is a process to establish and reinforce the professional identity of rehabilitation counselors. From its roots in historical legislation to ongoing introspection and empirical examination, the distinctiveness of rehabilitation counseling is grounded in the history and philosophies of the profession.[14] Through a defined scope and standard of practice, code of ethics, and knowledge base, rehabilitation counseling has established its uniqueness within the counseling field.[14] It is reasonable for the rehabilitation counselor educator to have the professional identity of a trained and practiced rehabilitation counselor grounded in the ethical, legal, and regulatory aspects of the profession. The rehabilitation counselor educator needs to integrate the scope of rehabilitation counselor practice into their teaching and supervision of students.

Rehabilitation counselor education and development is one of the primary building blocks of the professionalization process. Rehabilitation counselor education serves a critical function to promote and reinforce professional identity beginning in the formal educational and training phase throughout a rehabilitation counselor's work life. It is the responsibility of rehabilitation counselor educators to instill the principles, attitudes, knowledge, multicultural competency, and standards of practice of the profession and to function as role models for students and supervisees. The CRCC Code specifically defines ethical guidelines for educators as CRCs. The Code defines the distinction between educator, supervisor, and rehabilitation counselor roles.

H.5.a. PROGRAM INFORMATION AND ORIENTATION

Rehabilitation counselor educators recognize that orientation is a developmental process that continues throughout the educational and clinical training of students. Rehabilitation counselor educators have an ethical responsibility to provide enough information to prospective or current students about program expectations for them to make informed decisions about entering into and continuing in a program.

Student orientation is awareness of the expectations of a program. Much like informed consent, students need accurate information so that they can make decisions for themselves and the direction of their educational pursuits. Rehabilitation counselor educators need to assure that their programs provide adequate orientation and advise students so that they may navigate into and through academic programs with certainty.

CASE STUDY

Ellen wants to be a counselor and is thinking about attending graduate school. As an undergraduate, she majored in psychology and she wants to work with people. During her investigation of graduate programs, she discovers the field of rehabilitation counseling. She finds several programs in her state and contacts each of them for further information. One program has minimal information on its website about admissions and program requirements, accreditation, student learning outcomes, and graduate employment. She contacts the program and she is told by the department administrator that they are updating their written brochure and she will need to make an appoint to meet with the program coordinator. Ellen leaves several voicemails and emails for the coordinator over a period of time with no response. She contacts the department administrator as well as the department Chair, and Ellen is told that the coordinator will get back to her.

1. As CRC rehabilitation educators, what are their ethical obligations?

2. What steps can the program coordinator take to provide appropriate orientation for this potential student?

H.5.b. STUDENT CAREER ADVISING
Rehabilitation counselor educators provide career advisement to their students and make them aware of opportunities in the field.

H.5.c. SELF-GROWTH EXPERIENCES
Rehabilitation counselor educators are mindful of ethical principles when they require students to engage in self growth experiences. Rehabilitation counselor educators inform students they have the right to decide what information will be shared or withheld when other students are present.

Effective counselors possess characteristics that include the willingness to explore and grow as individuals. All persons including counselors have their own personal history and psychological stressors. Clients have the right to expect that their counselor cares about their own well-being and is psychologically healthy. In the counseling relationship, clients are encouraged to self-disclose. Therefore, it is only fair that the counselors in training experience the same process for themselves. The intensity of counselor training inherently triggers self-exploration and self-disclosure. While no student is expected to be a flawless human being, it is important that students are motivated to grow personally and are open to evaluating their own needs, values, and personality traits since these may have a bearing on their counseling effectiveness.[5]

Rehabilitation counselor educators have the responsibility to observe and evaluate student readiness and their progress in challenging areas of self-disclosure, self-care, and growth. CRC educators have an ethical obligation to delineate student self-disclosure from designed academic experiences and standards. They should inform students of the educators' responsibility to act when the student is exhibiting impairment that may impact their competencies.

CASE STUDY

Jocelyn is a student in a rehabilitation counseling program and is also in recovery from substance abuse. She has been sober for 5 years and has built a good network to support her recovery. Jocelyn is completing her internship in a homeless shelter for individuals who are using drugs and alcohol. Her responsibilities include intake interviews, development of rehabilitation plans, job placement, and case management. As a full time student and completing the internship, her stress level has increased and she is finding she is triggered by close contact with clients who are actively using drugs and alcohol.

She attends a weekly internship seminar with her professor and other graduate students. In her participation in the course, she discloses her recovery and emerging feelings of wanting to use again. She is fearful that her own personal and recovery issues are impacting her objectivity with her clients as well as her attention to course work.

ETHICAL CONSIDERATIONS

1.   What are Jocelyn's CRC internship instructor and faculty supervisor ethical responsibilities under this Code?

2.   What would you do as the instructor/supervisor working with Jocelyn?

H.5.d. STUDENT DISCLOSURE OF PERSONAL INFORMATION
Rehabilitation counselor educators do not require students to disclose highly personal and private information in course or program related activities, either orally or in writing (e.g. sexual history, history of abuse

and neglect, medical treatment, and relationships with parents, peers, and spouses or significant others).

CASE STUDY

Doug teaches a counseling theories and techniques course in a rehabilitation counseling program. One of the key assignments in the course asks students to apply a developmental theory to the stages of their lives. The assignment asks students to identify key events in their own development at different stages in their lives. Doug expects students to be open with their own exploration and reflection of their lives and how significant events may have impacted their development.

ETHICAL CONSIDERATIONS

1. How might this assignment conflict with this part of the code?

2. What are the ethical implications of this assignment?

H.5.e. DIVERSITY IN RECRUITMENT AND RETENTION

Rehabilitation counselor educators actively attempt to recruit and retain a diverse faculty and student body. Rehabilitation counselor educators demonstrate commitment to cultural diversity competence by recognizing and valuing diverse cultures and types of abilities that faculty and students bring to the training experience. Rehabilitation counselor educators provide appropriate accommodations as required to enhance and support the wellbeing and performance of students.

As CRCs, rehabilitation counselor educators are expected to recognize and actively advocate for cultural diversity within their programs. It is important for faculty to have clear recruitment and retention policies and plans that promote and respect cultural diversity. As the population of diverse consumers with disabilities expands, the need for trained rehabilitation counselors with cultural understanding and diverse backgrounds is imperative.

CASE STUDY

Greg teaches full time in a rehabilitation counseling program. As a CRC, Greg understands the importance of counselor training with multicultural awareness and competence. He is also dedicated to creating and maintaining a program of diversity with its students and faculty. However, Greg is having difficulty recruiting and retaining students with cultural differences. Greg finds it difficult to identify potential applicants to the program because the majority of the student body is Caucasian. The faculty is also Caucasian. He has joined a professional association focused on multicultural concerns in rehabilitation to expand his knowledge, has reached out to minority student groups on campus and community sources to advertise and recruit for his program.

ETHICAL CONSIDERATIONS

1. What steps might Greg need to take to address these ethical concerns?

2. How are his actions impacting his adherence with the intent of the ethical code?

H.5.f. TEACHING CULTURAL DIVERSITY

Rehabilitation counselor educators infuse material related to cultural diversity into all courses and workshops for the development of professional rehabilitation counselors.

Multicultural competencies in rehabilitation counseling are necessary due to the rapidly changing racial and ethnic profiles of persons with disabilities seeking services in the United States.[16] As a rehabilitation counselor educator, a CRC must be prepared to integrate information with regard to cultural diversity in courses, workshops, and other training to expose and prepare rehabilitation counselors to serve diverse populations.

CASE STUDY

Andrew is a CRC and teaching as an adjunct instructor in a continuing education workshop for state vocational rehabilitation (VR) counselors. He is responsible for training VR counselors about current assessment techniques to evaluate the job skills of consumers with disabilities. He is presenting material regarding job skills assessment and is asked by one of his trainees about the impact of educational deficits and language differences on the reliability of assessments. The VR counselor indicates that the majority of their caseload is from underrepresented groups and the VR counselors are struggling with applying traditional vocational assessment techniques with this population. Andrew has little experience working with such populations and struggles to answer the question.

ETHICAL CONSIDERATIONS

1. What are Andrew's ethical responsibilities to address his own deficits in cultural diversity?

2. How might he integrate cultural diversity into his training approach and materials?

H.5.g. TEACHING ETHICS

Rehabilitation counselor educators infuse ethical considerations throughout the curriculum and make students aware of their ethical responsibilities and standards of the profession.

The infusion of ethics and the professional code into the rehabilitation counseling curriculum is necessary in order to fully educate and prepare students to function as rehabilitation counselors. It is important for rehabilitation counselor educators to utilize curriculum and teaching materials that facilitate understanding of the ethical code but also allow students to process and analyze ethical scenarios and dilemmas. The ability of the rehabilitation counselor educator to teach and integrate ethics throughout the curriculum is optimal and results in student awareness of the standards, development of ethical decision-making processes, and builds ethical practice and competence in the application of the Code.

CASE STUDY

Students in a graduate rehabilitation program are required to take a comprehensive examination before completion of their program. The faculty of the program are all CRCs and teach various required academic courses and supervise practicum and internship seminars. The students take one ethics course that is shared with other counselor education programs (i.e., school counseling and mental health). After scoring the comprehensive exam, the faculty learns that most of their students fail the ethics portion of the exam. The faculty is shocked and unsure of how to handle the implications of these results for graduation requirements but also student competencies to practice.

ETHICAL CONSIDERATIONS

1. What issues are present that the CRC faculty need to address?

H.5.h. INTEGRATION OF STUDY AND PRACTICE

Rehabilitation counselor educators establish education and training programs that integrate academic study and supervised practice.

The foundation of education and training of rehabilitation counselors include academic and clinical preparation. Competent rehabilitation counselors need to be educated in the necessary knowledge and skills of professional practice. They also need to be capable of working directly with and providing proficient counseling services to individuals with disabilities in diverse settings. It is the responsibility of the CRC rehabilitation counselor educator and supervisor to assure well-balanced rehabilitation counseling education and training programs.

CASE STUDY

As a CRC, Beth is the new coordinator in a rehabilitation counseling program. As part of her responsibilities, she conducts a review of the existing program curriculum and clinical requirements for students. During her review, she finds inconsistencies in student field placements in terms of the number of hours students are completing, adequacy of supervision in the selected sites, and not receiving enough clinical practice with consumers. Beth is concerned because students need to document 600 hours of internship and be supervised by a CRC. Since Beth's program is in a rural area, there are limited community programs and agencies to place students and there is a lack of qualified CRC supervisors.

ETHICAL CONSIDERATIONS

1. What are Beth's responsibilities as an educator?

2. What are the ethical and professional implications of this scenario for students in Beth's program?

3. If you were Beth, how would you approach this dilemma to ensure students were receiving an integration of academic training and supervised practice?

H.5.i. USE OF CASE EXAMPLES
The use of client, student, or supervisee information for the purposes of case examples in a lecture or classroom setting is permissible only when: (1) the client, student, or supervisee has reviewed the material and agrees to its presentation; or (2) the information has been sufficiently modified to obscure identity.

H.5.j. STUDENT TO STUDENT SUPERVISION AND INSTRUCTION
Rehabilitation counselor educators make reasonable efforts to ensure the rights of students are not compromised when their peers lead experiential counseling activities in traditional, online, and/or hybrid formats (e.g. counseling groups, skills classes, clinical supervision). Rehabilitation counselor educators make reasonable efforts to ensure that students understand they have the same ethical obligations as rehabilitation counselor educators.

Many rehabilitation counselor education programs utilize peer counseling activities and supervision as a practice vehicle for student training. As an example, to learn and practice group counseling facilitation, many times students will lead and participate in group counseling with each other. For learning supervision skills, peer supervision can be used so students consult with peers to process and problem-solve clinical issues. It is the responsibility of the rehabilitation counselor educator to safeguard the ethical obligations of students since they are the same as practicing rehabilitation counselors, educators, and supervisors.

CASE STUDY

Kevin, a CRC, teaches an advanced group counseling methods course. One of the requirements of the course is for students to develop a specialized group and lead the group of their peers for three sessions. One of the student groups is led by Lisa. Lisa is very directive when leading the group and monopolizes a lot of group time. The group and Lisa become very frustrated with each other and conversations begin between students outside of class about the group process and Lisa as the leader. Kevin is unaware of what is happening outside of the class until Lisa comes to him and states her peers are "ganging up" on her, talking behind her back, and sabotaging her group. She is worried about her grade for the class.

1. What issues do you see arising in peer relationships?

2. What are Kevin's ethical obligations as an educator?

H.5.k. INNOVATIVE TECHNIQUES/PROCEDURES/MODALITIES

Rehabilitation counselor educators promote the use of techniques/procedures/modalities that are grounded in theory and/or have an empirical or scientific foundation. When rehabilitation counselor educators discuss innovative or developing techniques/procedures/ modalities, they explain the potential risks, benefits, and ethical considerations of using such techniques/procedures/modalities.

Many counseling methods have limited empirical evidence regarding their application and effectiveness when working with clients. However, counseling can be considered an art, thus techniques and approaches are evolving. In training rehabilitation counseling students, educators must present and teach well-balanced information regarding the strengths, limitations, possible risks, and ethical implications of utilizing techniques or procedures that have marginal theoretical or empirical evidence to support them.

CASE STUDY

Karen is a rehabilitation counselor educator teaching a mental health counseling techniques course. In her own counseling practice, Karen was trained in utilizing a new counseling approach to work with individuals who experience trauma. This approach employs controversial techniques

*and it has not been studied within the counseling or mental health field.
Karen strongly believes in this new approach to treatment and knows it
works for her private practice clients.*

*She teaches this approach in class and several of her students who are
also completing internship placements, begin to try to practice these
techniques with their clients. Karen receives several phones calls from site
supervisors questioning her about what she is teaching her students. They
are concerned that these inexperienced students lack the understanding of
the ethical implications of using this method and the limited efficacy of the
method. Students are seriously concerned about what they have been
taught and feel they were not given a balanced perspective.*

ETHICAL CONSIDERATIONS

1.   What are Karen's ethical obligations to her students?

H.5.1. FIELD PLACEMENTS

*Rehabilitation counselor educators develop clear policies within their
training programs regarding field placement and other clinical
experiences. Rehabilitation counselor educators provide clearly stated
roles and responsibilities for students, site supervisors, and program
supervisors. They confirm that site supervisors are qualified to provide
supervision and inform site supervisors of their professional and ethical
responsibilities in this role.*

It is necessary for rehabilitation counselor training programs to clearly develop
and document policies and procedures regarding clinical field experiences for
students. These policies can include requirements for hours, supervision, student
activities, evaluation, and supervisor qualifications. For example, many programs
document the roles and responsibilities of educators, students, and field
supervisors in practicum and internship handbooks that are distributed and
available to students and supervisors. Without a clear definition of roles and
responsibilities, there are risks that can compromise student learning and clinical
experiences. In addition, it is the task of the rehabilitation counselor educator to
evaluate the qualifications of field supervisors in order to ensure appropriate
supervision of students based on the ethical practices of the profession.

CASE STUDY

*In the case of Sylvia, the program coordinator, she also discovers in
her review of the program that there are no written policies and
procedure for the program field placements. There is also vague
information within a student handbook that is given to students and
supervisors regarding field placement requirements and processes. She*

learns that many students are not keeping hour logs nor receiving weekly
supervision. Further, she finds many of the field supervisors are not
master's level counselors or clinicians.

ETHICAL CONSIDERATIONS

1. Discuss the ethical implications for Sylvia as the coordinator of the
   program.

2. What step does she need to take in order to align her program with the
   intent of the Code?

H.5.m. STUDENT STATUS DISCLOSURE
Rehabilitation counselor educators make reasonable efforts to ensure
that clients at field placements are aware of the services rendered and the
qualifications of the students rendering those services. Rehabilitation
counselor educators reinforce the requirements for the student to disclose
their status as a student and how this affects the limits of confidentiality.

Professional disclosure as it applies to the rehabilitation counselor is also
necessary for counselors in training. As a rehabilitation counselor educator, it is
necessary to ensure that students in field placements understand and are prepared
to disclose their status as a student-trainee and their qualifications. The credentials
of the student's supervisor including relevant experience, confidentiality,
supervision process, and limits of confidentially in supervision needs to be
provided and explained to clients.

CASE STUDY

Jeremy is a graduate student in a rehabilitation counseling graduate
program. While in his internship with a community rehabilitation program
(CRP), Jeremy has been assigned to work with consumers regarding the
development of work skills. He conducts group and individual counseling
with each of his consumers. Jeremy is treated like one of the professional
staff at the agency and he does not disclose his student intern status to
consumers. An internship course requirement also required him to write
case concept papers about his consumers to hand in to his professor.
Although he maintains confidentially regarding consumer names, he uses
several examples and discusses in class the counseling issues that his
consumers are working on. He has not shared this fact with his
consumers.

1. What are the implications of Jeremy's actions?

2. As a rehabilitation counseling educator, what are his professor's
   responsibilities?

H. 6. REHABILITATION COUNSELOR EDUCATOR COMPETENCE

H.6.a. EDUCATOR KNOWLEDGE AND SKILL

Rehabilitation counselor educators who are responsible for developing, implementing, and supervising educational programs are knowledgeable, regarding the ethical, legal, and regulatory aspects of the profession, are skilled in applying that knowledge, and make students aware of their responsibilities. Rehabilitation counselor educators conduct counselor education and training programs in an ethical manner.

It is important that the rehabilitation counselor educators have the knowledge and specialized skills for teaching rehabilitation counseling. In addition to counselor education, rehabilitation counselor educators must be prepared to teach and supervisor students within rehabilitation settings and to work with a diversity of clients with disabilities regarding employment issues. Rehabilitation counselor educator competences also include serving as role models and to enhance the values of the profession to their students.

CASE STUDY

Before entering his doctoral training, Gerry was a special education teacher. He was accepted to a doctoral program focused on general counselor education with a specialization in rehabilitation. In order to become a CRC, Gerry had to complete an internship in a rehabilitation counseling setting because he had no experience in providing rehabilitation counseling services to individuals with disabilities.

Upon graduation, Gerry is hired as an assistant professor in a graduate rehabilitation counseling program. He is assigned to teach an introduction to rehabilitation counseling course. Though he passed the CRC exam and completed an internship, he has never practiced as a rehabilitation counselor.

1. Is Gerry qualified to teach as a rehabilitation counselor educator?

2. Is Gerry violating any ethical codes?

3. What must Gerry consider when developing his own knowledge and skill base for teaching and supervising?

4. What are the implications for Gerry's students?

H.6.b. TECHNOLOGY-ASSISTED EDUCATION

When using technology, rehabilitation counselor educators are competent in the use of that technology. Rehabilitation counselor educators take necessary precautions to protect confidential student information transmitted through any electronic means.

Much like rehabilitation counselor supervisors, educators are utilizing technology to teach, supervise, and communicate with students. Educators must understand and become proficient at using the different modalities of technology available to them such as online learning platforms (i.e. Blackboard, Canvas, Moodle) and become competent users of communication methods (i.e. email, video conferencing). Most educators have access and participate in specialized training in using different technology and how to protect confidential information is necessary.

CASE STUDY

Judy is a professor in a rehabilitation counseling program and has been teaching in the classroom for decades. During the COVID pandemic, her university abruptly shut down and all classes were to be taught online. Judy was not a savvy user of technology and struggled to pivot to online teaching and was seriously challenged using the University's online learning platform. She struggled with building the course and developing new ways to teach the content of her courses online. Students were frustrated with Judy's inability to set up and run live online classes. She was overwhelmed and confused.

1. What were Judy's ethical responsibilities regarding her own competencies in using technology for teaching?

2. What are possible resources for Judy to develop the skills to use technology for her teaching possibilities?

H.6.c. CULTURAL DIVERSITY IN REHABILITATION COUNSELOR EDUCATION

Rehabilitation counselor educators are sensitive to the role of cultural diversity in their relationships with students. Rehabilitation counselor educators understand and use culturally sensitive and competent teaching practices. They assist students in gaining the knowledge, personal awareness, sensitivity, disposition, and skills necessary for becoming a culturally competent rehabilitation counselor working with a diverse client population.

There has been much agreement regarding multicultural competency within the rehabilitation counseling field. Rehabilitation counseling accreditation standards, professional associations, and certification standards have accentuated the necessity of active integration of diversity into the student and faculty composition, diversity within the rehabilitation workforce, and infusion of multicultural and individual different competencies into rehabilitation counseling curriculum. **According to** Middleton, et al.,[17]

> *Professional multicultural rehabilitation competencies and standards are necessary if persons with disabilities from diverse ethnic backgrounds are to be well served by rehabilitation counselors. Current and future rehabilitation counselors must possess the necessary awareness, knowledge, and skills to practice their profession in an ethical, responsible, and competent manner with all consumers/clients.*[p.219]

As CRCs, educators must first assure that they are adequately prepared and possess multicultural competencies. Thoughtful and deliberate integration of cultural diversity competency into teaching and supervision is necessary in order to develop well-balanced and culturally competent rehabilitation counselors.

CASE STUDY

> *Karen is teaching a rehabilitation counseling course on job placement techniques for individuals with disabilities. She has prepared the course based upon available literature on the topic as well as her own placement experience as a rehabilitation counselor. The program that Karen teaches is in an urban area with many different races and ethnicities represented in the community. Most of her students in class live and work within the community. Karen teaches standard job placement theories and approaches. However, she does not expose her students to the possible challenges and considerations when working with a diverse consumer population, the influence of culture on workforce demands, or the impact of cultural differences between a client and rehabilitation counselor.*

ETHICAL CONSIDERATIONS

1. As a CRC, what does Karen need to address in her teaching approach and own cultural competencies?

2. What is the potential impact on her students?

H.7. ROLES AND RELATIONSHIPS BETWEEN EDUCATORS AND STUDENTS

H.7.a RELATIONSHIP BOUNDARIES WITH STUDENTS

Rehabilitation counselor educators are aware of the power differential in their relationships with students. They do not engage in electronic and/or in-person interactions or relationships that knowingly compromise the academic relationship. Rehabilitation counselor educators consider and clearly discuss the risks and benefits of extending boundaries with their students and take appropriate professional precautions to minimize the risk of harm to the student.

H.7.b. SEXUAL OR ROMANTIC RELATIONSHIPS WITH CURRENT STUDENTS

Rehabilitation counselor educators are prohibited from engaging in electronic and/or in-person sexual or romantic interactions or relationships with their current students.

H.7.c. EXPLOITATIVE RELATIONSHIPS

Rehabilitation counselor educators do not engage in exploitative relationships with their students.

Intimate or exploitative relationships between educators and current students are not appropriate. Given the many roles and power differential between educators and students, rehabilitation counselor educators need to have a keen awareness of how any interaction with a current student in the form of a sexual relationship or have potential for exploitation, is important to set clear boundaries. A rehabilitation counselor educator's ability to examine their own needs if they are sexually attracted to a current student is of the utmost importance. Seeking out their own supervision or consultation regarding these feelings or potential exploitation is necessary to set clear boundaries and ethical practice.

CASE STUDY

Kelly is a rehabilitation counselor educator. She has five rehabilitation counseling interns that she supervises. She has worked hard to develop relationships with each of her students and the class has developed a close comradery. The class frequently goes out together after class and Kelly has participated a few times with the group for dinner. One of her students, Mary is a good student. Kelly is finding herself thinking about Mary outside of class and feels she is becoming attracted to Mary. In their weekly internship class, Kelly finds herself preoccupied with Mary and giving her more attention. Kelly feels she is an ethical educator and is aware of her ethical code but feels that she is having difficulty managing her romantic feelings about the student.

ETHICAL CONSIDERATIONS

1. What are the ethical issues you feel Kelly needs to address?

2. How do you feel she can address these issues?

H.7.d. HARASSMENT
Rehabilitation counselor educators do not condone or participate in any form of harassment, including sexual harassment.

H.7.e. RELATIONSHIPS WITH FORMER STUDENTS
Rehabilitation counselor educators are aware of the power differential in their relationships with former students. Rehabilitation counselor educators discuss with former students potential risks when they consider engaging in romantic, sexual, or other intimate relationships.

CASE STUDY

Lynn has been Melissa's faculty advisor, professor, and internship supervisor. They have developed a close relationship over the three years that Melissa's has been in the graduate program. Lynn provided a positive reference for Melissa upon her graduation that allowed her to secure an excellent rehabilitation counseling position. Both Lynn and Melissa consider their relationship professional but also enjoy each other's company. After graduation, they become friends on a social level and have lunch dates. Lynn is extremely proud of Melissa's accomplishments and considers her more of a colleague now than a former student or supervisee. Melissa considers Lynn a professional mentor and friend.

ETHICAL CONSIDERATIONS

1. What issues do Lynn and Melissa need to consider in this evolving relationship?

H.7.f. ACADEMIC RELATIONSHIPS WITH RELATIVES AND FRIENDS
Rehabilitation counselor educators make every effort to avoid accepting close relatives, romantic partners, or friends as students. When such circumstances cannot be avoided, rehabilitation counselor educators utilize a formal review mechanism.

CASE STUDY

Mary is a professor in a graduate rehabilitation counseling program. She is frequently working closely in the field with other professionals in terms of training and presentations. She meets Beth who is a Transition Advocate with a non-profit agency. Mary is extremely impressed with Beth's professionalism, intellect, and commitment to working with individuals with disabilities. In the process of working on a project, Mary and Beth develop a friendship; they have lunch, go to yoga classes, and share their personal and family stories. They have children the same age; they live in the same community and have many of the same interests and goals in life. Mary learns that Beth wants to get a graduate degree in rehabilitation counseling. Mary teaches in the only program in the state. Mary feels Beth would be a great asset to the graduate program given her experience and drive.

ETHICAL CONSIDERATIONS

1. How can this situation be handled if Beth applies to Mary's graduate program?
2. What issues may need to be addressed prior to Mary's acceptance into the graduate program?
3. How can potential issues be addressed before accepting Beth to the program or if she is accepted into the program?

H.8. EDUCATION EVALUATION, REMEDIATION, AND ENDORSEMENT

H.8.a. EVALUATION OF STUDENTS

Rehabilitation counselor educators clearly state to students, prior to and throughout the training program, the levels of competency expected, appraisal methods, and timing of evaluations for both didactic and clinical competencies. Rehabilitation counselor educators provide students with ongoing feedback regarding their performance throughout the training program.

CASE STUDY

Casey is teaching a practicum course and supervising several students in field placements. One of her students, Olivia, has been struggling in her placement in terms of showing up on time, communication with her site supervisor, and overall performance with clients. Casey has been inconsistent with her oversight of Olivia, the difficulties she is having, and fails to follow up with Olivia's site supervisor. At the end of the semester, Olivia reviews the final site supervisor evaluation and talks with the site supervisor who reports Olivia did not do a good job with her placement and does not recommend she move onto internship. Casey communicates her concerns with Olivia who is upset with her evaluation and insists it was not her fault. She had a lot of personal issues going on during the semester which impacted her performance.

ETHICAL CONSIDERATIONS

1. What were Casey's ethical responsibilities regarding Olivia during her practicum placement?

H.8.b. GATEKEEPING AND REMEDIATION FOR STUDENTS
   Rehabilitation counselor educators, through ongoing evaluation, are aware of and address the inability of some students to achieve required competencies, which may be due to academic performance or personal concerns. Rehabilitation counselor educators do the following: (1) assist students in securing remedial assistance, including counseling, when needed; (2) seek professional consultation and document the decision to recommend dismissal or refer students for assistance; and (3) make reasonable efforts to ensure that students have recourse in a timely manner to address decisions requiring them to seek assistance, or to dismiss them and provide students with due process, according to institutional policies and procedures.

CASE STUDY

   Looking again at Casey's case study, please respond to the following questions.

ETHICAL CONSIDERATIONS

1. In the above case, what steps do you recommended Casey take to developing a remediation plan for Olivia?

2. What components of performance need remediation to assist Olivia?

3. Should Olivia be dismissed from the program?

H.8.c. REFERRING STUDENTS FOR COUNSELING
   If students request counseling or if counseling services are suggested as part of a remediation process, rehabilitation counselor educators assist students in identifying appropriate services. Rehabilitation counselor

*educators do not provide counseling services to currently enrolled
students but may address interpersonal competencies in terms of the
impact of these issues on academic performance, professional
functioning, and/or clients.*

CASE STUDY

*Karen is a full time faculty in a rehabilitation counseling program
and program coordinator. She works closely to develop relationships with
her students and support them within the program. She feels it is
important to provide her advisees with her cell number for ease of
communication while they are in the program. One student, Austin, has
begun texting Karen many times during the day. He is stressed and Karen
is trying to provide supportive texts. The texts from Austin increase into
the evening and become tangential and agitated. Karen starts to worry
about Austin's mental health status.*

ETHICAL CONSIDERATIONS

1. What are the ethical issues Karen needs to address regarding the situation with
    Austin?

2. What steps can Karen take regarding this student and her concerns?

H.8.d. ENDORSEMENT

*Rehabilitation counselor educators endorse students for certification,
licensure, employment, or completion of academic or training programs
based on satisfactory progress and observations while under supervision
or training. Regardless of qualifications, rehabilitation counselor
educators do not endorse students whom they believe to be impaired in
any way that would interfere with the performance of the duties
associated with the endorsement.*

CASE STUDY

*Linda is a program coordinator and provides references for new
graduates of her program when seeking employment. One of her students
who will be graduating soon has struggled in the program. The student
had many issues throughout the program including difficulties with
classmates, interpersonal challenges with faculty, and was fired from her
internship for significant interpersonal issues with co-workers and needed
a remediation plan to address her own personal and mental health issues
which were impacting her performance in the program. The remediation
plan was completed but Linda is not confident in the student's*

qualifications to work in the field. This student asks Linda for a reference she can utilize when looking for a job.

ETHICAL CONSIDERATIONS

1. Does Linda have an ethical obligation to endorse the student for graduation from the program? What issues need to be considered?

2. What is Linda's ethical obligation to provide a reference (endorsement) for this student?

3. What additional information do you need to make a decision to provide or not provide an endorsement?

REFERENCES

[1]Bernard, J. M., & Goodyear, R. K. (2004). *Fundamentals of clinical supervision* (5th ed.). Upper Saddle River, NJ: Pearson Education.

[2]Blackwell, T. L., Strohmer, D. C., Belcas, E. M., & Burton, K. A. (2002). Ethics in rehabilitation counselor supervision. *Rehabilitation Counseling Bulletin, 45*(4), 240–247.

[3]Campbell, J. M. (2006). *Essentials of clinical supervision.* Hoboken, NJ: John Wiley & Sons, Inc.

[4]Campbell, J. M. (2000). *Becoming an effective supervisor: A workbook for counselors and psychotherapists.* Ann Arbor, MI: Sheriden Books.

[5]Central Connecticut State University. (2014). Graduate student handbook for professional and rehabilitation counseling. New Britain, CT: Author.

[6]Commission on Rehabilitation Counselor Certification. (2014). *CRC certification guide.* Schaumberg, IL: Author.

[7]Council on Rehabilitation Education. (2010). *Standards for rehabilitation counselor education programs.* Schaumberg, IL: Author.

[8]Herbert, J. T., & Trusty, J. (2006). Clinical supervision practices and satisfaction within the public vocational rehabilitation program. *Rehabilitation Counseling Bulletin, 49*(2), 66–80.

[9]Herbert, J. T. (2004). Qualitative analysis of clinical supervision within the public vocational rehabilitation program. *Journal of Rehabilitation Administration, 28,* 51–74.

[10]Herbert, J. T. (2004b). Clinical supervision. In D. R. Maki & T. F. Riggar (Eds.), *Handbook of rehabilitation counseling* (pp. 289–304). New York: Springer.

[11]Herlinhy, B. (2006). Ethical and legal issues in supervision in *Essentials of clinical supervision (p.18-34).* Hoboken, NJ: John Wiley & Sons, Inc.

[12]Herlinhy, B. & Corey, G. (1997). Boundary issues in counseling: Multiple roles and responsibilities. Alexandria, VA: American Counseling Association.

[13]King, C. L. (2011). Rehabilitation counselor supervision in the private sector: A qualitative examination of long-term disability. *The Rehabilitation Professional, 19*(3), 83-92.

[14]King, C. L. (2009). *Rehabilitation counselor supervision in the private sector: An examination of the long term disability setting.* (Order No. 3345658, Boston University). *ProQuest Dissertations and Theses,* 238-n/a. Retrieved from http://0search.proquest.com.www.consuls.org/docview/ 304844230?accountid=9970. (304844230).

[15]Leahy, M. J. (1998). *Practitioner accountability: Professionalism, certification and licensure.* Paper for the 23rd Mary Switzer Seminar. Retrieved on May 17, 2008, from http://www.mswitzer.org/sem98/papers/leahy.html

[16]Matrone, K. F., & Leahy, M. J. (2005). The Relationship Between Vocational Rehabilitation Client Outcomes and Rehabilitation Counselor Multicultural Counseling Competencies. *Rehabilitation Counseling Bulletin, 48*(4), 233-244. DOI: 10.1177/00343552050480040401

[17]Middleton, R. A., Rollins, C. W., & Sanderson, P. (2000). Endorsement of professional multicultural rehabilitation competencies and standards: a call to action. *Rehabilitation Counseling Bulletin, 43*(4), 219-240. DOI: 10.1177/003435520004300407

[18]Scott, C. G., Nolin, J., & Wilburn, S. T. (2006). Barriers to effective clinical supervision for counseling students and postgraduate counselors: Implications for rehabilitation counselors. *Rehabilitation Education, 20*(2), 91–102.

[19]Schultz, J. C., Osokie, J. N., Fried, J. H., Nelson, R. E., & Bardos, A. N. (2002). Clinical supervision in public rehabilitation counseling settings. *Rehabilitation Counseling Bulletin, 45*(4), 213–222.

[20]Tarvydas, V. T. (1997). Standards of practice: Ethical and legal. In D. R. Maki & T. F. Riggar (Eds.), *Rehabilitation counseling: Profession and practice* (pp. 72–94) New York: Springer.

[21]Thielsen, V. A., & Leahy, M. J. (2001). Essential knowledge and skills for effective clinical supervision in rehabilitation counseling. *Rehabilitation Counseling Bulletin, 44*(4), 196

CHAPTER 12

RESEARCH AND PUBLICATION

ROXANNA N. PEBDANI

SECTION I: RESEARCH AND PUBLICATION

Research is an important part of rehabilitation counselling, and in order to conduct research in an ethical manner, rehabilitation counselors must be aware of their responsibilities with regard to research. Rehabilitation counselors who conduct research must do so in a culturally respectful and inclusive manner. Rehabilitation counselors are also encouraged to be research participants, where possible. Section I of the Code of Professional Ethics for Rehabilitation Counselors [1] has five distinct subsections relating to ethical research practices:

Research Responsibilities

➢ (I.1.), Rights of Research Participants

➢ (I.2.), Reporting Results

➢ (I.3.), Research Publications and Presentations

➢ (I.4.), Managing and Maintaining Boundaries

➢ (I.5.), all of which are discussed in depth in this chapter.

I.1 RESEARCH RESPONSIBILITIES

Standard I.1 relates to the responsibilities a rehabilitation counselor has when conducting research. Rehabilitation researchers should be culturally sensitive in their work (I.1.a.) and should adhere to ethical principles as well as legal and institutional requirements when conducting research with human participants (I.1.b.). Rehabilitation counselors should ensure that they have institutional approval prior to undertaking research (I.1.d.) where possible, however in some situations rehabilitation counselors may not have access to institutional approval (for example, those who work in a setting where research is not often conducted and, therefore, there is no method for obtaining institutional approval for research approval). Even in these instances where review is unavailable, rehabilitation counselors are expected to adhere to ethical and legal requirements regarding research (I.1.e.). Rehabilitation counselors undertaking research must understand the legal requirements of confidentiality and must adhere to these requirements (I.1.c.) and should ensure that the research they are undertaking interferes with the lives of research participants as little as possible (I.1.i.).

Rehabilitation counselors must do everything possible to protect research participants from injury throughout the research process (I.1.g.). If a rehabilitation counsellor finds themselves in a situation where they must act differently from normal research practice, they must seek consultation and ensure that the rights of their research participants are protected throughout the deviation (I.1.f.). All of these ethical principles ensure that research participants have adequate protection throughout the research process. Every member of the research team has a responsibility to act ethically throughout the research process, however the primary researcher has an ethical obligation to ensure adherence to these standards for themselves and the entire team (I.1.h.).

I.1.a. CULTURE AND DIVERSITY IN RESEARCH

Rehabilitation counselors plan, design, conduct, and report research in a manner that reflects cultural sensitivity. When possible, rehabilitation counselors take steps to include a diverse sample population.

This substandard speaks to the importance of representativeness in research. For many years, people with disabilities were excluded from research based on their disability. Clearly, this is not representative and led to under-representation of individuals with disabilities in published research. Rehabilitation counselors ensure that when they conduct research their sample is as diverse and representative of the population they are studying.

CASE STUDY

Matteo is conducting a research study on the impact of disability on access to health care in rural parts of the United States. Matteo takes a look at his survey responses as they come in and he realizes that his sample is primarily white and male. Matteo thinks to himself "hmm, that's odd, I know that there are people of color and women who live rurally and experience disability" but continues as he was.

Aneika is conducting a research study on the impact of fibromyalgia on the lives of women of color who disabilities. This study focuses on women of color, specifically, as the research shows that women of color tend to have different experiences in the medical system.

ETHICAL CONSIDERATIONS

1. Is Matteo acting ethically? Why or why not? What about Aneika? What makes the two situations different?

2. What should Matteo have done differently? Is there anything else he needs to keep in mind if he decides to change how he recruits in order to recruit a more diverse group of participants?

I.1.b. USE OF HUMAN SUBJECTS

Rehabilitation counselors plan, design, conduct, and report research in a manner that is consistent with pertinent ethical principles, applicable laws, host institutional regulations, and organizational and scientific standards governing research with human subjects. They seek consultation when appropriate.

When a rehabilitation counsellor designs a research study, it is essential that they adhere to ethical principles as set forth by all organizations involved. Generally, once a research project has been designed it is submitted to an Institutional Review Board (IRB) who provides feedback on the proposed project, including changes to make the project ethically responsible. When conducting research with an organization, the organization should also have input in the project and how it is carried out. Often, IRBs will require researchers to have an existing agreement with an organization prior to undertaking research within an organization.

CASE STUDY

Katie, a master's student in rehabilitation counseling, is collecting data for her master's thesis. She is surveying individuals who work in group homes, specifically state employees who work in group homes. To conduct her research, Katie obtains IRB approval and begins to solicit survey responses from state employees who work these settings. Much of the way through data collection, Katie finds out that her state's Department of Developmental Services (DDS) requires that she obtain DDS approval in order to survey their employees. However, Katie has been successful thus far and decides that since she only needs a few more responses, she will continue to collect her sample through her original approach.

ETHICAL CONSIDERATIONS

1. Which ethical principles apply here?

2. What should Katie have done differently to conduct research ethically?

3. How would you handle this if you were in Katie's place?

I.1.c. CONFIDENTIALITY IN RESEARCH

Rehabilitation counselors are responsible for understanding and adhering to applicable laws and organizational policies and applicable guidelines regarding confidentiality in their research practices.

Research participants have the right to have the information that they share or the data that comes from their participation in research to be confidential. As such, it is important that researchers do all that they can to protect this confidentiality. In some cases this will mean ensuring that data cannot be accessed by outside parties (storing data in password protected files on password protected computers, for example), but in other cases it will mean that ensuring that the data that is shared is not identifiable.

CASE STUDY

Nina has been conducting research for many years, as a professor in a research intensive institution. She is currently working on a qualitative research project that aims to understand how employers respond to employing individuals with disabilities. She has been lucky in recruitment and has been able to recruit major players in large and very well-known companies. Nina realizes that the way that the research participants are responding to questions makes it plainly obvious where each employee works. Still, Nina knows that the results and discussion sections of qualitative research must be supported by quotations from the interviews. Therefore, Nina proceeds with her work and publishes the article, using the identifying quotations to support her interpretation of the data.

ETHICAL CONSIDERATIONS

1. Which ethical standards apply in this situation?

2. What should Nina have done differently to conduct research ethically?

3. How would you handle this if you were in Nina's place?

I.1.d. INSTITUTIONAL APPROVAL

When institutional review board approval is required, rehabilitation counselors provide accurate information about their research proposals and obtain approval prior to conducting their research. They conduct research in accordance with the approved research protocols.

An IRB is a group of people tasked with ensuring that research conducted on behalf of or affiliated with an organization is conducted ethically. As discussed previously, once a research plan has been developed, researchers then submit their plan to the IRB. Once an IRB has approved a project, the researcher must follow the approved plan in conducting their research. If a researcher decides that they need to do something differently, they must apply for a modification to their research project which is submitted to the IRB. The researcher cannot make those changes until the IRB has approved it.

CASE STUDY

Remember Matteo from I.1.a.? He has decided that women and people of color are underrepresented in his research study on the impact of disability on access to health care in rural parts of the United States. He has realized that this largely has to do with where and how he is recruiting. He has IRB approval to recruit through seven specific Facebook pages, and he has noticed that these Facebook groups are targeted towards men. Matteo decides that he needs to make a change and starts looking for other Facebook groups to recruit from.

ETHICAL CONSIDERATIONS

1. Is what Matteo is doing ethical? Why or why not?

2. What should he do differently?

I.1.e. INDEPENDENT RESEARCHERS

When rehabilitation counsellors conduct independent research and do not have access to an institutional review board, they are bound to the same ethical principles and laws pertaining to the review of their plan, design, conduct, and reporting of research. Independent researchers not familiar with institutional review board standards seek appropriate consultation.

Some rehabilitation counsellors who are conducting research may work in an environment that does not have an IRB or a research approval body. Those researchers must still act ethically and adhere to legal requirements and should ask colleagues with more experience in research for help in designing and evaluating the appropriateness of a research project.

CASE STUDY

Amir works for a medium-sized non-profit organization that provides services to individuals who are homeless. He is interested in exploring the connection between posttraumatic stress disorder (PTSD) and homelessness and has devised a research project to explore the prevalence of PTSD in individuals who are homeless. This

293

is his first research project. He develops a research plan and begins to carry it out.

ETHICAL CONSIDERATIONS

1. Did Amir act ethically?

2. Why or why not?

3. What should he have done differently?

I.1.f. DEVIATION FROM STANDARD PRACTICES
Rehabilitation counsellors seek consultation and observe stringent safeguards to protect the rights of research subjects when a research-related problem indicates that a deviation from standard or acceptable practices may be necessary.

Very rarely, something will come up that requires that a researcher change their approach to their study. As we saw in I.1.d., acting ethically means seeking institutional approval and conducting research in accordance with the approval that has been obtained. However, in some cases, small changes must be made. When this is done, the researcher should seek consultation as soon as possible and report the changes to the IRB immediately.

CASE STUDY

Francis is a graduate student working on a large-scale research project run by his advisor. One of the projects that Francis is tasked with working on involves following-up with individuals who have had a negative experience in the workplace and conducting a brief telephone survey collecting information about their experience and how it was resolved. After a few follow-up calls, Francis realizes that asking research participants about these experiences is upsetting some of them, with some of the participants reporting psychological distress after completing the phone calls and revisiting their negative experiences. One participant makes a comment about suicide and then hangs up the phone, and Francis contacts local emergency services and asks them to conduct a welfare check.

ETHICAL CONSIDERATIONS

1. What does Francis need to do next in order to behave ethically?

2. How would you handle this if you were in Francis' place?

I.1.g. PRECAUTIONS TO AVOID INJURY

Rehabilitation counsellors who conduct research with human subjects are responsible for the welfare of participants throughout the research process and take reasonable precautions to avoid causing psychological, emotional, physical, or social harm to participants.

Just as in counselling, rehabilitation counsellor researchers are bound to the ethical principle of nonmaleficence–to do no harm. This was not always the case (see, for example, the Tuskegee Syphilis Study). Researchers should ensure that their proposed projects will not cause intentional harm and work to minimise the potential for inadvertent harm through their projects, as well.

CASE STUDY

Consider Francis' case above. What should Francis have done differently with regards to code I.1.g., Precautions to Avoid Injury?

I.1.h. PRINCIPAL RESEARCHER RESPONSIBILITY

The ultimate responsibility for ethical research practice lies with the principal researcher(s). All others involved in the research activities share ethical obligations and responsibilities for their own actions.

This substandard refers to the responsibility of individuals on a research team. Each researcher on a research team is responsible to ensure their own ethical behavior and follow all applicable ethical codes. However, a principal researcher, or the researcher in charge, is not only responsible for themselves, but they must also ensure that the entire research project is ethical–including the work of subordinate researchers.

CASE STUDY

Isabelle is a professor of rehabilitation counseling at a large research focused institution. She is the principal investigator on a large research grant for which she has one full time research assistant and four graduate research assistants. Isabelle is terribly busy and has tasked the full time research associate, Ned, to ensure that proper protocol is being followed in the study. Ned realizes that one of the graduate research assistants has been taking some of the research data home with her on a computer that is not password protected, which is not proper protocol according to the project's submission to the Institutional Review Board at their institution.

ETHICAL CONSIDERATIONS

1. Which ethical standards apply here?

2. What could the individuals in this case study have done differently?

3. How would you handle this if you were in their place?

I.1.i. MINIMAL INTERFERENCE

Rehabilitation counselors take precautions to avoid causing disruption in the lives of research participants or the setting in which research is conducted.

This substandard refers to the importance of making sure that rehabilitation counselors do everything in their power to ensure that the research they are conducting does not interfere with or disrupt the lives of their research participants.

CASE STUDY

Jonathan wants to study the prevalence of co-occurring disabilities in individuals with substance use disorders. He has trouble deciding which assessments to utilize in order to assess the co-occurring disorders and decides to begin collecting data and then decide which assessment is best for his population. Therefore, he decides to administer four surveys, which take a total of three hours of the participant's time. In addition to this, Jonathan decides that he does not have time to administer the assessments at the agency from which he is recruiting participants, so he requires research participants to come to his office–seven miles from the treatment facility–to take the assessments.

ETHICAL CONSIDERATIONS

1. Which ethical standards apply in this situation?

2. What should Jonathan have done differently to conduct research ethically?

3. How would you handle this if you were in Jonathan's place?

Section one of the Research and Publication section of the Code of Professional Ethics [1] ensures that the research we conduct is representative, fair, appropriate, and minimally invasive. Research standards have evolved over the years to become more inclusive, less invasive, and even less harmful.

However, it is up to all of us to ensure that we are acting ethically as we conduct research.

I.2: RIGHTS OF RESEARCH PARTICIPANTS

Rights of Research Participants, section I.2., further speaks to the importance of protecting human participants in research. Rehabilitation counselors undertaking research will make certain commitments–protection of confidentiality, how the research will be conducted, how data will be managed– and ethical rehabilitation counselors honor these commitments at all times (I.2.g.). Part of this commitment includes the concept of informed consent, which is the process by which research participants are given information about how the research will be conducted, potential risks, potential benefits, and limitations on confidentiality, among other things. Informed consent information is given prior to participants agreeing to participate in the research, and informed consent also assures that their participation is entirely voluntary (I.2.a.). Research participants have the right to expect that the information gained from research they participate in maintain their confidentiality (that their personal information is not shared)–and if confidentiality cannot be protected, the researcher must inform the participants during the informed consent process (I.2.e.).

These ethical principles apply to all research participants, including students, supervisees, and clients, all of whom have the right to choose whether or not they wish to participate in a research study, with no negative repercussions for not participating (students and supervisees: I.2.c, clients: I.2.d.). In some cases, research will be conducted on individuals who are not capable of giving informed consent. When that is the case, rehabilitation counselors instead get consent from someone authorized to give consent on their behalf (I.2.f.).

Though there was a time when deception was more commonly utilized in research, rehabilitation counselors should avoid using deception in their research projects unless there is no other way to study the topic they are studying. If they must use deception, then they also must debrief the research participants and explain both the deception and the reasons for deceptions as soon as possible (I.2.b.)

Lastly, though section I.2.–Rights of Research Participants–largely pertains to the rights of people who are participating in research, there are also three ethical requirements pertaining to research collaborators and sponsors. Rehabilitation counselors who are conducting research with colleagues should, prior to beginning the research project, discuss with their collaborators who will undertake which tasks, who will be included in subsequent publications, and who will be included in the article acknowledgement (I.2.h.). Similarly, sponsors and other invested entities should be informed of how the research will be undertaken and of the results of the research. They should also be acknowledged for their support in subsequent publications (I.2.i.). Finally, rehabilitation counselors should have a colleague to whom they can transfer their research data in the case that they can no longer manage the data (I.2.j.). This ensures that the data remains protected and that collected data is still able to be used. However, in order for this to be done ethically, this plan should be developed prior to undertaking the research and the transfer of data should be included in the informed consent.

I.2.a. INFORMED CONSENT IN RESEARCH

Individuals have the right to consent to or decline requests to become research participants. Rehabilitation counsellors obtain consent from participants prior to initiating research. In seeking consent, rehabilitation counsellors:

1. *Accurately explain the purpose and procedures to be followed.*

2. *Identify any procedures that are experimental or relatively untried.*

3. *Describe any attendant discomforts and risks.*

4. *Describe any benefits or changes in individuals or organizations that might be reasonably expected.*

5. *Disclose appropriate alternative procedures that would be advantageous for participants.*

6. *Offer to answer any inquiries concerning the procedures.*

7. *Describe any limitations on confidentiality.*

8. *Describe formats and potential target audiences for the dissemination of research findings.*

9. *Instruct participants they are free to withdraw their consent and to discontinue participation in the project at any time without penalty.*

This subsection of the Code [1] refers to informed consent; the idea that research participants should have all pertinent information about the research project prior to agreeing to participate. Participants also have the opportunity to withdraw from the study at any time, if they so choose. More specific information about informed consent and what is included can be read above.

CASE STUDY

Shareese is a professor of rehabilitation counseling who conducts research on pedagogy in counselor education. Every year when she teaches the group counseling course, she requires her students to write weekly journals on their experiences in class. Last year, Shareese decided that she would change the format of this course, however she continued the course requirement of a weekly journal. Shareese believes that the change she made to the course is novel and interesting and decides to do a content analysis on her students' journals, comparing last year's journals (before the change) to the current year. She then writes up her analysis of the journals and submits it for publication.

ETHICAL CONSIDERATIONS

1. Which ethical principles apply in this instance?

2. What should Shareese have done differently to conduct research ethically?

3. How would you handle this if you were in Sharcese's place?

I.2.b. DECEPTION

Rehabilitation counselors do not conduct research involving deception unless alternative procedures are not feasible. If such deception has the potential to cause physical or emotional harm to research participants, the research is not conducted, regardless of prospective value. When the methodological requirements of a study necessitate concealment or deception, the investigator explains the reasons for this action as soon as possible during the debriefing.

Rehabilitation counselors conducting research with human subjects do everything they can to avoid deceiving their participants. This means that research projects that involve lying to participants or keeping information from participants should be avoided, unless there is no alternate way to conduct the research. In cases where this deception can lead to harm to the participant, rehabilitation counselors do not conduct this research. If it is determined that the deception has no potential for harm to research participants, and that there is no other way to gather information about the phenomena in question, then deception is acceptable. However, if a rehabilitation counselor uses deception as a tool in their research, they must provide participants with information about the deception and why it was undertaken as soon as possible, generally during a post data collection debriefing.

CASE STUDY

Aisha is a graduate student in rehabilitation counseling who has just completed and published her thesis, a research project with participants who have intellectual disabilities. Aisha was interested in studying whether or not people with intellectual disabilities were as susceptible to the bystander effect as people without intellectual disabilities. To conduct this study, Aisha collapsed in a waiting room in front of people with intellectual disabilities who were by themselves, as well as in front of people with intellectual disabilities who were in a room full of others. She did the same in front of individuals without intellectual disabilities. All of the participants believed that they were participating in a different study, which was why they were waiting in the lobby.

Aisha used the same informed consent form for all of the participants, and dismissed the participants after the fall, without any more information. She has since published the study in a peer-reviewed journal but has had no contact with any of the research participants since the day of their participation.

ETHICAL CONSIDERATIONS

1. Which ethical standards apply in this situation?

2. What could Aisha have done differently to conduct research ethically?

3. How would you handle this if you were in Aisha's place?

I.2.c. STUDENT/SUPERVISEE PARTICIPATION

Rehabilitation counselors who involve students or supervisees in research make clear to them the decision regarding participation in research activities does not affect their academic standing or supervisory relationship. Students or supervisees who choose not to participate in research are provided with an appropriate alternative to fulfill their academic or clinical requirements.

This subsection of the Code [1] ensures that students and supervisees have rights regarding research participation. This is especially important given the hierarchical relationships between teachers and students and supervisors and supervisees. Students and supervisees should be informed that they are not required to participate in research, and that there are no negative effects of choosing not to participate. In a case where research participation is intended to be a part of a class, students who do not want to participate should be given an alternative task in lieu of their research participation.

CASE STUDY

Jesus is teaching an undergraduate course on assessment to two hundred undergraduate students. He is also simultaneously teaching a graduate level course on developing assessment instruments. He decides to allow his graduate students to pilot their assessment instruments on his undergraduate class. One day, his undergraduate students show up to class, only to find out that they will be spending the day taking assessments developed by Jesus' graduate students. The undergraduate students are told that they do not have to stay, however the day's work counts as part of their participation grade.

ETHICAL CONSIDERATIONS

4. Which ethical standards apply in this situation?

5. What should Raymond have done differently to conduct research ethically?

6. How would you handle this if you were in Raymond's place?

I.2.d. CLIENT PARTICIPATION

Rehabilitation counselors conducting research involving clients make clear in the informed consent process that clients are free to choose whether to participate in research activities and are free to withdraw from research studies without adverse consequences.

Similar to subsection I.2.c., when research involves unequal relationships, such as when rehabilitation counselors are conducting research with their clients, it must be clear to the client that they do not have to participate in the research study and can withdraw at any time.

CASE STUDY

Tamika is a rehabilitation counselor working with an OBGYN group who supports women with disabilities throughout their pregnancies. Tamika would like to explore how their OBGYN services, specific to women with disabilities, affects confidence in future pregnancies. She develops a postnatal confidence survey for women with disabilities and applies for IRB approval. Her informed consent form states that her clients do not have to participate in the study and that participants have the right to withdraw from the study without penalty at any time. After obtaining informed consent, she administers the survey to her clients when they come in for their six-week follow up. As approved in her IRB proposal she also asks a number of OB nurses to administer the same postnatal confidence survey to women without disabilities who have recently given birth, however they fail to emphasize the voluntary nature of the research and do not tell their participants that they are able to withdraw at any time.

ETHICAL CONSIDERATIONS

1. Which ethical principles are present in this case study?

2. Has Tamika done anything wrong? What about her research partners?

3. What should have been done differently in this case in order to act ethically?

I.2.e. CONFIDENTIALITY OF INFORMATION

Confidential information obtained about research participants during the course of research remains confidential. When the possibility exists that others may obtain access to such information, ethical research practice requires the possibility, together with the plans for protecting confidentiality, be explained to participants as part of the procedures for obtaining informed consent.

This subsection relates to the idea that rehabilitation counselors should work to protect sensitive information about research participants throughout the research process. The information that rehabilitation counselors gain about participants during a research project is protected and identifying information should not be shared. If there is a chance that this information might be shared, research participants should be warned. When developing a research project and providing information about the study so that participants can give informed consent to participate in the research project, these potential breaches of confidentiality and the steps that the rehabilitation counselors will take to protect that confidentiality should be discussed.

CASE STUDY

Mayra is conducting follow-up research on the employment of individuals who have completed a substance abuse treatment program. To collect data, she is following her research participants through their place of employment, by calling them at work. This has become an arduous task; therefore, she employs a young undergraduate student named Samantha to make these phone calls and collect data. She briefly trains Samantha, and then leaves her to work independently. A few weeks later, Mayra happens to walk by as Samantha leaves a message with one of the research participant's

*coworkers. Jennifer overhears her saying "This is Samantha with
Flowers Chemical Dependency Treatment Services I'm calling to
follow-up on his treatment. Would you please have him call me back at
his earliest convenience?"*

ETHICAL CONSIDERATIONS

1. Which ethical standards apply in this situation?

2. What could the individuals in this case study have done differently?

3. How would you handle this if you were in their place?

I.2.f. RESEARCH PARTICIPANTS NOT CAPABLE OF GIVING INFORMED CONSENT

*When research participants are not capable of giving informed
consent, rehabilitation counselors obtain informed consent from a
legally authorized representative.*

Informed consent occurs when sufficient information about the research
project, related benefits and risks, limitations of confidentiality, and ability to
quit the study at any time are provided to the participant. This relates to section
I.2.a. of the Code [1], discussed earlier in the chapter. When conducting
research with certain populations, for example some people with intellectual
disabilities, rehabilitation counselors should explain the information included in
the informed consent in language that is appropriate to their target population.
In addition, they should obtain informed consent from the research participant's
legal guardian or someone who can legally give consent on the participant's
behalf.

CASE STUDY

*Sara's research is on the inclusion of people with disabilities in the
community. She has always done her research with willing adult
participants, however this year she has become more interested in
inclusion in childhood. She develops a research project in which she
watches children with and without disabilities play on the playground
during recess, to see how inclusive the recess environment is of
students with disabilities. Sara obtains IRB approval from her home
institution, and also receives approval from the school board. When
the time comes, she sends an informed consent form home with
students that explains that parents can opt-out of this research, but not
responding to the consent form is opting-in to having their children's
playground behavior studied. She also has teachers read the consent
form to the children before they go out to play.*

ETHICAL CONSIDERATIONS

1. Which ethical principles apply here?

2. What should Sara have done differently to conduct research ethically?

3. How would you handle this if you were in Sara's place?

I.2.g. COMMITMENTS TO PARTICIPANTS
Rehabilitation counselors take reasonable measures to honor all commitments to research participants.

When conducting research, rehabilitation counselors may make certain commitments to their research participants. This can be reimbursement for time spent, incentives for participation, or that they will share certain information with participants by a certain time. Rehabilitation counselors who are acting ethically will do everything they can to honor these commitments.

CASE STUDY

Lizzie is working on a research project for which she is offering the chance to win a $50 gift card to a local store for participating. In her recruitment materials, she states that participants who complete the survey by a certain date will have the opportunity to win the gift card in a raffle completed on that date. However, that date has come and gone, and Lizzie is still short on participants. She decides to extend her recruitment and does not hold the raffle on the date she initially shared with participants.

ETHICAL CONSIDERATIONS

1. Which ethical principles apply in this case?

2. What should Lizzie have done differently to conduct research ethically?

3. How would you handle this if you were in Lizzie's place?

I.2.h. AGREEMENT OF CONTRIBUTORS
Rehabilitation counselors who conduct joint research establish agreements in advance regarding allocation of tasks, publication credit, and types of acknowledgment received and incur an obligation to cooperate as agreed.

When working with multiple researchers, determinations about who will complete which task, what will qualify for credit for publication, and how the research will be disseminated should be made prior to completion of the project. Similarly, these agreements should specify what types of acknowledgements will be made (acknowledging partners in research). Rehabilitation counselors should comply with previously made agreements regarding these decisions.

CASE STUDY

Syrah, John, Terri, and Kate are graduate students working together on a manuscript. Early on, they make determinations about who will conduct what parts of the research, and who will write which parts of the manuscript. In this conversation, they also determine author order, based on the level of contribution of each group member. Halfway through the project, Kate–initially first author–begins to miss deadlines and eventually decreases her level of participation on the project. Syrah steps up and takes on many of Kate's responsibilities. However, when the article is finally submitted, Kate does the submission, and puts herself as first author.

ETHICAL CONSIDERATIONS

1. Which ethical principles apply in this case?

2. What should have been done differently to conduct research ethically?

3. How would you handle this if you were in this situation?

I.2.i. INFORMING SPONSORS

Rehabilitation counselors inform sponsors, institutions, and publication channels regarding research procedures and outcomes. Rehabilitation counselors make reasonable efforts to ensure that appropriate bodies and authorities are given pertinent information and acknowledgment.

Researchers who receive support for their work from sponsors have an ethical obligation to ensure that their sponsors are aware of their results. Similarly, the institutions with whom the rehabilitation counselors are affiliated, as well as the organizations that publish the articles from these research projects, should be provided with these results. These institutions and publication organizations should also have information about sponsoring agencies and institutions, and rehabilitation counselors should ensure that these sponsors are appropriately acknowledged.

CASE STUDY

Amelia is working on a manuscript about research she conducted on interagency collaboration for transition from high school to college for youth with disabilities. Her research was financially supported by one of the transition support programs, whom she did not find to be particularly helpful for students in transition. She decides that because she found unfavorable results regarding the work of this support program, she should not acknowledge the agency's funding in her manuscript. She also decides that she does not want to inform the agency of her results, because she is worried about their reaction.

ETHICAL CONSIDERATIONS

1. Which ethical principles apply in this scenario?

2. What should Amelia have done differently to conduct research ethically?

3. How would you handle this if you were in Amelia's place?

I.2.j. RESEARCH RECORDS CUSTODIAN

As appropriate, rehabilitation counselors prepare and disseminate to an identified colleague or records custodian a plan for the transfer of research data in the case of their incapacitation, retirement, or death.

Sometimes, things can happen that are out of our control, or life circumstances mean that we must (or can) move on from research. Rehabilitation counselors who conduct research should make a plan for how data will be handled if they are no longer able to handle it themselves. This likely means handing the data over to a colleague who can be the new guardian of the data. It is important to remember that data are protected, and this plan for transfer of data must be approved by the IRB or approving body.

CASE STUDY

Martin has been doing research for the last 38 years in his role as professor and educator in a rehabilitation counselling program. As he nears retirement he realizes that he does not have a plan in place regarding what will happen to his data when he retires.

ETHICAL CONSIDERATIONS

1. What should Martin do in order to act ethically?

2.   Which ethical principles apply here?

I.3: REPORTING RESULTS

Section I.3. of the Code [1] specifies ethical principles related to reporting the results of research. When reporting research results, rehabilitation counselors must ensure that the reporting of these results are accurate and not misleading in any way (1.3.a.). Therefore, when rehabilitation counselors have results that reflect poorly on the organizations being studied, counselors still must report these results (I.3.b.). Similarly, if a counselor realizes after publication that a significant mistake was made in the research, they correct these errors through the publication (I.3.c.). Rehabilitation counselors must also provide enough information to allow for replication of any research project they publish (I.3.e.), and rehabilitation counselors must take every precaution to disguise and protect the identity of research participants (I.3.d.). Finally, researchers must explain the generalizability of the research–how valid the results are in diverse populations (1.3.a.) when disseminating their research results.

I.3.a. ACCURATE RESULTS

Rehabilitation counselors plan, conduct, and report research accurately. They provide thorough discussions of the limitations of their data and alternative hypotheses. Rehabilitation counselors do not engage in misleading or fraudulent research, distort data, misrepresent data, or deliberately bias their results. They explicitly mention all variables and conditions known to the investigator(s) that may have affected the outcome of studies or interpretations of data. They describe the extent to which results are applicable to diverse populations.

This subsection informs us that when conducting research in rehabilitation counseling, it is important that rehabilitation counselors act honestly and truthfully. This means that when developing a research project, carrying it out, and writing about it, rehabilitation counselors ensure that they are presenting an accurate and honest representation of the research and results. This also means that when explaining their research, rehabilitation counselors identify and discuss alternate explanations for why certain results were obtained, including extraneous variables that may have impacted the study. They also ensure that their research is not misleading or inaccurate in any way, work to eliminate bias from their research, and are certain to include information as to how generalizable the research is to individuals from different backgrounds.

CASE STUDY

Jacob is developing an assessment instrument that identifies the prevalence of depression in older adults with disabilities. He begins his project with review of the relevant literature and develops a draft survey using this information. He then convenes a group of experts in the field who address depression, the lives of older adults, the lives of individuals with disabilities, and various intersections of these topics. With this group, he formalizes his survey and then pilots it on a group of undergraduate students at the University where he works. After the pilot, he then administers the survey to 200 undergraduate students and assesses the reliability and validity of his instrument. He then publishes his results in an article entitled "A survey of depression for older adults with disabilities: Measures of reliability and validity."

ETHICAL CONSIDERATIONS

1.　Which ethical standards apply in this situation?

2.　What should Jacob have done differently to conduct research ethically?

3.　How would you handle this if you were in Jacob's place?

I.3.b. OBLIGATION TO REPORT UNFAVORABLE RESULTS
　　　Rehabilitation counselors report the results of any research of professional value, regardless of outcomes. Results that reflect unfavorably on institutions, programs, services, prevailing opinions, or vested interests are not withheld.

When rehabilitation counselors have conducted research that is of importance to the field, they must share the results of this research. Even when these results may lead to negative views of the organizations being studied, rehabilitation counselors have an obligation to share their research.

CASE STUDY

Davide is currently employed in a substance abuse treatment facility where he works with clients but also conducts research on the program. Last year, his treatment facility instituted a new approach to substance abuse rehabilitation that has been well received by the community. People who attend the facility are excited about their potential treatment outcomes under these changes. Additionally, the mayor and several local agencies are pleased with the change and its potential to reduce substance use in the city, and therefore have provided Davide's agency with funding to support the change in format. Davide has written grant proposals on the topic and has published a number of peer-reviewed research articles on the innovative changes his agency has implemented.

Davide has been conducting research on the outcomes of this change in format and recently realized that it is, in fact, increasing substance use in the city. While people who have attended the program cease to use substances by the time of program completion, at three and six month follow-up, they are 50% more likely to have relapsed than individuals who completed the original treatment program. Davide is disappointed and tells his agency supervisor of his results. His agency supervisor tells him that he should keep this information to himself and not publish these results. His supervisor tells him "we have had so much positive feedback related to this program, the mayor is happy, the community is happy, clients are happy. Don't rock the boat, Davide, just let it be."

ETHICAL CONSIDERATIONS

1. What ethical standard(s) did Davide violate?

2. What ethical standard(s) did Davide uphold?

3. What ethical violations did Davide's agency supervisor violate or uphold?

4. What could Davide have done differently to conduct research ethically?

5. How would you handle this if you were in Davide's place?

I.3.c. REPORTING ERRORS

If rehabilitation counselors discover significant errors in their published research, they take reasonable steps to correct such errors in a correction erratum or other appropriate publication means.

If, after publication, a rehabilitation counselor finds that they have made mistakes in their report or in their results, they must work to correct these errors. This may be done by submitting a correction to the editor of the journal in which the research was published, or by submitting an erratum (a published explanation of the mistake and correction), a whole or partial retraction (where the rehabilitation counselor makes a written statement in which they withdraw all or part of the article), or by taking other steps that are appropriate in rectifying the incorrect publication.

CASE STUDY

Mike is a doctoral student in his second year of his Ph.D. program. Mike published his first peer-reviewed research article this year, and he has finally received a hard copy of his work. He is excited and shares it with a friend of whom he bounced research ideas all year. His friend reads the article and notices a large omission that Mike made in his publication. In his rush to publish his article, he completely forgot to include one of the themes that developed from his data, which means the article is not painting a full picture of the research results.

ETHICAL CONSIDERATIONS

1. Which ethical standards apply in this situation?

2. What should Mike have done differently to conduct research ethically?

3. How would you handle this if you were in Mike's place?

I.3.d. IDENTITY OF PARTICIPANTS

Rehabilitation counselors who supply data, aid in the research of another investigator, report research results, or make original data available take due care to disguise the identity of respective participants in the absence of specific authorization from the participants to do otherwise. In situations where participants self-identify their involvement in research studies, researchers make reasonable efforts to ensure that data are adapted/changed to protect the identities and welfare of all parties and that discussion of results does not cause harm to participants.

Research participants have a right to remain anonymous, and it is the rehabilitation counselor's job to ensure that this happens. When working with data related to an individual (or many individuals), rehabilitation counselors take precautions to anonymize the data and ensure that they include no information that may identify research participants. However, there are situations, particularly in qualitative research, where participants may allow the researchers to identify them. In these rare cases, researchers ensure that the potential to be identified, and how this will be handled, is clearly stated in the informed consent. Special care should be taken when working with participants whose identity will be shared in research, and when possible, participants can choose pseudonyms or other anonymizers to further protect their identity.

In other cases, individuals may self-identify as research participants. When individuals self-identify, rehabilitation counselors still take precautions to protect the identities of these research participants, and work to protect research participants from harm related to the discussion of results of the research project.

CASE STUDY

Maggie, a professor of rehabilitation counseling at a large research focused institution, is conducting a qualitative case study with a professor of speech language pathology on a research participant who is trilingual but has aphasia in all three languages. Working together, the professors are trying to understand what it is like for the participant to return to work given his language difficulties. The research participant, a popular news anchor who sustained a traumatic brain injury approximately one year ago in a very publicized accident, is having a particularly difficult time returning to his work due to the limitations of his aphasia. Both researchers travel to a local conference to present their case study research, and one of the researchers describes the participant as a "35-year old male news anchor in the area who sustained a TBI in a car accident approximately one year ago, resulting in Broca's Aphasia."

ETHICAL CONSIDERATIONS

1. Which ethical standards apply in this situation?

2. What could the researchers have done differently to conduct research ethically?

3. How would you handle this if you were in the place of these researchers?

I.3.e. REPLICATION STUDIES

Rehabilitation counselors make reasonable efforts to make available sufficient original research information to qualified professionals who may wish to replicate the study.

At times, researchers may have interest in conducting a study that is similar to (or the same as) a previous study, called a replication study. In order to facilitate this, rehabilitation counselors should provide adequate information and data to other researchers who are interested in replicating their work. This may mean providing adequate information for other researchers to set up a study with the same procedures, or it may mean sharing research data with other researchers who want to use that data to replicate the study.

CASE STUDY

John is a professor at a large university in the Southwestern United States. For the last ten years, he has had two iterations of a large grant that allowed him to collect longitudinal data about health insurance access for individuals with disabilities who are self-employed. Last year he published a controversial article about health insurance access for people with disabilities, using his longitudinal data. A few researchers have decided that they want to replicate his study but need more information to do so. They ask him to share the surveys that he used, as well as some of the data that he has collected. John decides that he has spent too much time working on this data to share it with other researchers, and that he is not done with it. He does not respond to their request.

ETHICAL CONSIDERATIONS

4. Which ethical standards apply in this situation?

5. What should John have done differently to conduct research ethically?

6. How would you handle this if you were in John's place?

I.4. PUBLICATIONS AND PRESENTATIONS

How to publish research and conduct presentations ethically are the two main foci of section I.4. of the Code [1]. Rehabilitation counselors ensure that they recognize the work of others on the topic on which they are conducting research (I.4.c.) and they never present the work of another as their own (I.4.a.). Similarly, when publishing research, they ensure that the work they have submitted for publication is not submitted for publication elsewhere, nor has it been published elsewhere, in whole or in part (I.4.f.). Similarly, rehabilitation counselors ensure that editors are aware when a submission includes information that has been published elsewhere (I.4.f.). Through the publication process, reviewers of peer-reviewed publications should keep submissions confidential and should complete reviews comprehensively and quickly (I.4.g.).

When conducting research with others, rehabilitation counselors ensure that credit is given to contributors, and that those who contributed most are listed first in author order (I.4.d.). Similarly, when publishing student-conducted research, students should be given primary authorship (I.4.e.). Finally, when using case studies in research, ethical researchers ensure that either the subject(s) of the case studies are aware and agree to be the subject of the case studies or that the case studies have been anonymized so that the subject of the case studies cannot be identified (I.4.b.).

I.4.a. PLAGIARISM

Rehabilitation counselors do not plagiarize. Rehabilitation counselors should never copy another author's work. In addition, rehabilitation counselors ensure that credit is given where it is due, and not present the ideas or work of another individual as their own.

CASE STUDY

Levi is a professor in a large research-intensive university. He has been working with a graduate student, Kate, on a research project for approximately one year. Kate presents her results to the department and Levi decides that their research is ready to be presented at a conference. Levi then writes a conference proposal that is accepted for submission and presents at the conference. Kate finds out about the conference and is upset that Levi never told her about the conference, nor did he invite her to attend.

ETHICAL CONSIDERATIONS

1. Which ethical standards apply in this case?

2. What should Levi have done differently to conduct research ethically?

3. How would you handle this if you were in Levi's place?

I.4.b. USE OF CASE STUDIES

The use of information from participants, clients, students, or supervisees for the purpose of case examples in a presentation or publication is permissible only when: (1) participants, clients, students, or supervisees have reviewed the material and agreed to its presentation or publication; or (2) the information has been sufficiently modified to obscure identity.

Rehabilitation counselors may undertake research or write publications that include case studies (for example, a book that includes multiple case studies in different contexts). If a researcher provides a case study, they must either have permission from the subjects of the case study or they must ensure that the case study does not include identifiable information.

CASE STUDY

Roxanna is writing a book chapter that includes numerous case studies to demonstrate different concepts in chapter. She includes real-life examples but changes the names and key details of the cases so that the subjects of the case studies cannot be identified.

ETHICAL CONSIDERATIONS

1. Did Roxanna act ethically?

2. Why or why not?

I.4.c. ACKNOWLEDGING PREVIOUS WORK

When conducting and reporting research, including replication studies, rehabilitation counselors are familiar with and give recognition to previous work on the topic, observe copyright laws, and give full credit to those to whom credit is due.

Rehabilitation counselors should be aware of those who stood before them. When working on research, it is important that rehabilitation counselors include work that others have done on the topic. In this, rehabilitation counselors must give credit for ideas where they are due, and they must also be aware of copyright laws and how they apply to the rehabilitation counselor's work.

CASE STUDY

Elroy is working on a manuscript on a topic that has not been well-researched in rehabilitation counseling. He is excited about this project, because it is particularly applicable to his work, however, when writing his introduction and literature review section, he leaves out any literature on the topic that is not from the field of rehabilitation counseling.

ETHICAL CONSIDERATIONS

1. Which ethical standards apply here?

2. What should Elroy have done differently to conduct research ethically?

3. How would you handle this if you were in Elroy's place?

I.4.d CONTRIBUTOR(S)

Rehabilitation counselors give credit through joint authorship, acknowledgment, footnote statements, or other appropriate means to those who have contributed significantly to research or concept development in accordance with such contributions. Principal contributors are listed first and minor technical or professional contributions are acknowledged in notes or introductory statements.

When working in a research group, rehabilitation counselors should ensure that proper credit is given to contributors on a research project. This means that people who contributed to a project should be acknowledged in one of many ways. Their contribution may warrant joint authorship - that they be one of the authors on the research publication (with the author who contributed most serving as first author). Other individuals who have contributed less can be recognized in the acknowledgements section or in a footnote in the paper. Ideally, what constitutes being considered an author on the paper will be determined prior to undertaking the study.

CASE STUDY

Emmanuel is a doctoral student in rehabilitation counseling who has been working on a research project to fulfill a thesis requirement for his program. For this, he has been working with his faculty advisor but has also had two undergraduate students serve as research assistants on the project. Both undergraduate students contributed equally. However, come time for publication, one of the undergraduate students realized that author order was: Faculty advisor, graduate student, and undergraduate research assistant. The other undergraduate research assistant did not receive authorship credit, nor was she acknowledged in the paper.

ETHICAL CONSIDERATIONS

1. Which ethical standards apply in this situation?

2. What could the individuals in this case study have done differently to conduct research ethically?

3. How would you handle this if you were in the place of the individuals in this case study?

I.4.e. STUDENT RESEARCH
Manuscripts or professional presentations in any media that are substantially based on a student's course papers, projects, dissertations, or theses are used only with the student's permission and list the student as lead author.

When publishing an article that originated from a student research project of any kind, the student should be the primary author. This means that as long as the student has done a majority of the work, even if they are working with a researcher who is at a higher level (for example, a student who is doing a thesis related to work they do on a larger research project), the student should have first authorship.

CASE STUDY

Abdullah is a third year doctoral student conducting research in rehabilitation counseling. His advisor and boss, Dr. Sesay, has a five-year grant project that she is working on, and Abdullah is employed on this project. Abdullah's thesis is a sub-project of Dr. Sesay's grant work, but Abdullah has taken the lead on this project, with Dr. Sesay monitoring his work. When the time comes for publication, one of the more advanced graduate students in the department tells Abdullah that it is customary in their department for the supervising faculty member to have first authorship on all articles that come out during a student's tenure, so Abdullah submits the article with Dr. Sesay as first author.

ETHICAL CONSIDERATIONS

1. Which ethical standards apply here?

2. What should have been done differently to conduct research ethically?

3. How would you handle this if you were in this situation?

I.4.f. DUPLICATE SUBMISSION

Rehabilitation counselors submit manuscripts for consideration to only one journal at a time. Manuscripts that are published in whole or in substantial part in another journal or published work are not submitted for secondary publication without acknowledgment and permission from the original publisher.

When a rehabilitation counselor is submitting a manuscript for publication, they must ensure that what they are submitting has not been submitted or published elsewhere. This means that a rehabilitation counselor will not submit the same article for publication to multiple journals at the same time. This also means that when a rehabilitation counselor submits a journal article, it should not have research that has been published elsewhere included in the manuscript. If a situation necessitates reprinting work that has been published elsewhere, the rehabilitation counselor first obtains permission from the original publication and also formally acknowledges this reprint in the new publication.

CASE STUDY

Warren is a graduate student in rehabilitation counseling who has been working hard on a research manuscript that is finally ready for publication. He has heard that it is difficult to get publications through the peer review process, and that he will probably get a few rejections on this manuscript before it is published. To hedge his bets, Warren

decides to submit his manuscript to two journals simultaneously,
assuming that it will definitely be rejected by one of them.

ETHICAL CONSIDERATIONS

1. Which ethical standards apply here?

2. What should Warren have done differently to conduct research ethically?

3. How would you handle this if you were in Warren's place?

I.4.g. PROFESSIONAL REVIEW
   Rehabilitation counselors who review material submitted for publication, research, or other scholarly purposes:

1. *Respect the confidentiality and proprietary rights of those who submitted it;*
2. *Avoid personal biases;*
3. *Make publication decisions based on valid and defensible standards; and*
4. *Review only materials that are within their scope of competency.*

As a part of their professional service as rehabilitation counselors who conduct research, they may be asked to review manuscripts that have been submitted to journals for peer-review. Rehabilitation counselors who are reviewing manuscripts should ensure that they maintain confidentiality about the articles they are reviewing. When they are conducting these reviews, they should make decisions about the quality of submission based on the project and how it was completed (the appropriate use of research methods and statistics), as well as the scope of the article and how it fits within the field. Rehabilitation counselors serving as reviewers should, to the extent possible, only review work that they have the background knowledge and understanding to review. For example, a reviewer who has never worked with exploratory factor analysis and does not have a knowledge base in the statistical method should not be reviewing an article that uses that methodology. Lastly, it is important that rehabilitation counselor reviewers do everything they can to ensure that their review is completed and returned to the editor within an appropriate time-frame.

CASE STUDY

Kia is a third year doctoral student at a large university in the Midwest. He has published a few articles and enjoys doing research very much. Therefore, when he receives a request from a journal he reads regularly, requesting that he be a peer-reviewer he is pleased and jumps on the idea. Kia begins the review very quickly because he is so excited. As he reads, he realizes that he is unfamiliar with the topic of the research, but he decides that he can make up for that by doing a little homework. Then, Kia realizes that the statistical analysis method the authors use in the manuscript are an approach he has never used before. Therefore, Kia decides to spend some time learning about the statistical method and the background of the article. This causes the review to be more work than he anticipated, and he falls behind on his review. Three months later, he receives a reminder from a very impatient editor about his incomplete review.

ETHICAL CONSIDERATIONS

1. Which ethical standards apply here?

2. What should Kia have done differently to conduct research ethically?

3. How would you handle this if you were in Kia's place?

I. 5: MANAGING AND MAINTAINING BOUNDARIES

Just like any counseling relationship, the research relationship has important boundaries that must be maintained. Ethical rehabilitation counselors will ensure that they maintain appropriate boundaries in their research, within reason (I.5.a.). They also do not ever engage in sexual or romantic relationships with research participants (I.5.b.) and never subject research participants to any type of harassment (I.5.c.).

I.5.a. BOUNDARY CONSIDERATIONS IN RESEARCH

Rehabilitation counselors consider the risks and benefits of extending current research relationships beyond conventional parameters. When a non-research interaction between researchers and research participants may be potentially beneficial, researchers must document, prior to the interaction (when feasible), the rationale for such interactions, the potential benefits, and anticipated consequences for research participants. Such interactions should be discussed and are initiated with appropriate consent of research participants. Where unintentional harm occurs to research participants, researchers must show evidence of an attempt to remedy such harm.

Rehabilitation counselors must work to ensure that they maintain appropriate boundaries in their research relationships. This can be complicated in some research settings. For example, individuals conducting ethnographic research may inadvertently become emotionally close to some of the individuals being studied. If this happens, the researcher first must determine that this relationship is beneficial to the participant (otherwise it should be stopped). If the researcher determines that the relationship is not harmful to the client and that it will continue, the researcher should, to the extent possible, record why they will be engaging in this relationship, how it will benefit the participant, and what outcomes may come of this relationship. Where possible, this record should be made prior to entering the relationship. Finally, if these nonprofessional relationships do ultimately have a negative impact on the research participants, the researcher should be able to demonstrate that they worked to rectify this and reduce the harm to participants.

CASE STUDY

Elijah works for an agency for whom advocacy is a big piece of their work. Elijah is tasked with conducting research to ensure that the agency is serving the needs of their clients. To approach this, Elijah begins a qualitative study in which he conducts interviews in the agency and then observes clients in the field as they self-advocate. One day, after a particularly long and exhausting protest, a few of the research participants ask Elijah to join them for dinner.

ETHICAL CONSIDERATIONS

1. What should Elijah do to ensure that he is acting ethically?

2. Which ethical standards apply to Elijah's situation?

3. How would you handle this if you were in Elijah's place?

I.5.b. SEXUAL OR ROMANTIC RELATIONSHIPS WITH RESEARCH PARTICIPANTS

Rehabilitation counselors are prohibited from engaging in electronic and/or in-person sexual or romantic interactions or relationships with current research participants.

Rehabilitation counselors should never enter into romantic relationships with research participants. This also means that sexual relationships with research participants should be avoided, regardless of who (the researcher or participant) initiated the relationship.

CASE STUDY

Ariel is a rehabilitation researcher conducting ethnographic research on Deaf Culture in Fredrick, Maryland. She is fluent in American Sign Language and quickly and easily inserts herself into the Deaf Community. After a few months, she realizes that one of her consented research participants, Ted, has romantic feelings for her. Ariel realizes that she, too, has romantic feelings for Ted. They begin a romantic relationship. However, Ariel is careful to record the relationship in the context of her research, weighing the positives and negatives of beginning a relationship with Ted while conducting this ethnographic study.

ETHICAL CONSIDERATIONS

1. Which ethical standards apply in this situation?

2. What should Ariel have done differently to conduct research ethically?

3. How would you handle this if you were in Ariel's place?

I.5.c. HARASSMENT

Rehabilitation counselors do not condone or subject research participants to any form of harassment, including sexual harassment.

Rehabilitation counselor researchers do not allow for any harassment to occur towards their research participations. This includes sexual harassment or any other type of harassment.

CASE STUDY

Emilia is a graduate student working with her advisor on a research project for which they are surveying college students. Due to time constraints, Emilia and her advisor share the responsibility of administering the survey to students, however it is Emilia's job to come at the end of the research session and collect all of the materials used for the project and return them to her office for storage. One day, as Emilia enters the room to collect the materials from her advisor, she overhears him saying to a participant "you're looking particularly sexy today." Emilia walks in and her advisor's face goes red, but he says nothing. Emilia is concerned but says nothing.

ETHICAL CONSIDERATIONS

1. Which ethical standards apply here?

2.   What should have been done differently to conduct research ethically?

3.   How would you handle this if you were in Emilia's place?

CONCLUSION

There are many interconnected standards that explain how to conduct research ethically. Rehabilitation counselors should do everything in their power to protect their participants and ensure that they are fully informed of their rights as research subjects. Similarly, rehabilitation counselors have an ethical responsibility to ensure that their research is accurate, and that even unfavorable research is presented to the public. Rehabilitation counselors must also ensure fairness in publication and presentation, ensuring that all contributors are acknowledged in their work. Lastly, Rehabilitation counselors must follow all applicable guidelines with regards to conducting research, including, but not limited to the Code [1].

DISCUSSION QUESTIONS

1.   Which research ethics standards do you think are most complicated? What do you think is complicated about the standard?

2.   In your opinion, which research ethics standard has the most ambiguity? What is ambiguous about the standard? How will you ensure that you act ethically with regards to this standard?

3.   There was a time where informed consent was not required in research. How do you think that affected research participation?

4.   Look up an article about Henrietta Lacks–read about her situation and think about which ethical principles were not adhered to in her situation.

5.   Look up an article about the Tuskegee Syphilis Study–which ethical principles were not adhered to in that experiment.

6.   Look up the Stanford Prison Experiment–do you think that experiment would have been allowed to take place today? Why or why not?

REFERENCE

[1]Commission on Rehabilitation Counselor Certification, Code of professional ethics for rehabilitation counselors. 2017, Schaumburg, IL: Author.

CHAPTER 13

TECHNOLOGY, SOCIAL MEDIA, & DISTANCE COUNSELING

JOSEPH F. STANO

SECTION J. TECHNOLOGY, SOCIAL MEDIA, & DISTANCE LEARNING

J.1. COMPETENCE & LEGAL CONSIDERATIONS

The new preamble to Section J of the *Code of Professional Ethics for Rehabilitation Counselors* highlights the expectation for rehabilitation counselors to "actively attempt to understand the evolving nature of technology, social media, and distance counseling and how such resources may be used to better serve their clients."[1,p.31] Beyond the aspirational preamble, Section J.1. of the Code contains two enforceable standards that serve to underscore the unique competencies and legal considerations specific to distance counseling and the use of technology.

Ethical standard J.1.a explains that "rehabilitation counselors are held to the same level of expected behavior and competence as defined by the Code regardless of technology used"[1,p.31] Taken with the section introduction, this standard ensures that any technology used by the rehabilitation counselor is subject to the same level of expected behavior and competence as traditional face-to-face counseling.

Moreover, ethical standard J.1.b begins to unpack the growing trend for state licensure laws to define competence as the legal ability to provide counseling services. With this as a reference point, J.1.b explains that distance services that cross state lines are subject to laws in both the client's place of residence as well as the rehabilitation counselor's practicing location. Furthermore, it is necessary to make sure that client rights and safety are protected even when providing distance services to a client within the state where the rehabilitation counselor lives and practices.

CASE STUDY

Eric is a national certified rehabilitation counselor and independent licensed professional counselor within his state. Over the last four years, he has been providing in-person services to youth and adults with disabilities related to behavioral management/support services, social skills development, personal management, and pre-vocational training. In the past, he has talked with clients over the telephone but is unsure whether this counts as distance counseling. In this state, licensed counselors are allowed to provide telehealth, although he is unsure about all the details. He has not had any formal telehealth training or supervised practice but enjoys using Zoom and other technology to interact with family and friends.

Eric has started to provide services to a new client, who has struggled to attend in-person counseling sessions. A few months earlier, the client was in a car accident and is uncomfortable with driving. The client has asked Eric if it would be okay to receive services over Zoom. Eric rationalizes that services over Zoom would be fine given that he is an experienced rehabilitation counselor and genuinely enjoys using Zoom in his private life. It seems like everyone is communicating online these days, and how different can it be to provide distance services?

After two sessions, Eric is finding distance services to be much different than expected. The client appears easily distracted, and at times moves around so much that Eric has trouble following his nonverbals on Zoom. At one point, the client becomes emotionally upset, and Eric is unsure how to express empathy and support over Zoom. Eric knows how he would handle situations like this in-person but is struggling with how to translate his in-person skills to a distance setting.

Despite a growing list of reservations, Eric still wants to provide distance services to the client. However, he is unsure how to make the sessions more effective or where to find additional training and supervision resources. Eric wants to expand his practice to include tele-health but is in need of help.

DISCUSSION QUESTIONS

1. What are the additional competencies necessary for providing distance services? How would a rehabilitation counselor know if they were competent to provide distance services?

2. What action steps could Eric take to become competent to provide distance services? Where would he find the information necessary to ensure he was practicing effectively and ethically?

3. In addition to the state licensure law, what other laws and legislation would regulate a rehabilitation counselor providing distance services to a client in the same state?

4. What factors would determine whether a client was appropriate or not appropriate to receive distance services? In other words, what types of clients or client situations would not be appropriate for distance services?

5. What procedures are necessary for client safety when providing distance services? What information would a rehabilitation

counselor need in case of a technology failure or a client emergency?

J.2. ACCESSIBILITY

Access and accessibility are necessary for individuals with disabilities to experience the benefits of digital technology. A focus on accessibility is critical because the use of technology has the power to breakdown traditional barriers to communication, interaction, and access to information for persons with disabilities. With this in mind, the CRCC (2017) Code now requires reasonable efforts be made by rehabilitation counselors to ensure that any technology used, purchased, or recommended is not only consistent with current legal standards of accessibility but also is appropriate for the client's needs and capabilities with technology and language preferences (J.2.a.). Moreover, standard J.2.a underscores the need to review limitations of technology with clients, particularly when recommending software used to assist in language translation.

When providing technology assisted services, ethical standard J.2.b ensures that rehabilitation counselors guide clients in obtaining reasonable access to pertinent applications. Taken together, J.2.a. and J.2.b clarify the importance of determining both the suitability of the technology being considered from a legal perspective, but also the unique requirements of individual clients.

CASE STUDY

Pablo is a certified rehabilitation counselor who works for a state vocational rehabilitation services program. Pablo provides both face-to-face and Internet counseling with clients who have a wide range of disabilities. Pablo recently began counseling a client online who has a moderate case of rheumatoid arthritis. The client initially reports to Pablo that she has minor to moderate joint pain, stiffness, and inflammation in her wrists and fingers, and general fatigue in her hands. The client reveals to Pablo that she uses prescription medication to control the pain and inflammation and has been following an exercise plan prescribed by her physical therapist to help with the stiffness she experiences.

The typical counseling session between Pablo and his client takes place via a secure text/chat modality. The initial sessions went very well and typing on a keyboard did not seem to be an issue for the client. Recently, the client has been experiencing more severe pain in her wrists and fingers. She reveals this information to Pablo, who in turn recommends that she use a voice to text software program during their counseling sessions to lessen the use and activity of her wrists and fingers. Pablo arranges for the state vocational agency to purchase the software for his client and to be sent to her home. He felt using the software would make the counseling sessions easier and more productive. The client had never used speech to text software before, but Pablo felt there was a small learning curve and did not provide an orientation to the software.

During his first session with the client using the speech to text software, Pablo found he was having problems deciphering her questions. Pablo found it difficult to understand what she was saying and to make sense of her responses. With no training or orientation to the software, the client became extremely frustrated. At this point, she was unable to type her responses, and decided to terminate her counseling sessions with Pablo and find a rehabilitation counselor she could meet with face-to-face.

DISCUSSION QUESTIONS

1. What may have been important for Pablo to discuss in the informed consent process during sessions with the client?

2. What do you see as your boundaries of competence in determining both the suitability of the technology being considered from a legal perspective, but also the unique requirements of individual clients? How would you determine your level of competence?

3. If you were the client, what would you have wanted Pablo to do in this scenario?

4. What steps could Pablo have taken to ensure that the technology was appropriate for the client's needs and capabilities?

5. What factors do rehabilitation counselors need to consider when deciding whether or not technology is appropriate for a client's needs and capabilities?

J.3. CONFIDENTIALITY, INFORMED CONSENT, & SECURITY

Informed consent is an essential first step in ensuring that clients are able to make informed and autonomous decisions. Revisions to the CRCC Code (2017) have clarified that clients have the right to decide whether they wish to use distance-based technologies and that they be fully informed about considerations specific to this choice and to the use of digital technology in counseling. These considerations must be included in the informed consent process in addition to those addressed in the usual and customary informed consent protocol[1,p. 31] (J.3.a). Consistent with other related codes of ethics such as the Code of Ethics of the American Counseling Association[2] (ACA), rehabilitation counselors must explain to clients how to manage technology failure, response time, referral information for emergencies, and general considerations regarding overall risks and benefits, cultural and language concerns, and logistical concerns specific to the use of technology in counseling.

In addition to delineating the potential issues unique to technology-based distance counseling and enforcing the need to address these concerns as part of the informed consent process, Section J.3 emphasizes the importance of ensuring the confidentiality of protected health information and the need for rehabilitation counselors to inform clients about the privacy and confidentially-related risks and limitations of using technology to transmit confidential information. The CRCC (2017) Code now mandates the security of electronic confidential information transmitted or stored, including encryption and password protection (J.3.b. & J.3.c.).

Concerned with client safety, one other unique consideration for distance counseling is the need to verify the identity and physical location of the client. It is thus important for rehabilitation counselors to verify the client's identity at the beginning of each session[1] (J.3.d., p. 32). According to this standard, verification can include, but is not limited to, using code words, numbers, graphics, or other nondescript identifiers.

Taken together, the standards in this section help to highlight the importance of ensuring that precautions and safeguards are instituted by a rehabilitation counselor to protect the client against those risks.

CASE STUDY

Meghan works for a vocational rehabilitation agency in a Southwestern state that has a large catchment area, including several rural counties that have sizeable Latinx and tribal populations. The agency has decided that to ensure better access to counseling, it will switch from in-person counseling to the use of distance counseling for their clients in some of the more remote, rural areas. They reason that this will be a win-win as it is more cost-effective, they can use a translation program so that they will be able to counsel in the clients' preferred language without the use of a live interpreter, and the problems of access due to transportation limitations will be minimized. Meghan contacts her client, Paloma, who injured her back 4 months ago while working as a home health aide for an elderly, disabled woman. Paloma lives with her family in a multi-generational household, including her mother, her 2 teen-aged children, her recently separated oldest daughter, and her daughter's 2 children. Meghan discusses the new plans to use distance technologies and shares that they will be purchasing a new computer for her use. Paloma shares that she is concerned that there is not a reliable internet connection in their home, and no private space due to their large family, and that when family members need to get online, they have to travel to a small nearby town to use their library's computers, which are co-located in the library's computer lab room. Paloma shares that because she cannot connect to the internet at home, she will still need to use the library's internet or use the internet at the coffee shop down the street from the library. While this is not very convenient, Paloma is delighted that she will be getting a new computer, and it is easier for her to get to the library than to travel the 65 miles to the counselor's office. She is also excited about being able to use the computer's translation program, as her English has improved quite a bit since arriving from El Salvador 3 years earlier, but she still struggles with finding the right English words sometimes. She is a little bit concerned about privacy, but Meghan suggests that she can talk in a low voice and discuss anything really private using the chat function.

DISCUSSION QUESTIONS

1. What responsibilities do rehabilitation counselors have to ensure confidentiality during sessions? How might the appropriate use of technology in this case study be a challenge?

2. What might be some ethical concerns regarding how Meghan is proceeding with the transition to distance counseling in this case?

3. Meghan's agency is planning to use a translation program, rather than using a live interpreter or a Spanish-speaking counselor. Is this an acceptable and ethical plan? Why or why not?

4. How might you need to modify your informed consent process before changing to distance counseling in this case?

J.4. SOCIAL MEDIA

Rather than being static, the need for ethical guidance on technology has grown over the years. In particular, the need for clarity related to the use of social media in the rehabilitation counseling process has become apparent. In response to the rapid growth in social media use as a society, the 2017 Code revisions have provided additional guidance on how to manage affordances and constraints of social media platforms media for the first time.

When rehabilitation counselors use social media professionally, a new requirement in the CRCC (2017) Code is that rehabilitation counselors "separate professional and personal pages and profiles to clearly distinguish between the two kinds of electronic presence."[p.32] (J.4.a.). It is the responsibility of individual rehabilitation counselors to ensure they are using social media in ways that are professional and intended to enhance the delivery of rehabilitation services. Moreover, rehabilitation counselors must recognize the largely permanent nature of information posted to social media and take reasonable steps to monitor for and remove or correct potentially harmful information.

The larger point of J.4. and J.4.b is that rehabilitation counselors must be adept at maintaining virtual relationship boundaries for themselves and others in digital spaces and monitoring these spaces to ensure the appropriateness of posted content. To support these mandates, new ethical standards in the CRCC Code 2017 require rehabilitation counselors to work within their organizations to develop and communicate a social media policy that addresses the potential benefits, limitations, and boundaries when social media is used (J.4.c. & J.4.d.). It is thus important that rehabilitation counselors are able to apply guidelines such as the CRCC Social Media Policy and Social Media Code of Conduct[3].

A new standard in the CRCC (2017) Code has required rehabilitation counselors to "respect the privacy of their client's presence on social media and avoid searching a client's virtual presence unless relevant to the rehabilitation counseling process."[p.32] (J.4.d.) In other words, it is unethical for rehabilitation counselors to *google* their clients because it violates privacy. While there may be exceptions searching online for client information is something that must be disclosed in advance as part of informed consent.

In addition to privacy, the CRCC (2017) Code requires rehabilitation counselors to "protect the confidentiality of clients by avoiding the posting of any personally identifiable information," and "in no circumstance should protected or extremely sensitive information be shared via social networking platforms."[p.32] (J.4.e.)

CASE STUDY

Alyia is a certified rehabilitation counselor who has worked as an independent forensic expert for many years. Alyia is typically hired as a consultant by insurance carriers or law firms in matters concerning employability, labor market access, wage loss analysis, and wage-earning capacity. She is a member of a professional association with a large group of rehabilitation professionals interested in private sector rehabilitation. The professional organization offers a number of benefits to professionals including regional and national conferences, a variety of continuing education opportunities, and a peer-reviewed journal. The organization also offers its members a strong online presence via a website, newsletter, and other social media platforms that serve as information sources for private sector rehabilitation professionals.

Several online resources of the professional organization that Alyia often uses are the extremely active member forums, ListServs (i.e., automated emailing lists), and social media outlets, utilized by thousands of members across the country. Alyia finds these social networking platforms extremely helpful when she requires consultation on a difficult case. Because Alyia works alone and is the self-proprietor of her rehabilitation consulting firm, she has no one with whom she can consult directly in person. Alyia often uses the online resources to request information on a topic, or to ask her peers questions regarding potential solutions to problems she is facing on a particular case.

Alyia is often requested to present live testimony and explain the methodology of the vocational examination process she uses to make decisions about a particular client. She recently was working on a multifaceted case and encountered what she thought was an ethical issue. Turning to the professional organization's ListServ and other social networking outlets, Alyia solicited the advice of her fellow vocational experts. To give her peers a better idea of the intricacies of the case, when posing her question regarding the ethical dilemma, she included the client's initials, date of birth, hometown, and place of employment. Alyia was facing a strict deadline and was hoping to receive some perspective on her case as quickly as she could.

DISCUSSION QUESTIONS

1. How might members of the professional organization's Listserv and other social media outlets contribute to the safe and ethical use of these online resources?

2. What policies and practices do you need (or will need in the future) for regulating your social networking to maintain your personal and professional boundaries?

3. If you were Alyia in this case, what might you consider doing differently in this scenario?

4. Utilizing professional networking sites for case consultation provides many benefits, but also unique ethical challenges. How can risks be minimized when using these types of online resources?

5. How should the professional organization deal with clear ethical violations on their social networking platforms? What is the professional organization's obligation to monitor the content? What about the other professionals utilizing the social networking platforms?

REFERENCES

[1] American Counseling Association (2014). *Code of ethics.* Retrieved from www.counseling.org

[2] Commission on Rehabilitation Counselor Certification (CRCC). (2017). *Code of professional ethics for rehabilitation counselors.* Retrieved from https://www.crccertification.com/code-of-ethics-3

[3] Commission on Rehabilitation Counselor Certification (CRCC). *Social media policy.* Retrieved from https://www.crccertification.com/social-media-policy

CHAPTER 14

BUSINESS PRACTICES

CHERIE L. KING

SECTION K: BUSINESS PRACTICES

The business and administrative aspects of rehabilitation counseling practice are usually not a significant part of rehabilitation counselor training. However, once a rehabilitation counselor is working in the field, attention to the aspects of business practice is necessary. The CRC Code contains several cannons related to appropriate and ethical business and administrative practices that are expected of a Certified Rehabilitation Counselor (CRC). First and foremost, CRCs must be aware of the ramifications of improper or inappropriate practice related to several areas of business procedures including advertisement, client record keeping, case documentation, and billing. Some CRCs may work within agencies or programs that have recognized administrative processes and procedures but CRCs must be aware of the suitability and consistency of these processes and policies relative to the CRC code. For CRCs as sole practitioners, establishing administrative business practices with the CRC Code in mind is considered a best practice.

K.1: ADVERTISING AND SOLICITING CLIENTS

K.1.a. ACCURATE ADVERTISING
When advertising or otherwise representing their services to the public in any form of media, rehabilitation counselors identify their credentials in an accurate manner that is not false, misleading, deceptive, or fraudulent.

K.1.b. TESTIMONIALS AND STATEMENTS
Rehabilitation counselors who use testimonial do not solicit them from current or former clients or evaluees, or any other persons who may be vulnerable to undue influence. When considering the use of unsolicited testimonials for clients or evaluees, rehabilitation counselors discuss the implications and obtain permission for such use. Testimonials from those who are not current or former clients or evaluees (e.g. partner organizations, placement sites) may be used. Regardless of the sources of the testimonial, rehabilitation counselors make reasonable efforts, whenever feasible, to ensure that statements made by others about them or about the profession are accurate.

It is acceptable for rehabilitation counselors to advertise their services, although rehabilitation counselors in private practice settings are more likely to employ this practice to solicit referrals. The Code indicates that rehabilitation counselors who do advertise must ensure that the content of the representation of their credentials and expertise to provide services must be accurate and not misleading. Rehabilitation counselors presenting false, deceptive, or ambiguous information regarding their education, skills, experience, and credentials are violating this ethical code. Similarly, to other businesses, rehabilitation counselors will use testimonials in advertising to provide credibility to services by using referral sources such as other professionals (attorneys, professional peers, etc.). This is an acceptable practice as long as the rehabilitation counselor does not solicit testimonials from current or former clients or other vulnerable persons. Requesting testimonials from these persons is inappropriate and crosses an ethical line when influencing a potentially vulnerable client to provide statements to assist a rehabilitation counselor in advertising or soliciting additional business.

CASE STUDY

Rick is a private rehabilitation consultant who has had consistent referrals from local attorneys and insurance carriers to provide forensic assessments and case management services. Over the last six months, referrals have been low and Rick has needed to start marketing his services in a new way. He has maintained his CRC status and has completed the required continuing education units (CEUs). However, Rick wants to solicit business from other areas of legal practice such as divorce cases.

Rick has experience and training in forensic vocational assessment and evaluation primarily in Workers' Compensation and Social Security but has no experience in providing expert testimony in divorce cases and has not received any training, mentoring, or supervision regarding the differences and nuances of working as an expert within this legal realm. Rick's business is slowing and he is anxious about his financial stability and needs to get the attention of these potential referral sources. He develops marketing materials and a website indicating that he has experience in providing services as an expert witness in divorce cases.

ETHICAL CONSIDERATIONS

1. What are the ethical issues related to this marketing effort and what impact does this have on Rick's ethical practice and his professional credibility?

K.1.c. RECRUITMENT THROUGH SELF-REFERRAL
Rehabilitation counselors working in an organization that provides rehabilitation counseling services do not refer clients to their private practice unless the policies of a particular organization makes explicit provisions for self-referrals. In such instances, clients must be informed of other available options for services.

CASE STUDY

Tina is a vocational rehabilitation counselor in a state Vocational Rehabilitation (VR) agency. She is also a licensed professional counselor in her state and has a private mental health counseling practice. She works with many VR clients who are in need of a therapist. Tina is frustrated with the lack of qualified therapists who understand disability and employment issues and the impact on mental health. Since this is her area of expertise, she informs selected clients that she is a licensed therapist and can offer mental health services outside her role as a VR counselor.

ETHICAL CONSIDERATIONS:

What does Tina need to address?

1.   relative to her organization?

2.   What ethical issues does this scenario present?

K.1.d. PROMOTION OF PRODUCTS AND TRAINING EVENTS
Rehabilitation counselors who develop products related to their profession or conduct workshops or training events make reasonable efforts to ensure that advertisements concerning these products and events are accurate and disclose adequate information so clients or consumers may make informed choices. Rehabilitation counselors do not use counseling, teaching, training, or supervisory relationships to promote their products or training events in a manner that is deceptive or would exert undue influence on individuals who may be vulnerable. Rehabilitation counselor educators may adopt textbooks they have authored for appropriate instructional purposes.

CASE STUDY

Steven is a private rehabilitation counselor and has developed a job seeking skills training event for clients with disabilities. The focus of the training is to provide individual job seekers with disabilities new skills to find employment. Steven advertises this training workshop to the public and promotes it to his current and past clients as an "extra" service to help them find jobs. He is offering a reduced rate for clients to attend. Many of his clients are vulnerable and feel pressured by Steven to attend and pay reduced rate. Several are still unemployed or underemployed and Steven advertises that the skills they will learn in the training will guarantee they find a job quickly.

ETHICAL CONSIDERATIONS

1. What are the ethical concerns regarding Steven's promotion of the training workshop?

2. What are the implication for his current and past clients?

K.2. CLIENT RECORDS

The legal and ethical standards for case documentation and record keeping are a critical function of a rehabilitation counselors' practice in any work setting. For rehabilitation counselors working for institutions and agencies, established protocols and procedures for client documentation and record keeping for clinical and insurance billing purposes are a cornerstone of business operations and clinical practice. The CRC Code has several ethical standards devoted to specific areas of client records to which a rehabilitation counselor must be familiar and must integrate into their daily practice whether in private practice or working for an employer.

For counselors working within agencies or programs that receive public and/or private funds, required documentation practices and procedures are usually well established but there may be circumstances when a rehabilitation counselor is faced with procedures that conflict or compete with ethical standards. This is also true for private rehabilitation counselors who may not have well-established processes in place for client record documentation and record keeping.

It is important to utilize a system of caseload documentation and record keeping that aligns with standard professional practice as well as legal and ethical standards. Most rehabilitation counselors are trained on various case or progress note methods (i.e., SOAP notes, DAP notes, or to use Electronic Medical Records (EMR) systems). Attention to appropriate and timely case notes in client files (paper or electronic) is important. Case notes are evidence of services provided, client issues, progress, or lack of progress with services, and that the case notes document and justify the services provided for billing and reimbursement purposes. Many programs and agencies have internal quality assurance (QA) reviews in order to maintain a consistent process and system of case documentation as required by state and federal reimbursement requirements (e.g., Medicaid and Medicare). This is also important for internal and external auditing purposes.

K.2.a. RECORDS AND DOCUMENTATION

Regardless of format, rehabilitation counselors create, protect, and maintain documentation necessary for rendering professional services. Rehabilitation counselors include sufficient and timely documentation to facilitate the delivery and continuity of services. Rehabilitation counselors make reasonable efforts to ensure that documentation accurately reflects client progress and the services provided, including who provided the services. If records and documentation need to be altered, it is done so according to organizational policy and in a manner that preserves the original information. Alternations are accompanied by the date of change, the identity of who made the change, and the rationale for the change.

CASE STUDY

Lisa is working as a counselor in a community mental health clinic that serves many clients receiving federal Supplemental Security Income (SSI). Her agency is primarily funded by both the State Department of Mental Health and federal Medicaid reimbursement. Lisa has a caseload of over 50 clients and is responsible for several therapy groups with an average of 10 clients in each group. She is required to document via the agency's computer based case management system, weekly progress notes on each client. Lisa is overworked and overwhelmed and is having significant trouble keeping up with her paperwork and case notes. She goes to her supervisor about this problem and she is told to find a way to make it work. Lisa is feeling even more pressure to get the progress notes completed so that the agency can generate billing for payment. Lisa begins to input case notes on each of her clients with little regard for appropriate detail and content specific to each of her clients. In some cases, she cannot remember what was discussed in the client sessions.

ETHICAL CONSIDERATIONS

1. What potential ethical and legal issues arise from Lisa's actions?

K.2.b. PRIVACY
Documentation generated by rehabilitation counselors protects the privacy of clients to the extent possible and includes only relevant or appropriate information.

CASE STUDY

Peter is a vocational rehabilitation counselor with the State VR agency. He is working with his client, Susan, who is seeking services to return to employment after a long illness and subsequent physical limitations. They have worked together over six months to develop an employment plan. In their most recent session, Susan discloses she recently had an abortion. She is receiving post procedure counseling,

*and Susan indicates this will not impact her plans to return to work.
After their meeting, Peter is required to document the results of the
session on the agency's electronic case management system.*

ETHICAL CONSIDERATIONS

1. What is Peter's ethical obligation in terms of appropriate case
    documentation with respect to client privacy and confidentially?

K.2.c. RECORD MAINTENANCE

*Rehabilitation counselors securely maintain records necessary for
rendering professional services to clients and as required by appliable
laws and organizational polices. Subsequent to file closure or
termination of services, records are stored in a secure manner that
ensures reasonable future access for record retrieval. Records are
destroyed in a manner assuring preservation of confidentiality.
Rehabilitation counselors apply careful discretion and deliberation
before destroying records that may be needed by a court of law.*

CASE STUDY

*Sarah is a private rehabilitation consultant who works from home.
Her office is in her dining room and she has client files spread around
the room. She has a file cabinet with a lock but cannot find the key.
Her children bring many friends home. One day as a joke, one of
Sarah's children and their friend see a pile of files on the table and
start looking through them. They are able to read one of Sarah's
client's medical and psychiatric records. Although Sarah's child and
her friend do not copy or take information from the file, they have read
the details.*

ETHICAL CONSIDERATIONS

1. What is Sarah's dilemma regarding this situation?

2. What steps should she have taken to manage the records and case
    files?

K.2.d. CONTINGENCY PLANNING

*Rehabilitation counselors prepare and disseminate to identified
colleagues or record custodians a plan to transfer of clients and files
in the cases of their incapacitation, death, or termination of practice.*

K.3. FEES, BARTERING, AND BILLING

Many rehabilitation counselors are not prepared for the business aspects of practice. If working for an agency, most rehabilitation counselors are not involved with the setting of fees, billing, or the need for bartering. However, many situations can arise within private practice that require a rehabilitation counselor to be involved in determining fees, creating invoices, negotiating slide scale fees, and the collection of accounts payable. Determining fees for services must be handled carefully and with the market in mind. Considerations include what is the going rate for rehabilitation counseling service. Are services billed on an hourly basis? Is a flat rate an expected manner to bill for services? Rehabilitation counselors are sometimes subject to fees or an hourly rate pre-determined by a referral (e.g., an insurance carrier). However, in practice (e.g., forensic rehabilitation), the rehabilitation counselor must know the general billing rates for the services they are qualified to perform and what the market will bear. When directly billing for services to clients with disabilities, rehabilitation counselors must take into consideration what clients are able to afford and be willing to either fairly negotiate fees or help the client to find another alternative service that is financially appropriate for the client. It is also necessary for rehabilitation counselors to disclose and clearly discuss all financial matters with clients. Many rehabilitation counselors include their billing and financial policies in a professional disclosure document so their clients are informed of collection and possible legal actions for non-payment.

K.3.a. UNDERSTANDING OF FEES AND NONPAYMENT OF FEES
Prior to providing services, rehabilitation counselors clearly explain to the clients or evaluee and/or responsible party all financial arrangements related to professional services. If a third party is paying for services, the rehabilitation counselor explains that arrangement to the client or evaluee and /or responsible party. If rehabilitation counselors, or their employer, intend to use collection agencies or take legal measures to collect fees when payment is not received as agreed upon, they include such information in their professional disclosure statement or retainer agreement. If collection actions are considered, the rehabilitation counselor first informs the clients, evaluee, or responsible party of intended actions in a timely fashion.

CASE STUDY

Mark is a vocational expert working on a divorce case. His client, the wife, paid Mark his retainer, but only paid a small portion of the balance prior to trial. Mark had specifically outlined his payment policy in writing when taking the case. Mark told the client and her attorney that he would not attend the trial unless he was paid the balance owed to him. The attorney said that the client was not able to pay him but asked if Mark would accept a formal lien against her portion of her husband's retirement account, in which the state law guaranteed her half. Mark agreed and the client was aware that her attorney was formally drawing up an agreement putting that lien in place.

The trial went forward; however, the client felt that she did not do as well in court as she might have. She fired her attorney and refused to pay Mark. She then declared bankruptcy. Mark spoke to his own counsel and determined that his lien superseded her declaration of bankruptcy. Mark offered to arrange a court appointed schedule so the client could pay him in full.

At the time Mark anticipated receiving his first payment, she withdrew her bankruptcy claim and said she was ending the court appointed payment arrangement. Mark still had an enforceable lien and engaged in additional litigation. He was advised by his attorney that he could consider pressing for the client's incarceration for violating the legal agreement.

ETHICAL CONSIDERATIONS

1.   What ethical issues is Mark faced with in this situation?

K.3.b. ESTABLISHING FEES

If a rehabilitation counselor's usual fees create undue hardship for the clients, the rehabilitation counselor may adjust fees, when legally permissible, or assist the client in locating comparable, affordable services.

K.3.c. UNACCEPTABLE FEE ARRANGEMENTS

Rehabilitation counselors do not participate in fee splitting, nor do they give or receive commissions, rebates, or any other form of renumeration when accepting referrals or referring clients for additional professional services.

K.3.d. LIENS AND OUTCOME BASED PAYMENTS

Liens and payments based on outcomes are acceptable when it is standard practice within the particular practice setting. In a forensic setting, payment for services is never contingent on an outcome of a case or award.

K.3.e. BARTERING DISCOURAGED

Rehabilitation counselors ordinarily refrain from accepting goods or services from clients in return for rehabilitation counseling services because such arrangements may create inherent potential for conflicts, exploitations, and distortion of the professional relationship. Rehabilitation counselors may barter only if the client request it, if such arrangements are acceptable practice in the community, and if the bartering does not result in exploitation or harm. Rehabilitation counselors consider the cultural implication of bartering, discuss relevant concerns with clients, and document such arrangements in writing.

Although bartering for goods and services is reappearing in many communities and commonplace in many cultures, rehabilitation counselors need to be aware of the potential pitfalls and ethical concerns for bartering with clients in exchange for rehabilitation counseling services. This practice can create potential conflicts such as exploitation of clients. The Code discourages rehabilitation counselors from engaging in bartering with clients but in cases where it may be necessary or customary in a community, rehabilitation counselors are strongly encouraged to enter into a written agreement with the client that specifically outlines the expectations of the arrangement.

CASE STUDY

Mary works closely with many clients in the Native American community. She is the only rehabilitation counselor within 200 miles of the Native American community and spends at least one day per week working with clients on vocational rehabilitation and counseling issues. She has established a sliding scale fee for her clients based on their ability to pay but recently she is being requested to accept traditional healing sessions and household maintenance services (lawn mowing, housecleaning, and repairs) in exchange for her services. Mary is an accepted and trusted professional in their community and she understands that trading services is customary within the Native American culture. She is worried that if she does not accept these barter arrangements, she will be seen as disrespectful of their cultural traditions.

ETHICAL CONSIDERATIONS

1. How can Mary maintain her credibility and connection to her clients and their cultural traditions and not violate the Code?

K.3.f. WITHHOLDING RECORDS FOR NONPAYMENT

Rehabilitation counselors may not withhold records under their control that are requested and needed for emergency medical/psychiatric treatment of clients solely because payment has not been received.

K.3.g. BILLING RECORDS AND INVOICES

Rehabilitation counselors maintain billing records that are confidential, accurately reflect the services provided and fees charged, and identify who provided the services. Invoices accurately reflect the services provided.

K.4. TERMINATION AND REFERRAL

Rehabilitation counselors in fee for service relationships may terminate client services due to nonpayment of fees under the following conditions: (1) clients were informed or payment responsibilities and the effects of nonpayment or termination of payment by third parties; and (2) clients do not pose an imminent danger to themselves of others. As appropriate, rehabilitation counselors refer clients to other qualified professional to address issues unresolved at the time of termination.

The Code states that rehabilitation counselors in fee-for-service arrangements may terminate services with clients due to nonpayment under specific conditions. Many situations have occurred in which rehabilitation counselors are hired to provide vocational rehabilitation services to a client and then are not paid for services rendered. Rehabilitation counselors must fully inform clients regarding their policies for non-payment by a third party (i.e. insurance company). The counselor can terminate the client only if doing so does not pose a danger to self or others. In these circumstances, it is the rehabilitation counselors' ethical responsibility to refer the client to other appropriate and qualified professionals if necessary.

CASE STUDY

Lila has been working on a referral from a Workers' Compensation carrier to provide job placement services to an injured worker, John. After working with John for over 4 months, she assisted him in developing a new resume, helped him improve his job seeking and interviewing skills, and provided many job leads as a result of hours of labor market survey work.

Her billing policy is to send an invoice with a report for services rendered to the referral source every 30 days. Her policy also includes an expectation of payment within 10 days of receipt. After sending invoices for over 40 hours of work with John, she has not received any payments. She has sent emails and left voicemails for the claim adjuster but has not received a return call. The injured worker, John, is still looking for work and has been very motivated in his job search.

In her most recent follow up with John, she explains that she will be unable to continue working with him because she has not been paid by the insurance carrier. She informs him that she is terminating services and wishes him luck in his job search. John is angry and says she is abandoning him and he needs her continued help.

ETHICAL CONSIDERATIONS

1. What issues is Lila dealing with regarding the ethical code related to the termination of a client due to non-payment for services?

AUTHOR NOTE

The author would like to express her appreciation to several of her colleagues who shared their stories about ethical situations they have experienced. Names have been change to protect the innocent.

REFERENCE

[1]Commission on Rehabilitation Counselor Certification. (2016). *Code of professional ethics*. Retrieved from https://crccertification.com/code-of-ethics-4/

CHAPTER 15

RESOLVING ETHICAL ISSUES

ERICA L. WONDOLOWSKI

SECTION L: RESOLVING ETHICAL ISSUES

Rehabilitation counselors behave in an ethical and legal manner. They are aware that client welfare and trust in the profession depend on a high level of professional conduct. They hold other rehabilitation counselors to the same standards and are willing to make reasonable efforts to ensure that standards are upheld. Rehabilitation counselors strive to resolve ethical dilemmas with direct and open communication among all parties involved and seek consultation with colleagues and supervisors when necessary. Rehabilitation counselors incorporate ethical practice into their daily professional work and engage in ongoing professional development on current topics in ethical and legal issues in counseling. Rehabilitation counselors become familiar with the CRCC Guidelines and Procedures for Processing Complaints[1] and use it as a reference for assisting in the enforcement of the Code.[2, p.34]

One should note the language used in the introductory statement to Section L of the Commission on Rehabilitation Counselor Certification (CRCC) Code of Professional Ethics.[2] The tone is affirmative, rather than suggestive using terms such as *are* instead of *should*. What is provided are not recommendations, nor are they to be treated as professional development goals to be striven for over time. No, the CRCC plainly communicates that those who have earned the designation of Certified Rehabilitation Counselor (CRC) or Canadian Certified Rehabilitation Counselor (CCRC) are immediately held to a set of clearly outlined standards of conduct.

Often, ethical issues that arise over the course of one's professional career fall within a perceivable gray area, where no single subsection wholly addresses the situation at hand. To attempt to address every potential ethical concern in the Code would not only be a lofty and burdensome undertaking for the CRCC, but also prove to be highly limiting and restrictive to the rehabilitation counseling professional. To aid in comprehension, case studies are provided for each subsection of Section L throughout this chapter. It is highly recommended that one also peruses the CRCC Advisory Opinions[3] to learn of more complex allegations, how the ethical standards can intersect, and the opinions of the CRCC Ethics Committee with regard to addressing the allegation.

L.1. KNOWLEDGE OF ETHICAL STANDARDS AND THE LAW

L.1.a. KNOWLEDGE OF THE CODE

Rehabilitation counselors are responsible for reading, understanding, and following the Code, and seeking clarification of any standard that is not understood. Lack of knowledge or misunderstanding of an ethical responsibility is not a defense against a charge of unethical conduct.[2,p.34]

It is the rehabilitation counselor's duty to make sure that they are knowledgeable of the ethical conduct which governs practice. Rehabilitation counselors who neglect to understand or misuse the Code are subject to the consequences of their actions. The realistic consequences of substantiated unethical conduct may include, but are not limited to:

1. removal from the profession,

2. demotion of professional position,

3. appropriate disciplinary actions,

4. written or oral reprimand,

5. suspension,

6. salary reduction,

7. loss of benefits, and

8. stagnation of upward mobility.

CASE STUDY

Ken, a rehabilitation counselor, works for his local area office for the state Vocational Rehabilitation organization. This organization frequently refers its clients to Speak Freely, a public speaking group to enhance interviewing skills and social skill development. These referrals help Speak Freely financially by generating more income for their establishment. There is no formal agreement between the two organizations. A contact that works at Speak Freely treats Ken to lunch on a weekly basis so that they can discuss future referrals. The rehabilitation counselor proceeds to allow and begins to expect that the contact from Speak Freely to pay for lunch every time they meet.

Eventually, Ken's supervisor becomes aware of the arrangement and approaches him about accepting free lunches for referrals. The supervisor verbally reprimands Ken, stating that their behavior is unethical, and the "free lunches" need to stop immediately.

Ken ignores the supervisor's warning and decides to continue accepting free meals at Speak Freely's expense, to save money. The supervisor confronts Ken again and sternly explains that this behavior violates his ethical code of conduct. The supervisor indicates that they will be reporting Ken to the executive director of the organization, who will decide the appropriate disciplinary action to take.

The executive director notifies the CRCC about this ethical issue, the desire to resolve it informally, and, in the end, the executive director determines that Ken should be terminated for his unethical behavior. Ken is devastated over the loss of his job as well as the added potential of losing his CRC credential. Ken tries to justify his behavior by rationalizing that he did not know accepting free lunches from a referral source on a weekly basis was unethical.

Ken is terminated and is having difficulty finding work at another agency. In addition, the rehabilitation counselor is placed on probation with the CRCC; all because of his erroneous belief that they did not know what they were doing was unethical.

L.1.b. KNOWLEDGE OF RELATED CODES OF ETHICS

Rehabilitation counselors understand applicable ethics codes from other professional organizations or from certification and licensure bodies of which they are members. Rehabilitation counselors are aware the Code forms the basis for CRCC disciplinary actions, and understand they are held to the CRCC standards if there is a discrepancy between codes.[2,p.34]

It is expected that rehabilitation counselors know their own Code, but it is of equal importance for a rehabilitation counselor to be aware of Codes governing related professions. The utilization of integrated healthcare and care team service provision models are creating increasingly more opportunities where the rehabilitation counseling professional may find themselves working alongside professionals in a wide variety of fields. An awareness and working knowledge of the roles, functions, and scope of practice for these professions, and how they may or may not align with that of the rehabilitation counselor can greatly assist one in navigating the precarious ethical positions that may arise. For example, rehabilitation counselors may work within a hospital setting where they work on a treatment team with physical therapists and massage therapists. Both latter professions legally touch people as a component of treatment and their own ethical codes allow such touching. CRC and CCRC holders, however, are expected to have minimal physical contact with clients (e.g., shaking hands, giving someone a high five). Contact beyond such common expressions of social etiquette may find themselves on the receiving end of disciplinary action under the Code.

CASE STUDY

Ralph is a rehabilitation counselor working in a hospital setting. His role and function require that he meet with persons who recently underwent surgery following trauma to assist them in returning to their past employment or to seek alternative employment. Ralph is aware that his clients meet with physical therapists to strengthen body function (e.g., use of arms or wrists) and that his clients also meet with massage therapists to reduce tension and general anxiety following the recent surgery as well as related pain while undergoing physical rehabilitation. Ralph's client, Harold, tells him that his neck hurts badly, especially after physical therapy. He tells Ralph that the massage therapist helps in the moment at which it is happening but that the pain quickly returns afterwards and makes it hard to concentrate. When working with Ralph, Harold states that the pain makes it difficult to consider decisions pertaining to work. Harold proceeds to ask Ralph if he could massage his neck to reduce the pain, and so that they could continue to discuss employment. Ralph viewed this as a harmless behavior and started massaging Harold's neck. The conversation quickly turned to work, and Ralph was pleased with Harold's progress in reviewing a return to employment.

One day, Marie, a massage therapist, accidentally walked into Ralph's office and immediately noted that Ralph was massaging Harold's neck. In her best professional tone, Marie advised Ralph to stop massaging Harold's neck since Ralph was not trained in professional techniques related to Harold's injuries or massage in general. Ralph informed Marie that he saw no harm in his behavior since it helped his client concentrate on employment.

Marie reported the incident to the program director. Ralph was disciplined for his inappropriate behavior and the hospital's ethics committee decided to report Ralph to the CRCC since they were aware that the applicable code of ethics did not allow the practice of massaging or touching beyond acceptable social conventions such as shaking hands. After review, it was decided that Ralph would be terminated from his employment as a rehabilitation counselor at the hospital and the CRCC concluded that his CRC would be revoked for inappropriate and unprofessional behavior.

L.1.c. CONFLICTS BETWEEN ETHICS AND LAWS
Rehabilitation counselors obey the laws of the legal jurisdiction in which they practice unless there is a conflict with the Code. If ethical responsibilities conflict with laws, rehabilitation counselors make known their commitment to the Code and take steps to resolve conflicts. If conflicts cannot be resolved by

such means, rehabilitation counselors may adhere to the requirements of law.[2,p.34]

Conflict and discrepancy may exist between what local, state, and/or federal laws do and do not allow, and the standard of conduct, role and function of a rehabilitation counselor as outlined by the Code. The rehabilitation counselor must have a working knowledge of pertinent federal, state, and local laws that might impact the practice of rehabilitation counseling, as well as such laws that may impact the environments where a rehabilitation counselor may take place. It is incumbent upon rehabilitation counselors to review applicable statutes, to anticipate and avoid potential conflicts, if possible, as well as adhere to the legal requirements of their specific place of employment provided that such conflicts represent accepted local legal governance.

The field of addictions and substance abuse counseling has employed many a rehabilitation counselor. While substance abuse treatment is a necessary and beneficial service, certain intervention techniques may directly conflict with state and federal laws such as those requiring any person aware of the use or misuse of illegal substances to be reported to proper authorities. There are individuals providing services in the field of addictions who understand relapse, or the resumption of substance use following a period of sobriety, as an expected component of treatment. The goal is that following this period of relapse, that the client will again cease to use substances, re-accept treatment, and pursue a longer period of sobriety.

Professionals within rehabilitation counseling and other fields have come to view the harm reduction model of treatment as viable and successful. This model asks that the counselor support and assist the client, despite their continued use. The counselor is asked to provide safe alternatives without requiring the client to cease using. For example, rather than asking a client to go through a medical detox program to help safely rid their body of the opioids they had been injecting for years, the counselor can reduce the harm that the client may find themselves in by providing them with clean syringes. The harm reduction model accepts the client in their current state, seeks to keep them as safe as possible until such time as they choose to cease using of their own volition. This model can create a conflict between laws and practice since federal, state, and local laws perceive the use and abuse of chemicals as illegal and often perceive persons who aid and abet such behavior as accomplices to the act.

The rehabilitation counselor can and should work with their local professional association for assistance in contacting their state's alcohol and drug addiction service to assess the legality and acceptance of the harm reduction model. The counselor may continue working with their client using the harm reduction model only if the applicable governing bodies grant permission to do so. However, if the applicable governing bodies do not accept harm reduction as a valid model by which to intervene, the rehabilitation counselor may choose to abdicate their professional position and credentials, in order to advocate for change under their rights as a citizen.

Readers who wish to see a specific and detailed case history related to this section should look at the Advisory Opinions[3] provided for in subsection L.2.f., Organization Conflicts, as it covers much of the same topic as presented in this subsection of the Code.

L.2. ADDRESSING SUSPECTED VIOLATIONS

L.2.a. ETHICAL DECISION-MAKING MODELS AND SKILLS
Rehabilitation counselors recognize underlying ethical principles and conflicts among competing interests. They apply appropriate decision-making models and skills to resolve dilemmas and act ethically.[2,p.34]

Successful rehabilitation counseling professionals seek to ensure a high quality of service provision and care, so that clients reach their identified care goals and continue to succeed following the closure of their case. Frequently confronted with situations where they will need to utilize their professional judgment in determining whether a particular scenario is ethically sound, rehabilitation counselors must actively and consistently apply the Code, subsequently assisting them to identifying any ethical dilemmas that may arise and providing a foundation for how to proceed appropriately.

While diligent and proactive comprehension may position one to efficiently execute the decision-making process, the CRCC also provides designees with a resource outlining several contemporary decision-making models.[4]

TABLE 1

CONTEMPORARY DECISION-MAKING MODELS[4]

TARVDAS & HARTLEY[5]	COTTONE[6]	GARCIA, CARTWRIGHT, BORCHUKOWSK[a7]	COREY COREY COREY, & CALLANAN[8]	HERLIHY & WATSON[9]
Interpret situation	Obtain information from those involved.	Awareness & fact finding-enhancing sensitivity & awareness means not only being aware of a dilemma but also how that dilemma may affect the different stakeholders involved who may have different or opposing worldviews. It is the counselor's responsibility to know the difference.	Identify the problem or dilemma.	Discernment
Formulating an ethical decision	Assess the relationships-conflicting opinions? Adversarial?	Formulation of an ethical decision- review potential discriminatory laws or institutional regulations. Make sure potent courses of action reflect the different worldviews involved: consider the positive and negative consequences of opposing course of action from the parties involved. Consult with cultural experts. If necessary; select a course of action that best represents an agreement of the parties involved in the case.	Identify the potential issues involved	Respectful-ness
Selecting an action by weighing competing, nonmoral values	Consult valued colleagues and expert opinion including ethical standards.	Arbitration-parties may not always agree. In that case, the parties may seek arbitration if disagreement persists. This is similar to negotiating where a third party can make the final decision or assist in coming to an agreement. Process	Review the relevant ethics codes.	Acknowled-gment of emotiions in decision-making
Planning and executing the selected course of action	Negotiate if necessary.		Know the applicable laws and regulations.	Self-reflection: "Who shall I be?"

TARVDAS & HARTLEY[5]	COTTONE[6]	GARCIA, CARTWRIGHT, BORCHUKOWSK[a7]	COREY COREY COREY, & CALLANAN[8]	HERLIHY & WATSON[9]
	Consensualize			Obtain consultation Consider possible and probable courses of action.	Community consider- ation Consultation
	Interactive Reflection (when consensual- ization fails)				
	Arbitrate if Necessary			Enumerate the consequences of various decisions. Choose what appears to be the best course of action.	

CASE STUDY

Dante, a rehabilitation counselor, is working with Cathryn who is diagnosed with Major Depressive Disorder and a substance use disorder. She displays many barriers to employment such as lack of education, minimal work history, ambiguous interests, history of alcohol abuse, and minor legal issues. Dante works with her and prepares her to become an integrated member of society. Near the end of her treatment, she starts to display great improvements in many areas of her life.

Cathryn successfully graduates from her addiction treatment program and Dante does not see or hear from her until 2 years later, when he attends a fundraiser to help local charities rebuild parks. He discovers that the person in charge of setting up the fundraiser is Cathryn, who he worked with a couple years earlier in his career. He respects what she is doing and plans to donate money to the fundraising event. During a discussion with her, Cathryn asks Dante if he would like to have dinner after the fundraiser ends. Dante contemplates the idea and rationalizes that her treatment ended a few years ago. He also feels that they are both consenting adults and there is no planned or discussed sexual contact. The counselor is still apprehensive about accepting the offer, however. After careful consideration of the ethical principles involved, Dante respectfully declines the invitation. He feels that it would be ethically irresponsible to have contact outside of treatment, and that instead of promoting Cathryn's welfare, it could prove potentially harmful.

L.2.b. CONSULTATION

When uncertain as to whether particular situations or courses of action may be in violation of the Code, rehabilitation counselors consult with other professionals who are knowledgeable about ethics, with supervisors, colleagues, and/or with appropriate authorities, such as CRCC, licensure boards, or legal counsel.[2,p.34]

There are several courses of action that a rehabilitation counselor can employ when resolving ethical issues. It is the responsibility of the rehabilitation counselor to make sure they have gathered and verified all pertinent information before determining the nature of the dilemma. One must engage in this process humbly and modestly. Doing so increases the likelihood that appropriate outside consultation, within the confines of confidentiality, will be sought and that one's pride or insecurity does not stand in the way. Additionally, active engagement in reviewing relevant and current literature can assist those rehabilitation counselors in exploring a situation and the different courses of actions, wholly. Knowledge of the numerous resources that one has, including appropriate consultants, means by which to obtain current and applicable literature, and regularly taking a self-inventory to address those barriers that may hinder one's ability to seek consultation, will expedite the identification, assessment, and resolution of ethical dilemmas.

CASE STUDY

Nancy, a rehabilitation counselor, has been providing individual counseling to John Delaney for several months during which they have discussed various vocational concerns such as barriers to employment, life stressors, and work readiness. John expresses his desire to work but is apprehensive to move forward due to his legal history. Nancy has been supportive of John throughout this process and has provided him the guidance to work on his issues.

One day, Nancy receives a telephone call from her son who announces that he will be bringing his new girlfriend, Dana Delaney, to dinner over the weekend to meet the family. While Nancy briefly hesitates at the last name of Delaney, she quickly brushes it off as a mere coincidence of two individuals with a common last name, and one just happens to be a client.

In the next session with Mr. Delaney, John expresses elation that his daughter, Dana, has met a young man and is visiting his parents for the weekend. Then, John chuckles and shares, "His last name is the same as yours! How funny is that?" Nancy smiles awkwardly as she begins to realize that the boy her client's daughter is dating, is her son. After the session, Nancy regroups; while she understands the complexity of the situation and is aware this could be unethical, she is unsure how to proceed. Nancy is conflicted because of the dual relationship that just established itself and is unsure how to discuss it with John.

Nancy confides in a trusted colleague who she believes may be able to provide more insight on how to continue. The colleague presents possible scenarios to gain different perspectives. The colleague postulates that the relationship between the two children could end tomorrow and the issue would be resolved, or the potential of a long-term romance could interfere with the professional help being provided to John.

The colleague suggests that Nancy meet with the client and discuss the issue regarding their children dating prior to referring him to a different counselor who does not have a conflicting interest but may be able to provide quality service to John. At their next meeting, Nancy shares what she had concluded regarding their children dating, with John. As they discussed the possibilities and the ethical ramifications of this relationship, the two agree that a referral would be best as it would allow for their children to date while also not jeopardizing John's care or Nancy's credentials.

L.2.c. INFORMAL RESOLUTION

When rehabilitation counselors have reason to believe that another rehabilitation counselor is violating or has violated an ethical standard, they attempt to resolve the issue informally by direct communication with the other rehabilitation counselor if feasible and provided such action does not violate confidentiality rights that may be involved.[2,p.34-35]

Whether a rehabilitation counselor finds themselves working in the private-for profit, public and state-federal, or non-profit sectors, the likelihood that an ethical dilemma will arise remains. The organizational culture that exists may foster friendships between colleagues and emphasize the importance of group successes, or it may cultivate a more divisive, and competitive climate that pits one against another. While it would stand to reason that the more toxic work environments may see greater incidence of ethical dilemmas, no workplace is immune.

When applying for the designation of CRC or CCRC, each rehabilitation counselor assumed the duty of a mandated reporter for clients as well as the colleagues that they work with. As social beings, some individuals may feel the inclination to discuss events of a questionable nature, informally, with others. While this is often unethical, in and of itself, it also significantly increases the chances of misinformation and falsehoods being perceived as truth. One may witness first-hand a potential ethical violation taking place. Whether this information is second-, third-, or first-hand knowledge per subsection L.2.c., after determining the credibility of the information all rehabilitation counselors must make the first crucial decision in asking whether what was heard or observed can be addressed informally, without violating confidentiality rights.

Going to a colleague to discuss their behavior, especially when their ethics are called into question, is not often an easy conversation to have. This informal approach to concerns, however, may prove to be the redirection a wayward or misinformed colleagues needs. The goal of the informal resolution is to help cease current and future ethical violations, to educate when appropriate, and to support the colleague in question.

If a toxic or competitive culture exists in the workplace, or the colleague in question tends to act in an aggressive or antagonistic manner, this well-meaning conversation may not be well received. The rehabilitation counselor should then bring the information to the colleague in question's supervisor, allowing them to address it from an organizational standpoint. One cannot, however, ignore the existing American social more that recriminates those perceived as "snitching," and the potential fallout which may occur with the colleague in question or the overall workplace environment. Identified violations which are more serious in nature, has or is likely to substantially harm persons or organizations, or was not successfully resolved informally, will require the rehabilitation counselor to pursue further action, outlined in subsection L.2.d.

CASE STUDY

Gloria has been working with Angela a 35-year-old for almost a year, assessing her rehabilitation needs to productively integrate back into society. Angela has accomplished many goals during the course of her treatment and, with the help of Gloria, has obtained her GED and increased her professional skills. Angela will soon graduate from her treatment program and has been accepted at a local community college with a declared marketing major. For Angela, attending college will be a milestone she did not foresee a year ago and she is thankful to Gloria for helping her get to this point.

During their last session, Angela hands Gloria a gift certificate of $350.00 to a local clothing store in a show of appreciation. Gloria *accepts the gift certificate as the Christmas holiday is only a few months away and says, "thank you." Jaclyn, another rehabilitation counselor who shares an office with Gloria, hears her accept the gift certificate without informing the client that she cannot accept such gifts due to ethical reasons. Jaclyn has witnessed such gift exchanges before between Gloria and other clients, but the gifts were small with no real monetary value. While in those instances, Jaclyn did not think much about confronting Gloria's questionable behavior, she is now placed in a predicament of intervening and addressing this behavior with Gloria.*

After careful consideration, Jaclyn attempts to resolve the issue informally by discussing the current situation with Gloria in hopes that it will not lead to any further unethical exchanges of money for services. Jaclyn does not want to cultivate a conflict and addresses the issue as professionally as possible, while trying to get her point across. Gloria, after discussing gifts from clients with Jaclyn, realizes that accepting the gift certificate violated ethical standards by crossing boundaries with a client. Gloria asks to meet with Angela again, respectfully declines and returns the gift certificate, and expresses that she cannot accept the gift due to ethical reasons.

L.2.d. REPORTING ETHICAL VIOLATIONS

When an informal resolution is not appropriate or feasible, is not resolved, or if an apparent violation has substantially harmed or is likely to substantially harm persons or organizations, rehabilitation counselors take further action appropriate to the situation. Such action might include referral of the matter to applicable committees on professional ethics (e.g., voluntary certification bodies, licensure boards, organizational authorities). Referral may not be appropriate when the reporting would violate confidentiality rights (e.g., when clients refuse to allow information or statements to be shared) or when rehabilitation counselors have been retained to review the work of another rehabilitation counselor whose professional conduct is in question (e.g., consultation, expert testimony).[2,p.35]

Rehabilitation counselors may need to report unethical behaviors or actions beyond the realm of informal resolution. An example of such an event could be witnessing or gaining knowledge of any illegal or inappropriate activity occurring within the organization. Rehabilitation counselors need to follow necessary protocols to make sure they take all appropriate actions. These steps may include contacting professional governmental officials, state licensure organizations, or the CRCC[1].

The rehabilitation counselor must also consider violation of client confidentiality rights if certain events are brought forward to the agency or a governing body. The information about a given client or group of clients may be made public to investigate the identified ethical concern, or the client may not provide their permission to discuss their involvement.

While it may seem that the best person to review the work of a rehabilitation counselor alleged to have acted unethically would be another rehabilitation counselor, subsection L.2., *Addressing Suspected Violations*, makes it clear that this is incorrect. The unethical concern must be brought to the organization's chain of command or through outside organizations as discussed above.

CASE STUDY

Helen has been working as a rehabilitation counselor for three years in a therapeutic community center that provides housing for formerly incarcerated women who have a history with substance abuse and family conflict. Helen and Connie, another rehabilitation counselor, have been friends since Helen started working for the agency several years ago. Connie has been with the agency one year longer than Helen, and she was the person who assisted getting Helen acclimated to her role in the agency. They have both supported one another and developed a genuine bond inside the workplace.

One day, Connie was in a counseling session with her client, Beatrice, discussing her vocational goals when she inexplicably discloses that she is intimately involved with a rehabilitation counselor in the agency named Helen. Beatrice confesses that the relationship has been going on for almost a year and though it was simply platonic at the beginning, it turned sexual after they started meeting outside of the agency. She reveals that she meets Helen at her apartment some nights during the workweek and on occasional weekends. Beatrice confesses that she is falling in love with Helen and is confused about her feelings towards her.

Connie is utterly flabbergasted by this news and is stupefied about how to address this matter without breaking confidentiality and trust with the client. Connie knows that some action must be implemented because a boundary between counselor and client has been blatantly violated and the therapeutic relationship has been breached, causing potential harm to the client.

Connie begins the process by first consulting with her other colleagues who may know how to proceed better than she does while preserving the confidentiality of the client. Many of her colleagues suggest that the rehabilitation counselor in question is taking advantage of the dynamics of counseling and is exploiting the client, potentially causing them harm. They conclude that this behavior cannot be addressed by attempting an informal resolution but rather, these colleagues feel the best solution is to take further action appropriate to the situation, even if it means potentially losing a friendship. Connie is aware of the seriousness of the situation and the consequences it may have on her friendship with Helen but knows her colleagues are ethically correct. Connie is obligated to examine the proper channels of decision-making and the principles that govern the ethical dilemma by informing her superiors that an investigation into this matter is the appropriate action.

The superiors gather information to ensure the allegations are correct and then proceed to speak with Helen about her unethical behavior with a client. Helen admits to her indiscretion after realizing the evidence against her is too much to dispute. Helen is suspended from her agency for violating ethical boundaries with a client and is scheduled to meet with her agency's executive director and the CRCC Ethics Committee for further investigation. The executive director at her agency decides that Helen is to be terminated immediately. The agency's legal department felt that police charges against Helen did not appear appropriate despite the counseling relationship since both she and the client were consenting adults and pursuing a police investigation might well disclose information about the client.

After meeting with the CRCC Ethics Committee, a conclusion has been drawn that Helen has directly violated her professional role as a rehabilitation counselor by destroying the therapeutic relationship with a client. Subsequently, her CRC credential is terminated. At all points throughout the investigation, the client's name was not included and remained anonymous.

L.2.e. SELF-REPORTING

Rehabilitation counselors shall immediately notify CRCC when sanctioned for violations of ethical codes by any applicable counselor licensure, certification, or registry boards; other mental health licensure, certification, or registry boards; and voluntary national certification boards or professional associations with which they are affiliated. Rehabilitation counselors notify CRCC if they are found to have violated another organization's professional code of ethics, violated laws in relation to their practice in the field of rehabilitation counseling, or are convicted of offenses that constitute violations of the Code.[2,p.35]

As a CRC or CCRC, rehabilitation counselors are expected to uphold a high standard of ethical conduct. While this includes assisting others in identifying their missteps, it especially requires one to always hold themselves accountable. Subsection L.2.e. reinforces this duty in explicitly outlining that while the CRCC may not be the sanctioning body for verified violation of law or ethics, CRC and CCRC designees *must* report these charges and sanctions immediately. In other words, the rehabilitation counselor cannot hope that the CRCC does not find out, in hopes of maintaining their credential. It is equally important that the rehabilitation counselor also note that they do not have to been found in violation of the CRCC Code, but the ethical codes of *any* applicable licensure, certification or registry boards, professional organizations, or laws, as it applies to their practice as a rehabilitation counselor.

L.2.f. ORGANIZATIONAL CONFLICTS

If the demands of organizations with which rehabilitation counselors are affiliated pose a conflict with the Code, rehabilitation counselors specify the nature of such conflicts and express their commitment to the Code to appropriate responsible officials. When possible, rehabilitation counselors work to create change within organizations to allow full adherence to the Code. If the conflict cannot be resolved, rehabilitation counselors evaluate the risks and benefits of continued affiliation with the organization.[2,p.35]

Rehabilitation counselors must know and comprehend the role and function of the organization or organizations for which they work and the degree to which they align with the expectations outlined in the Code. Organizational policy, particularly in those which house different specialties, may not have been developed in a manner that fully aligns with the role and function of a rehabilitation counselor or the CRCC credential. Proactive investigation and comprehension of organizational policies and expectations can assist the rehabilitation counselor in identifying potential contradictory expectations.

It is expected that rehabilitation counselors report such conflicts to their employer and, where possible, recommend changes within the organization to adhere to Code standards. It is strongly recommended that the rehabilitation counselor provide this feedback in writing so that a hard copy of the interaction is memorialized, in the event that it is needed later. If the rehabilitation counselor and organization reach an impasse regarding what is being asked of them per policy and what they are ethically obligated to uphold, it may behoove the rehabilitation counselor to consider a change in employer.

CASE STUDY

Jerome, a current rehabilitation counselor, has a history of chemical dependency. He also has been clean of illicit substances for the last 5 years during which Jerome completed a master's degree in rehabilitation. He was always an excellent student and completed his graduate degree with a 3.7/4.0 GPA. He genuinely enjoyed his degree program and was eager to start working in the field of rehabilitation

counseling. Attending school gave him little time to think about drugs
and he was eager to remain clean and sober.

Jerome knew that he wanted to help individuals who had an active
addiction and took a position with a recovery program in a
neighboring state, which promoted the harm reduction model. For
Jerome, the position sounded like a great opportunity to help others
like him and to use the knowledge he had gained academically, as well
as personally.

The job began smoothly, and Jerome felt that he made the right
choice. He was invited to attend a meeting of the local community
group which sponsored the program. He was asked to prepare a
report discussing the clients with whom he worked and to share status
reports on their care. Jerome wrote his report and submitted it to the
agency executive director.

The executive director called Jerome into his office and told him,
"Why doesn't this report have any names listed? How will the local
community group know who was improving? If they do not know who
is improving, and it is just numbers on a spreadsheet, they may think
we're making it all up or worse, they could cancel our funding!"
Jerome stated that using client names went against his personal
ethical beliefs, confidentiality standards, and his professional code of
ethics. The executive director then informed Jerome that he would be
terminated from his position should he fail to follow protocol and
what was being asked of him.

Jerome considered the situation and wrote the executive director a
thorough email outlining the confidentiality issues at hand as well as
the purview of his role and function as a rehabilitation counselor per
the CRCC Code of Ethics. After reviewing the email, the executive
director told Jerome that he respected him for taking the time to better
educate him, and that Jerome would not be required to provide the
names of his clients. Jerome was pleased with the outcome and
attended the meeting. After the meeting ended, Jerome felt that the
community was supportive of each client presented, despite their
names being retracted from the data. Jerome could not, however,
accept the idea that it had been common practice that other employees
before him disclosed the names and levels of compliance of clients to
the community group members.

Jerome felt that he had resolved his confidentiality issues by
sending the email to the executive director, but he felt that he could no
longer keep the professional position since the techniques used by the
organization were in violation of his Code and everything he learned
while completing his graduate degree. Jerome decided to leave the
position and to seek a more standardized rehabilitation counseling
position in the same field. Jerome felt confident that he had resolved

any issue related to confidentiality in that situation, and that he had
complied with the Code standards.

L.3. CONDUCT IN ADDRESSING ETHICAL ISSUES

L.3.a. COOPERATION WITH ETHICS COMMITTEES

Rehabilitation counselors have a working knowledge of the Code
and assist in the process of enforcing it. Rehabilitation counselors
cooperate with investigations, requests, proceedings, and requirements
of the CRCC Ethics Committee or ethics committees of other duly
constituted associations or boards having jurisdiction over those
charged with a violation.[2(p35)]

It is incumbent upon every rehabilitation counselor to cooperate with any
duly organized body (e.g., CRCC or a state legal body), when asked to respond
to unethical or illegal behavior of others, providing information and appropriate
data pertaining to the alleged ethical or legal issue, and to follow the standards
of their own profession as well as those of any other body governing the
behavior of any rehabilitation counselor. The rehabilitation counselor must
follow Code standards in submitting this information,[1] as well as those
standards of other applicable bodies (e.g., state licensure boards).

CASE STUDY

Gale and Kristi are both CRC holders at a local non-profit,
providing services to housing insecure adolescents and teenagers.
Among the services available are a small collection of age-appropriate,
gently used clothes, a bay of showers where the young adults can wash
up, a food pantry, and part-time job placement for those who qualify.
Gale and Kristi have known each other throughout their undergraduate
and graduate degrees and consider each other their best friend. When
they are not working, they often can be caught on the phone or going
out to Karaoke with each other.

One day, Kristi is walking past the bay of showers when she sees
another rehabilitation counselor, Dale, quickly leaving one of the
shower stalls. Moments later, one of the young ladies who checked in
that morning leaves the same stall, wrapped only in a towel. Kristi
identifies that this is an egregious ethical violation, as well as a
potentially illegal act. She swiftly requests a private meeting with
Dale's supervisor and begins to outline what she observed. Visibly
shaken, Dale's supervisor seeks out the young lady to inquire as to
what occurred and to ensure her safety.

Dale's supervisor phones for law enforcement, and formal charges are pressed by the young lady against Dale for attempted sexual misconduct. Additionally, Dale's supervisor files a formal report with the CRCC outlining the allegations of gross ethical misconduct. Dale is immediately removed from the premises by law enforcement and his employment is suspended indefinitely, pending results of an investigation.

Kristi is asked to document what she observed for the CRCC Ethics Committee and, several months later, is subpoenaed to testify when criminal charges are brought against Dale in the County court. As is her duty as a CRC holder, she actively participates in all investigations and proceedings.

L.3.b. CONFIDENTIALITY

Rehabilitation counselors who are knowledgeable of and/or party to a complaint alleging violation of the Code maintain confidentiality of all information related to the complaint and to the adjudication of the complaint unless they are compelled to disclose information by a validly issued subpoena or when otherwise required by law or valid court order. [2, p.35]

There may be instances when a rehabilitation counselor is called upon to report an alleged ethical violation, provide additional information during inquiry, or engage with the formal proceedings. As such, the rehabilitation counselor may be privy to sensitive information including how the formal allegation investigation concluded and applicable sanctions. This information is not to be shared with others, whether professional or personal in nature, apart from being in receipt of a valid subpoena, court order, or otherwise compelled by law. Any information that one has pertaining to the proceedings of an alleged Code violation, should not be discussed otherwise.

CASE STUDY

In the previous case study, Kristi had witnessed the highly questionable behavior of her colleague Dale as he exited a shower stall, followed moments later by a young lady from the same stall. Kristi, after reporting what she saw to Dale's supervisor, cannot fully process the implications of the day's events. She wants desperately to confide in her best friend, Gale, but knows that it would be wrong of her to do so. She begins to discuss her day with her husband but stops when she realizes this would also violate confidentiality. When she is asked for a written statement from the CRCC Ethics Committee, and when she is subpoenaed to testify before the county court in the criminal trial, that Kristi finally is able to share what she observed that day.

L.3.c. UNWARRANTED COMPLAINTS

Rehabilitation counselors do not initiate, participate in, or encourage the filing of ethics complaints that are retaliatory in nature, made with reckless disregard or willful ignorance of facts that would disprove the allegation, or are intended to harm rehabilitation counselors rather than to protect clients or the public.[2,p.35]

Rehabilitation counselors, as any professional person, should responsibly review any allegations made against another rehabilitation counselor, or bring ethical charges under the false belief of protecting the public. While it is not the charge of the rehabilitation counselor to fully investigate an allegation, due diligence must be given toward verifying that the alleged misconduct occurred and that it violated one or more standards of the Code. False reports of ethical misconduct, the filing of a report that had superficial merit but can quickly be disproven or filing a report to harm or disparage a colleague rather than promote and protect the clients and general public, is unacceptable and may result in the original filer being accused of ethical misconduct.

CASE STUDY

Alphonse and Gabriel are both rehabilitation counselors working in a residential community program for persons diagnosed with developmental disabilities. Though Alphonse has been at this community program for 3 years and Gabriel started last month, Alphonse feels that the supervisors favored Gabriel. As a result, Alphonse grows increasingly jealous and spiteful of Gabriel. Recently, Alphonse concocted a plan which, he believed, would depict Gabriel in a less favorable light to their supervisors. When finally executed, Alphonse had filed a report falsely alleging that Gabriel was under the influence of illicit drugs while working with their clients in the community-based developmental disability program. While the allegation and investigation were quite troubling, Gabriel quickly saw his name cleared when the CRCC Ethics Committee reported that the allegations were unfounded.

Alphonse, days after Gabriel's name was cleared by the Ethics Committee, turns to Gabriel, and says in a whisper, "Maybe next time they'll find the drugs in your locker?" Gabriel, now suspecting that it was Alphonse who filed the false allegation report, contacts their supervisor to discuss the situation. The supervisor speaks with Alphonse privately, indicates that it is believed that Alphonse was the author of the false allegation report, and that not only would a written reprimand be going into his record of employment with the organization, but that the organization would be conducting an internal investigation, and the CRCC Ethics Committee would be notified. Alphonse, who had initially denied the allegation, conceded when the consequences were outlined before him by his supervisor.

L.3.d. UNFAIR DISCRIMINATION AGAINST COMPLAINANTS AND RESPONDENTS

Rehabilitation counselors do not disparage or retaliate against individuals by denying services, employment, advancement, admission to academic or other programs, tenure, or promotions based solely upon their having made or there being the subject of an ethics complaint. This does not preclude taking action based upon the outcome of such proceedings when rehabilitation counselors are found to be in violation of ethical standards.[2,p.35]

Similar to the U.S. criminal justice maxim of "innocent until proven guilty," where there is an assumption of innocence unless there is evidence beyond a reasonable doubt otherwise, the Code requires rehabilitation counselors to maintain the status quo within their respective environment as any necessary investigation or proceedings occur. Allegations being brought forth do not necessarily mean that there is not proof to the contrary. A person alleged of having committed ethical misconduct has the right to continue working as a rehabilitation counselor after ethical charges have been levied against them and they may continue in that capacity until such time that the charge is proven true and sanctions are issued, or the charge is unverifiable and they may continue in their position, if they so choose.

Should it be known that a person has filed an ethical misconduct allegation against another, their ability to function within their organization should not be jeopardized. The CRC or CCRC holder has a duty to report and therefore should not be penalized for doing so in any way. This is comparable to the process of whistleblowing, whereby unethical or illegal activity is reported, typically an individual within the organization. These persons, known as whistleblowers, are often protected from retaliation, and provided legal recourse under a variety of federal protection laws. In short, no rehabilitation counselor should experience retaliation of any nature for doing their duty as a CRC or CCRC designee.

CASE STUDY

Returning to the case of Alphonse for a moment, recall that there was to be an internal investigation as to whether it was Alphonse who filed the false allegation report, in addition to the proceeding by the

CRCC. In the interim, however, Alphonse was allowed to continue working. It was not until the internal investigation had concluded, that Alphonse was ultimately asked to resign from his position. Had he been asked to do so prior to the end of the investigation, Alphonse may have been able to bring charges against the organization for false accusation and/or discrimination, among others. Similarly, Alphonse was able to continue claiming the CRC credential until the allegations were deemed valid, and sanctions were issued.

THE FAR-REACHING SCOPE OF IMPLICATION

In closing, regarding the process by which potential ethical violations are identified, addressed, and resolved, one should direct their attention to the closing note of the entire Code of Ethics,[2] restated below. Here, the CRCC directly outlines the power, jurisdiction, and ultimate obligation to investigate any allegations of ethical misconduct, and to approve penalties, including revocation or suspension, for the CRC or CCRC holder who is found to have evidence substantiating those allegations against them.

While a verified ethical violation and subsequent penalty is clearly influential on the CRC or CCRC holder, impacting their professional standing and future employability as a rehabilitation counselor, it is important to understand the insidious impact that unethical behavior has within the system it occurs. Not only does it hold high probability of negatively impacting the client, but it can further permeate to create a poor reputation for the organization wherein it took place, and the overall profession. The CRC or CCRC holder, upon designation, is now a professional representative in *all* that they do, when they believe people are watching or not, regardless of whether they are in a professional or social environment. It behooves the future and current rehabilitation counseling professional to keep this in mind, especially considering the relative size of the field in comparison to others.

NOTE:

Rehabilitation counselors who violate the Code are subject to disciplinary action. Since the use of the Certified Rehabilitation Counselor (CRC®) and Canadian Certified Rehabilitation Counselor (CCRC®) designations are a privilege granted by the Commission on Rehabilitation Counselor Certification (CRCC®), CRCC reserves unto itself the power to suspend or to revoke the privilege or to approve other penalties for a violation. Disciplinary penalties are imposed as warranted by the severity of the offense and its attendant circumstances. All disciplinary actions are undertaken in accordance with published procedures and penalties designed to assure the proper enforcement of the Code within the framework of due process and equal protection under the law.[2,p.39]

REFERENCES

[1]Commission on Rehabilitation Counselor Certification. (2017). *Guidelines and procedures for processing complaints.* http://crccertification.com/wp-content/uploads/2020/10/CRCC_GuidelinesForComplaints.pdf

[2]Commission on Rehabilitation Counselor Certification (2017). *Code of professional ethics for rehabilitation counselors.* https://crccertification.com/wpcontent/uploads/2021/03/CRC_CodeEthics Eff2017-FinaLnewdiesign.pdf

[3]Commission on Rehabilitation Counselor Certification. (2020). *Advisory opinions from ethics committee minutes 1996-2020.* https://crccertification.com/wp-content/uploads/2020/12/AdvisoryOpinions-2020-08.pdf

[4]Commission on Rehabilitation Counselor Certification. (2021). *Contemporary decision-making models.* https://crccertification.com/code-of-ethics-4/decision-making-models/

[5]Corey, C., Corey, G., Corey, M. S., & Callanan, P. (2014). *Issues and ethics in the helping professions* (9th ed.). Brooks/Cole.

[6]Cottone, R. R. (2001). A social constructivism model of ethical decision-making in counseling. *Journal of Counseling Development*, 79, 39-45. https://doi.org/10.1002/j.1556-6676.2001.tb01941.x

[7]Garcia, J., Cartwright, B., Winston, S., & Borchukowska, B. (2003). A transcultural integrative ethical decision-making model in counseling. *Journal of Counseling and Development*, 81, 268-276. http://doi.org/10.1002/j.1556-6678.2003.tb00253.x

[9]Herlihy, B. & Watson, Z. E. (2007). Social justice and counseling ethics. In C.C. Lee (Ed.), *Counseling for social justice* (2nd ed., pp. 181-199). American Counseling Association.

[10]Tarvydas, V. M. (2018). Ethical decision-making processes. In R.R. Cottone & V. M. Tarvydas (Eds.), *Ethical and professional issues in counseling* (pp. 144-154). Prentice Hall.